akahashi

The spotlight on Rumiko Takahashi's career began in 1978 when she won an honorable mention in Shogakukan's annual New Comic Artist Contest for *Those Selfish Aliens*. Later that same year, her boy-meets-alien comedy series, *Urusei Yatsura*, was serialized in *Weekly Shonen Sunday*. This phenomenally successful manga series was adapted into anime format and spawned a TV series and half a dozen theatrical-release movies, all incredibly popular in their own right. Takahashi followed up the success of her debut series with one blockbuster hit after another—*Maison Ikkoku* ran from 1980 to 1987, *Ranma ½* from 1987 to 1996, and *Inuyasha* from 1996 to 2008. Other notable works include *Mermaid Saga*, *Rumic Theater*, and *One-Pound Gospel*.

Takahashi won the prestigious Shogakukan Manga Award twice in her career, once for *Urusei Yatsura* in 1981 and the second time for *Inuyasha* in 2002. A majority of the Takahashi canon has been adapted into other media such as anime, live-action TV series, and film. Takahashi's manga, as well as the other formats her work has been adapted into, have continued to delight generations of fans around the world. Distinguished by her wonderfully endearing characters, Takahashi's work adeptly incorporates a wide variety of elements such as comedy, romance, fantasy, and martial arts. While her series are difficult to pin down into one simple genre, the signature style she has created has come to be known as the "Rumic World." Rumiko Takahashi is an artist who truly represents the very best from the world of manga.

RIN-NE

VOLUME 13
Shonen Sunday Edition

STORY AND ART BY
RUMIKO TAKAHASHI

KYOKAI NO RINNE Vol. 13
by Rumiko TAKAHASHI
© 2009 Rumiko TAKAHASHI
All rights reserved.
Original Japanese edition published by SHOGAKUKAN.
English translation rights in the United States of America,
Canada, the United Kingdom and Ireland arranged with
SHOGAKUKAN.

Translation/Christine Dashiell
Touch-up Art & Lettering/Evan Waldinger
Design/Yukiko Whitley
Editor/Mike Montesa

Printed in Canada

Published by VIZ Media, LLC
P.O. Box 77010
San Francisco, CA 94107

10 9 8 7 6 5 4 3 2 1
First printing, November 2013

VIZ
media

SHONEN
SUNDAY

www.viz.com   WWW.SHONENSUNDAY.COM

Story and Art by
Rumiko Takahashi

RIN-NE

Characters

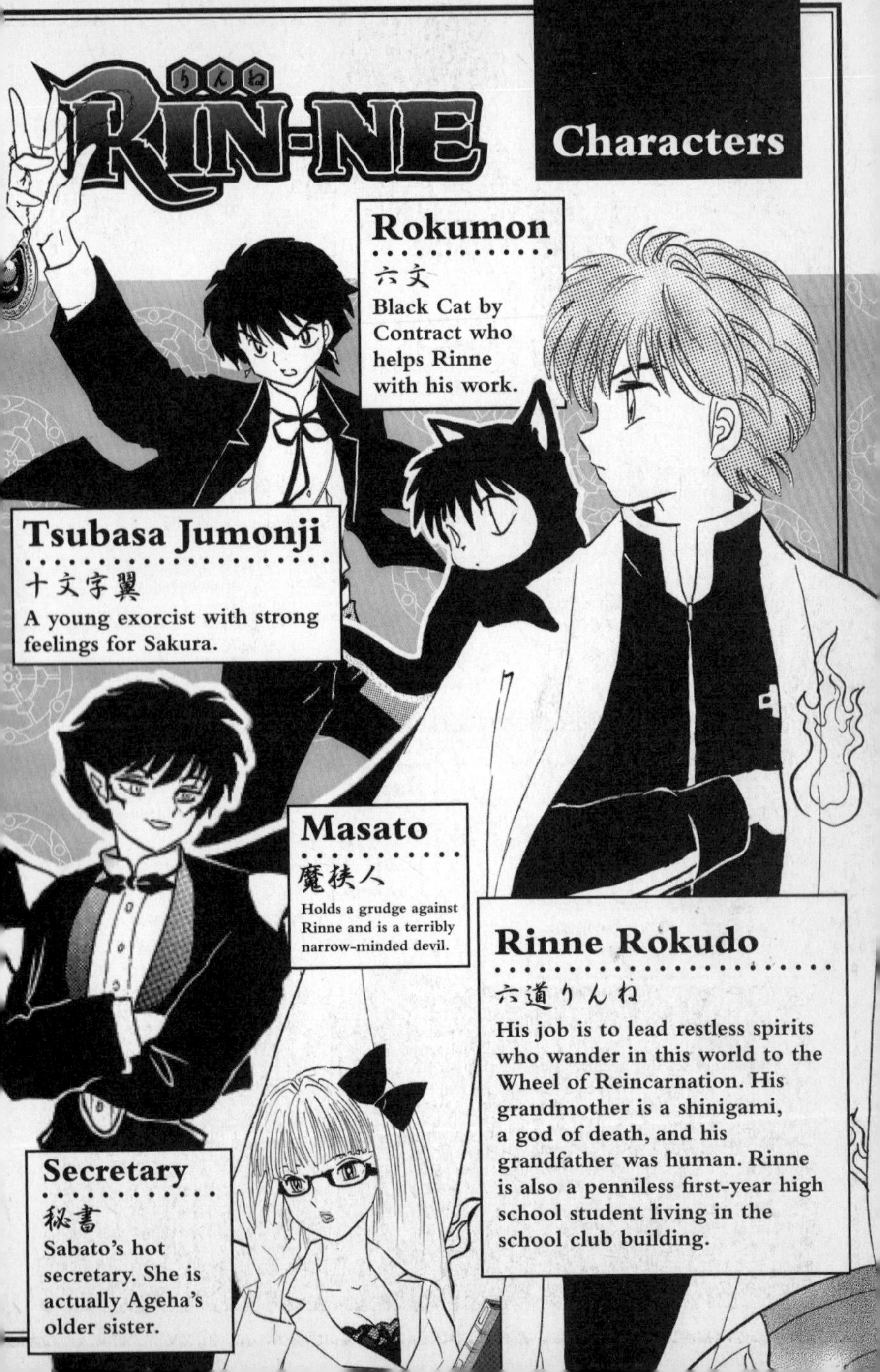

Rokumon
六文
Black Cat by Contract who helps Rinne with his work.

Tsubasa Jumonji
十文字翼
A young exorcist with strong feelings for Sakura.

Masato
魔狭人
Holds a grudge against Rinne and is a terribly narrow-minded devil.

Rinne Rokudo
六道りんね
His job is to lead restless spirits who wander in this world to the Wheel of Reincarnation. His grandmother is a shinigami, a god of death, and his grandfather was human. Rinne is also a penniless first-year high school student living in the school club building.

Secretary
秘書
Sabato's hot secretary. She is actually Ageha's older sister.

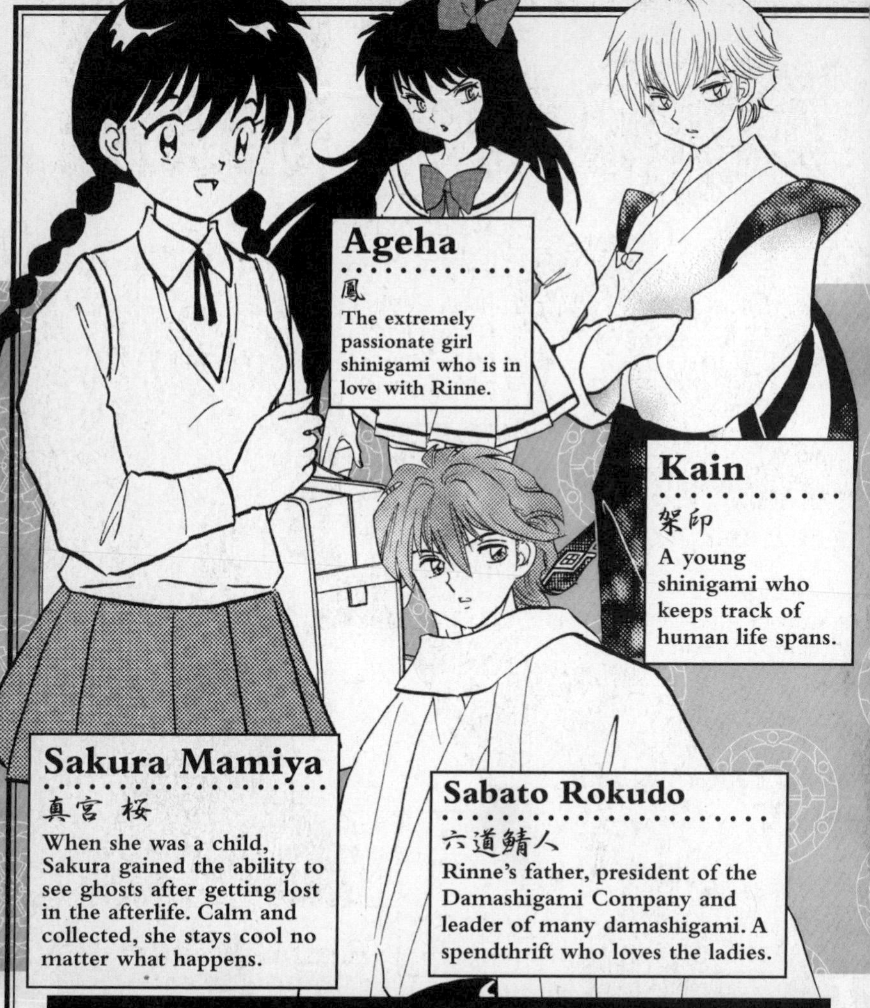

Ageha

鳳

The extremely passionate girl shinigami who is in love with Rinne.

Kain

架印

A young shinigami who keeps track of human life spans.

Sakura Mamiya

真宮 桜

When she was a child, Sakura gained the ability to see ghosts after getting lost in the afterlife. Calm and collected, she stays cool no matter what happens.

Sabato Rokudo

六道鯖人

Rinne's father, president of the Damashigami Company and leader of many damashigami. A spendthrift who loves the ladies.

The Story So Far

Together, Sakura, the girl who can see ghosts, and Rinne the shinigami (sort of) spend their days helping spirits that can't pass on reach the afterlife, and deal with all kinds of strange phenomena at their school.

Rokumon decides to take the Black Cat Ranking Exam. Rokumon battles fiercely to win when his rivals Oboro and Suzu also sign up. Since he paid Rokumon's exam fee, Rinne's very interested in the results.

Rinne's troubles seem to come and go with the seasons. What's in store for him next?

RIN-NE

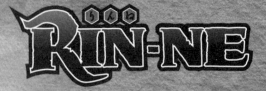

Contents

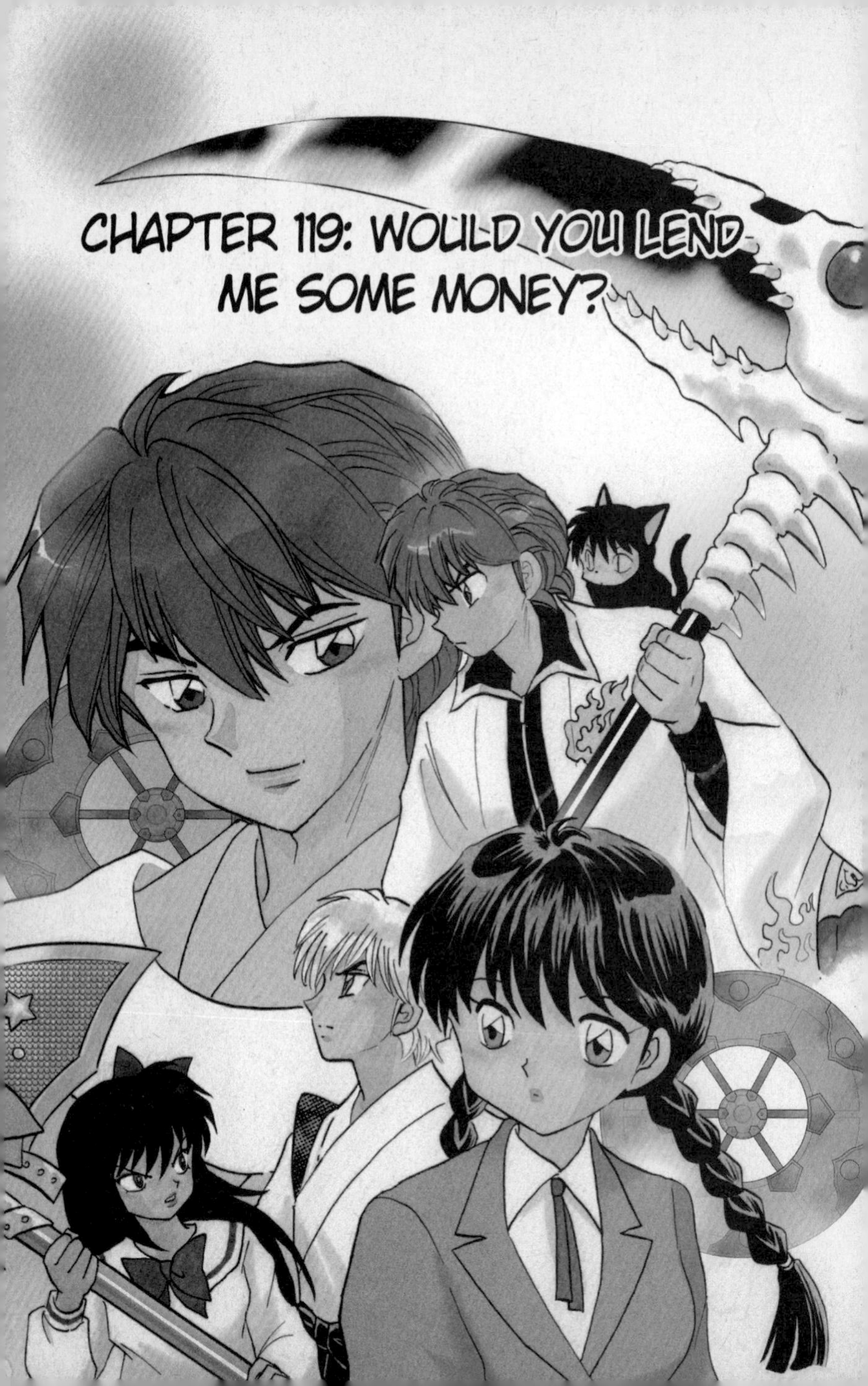
CHAPTER 119: WOULD YOU LEND ME SOME MONEY?

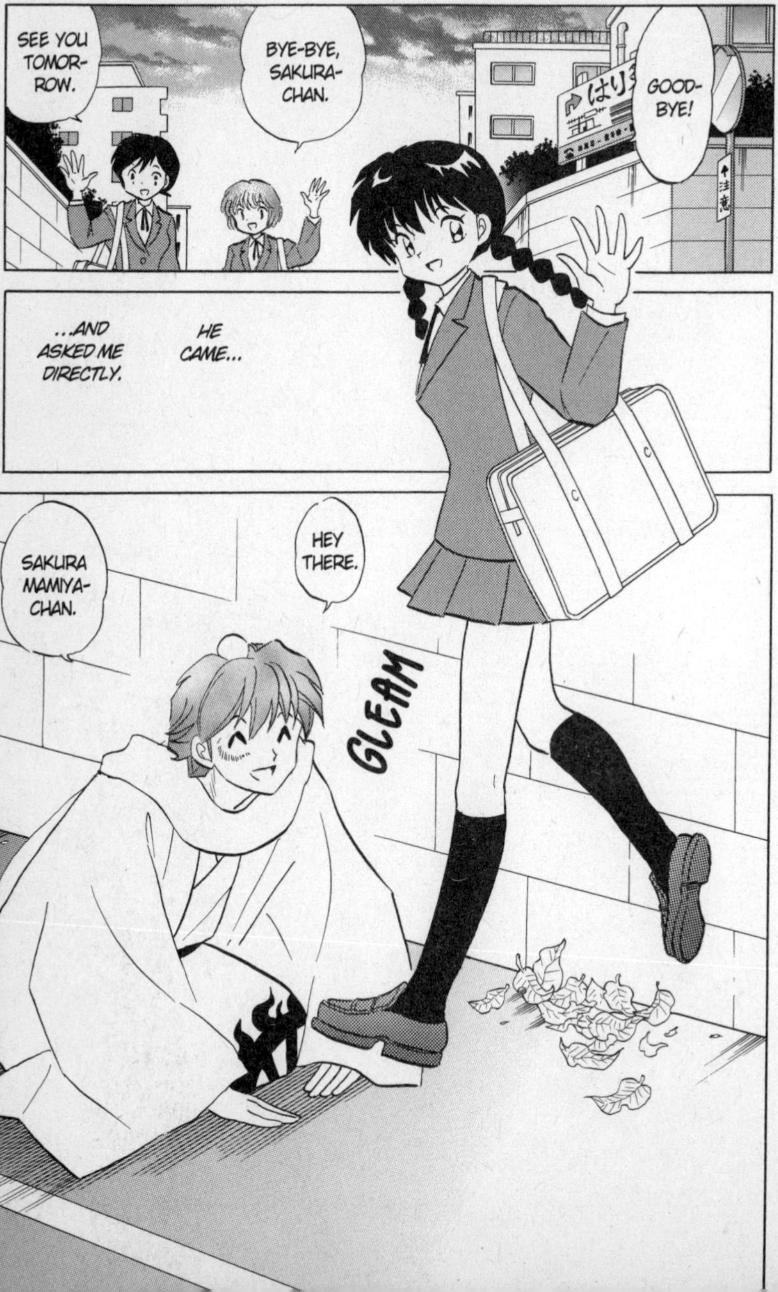
GOOD-BYE!
BYE-BYE, SAKURA-CHAN.
SEE YOU TOMORROW.
HE CAME...
...AND ASKED ME DIRECTLY.
HEY THERE.
SAKURA MAMIYA-CHAN.
GLEAM

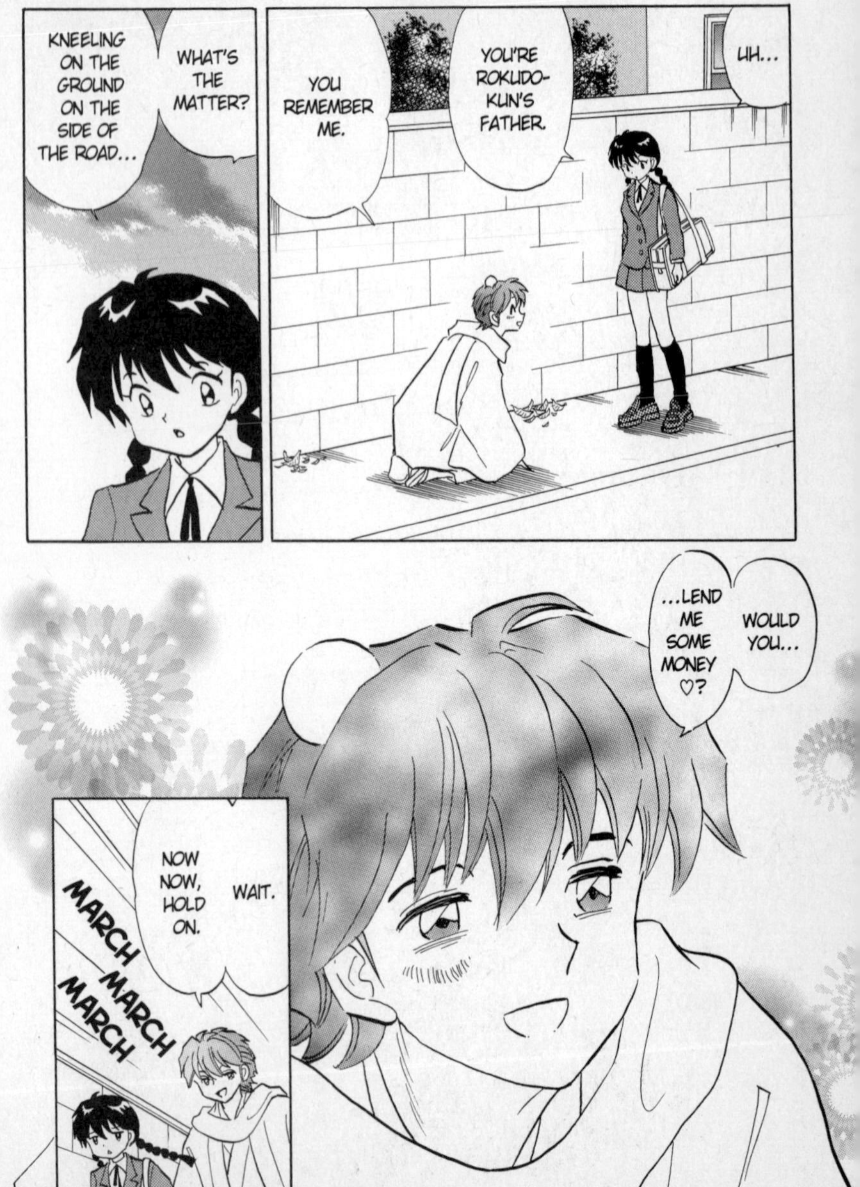
UH...
YOU'RE ROKUDO-KUN'S FATHER.
YOU REMEMBER ME.
WHAT'S THE MATTER?
KNEELING ON THE GROUND ON THE SIDE OF THE ROAD...
WOULD YOU...
...LEND ME SOME MONEY ♡?
WAIT.
NOW NOW, HOLD ON.
MARCH MARCH MARCH

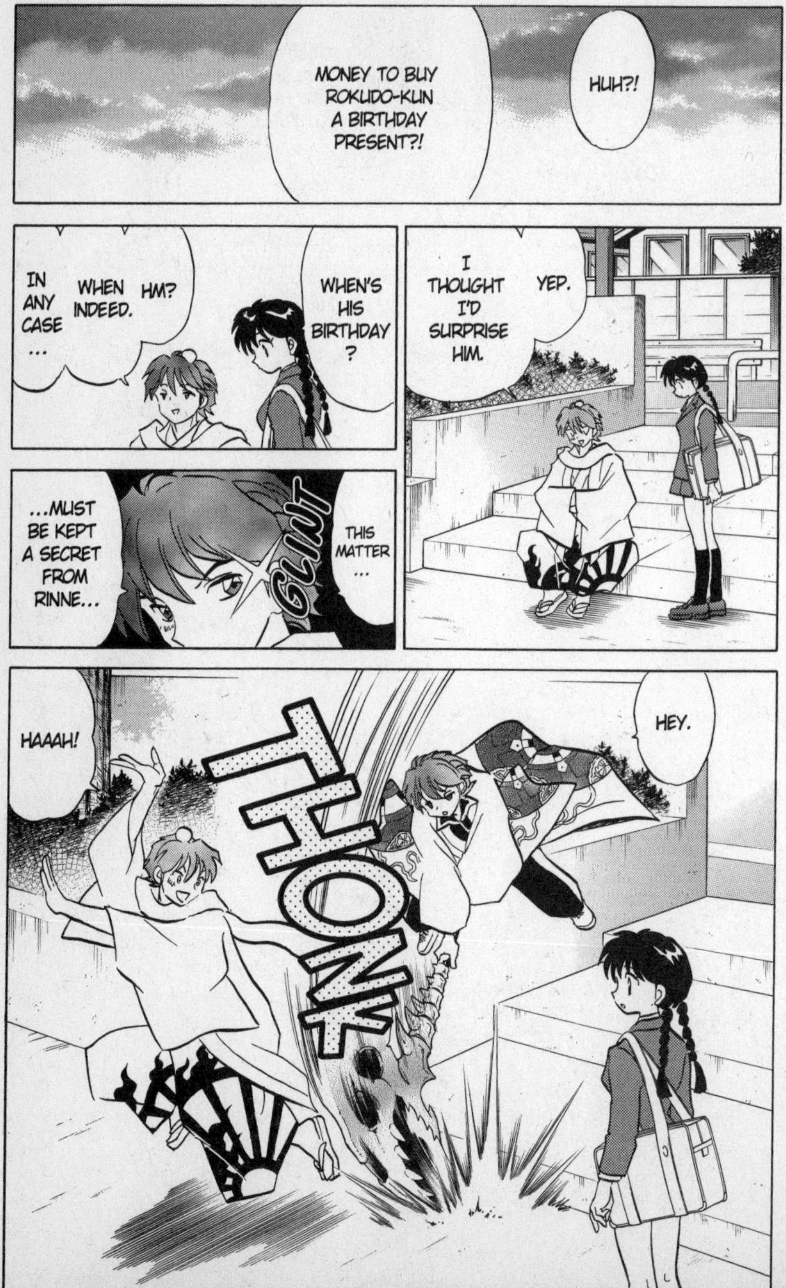
HUH?!
MONEY TO BUY ROKUDO-KUN A BIRTHDAY PRESENT?!
YEP.
I THOUGHT I'D SURPRISE HIM.
WHEN'S HIS BIRTHDAY?
HM?
WHEN INDEED.
IN ANY CASE...
THIS MATTER...
GLINT
...MUST BE KEPT A SECRET FROM RINNE...
HEY.
THONK
HAAAH!

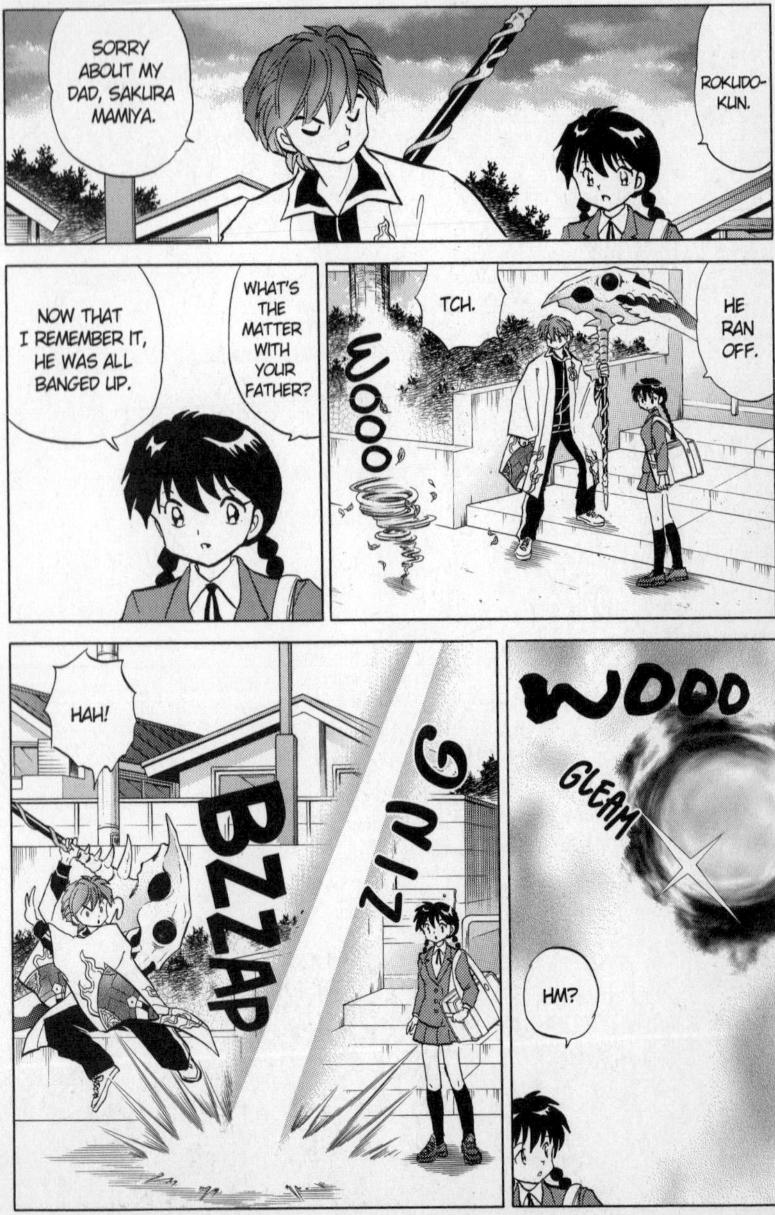
ROKUDO-KUN.
SORRY ABOUT MY DAD, SAKURA MAMIYA.
HE RAN OFF.
TCH.
WOOO
WHAT'S THE MATTER WITH YOUR FATHER?
NOW THAT I REMEMBER IT, HE WAS ALL BANGED UP.
WOOO
GLEAM
HM?
ZING
HAH!
BZZAP

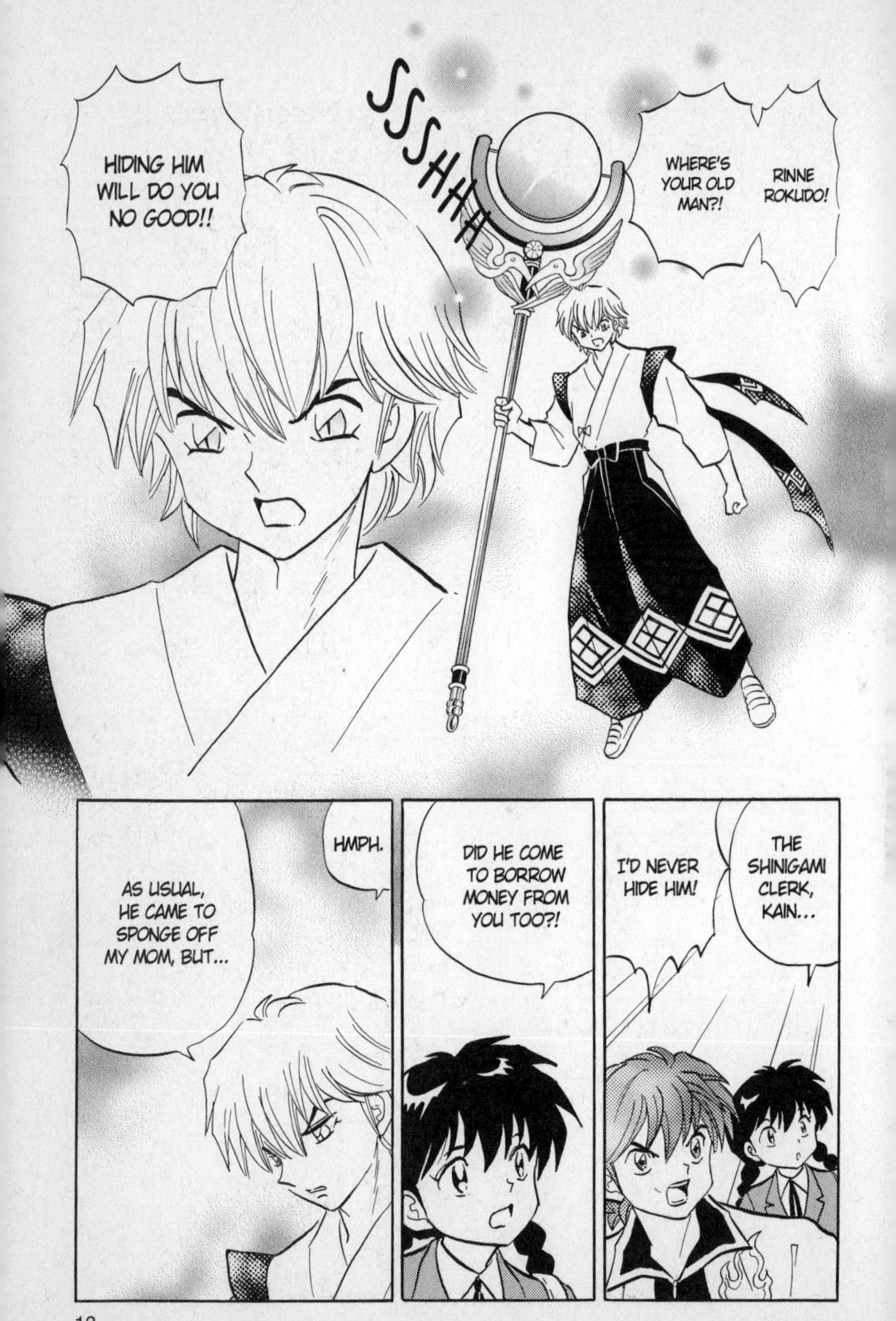
RINNE ROKUDO!
WHERE'S YOUR OLD MAN?!
SSSHHHH
HIDING HIM WILL DO YOU NO GOOD!!
THE SHINIGAMI CLERK, KAIN...
I'D NEVER HIDE HIM!
DID HE COME TO BORROW MONEY FROM YOU TOO?!
HMPH.
AS USUAL, HE CAME TO SPONGE OFF MY MOM, BUT...

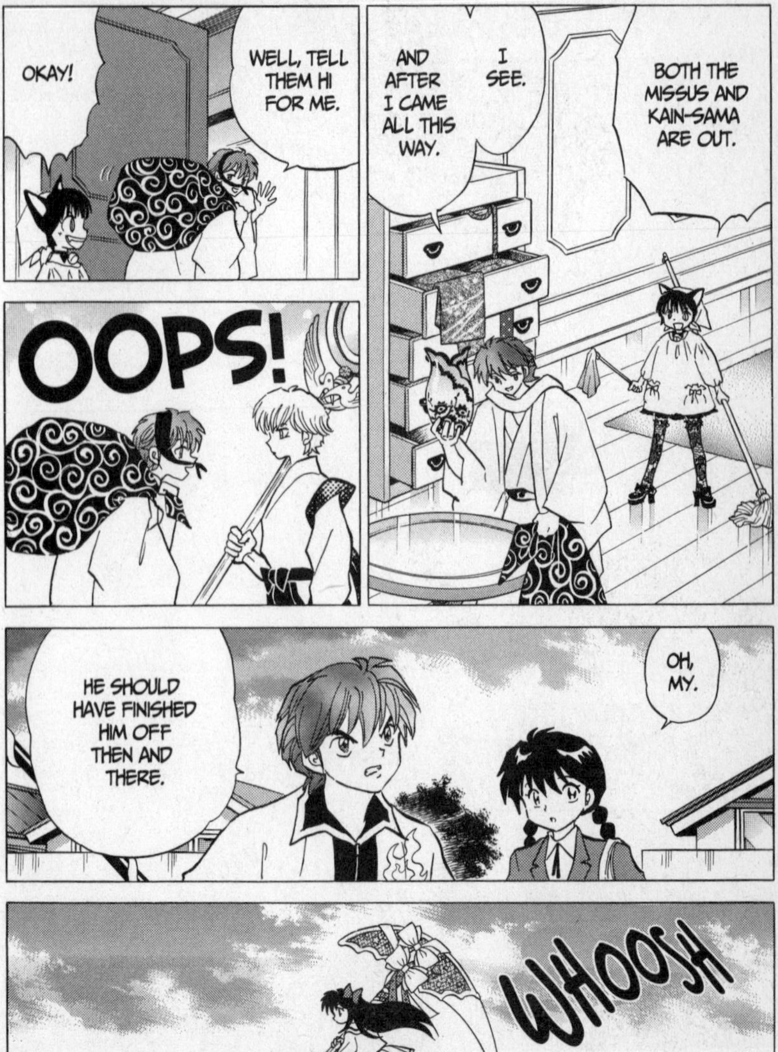
BOTH THE MISSUS AND KAIN-SAMA ARE OUT.
I SEE.
AND AFTER I CAME ALL THIS WAY.
WELL, TELL THEM HI FOR ME.
OKAY!
OOPS!
OH, MY.
HE SHOULD HAVE FINISHED HIM OFF THEN AND THERE.
WHOOSH

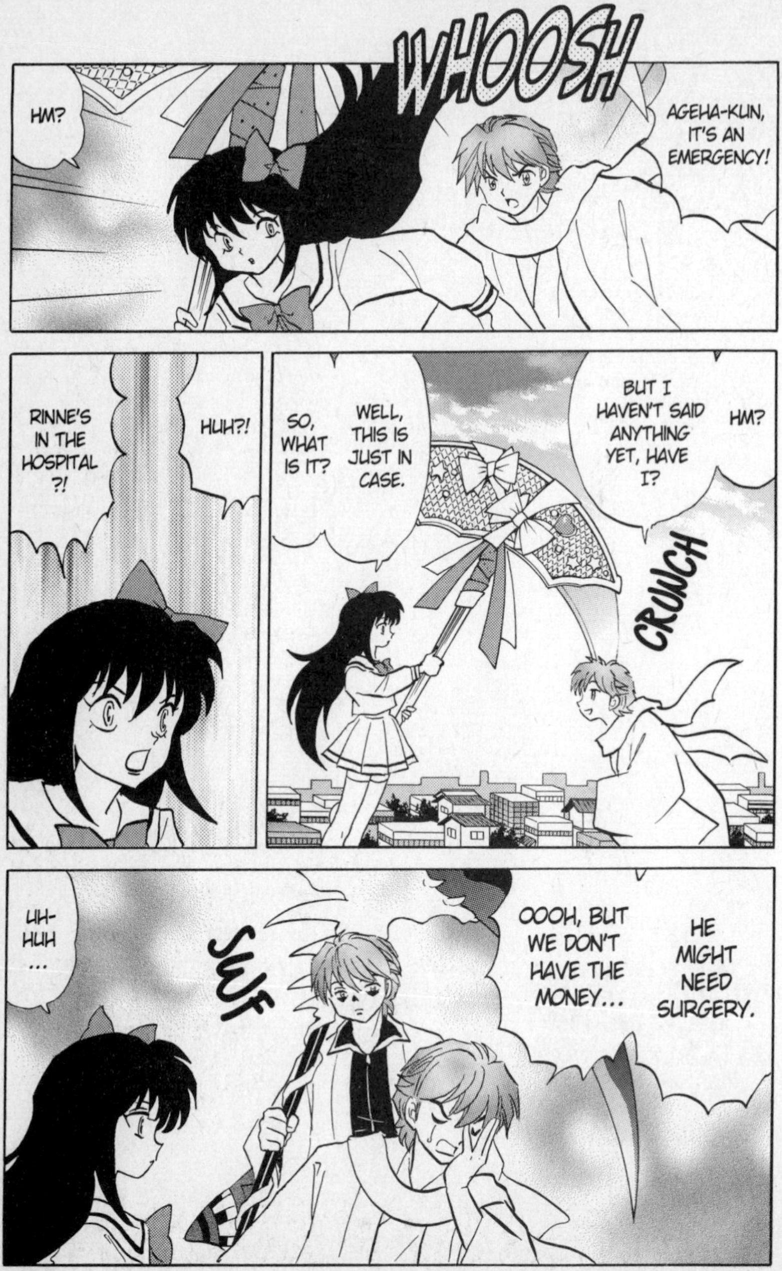
AGEHA-KUN, IT'S AN EMERGENCY!
WHOOSH
HM?
HM?
BUT I HAVEN'T SAID ANYTHING YET, HAVE I?
WELL, THIS IS JUST IN CASE.
SO, WHAT IS IT?
CRUNCH
HUH?!
RINNE'S IN THE HOSPITAL?!
HE MIGHT NEED SURGERY.
OOOH, BUT WE DON'T HAVE THE MONEY...
SWF
UH-HUH...

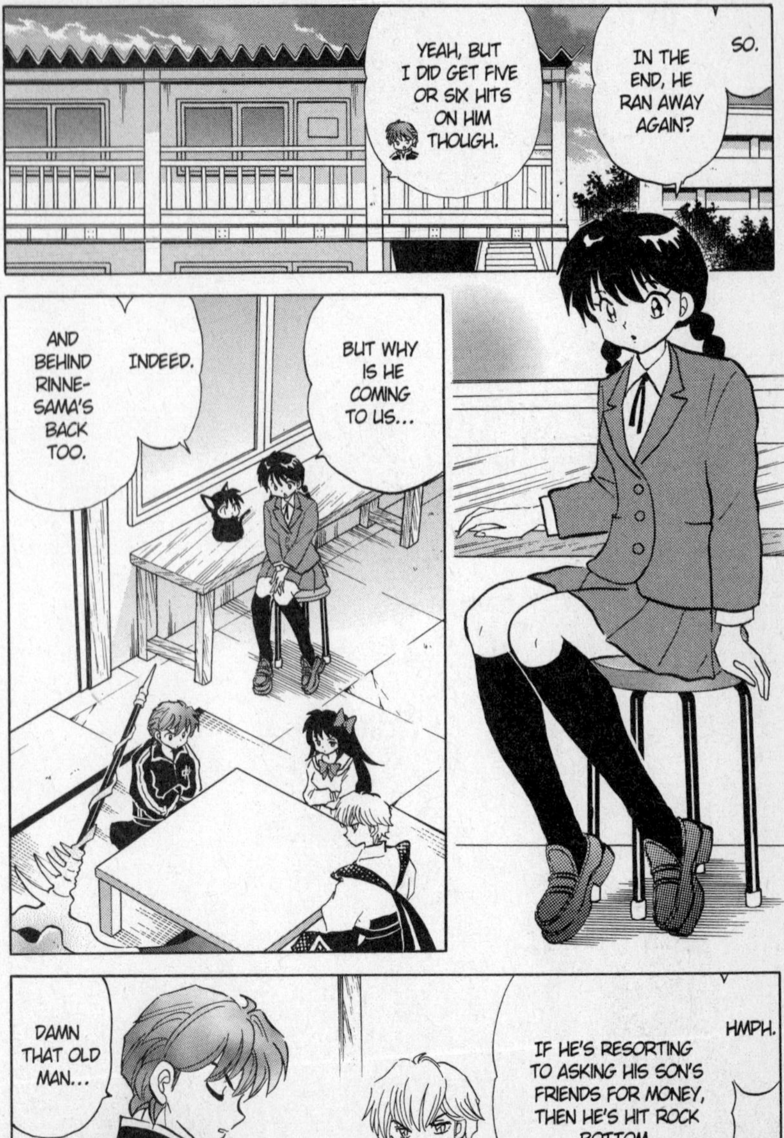
SO.
IN THE END, HE RAN AWAY AGAIN?
YEAH, BUT I DID GET FIVE OR SIX HITS ON HIM THOUGH.
BUT WHY IS HE COMING TO US...
INDEED.
AND BEHIND RINNE-SAMA'S BACK TOO.
HMPH.
IF HE'S RESORTING TO ASKING HIS SON'S FRIENDS FOR MONEY, THEN HE'S HIT ROCK BOTTOM.
DAMN THAT OLD MAN...

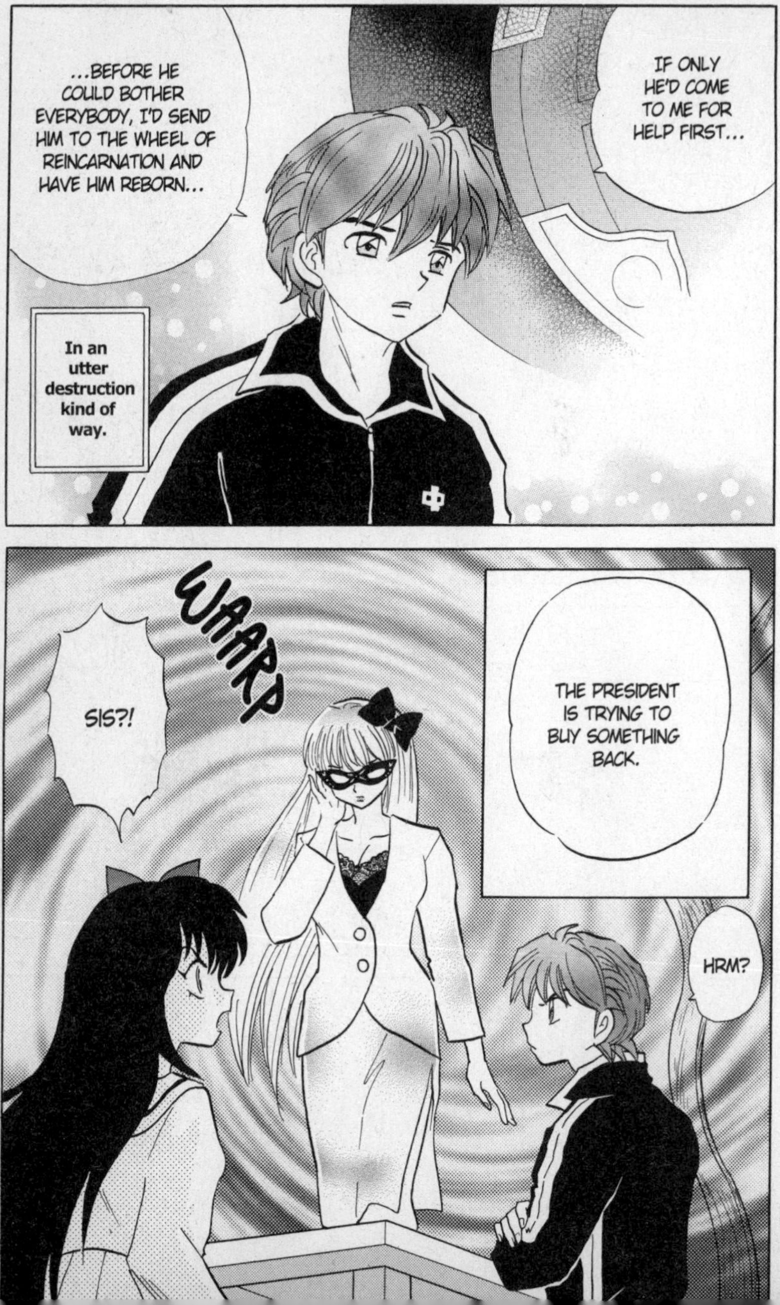
IF ONLY HE'D COME TO ME FOR HELP FIRST...
...BEFORE HE COULD BOTHER EVERYBODY, I'D SEND HIM TO THE WHEEL OF REINCARNATION AND HAVE HIM REBORN...
In an utter destruction kind of way.
THE PRESIDENT IS TRYING TO BUY SOMETHING BACK.
WAARP
SIS?!
HRM?

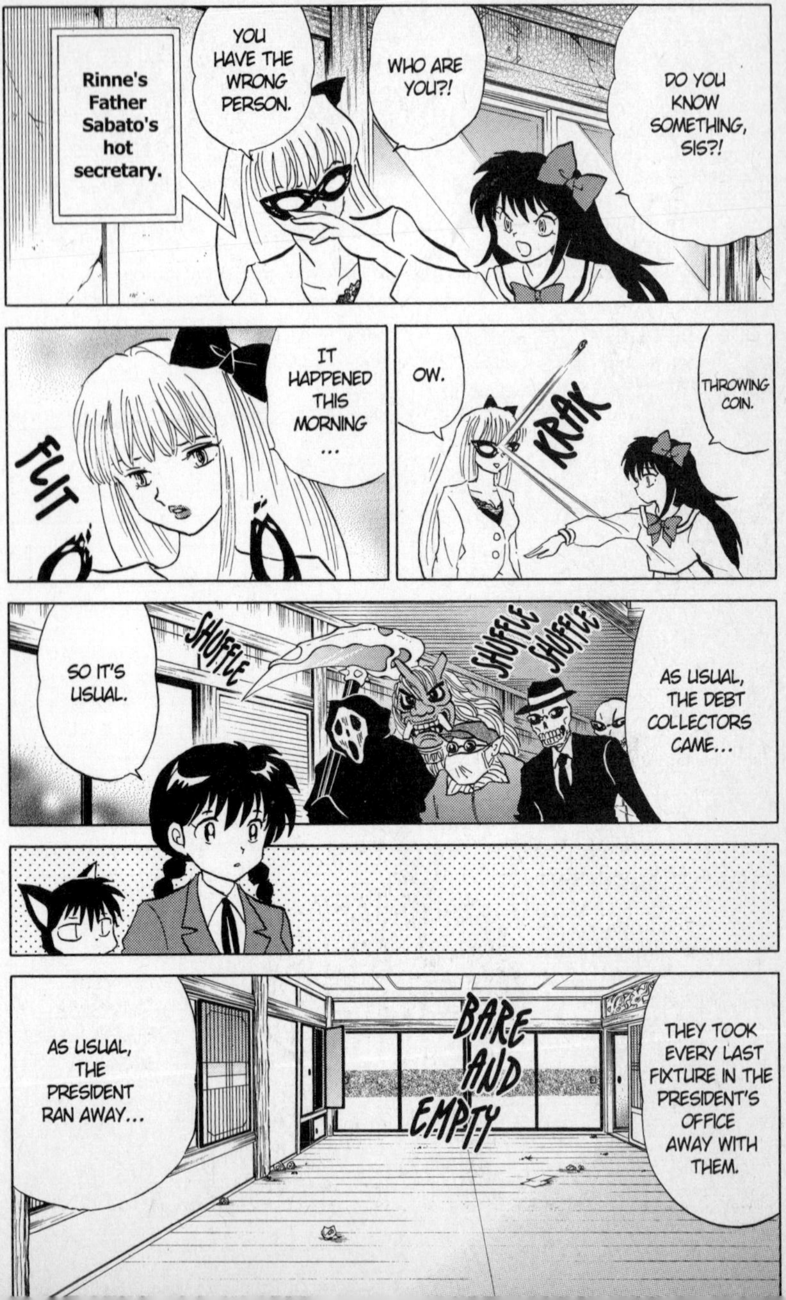
DO YOU KNOW SOMETHING, SIS?!
WHO ARE YOU?!
YOU HAVE THE WRONG PERSON.
Rinne's Father Sabato's hot secretary.
THROWING COIN.
KRAK
OW.
IT HAPPENED THIS MORNING ...
FLIT
AS USUAL, THE DEBT COLLECTORS CAME...
SHUFFLE SHUFFLE
SHUFFLE
SO IT'S USUAL.
THEY TOOK EVERY LAST FIXTURE IN THE PRESIDENT'S OFFICE AWAY WITH THEM.
BARE AND EMPTY
AS USUAL, THE PRESIDENT RAN AWAY...

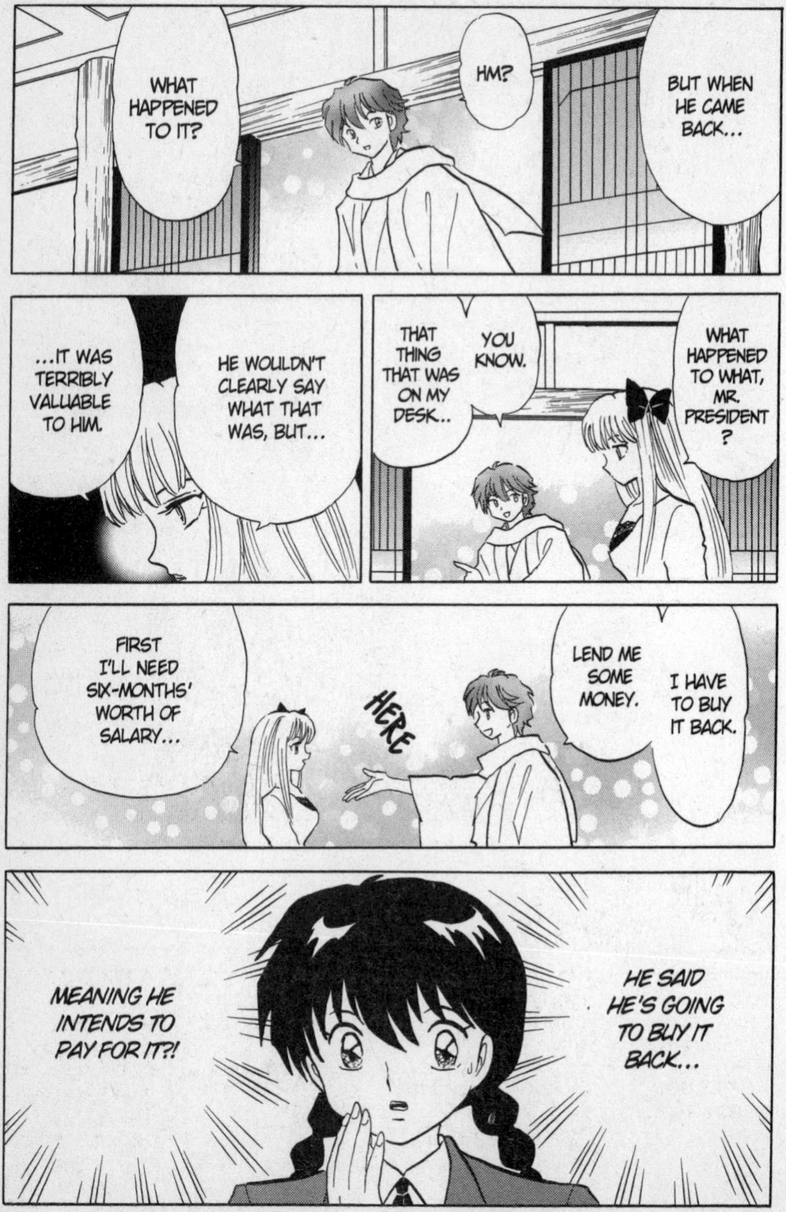
BUT WHEN HE CAME BACK...
HM?
WHAT HAPPENED TO IT?
WHAT HAPPENED TO WHAT, MR. PRESIDENT?
YOU KNOW.
THAT THING THAT WAS ON MY DESK...
HE WOULDN'T CLEARLY SAY WHAT THAT WAS, BUT...
...IT WAS TERRIBLY VALUABLE TO HIM.
I HAVE TO BUY IT BACK.
LEND ME SOME MONEY.
HERE
FIRST I'LL NEED SIX-MONTHS' WORTH OF SALARY...
HE SAID HE'S GOING TO BUY IT BACK...
MEANING HE INTENDS TO PAY FOR IT?!

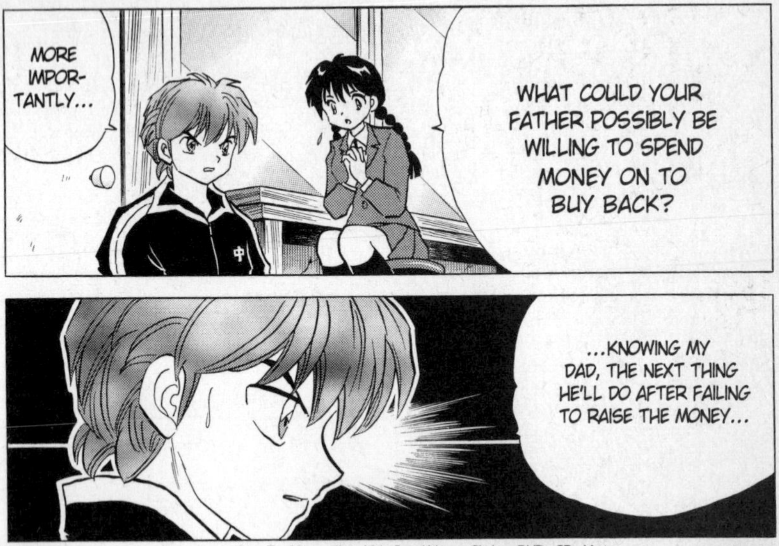
WHAT COULD YOUR FATHER POSSIBLY BE WILLING TO SPEND MONEY ON TO BUY BACK?
MORE IMPOR-TANTLY...
...KNOWING MY DAD, THE NEXT THING HE'LL DO AFTER FAILING TO RAISE THE MONEY...

Signs: Total Secondhand Sale Brand Names, Clothing, DVDs, CDs, Music

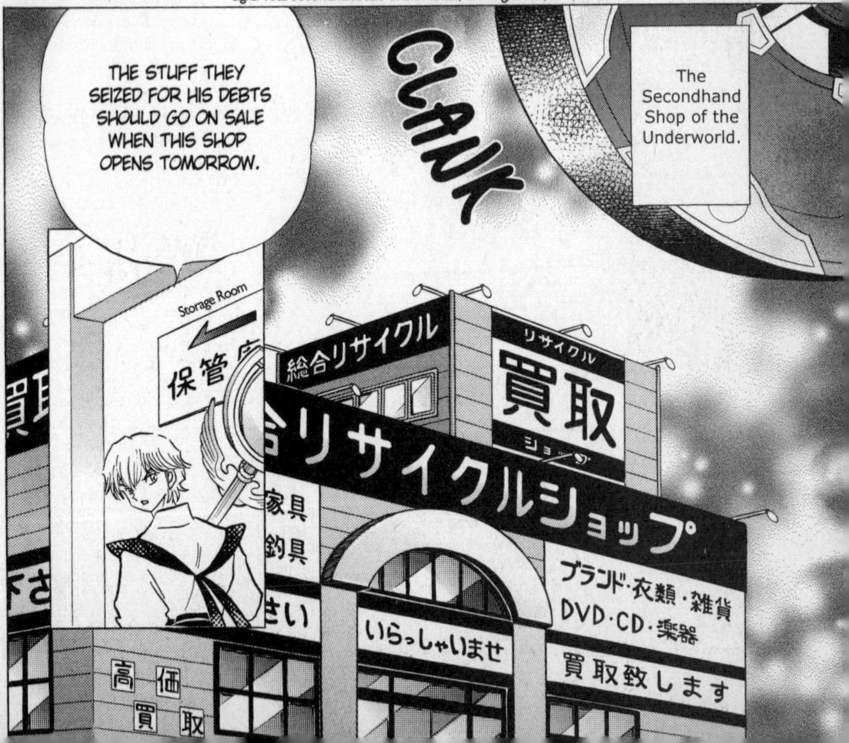
The Secondhand Shop of the Underworld.
CLANK
THE STUFF THEY SEIZED FOR HIS DEBTS SHOULD GO ON SALE WHEN THIS SHOP OPENS TOMORROW.
Storage Room
総合リサイクル
リサイクル
買取
家具
釣具
ブランド・衣類・雑貨
DVD・CD・楽器
いらっしゃいませ
買取致します
高価
買取

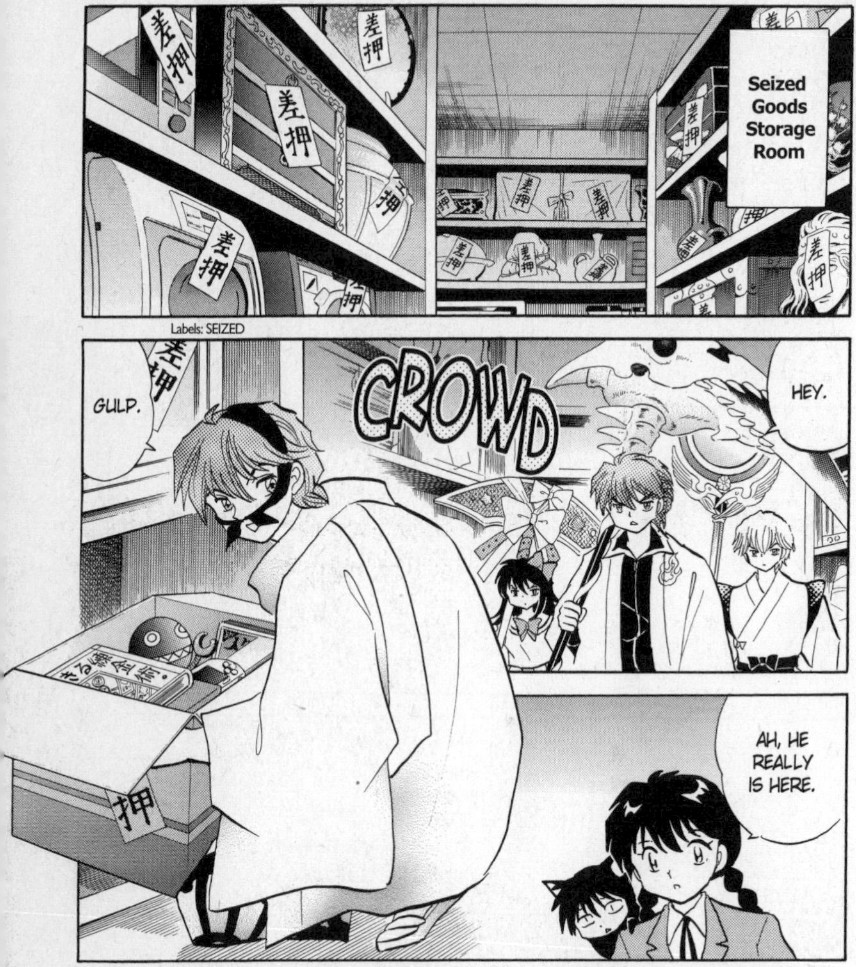
Seized Goods Storage Room
Labels: SEIZED
HEY.
CROWD
GULP.
AH, HE REALLY IS HERE.
LET ME ASK YOU ONE THING.
WHAT'RE YOU DOING?
HMPH, RINNE.
IN THE WORLD...

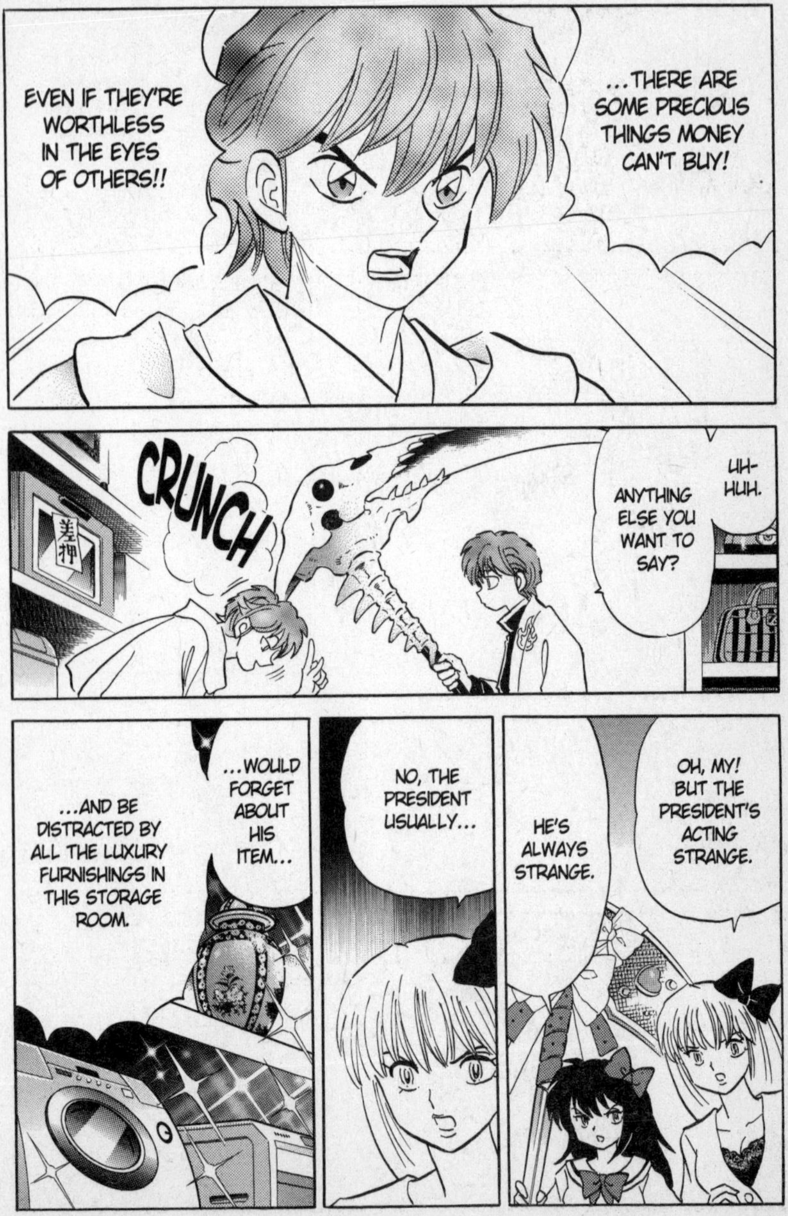
EVEN IF THEY'RE WORTHLESS IN THE EYES OF OTHERS!!
...THERE ARE SOME PRECIOUS THINGS MONEY CAN'T BUY!
UH-HUH.
ANYTHING ELSE YOU WANT TO SAY?
CRUNCH
差押
OH, MY! BUT THE PRESIDENT'S ACTING STRANGE.
HE'S ALWAYS STRANGE.
NO, THE PRESIDENT USUALLY...
...WOULD FORGET ABOUT HIS ITEM...
...AND BE DISTRACTED BY ALL THE LUXURY FURNISHINGS IN THIS STORAGE ROOM.

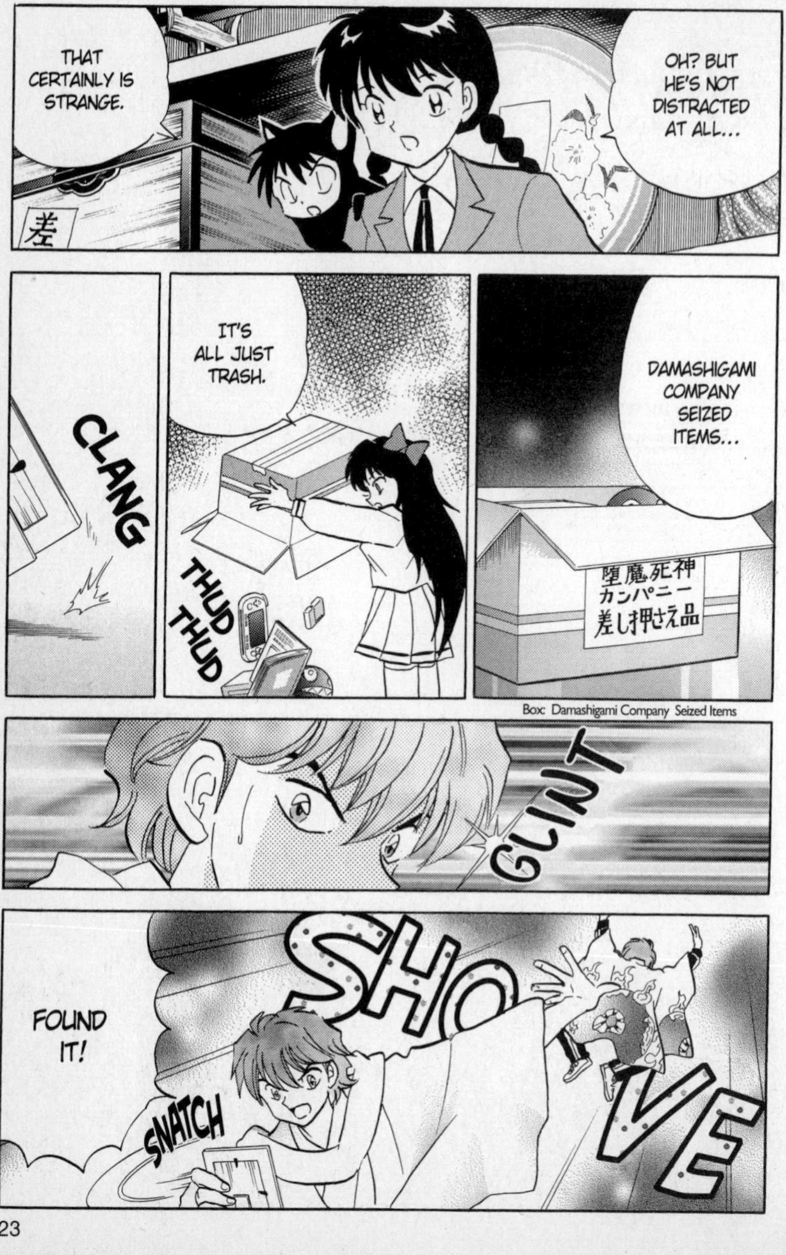
OH? BUT HE'S NOT DISTRACTED AT ALL...
THAT CERTAINLY IS STRANGE.
差
DAMASHIGAMI COMPANY SEIZED ITEMS...
堕魔死神 カンパニー 差し押さえ品
Box: Damashigami Company Seized Items
IT'S ALL JUST TRASH.
THUD THUD
CLANG
GLINT
SHOVE
FOUND IT!
SNATCH

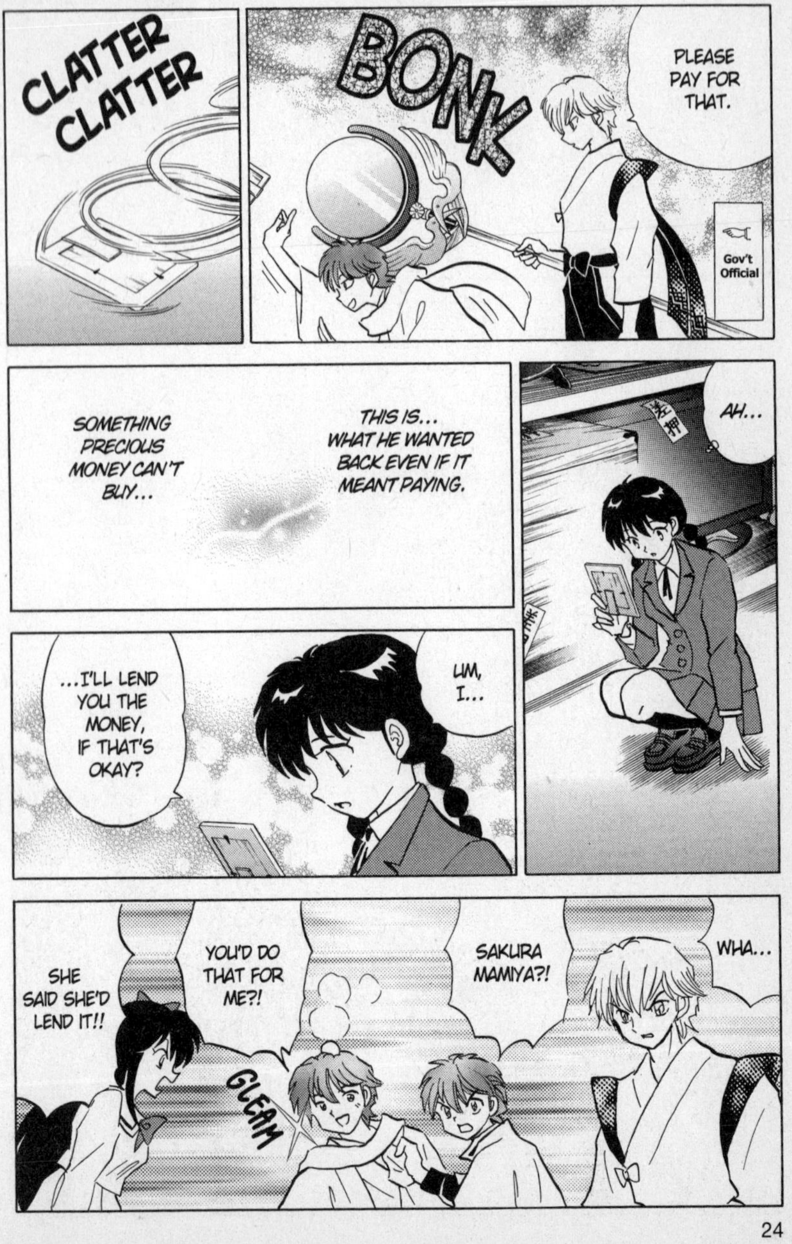
PLEASE PAY FOR THAT.
BONK
Gov't Official
CLATTER CLATTER
AH...
差押
THIS IS... WHAT HE WANTED BACK EVEN IF IT MEANT PAYING.
SOMETHING PRECIOUS MONEY CAN'T BUY...
UM, I...
...I'LL LEND YOU THE MONEY, IF THAT'S OKAY?
WHA...
SAKURA MAMIYA?!
YOU'D DO THAT FOR ME?!
GLEAM
SHE SAID SHE'D LEND IT!!

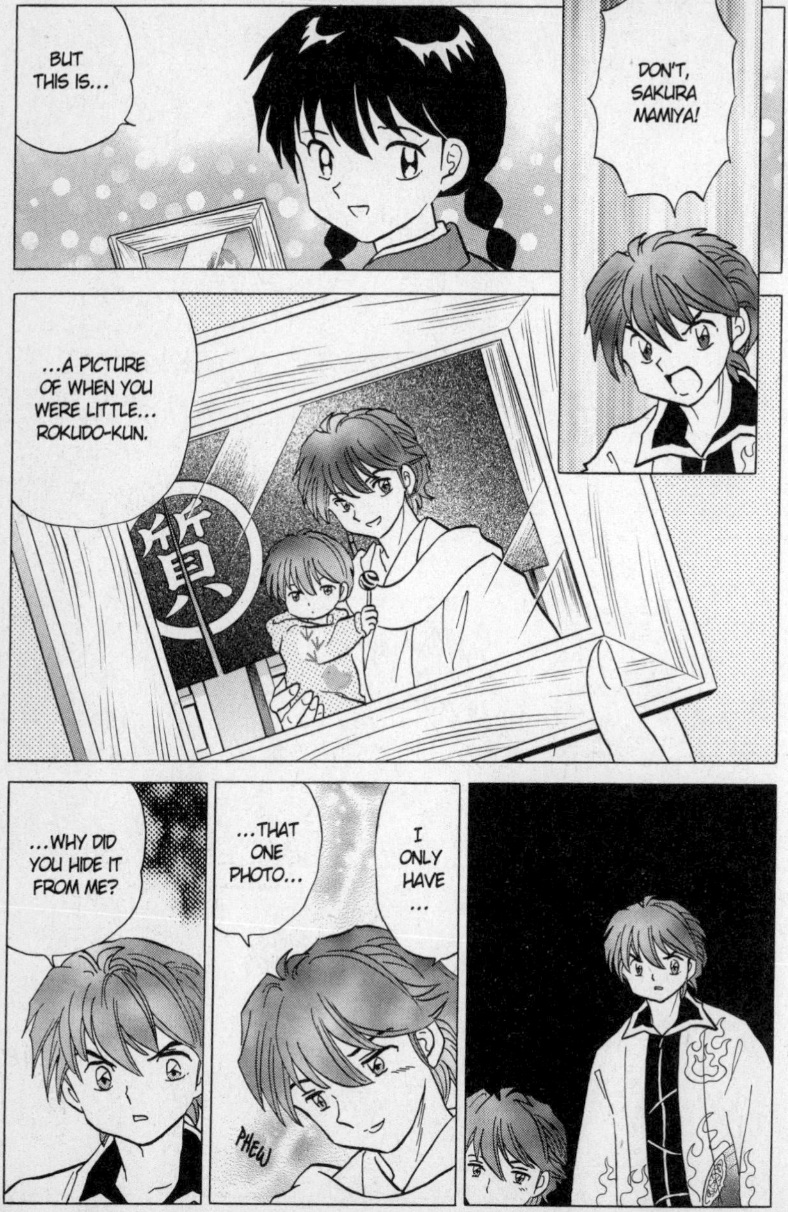

DON'T, SAKURA MAMIYA!
BUT THIS IS...
...A PICTURE OF WHEN YOU WERE LITTLE... ROKUDO-KUN.
I ONLY HAVE...
...THAT ONE PHOTO...
PHEW
...WHY DID YOU HIDE IT FROM ME?

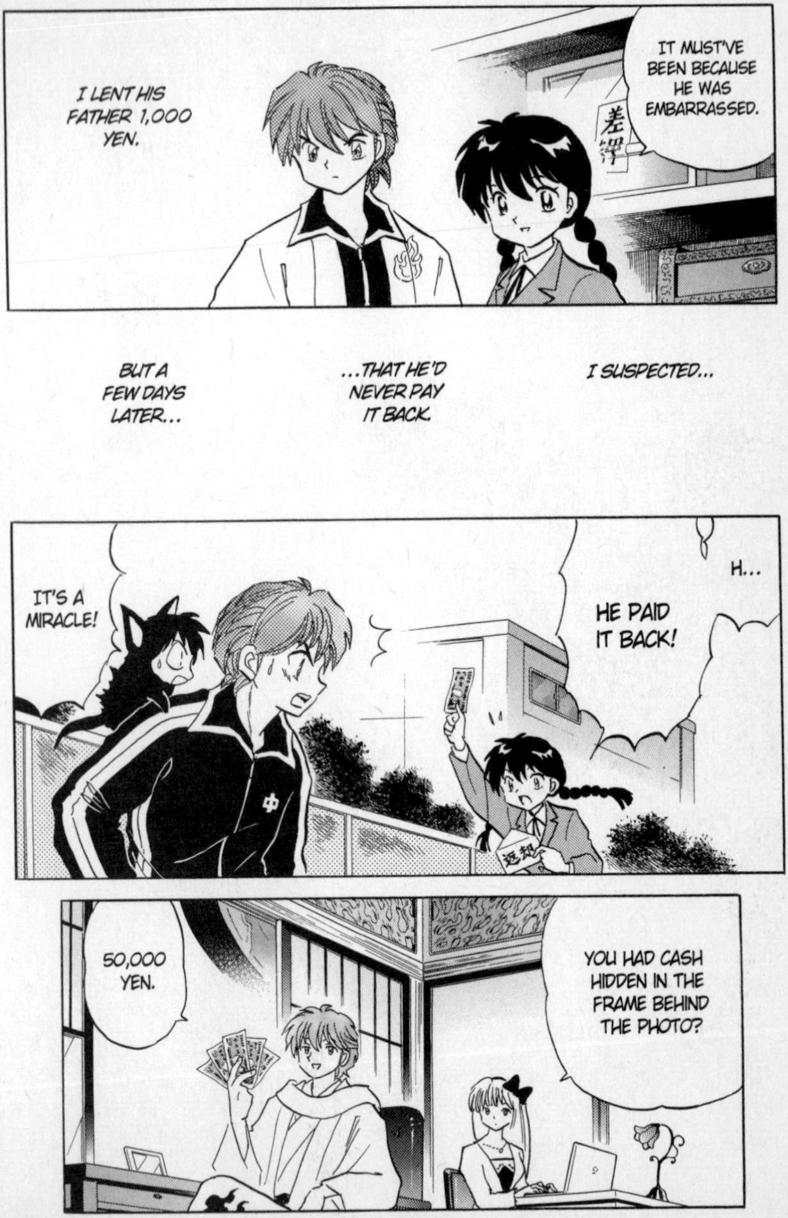
IT MUST'VE BEEN BECAUSE HE WAS EMBARRASSED.
I LENT HIS FATHER 1,000 YEN.
I SUSPECTED...
...THAT HE'D NEVER PAY IT BACK.
BUT A FEW DAYS LATER...
H...
HE PAID IT BACK!
IT'S A MIRACLE!
YOU HAD CASH HIDDEN IN THE FRAME BEHIND THE PHOTO?
50,000 YEN.

CHAPTER 120: WHEN IT COMES TO SCYTHES, COME TO THE CRESCENT MOON HALL

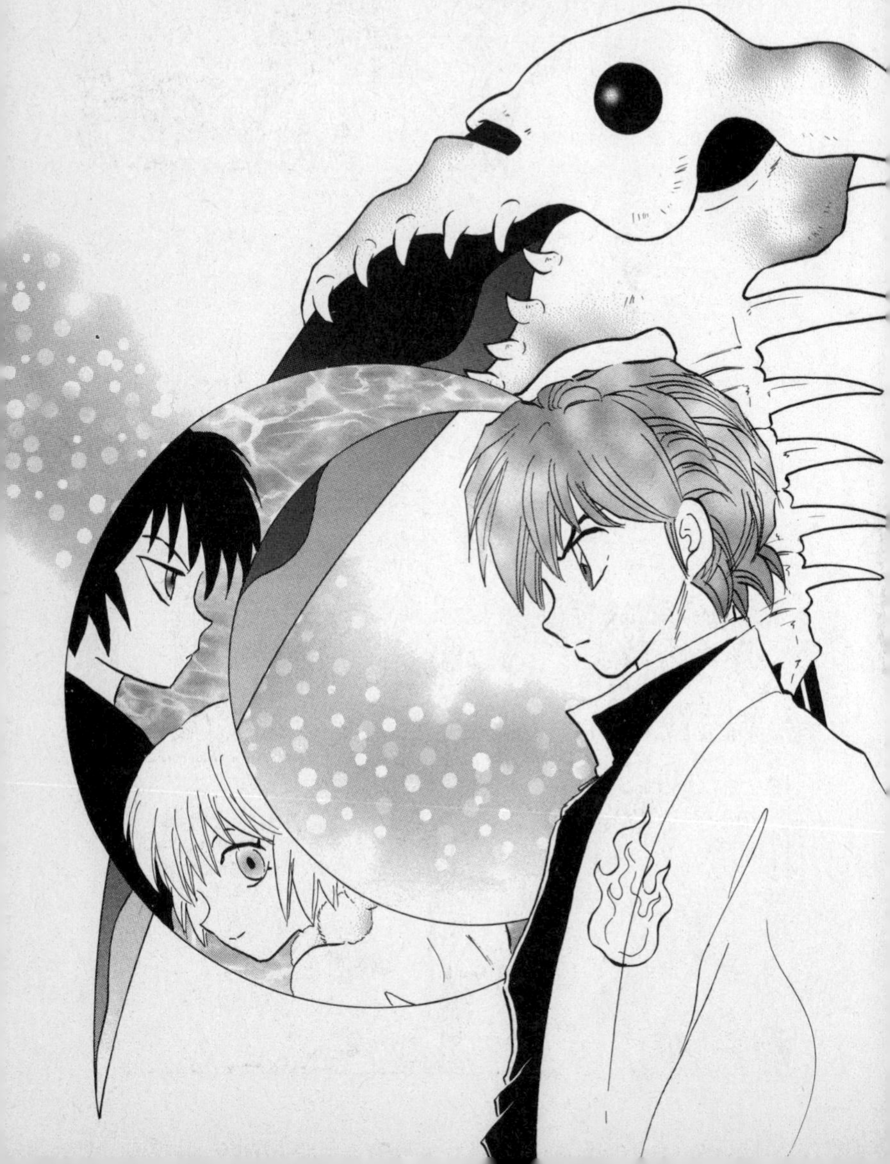

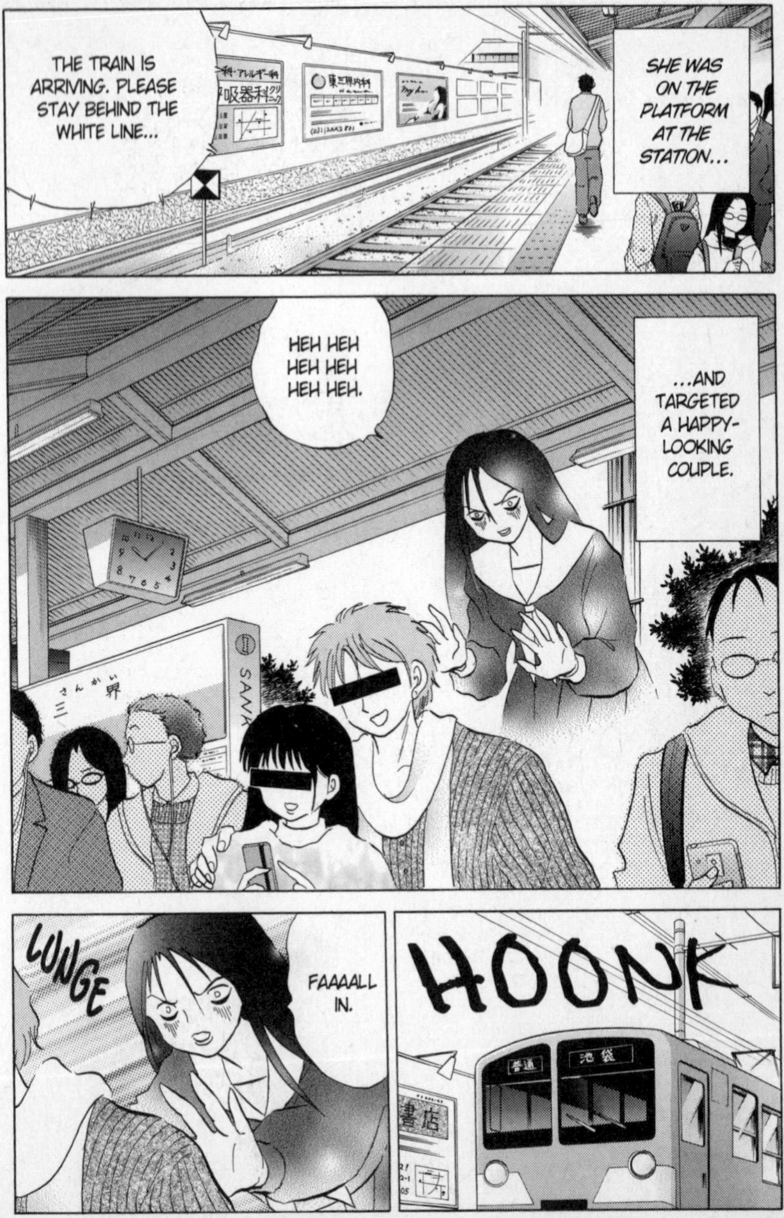
SHE WAS ON THE PLATFORM AT THE STATION...
THE TRAIN IS ARRIVING. PLEASE STAY BEHIND THE WHITE LINE...
...AND TARGETED A HAPPY-LOOKING COUPLE.
HEH HEH HEH HEH HEH HEH.
さんかい
三界
HOONK
普通
池袋
書店
FAAAALL IN.
LUNGE

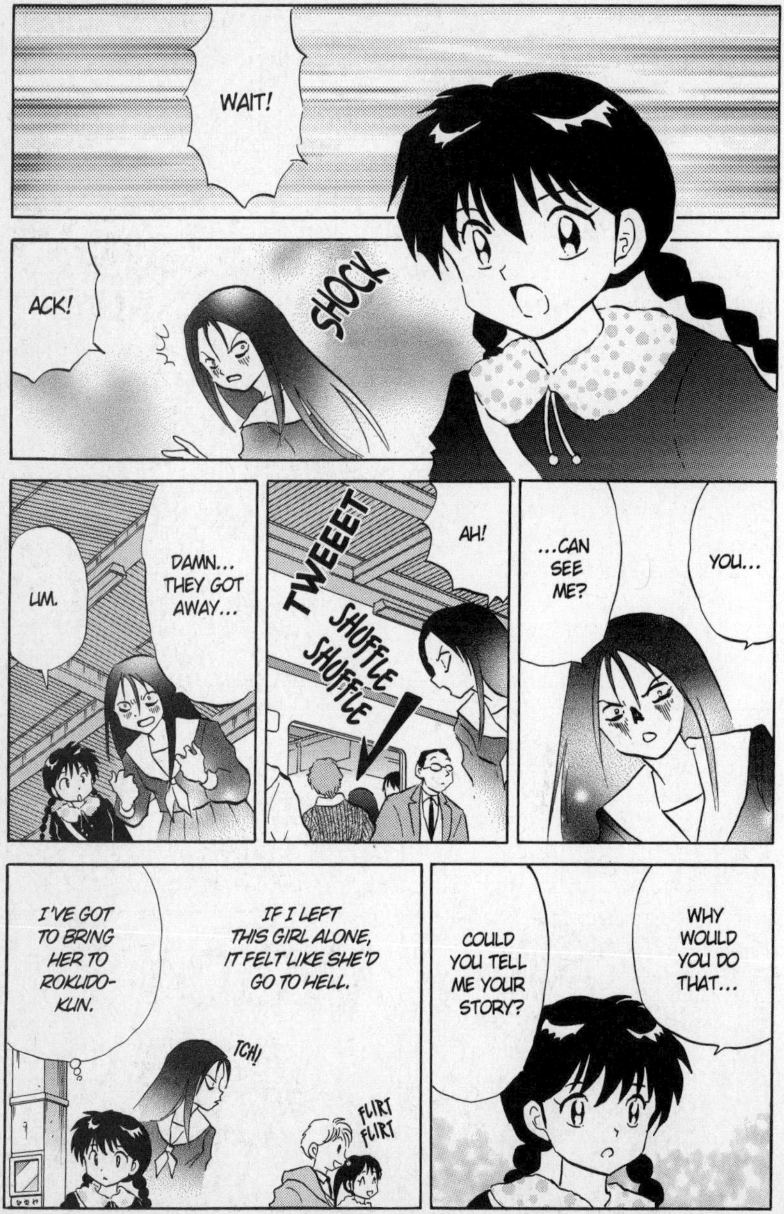
WAIT!
ACK!
SHOCK
YOU...
...CAN SEE ME?
AH!
TWEEEET
SHUFFLE SHUFFLE
DAMN... THEY GOT AWAY...
UM.
WHY WOULD YOU DO THAT...
COULD YOU TELL ME YOUR STORY?
IF I LEFT THIS GIRL ALONE, IT FELT LIKE SHE'D GO TO HELL.
I'VE GOT TO BRING HER TO ROKUDO-KUN.
TCH!
FLIRT FLIRT

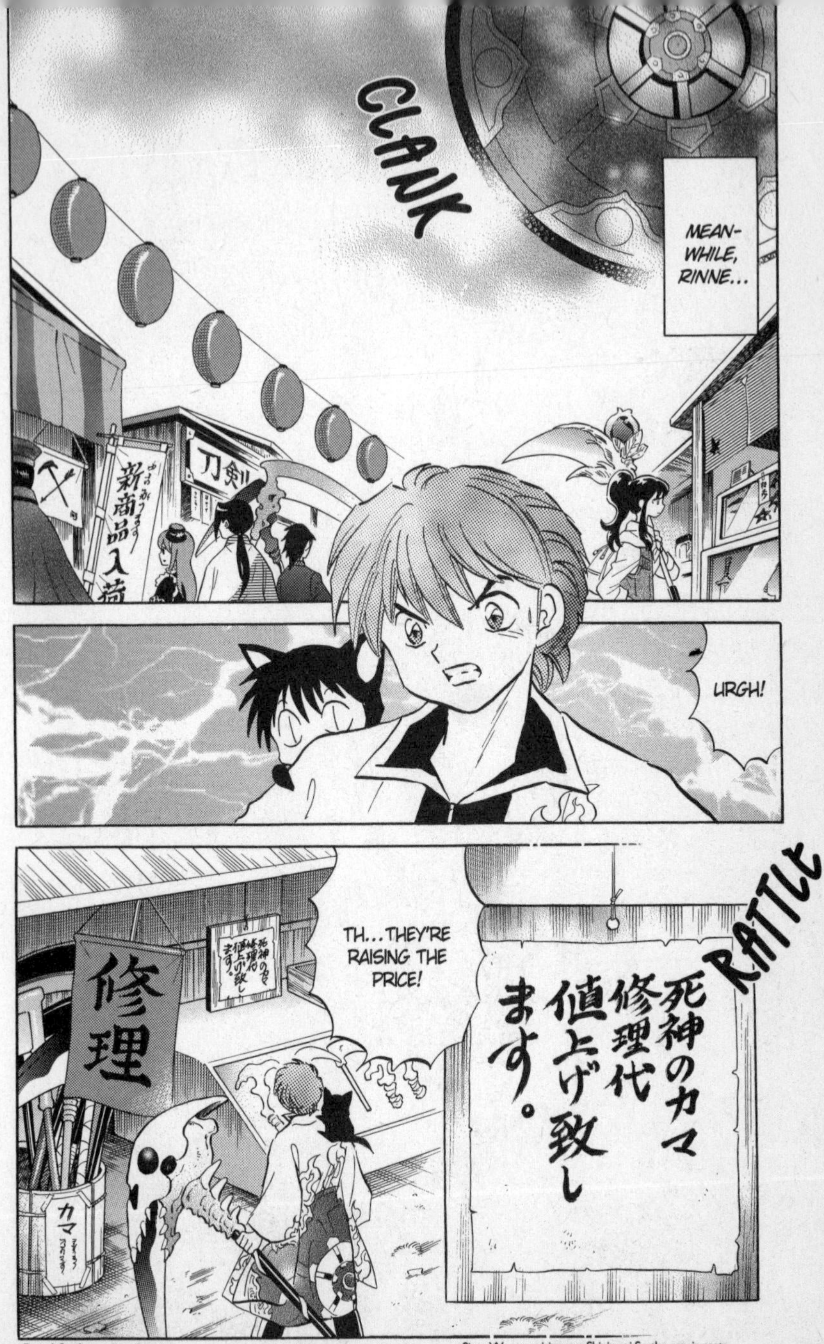
MEAN-WHILE, RINNE...
CLANK
刀剣
新商品入荷
URGH!
RATTLE
死神のカマ修理代値上げ致します。
TH...THEY'RE RAISING THE PRICE!
修理
カマ

Barrel: Scythes Sign: Repairs Sign: We are raising our Shinigami Scythe repair costs.

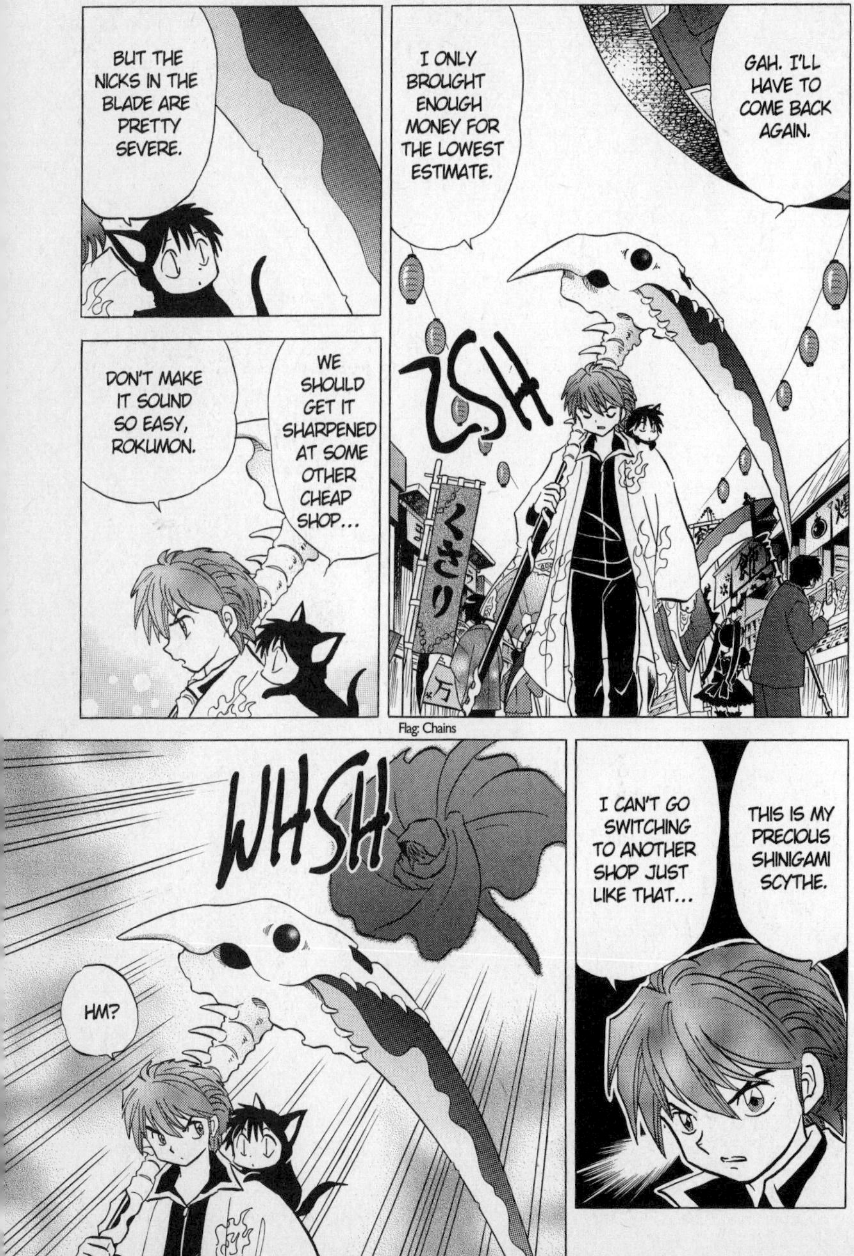
GAH. I'LL HAVE TO COME BACK AGAIN.
I ONLY BROUGHT ENOUGH MONEY FOR THE LOWEST ESTIMATE.
ZSH
くさり
BUT THE NICKS IN THE BLADE ARE PRETTY SEVERE.
WE SHOULD GET IT SHARPENED AT SOME OTHER CHEAP SHOP...
DON'T MAKE IT SOUND SO EASY, ROKUMON.
THIS IS MY PRECIOUS SHINIGAMI SCYTHE.
I CAN'T GO SWITCHING TO ANOTHER SHOP JUST LIKE THAT...
WHSH
HM?
Flag: Chains

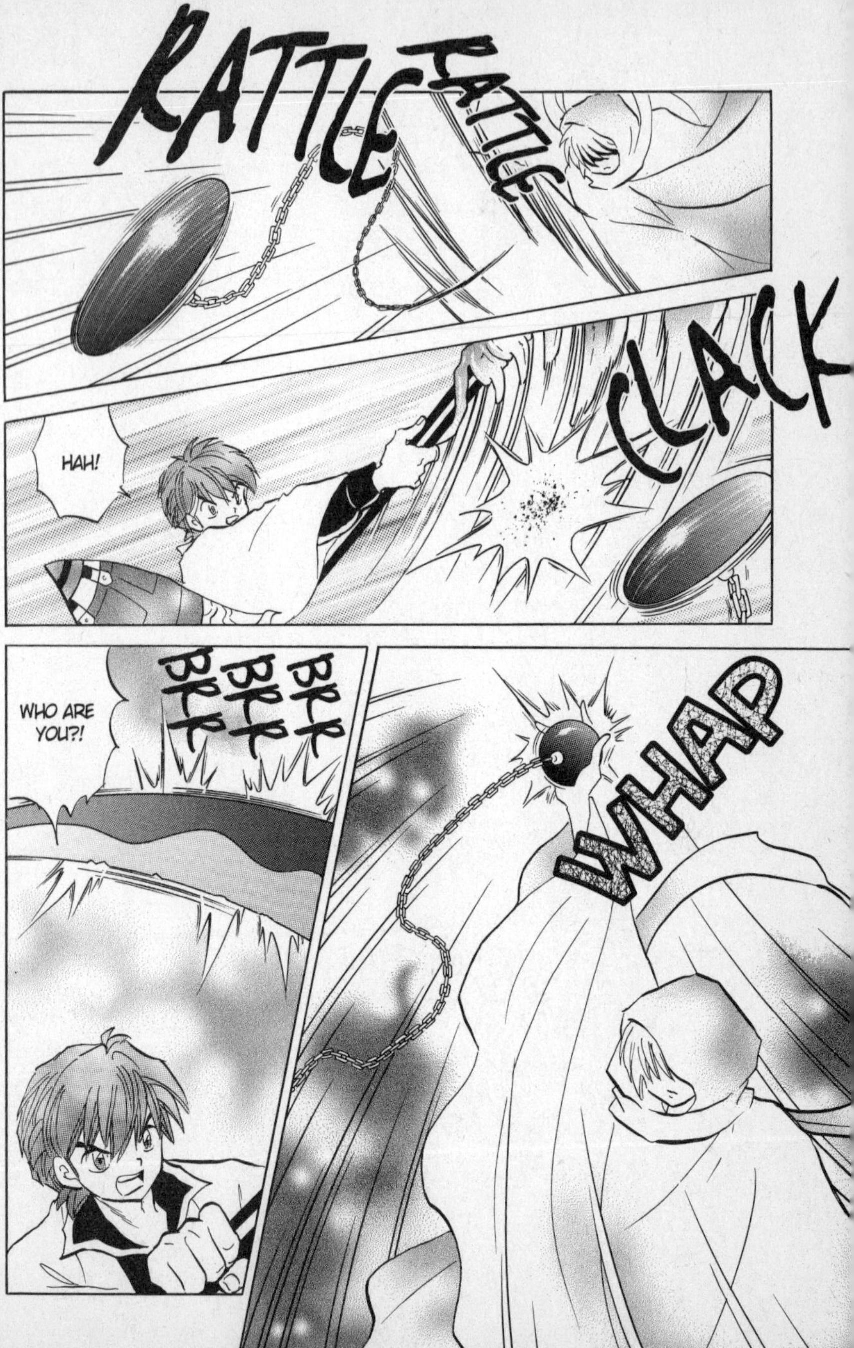
RATTLE
RATTLE
CLACK
HAH!
WHAP
BPPP BPPP BPPP
WHO ARE YOU?!

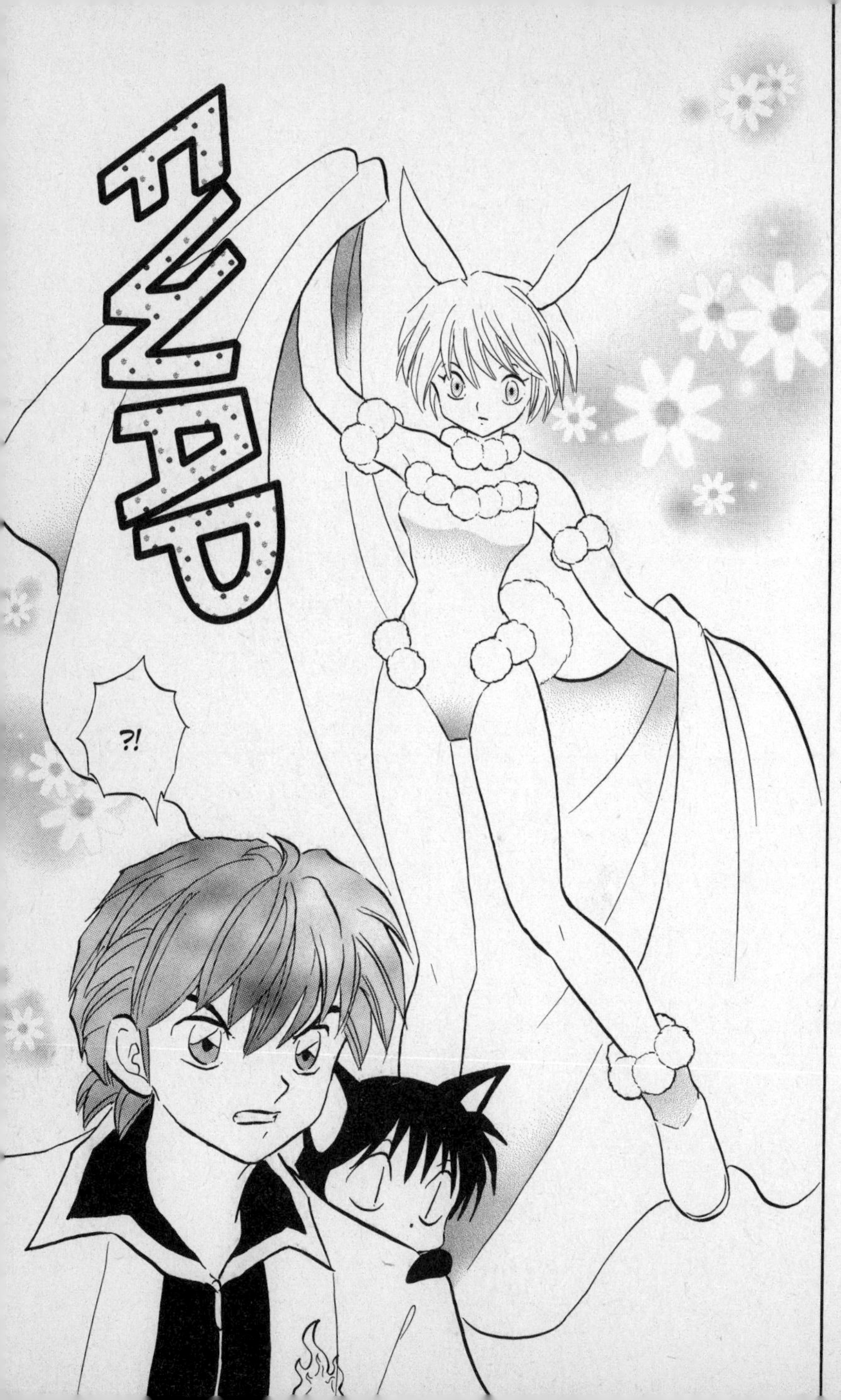
FWAP
?!

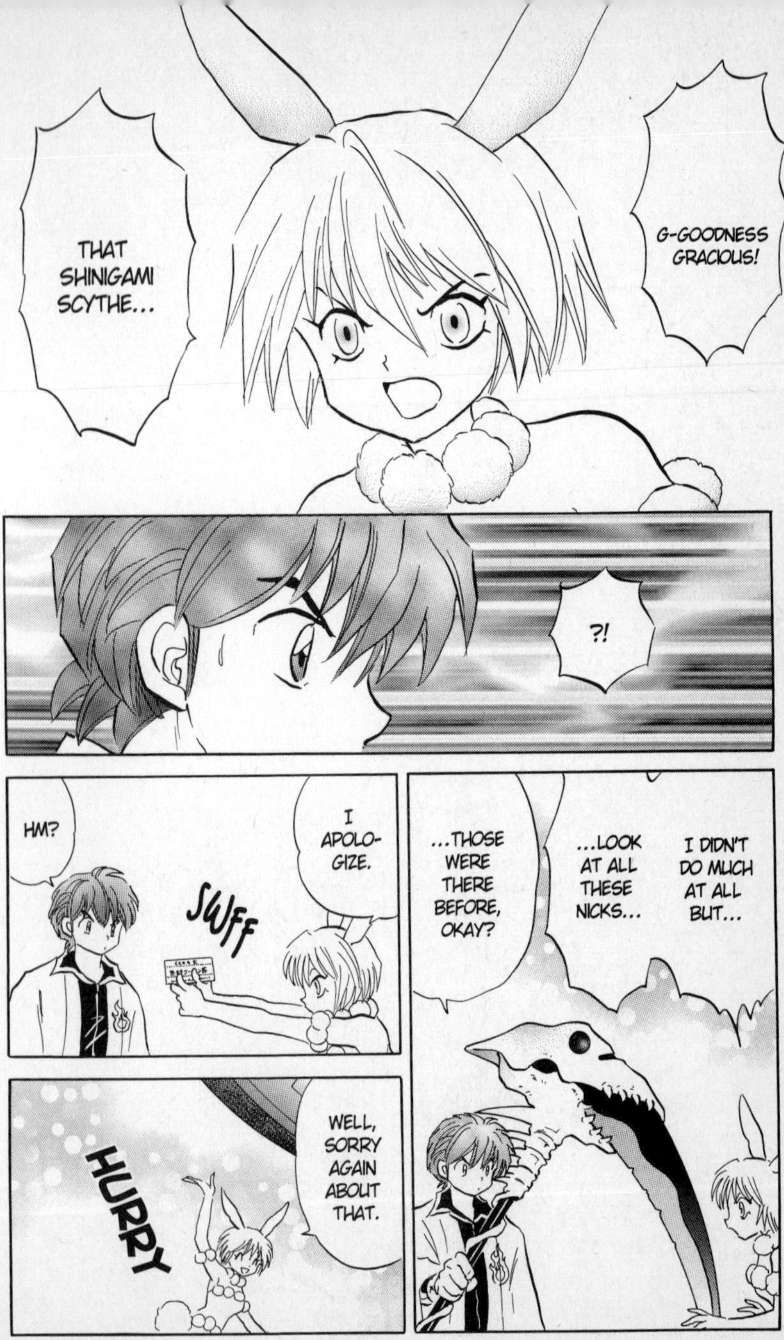
G-GOODNESS GRACIOUS!
THAT SHINIGAMI SCYTHE...
?!
I DIDN'T DO MUCH AT ALL BUT...
...LOOK AT ALL THESE NICKS...
...THOSE WERE THERE BEFORE, OKAY?
I APOLOGIZE.
SWFF
HM?
WELL, SORRY AGAIN ABOUT THAT.
HURRY

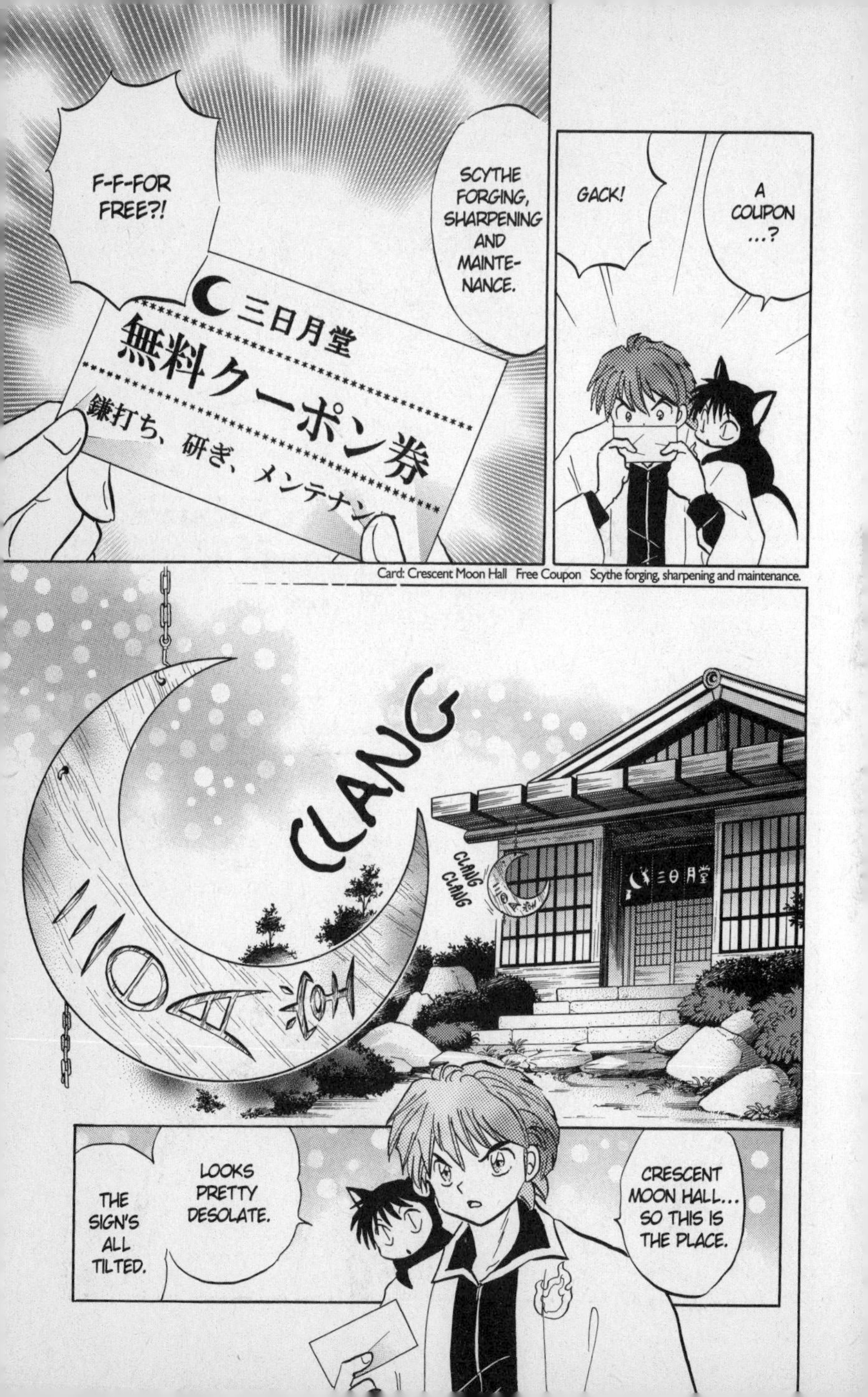
GACK!
A COUPON ...?
SCYTHE FORGING, SHARPENING AND MAINTE-NANCE.
F-F-FOR FREE?!
三日月堂
無料クーポン券
鎌打ち、研ぎ、メンテナン
Card: Crescent Moon Hall Free Coupon Scythe forging, sharpening and maintenance.
CLANG
CLANG CLANG
三日月堂
CRESCENT MOON HALL... SO THIS IS THE PLACE.
LOOKS PRETTY DESOLATE.
THE SIGN'S ALL TILTED.

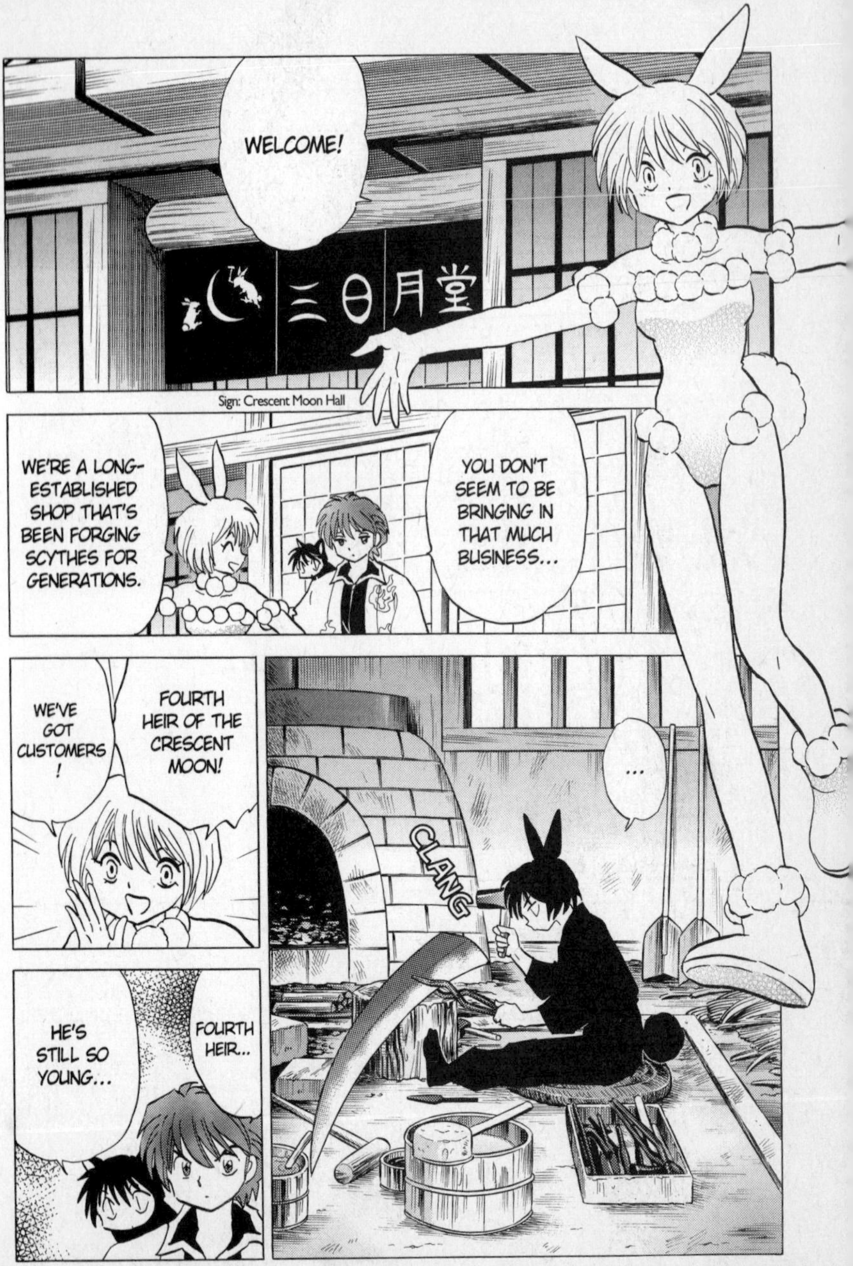
WELCOME!
三日月堂
YOU DON'T SEEM TO BE BRINGING IN THAT MUCH BUSINESS...
WE'RE A LONG-ESTABLISHED SHOP THAT'S BEEN FORGING SCYTHES FOR GENERATIONS.
...
CLANG
WE'VE GOT CUSTOMERS!
FOURTH HEIR OF THE CRESCENT MOON!
FOURTH HEIR...
HE'S STILL SO YOUNG...
Sign: Crescent Moon Hall

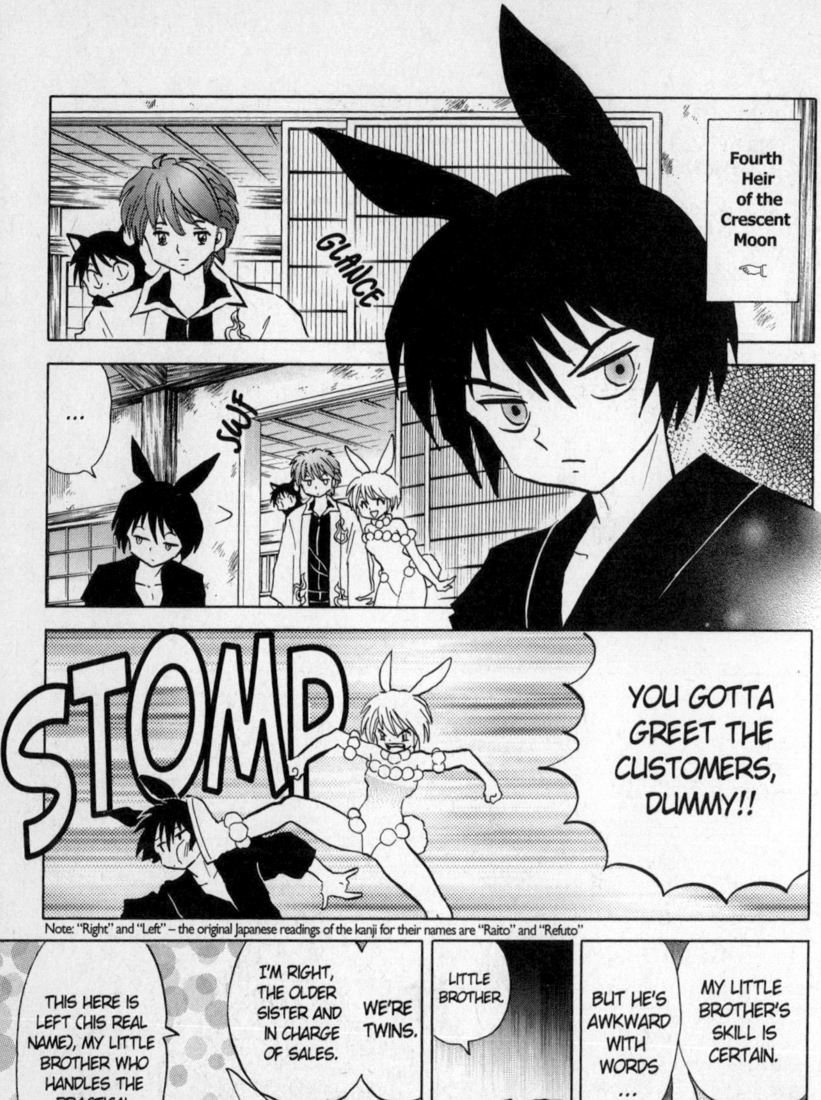
Fourth Heir of the Crescent Moon
GLANCE
...
SWF
YOU GOTTA GREET THE CUSTOMERS, DUMMY!!
STOMP

Note: "Right" and "Left" – the original Japanese readings of the kanji for their names are "Raito" and "Refuto"

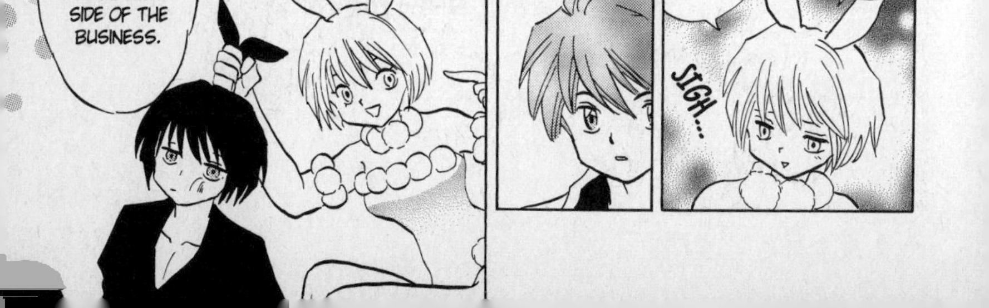
MY LITTLE BROTHER'S SKILL IS CERTAIN.
BUT HE'S AWKWARD WITH WORDS ...
SIGH...
LITTLE BROTHER
WE'RE TWINS.
I'M RIGHT, THE OLDER SISTER AND IN CHARGE OF SALES.
THIS HERE IS LEFT (HIS REAL NAME), MY LITTLE BROTHER WHO HANDLES THE PRACTICAL SIDE OF THE BUSINESS.

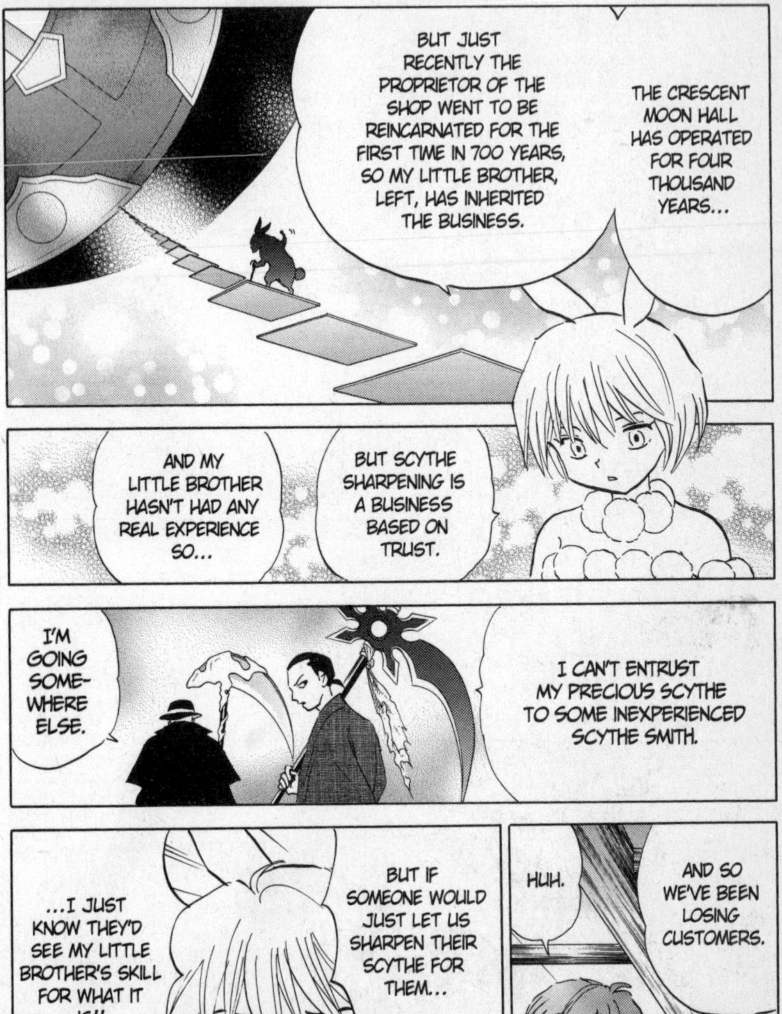
THE CRESCENT MOON HALL HAS OPERATED FOR FOUR THOUSAND YEARS...
BUT JUST RECENTLY THE PROPRIETOR OF THE SHOP WENT TO BE REINCARNATED FOR THE FIRST TIME IN 700 YEARS, SO MY LITTLE BROTHER, LEFT, HAS INHERITED THE BUSINESS.
BUT SCYTHE SHARPENING IS A BUSINESS BASED ON TRUST.
AND MY LITTLE BROTHER HASN'T HAD ANY REAL EXPERIENCE SO...
I CAN'T ENTRUST MY PRECIOUS SCYTHE TO SOME INEXPERIENCED SCYTHE SMITH.
I'M GOING SOME-WHERE ELSE.
AND SO WE'VE BEEN LOSING CUSTOMERS.
HUH.
BUT IF SOMEONE WOULD JUST LET US SHARPEN THEIR SCYTHE FOR THEM...
...I JUST KNOW THEY'D SEE MY LITTLE BROTHER'S SKILL FOR WHAT IT IS!!

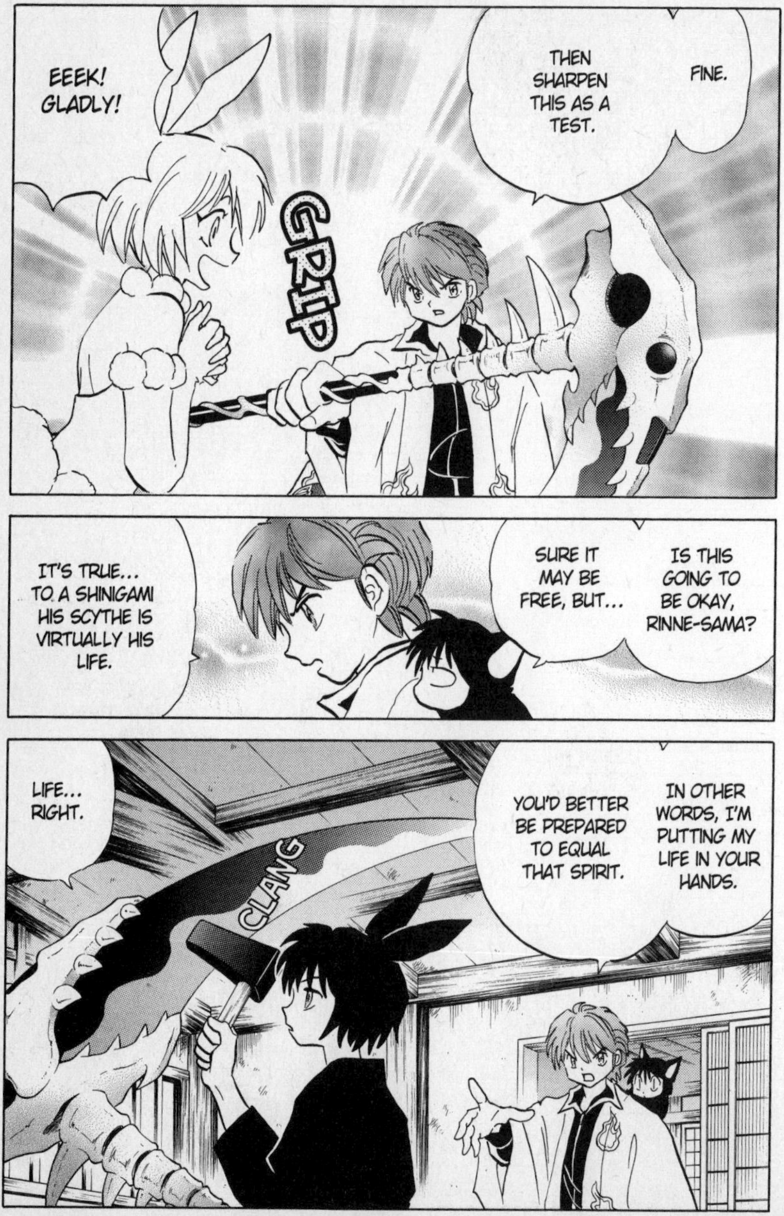
FINE.
THEN SHARPEN THIS AS A TEST.
GRIP
EEEK! GLADLY!
IS THIS GOING TO BE OKAY, RINNE-SAMA?
SURE IT MAY BE FREE, BUT...
IT'S TRUE... TO A SHINIGAMI HIS SCYTHE IS VIRTUALLY HIS LIFE.
IN OTHER WORDS, I'M PUTTING MY LIFE IN YOUR HANDS.
YOU'D BETTER BE PREPARED TO EQUAL THAT SPIRIT.
LIFE... RIGHT.
CLANG

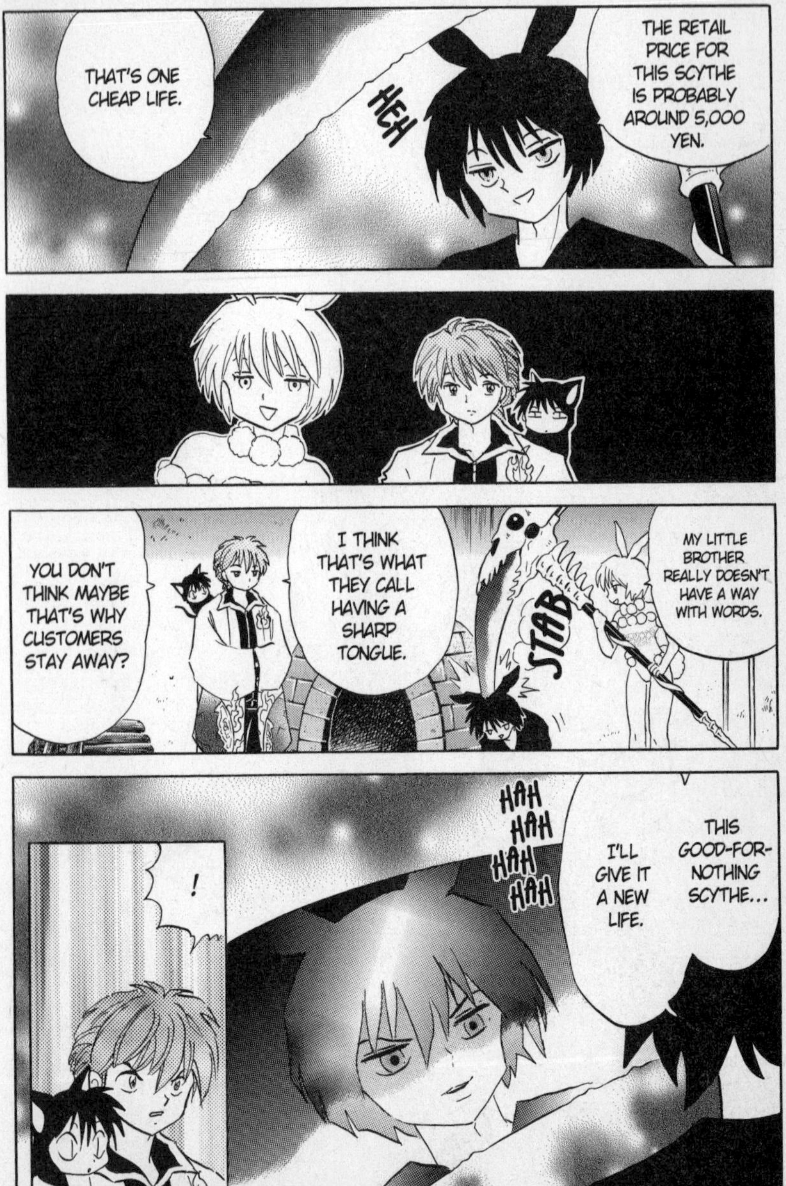
THE RETAIL PRICE FOR THIS SCYTHE IS PROBABLY AROUND 5,000 YEN.
HEH
THAT'S ONE CHEAP LIFE.
MY LITTLE BROTHER REALLY DOESN'T HAVE A WAY WITH WORDS.
STAB
I THINK THAT'S WHAT THEY CALL HAVING A SHARP TONGUE.
YOU DON'T THINK MAYBE THAT'S WHY CUSTOMERS STAY AWAY?
THIS GOOD-FOR-NOTHING SCYTHE...
I'LL GIVE IT A NEW LIFE.
HAH HAH HAH HAH
!

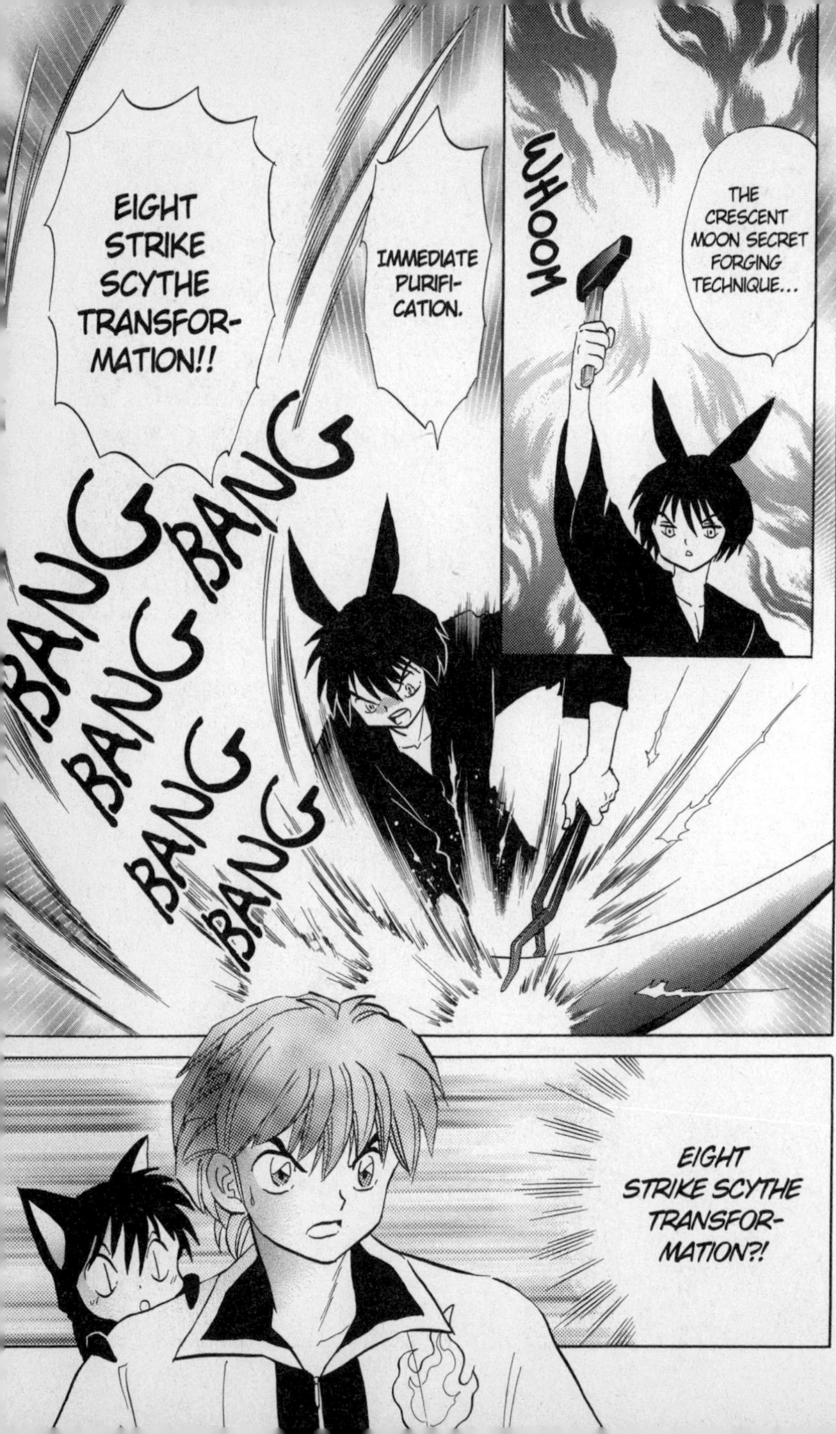
THE CRESCENT MOON SECRET FORGING TECHNIQUE…
WHOOM
IMMEDIATE PURIFI-CATION.
EIGHT STRIKE SCYTHE TRANSFOR-MATION!!
BANG BANG BANG BANG BANG BANG
EIGHT STRIKE SCYTHE TRANSFOR-MATION?!

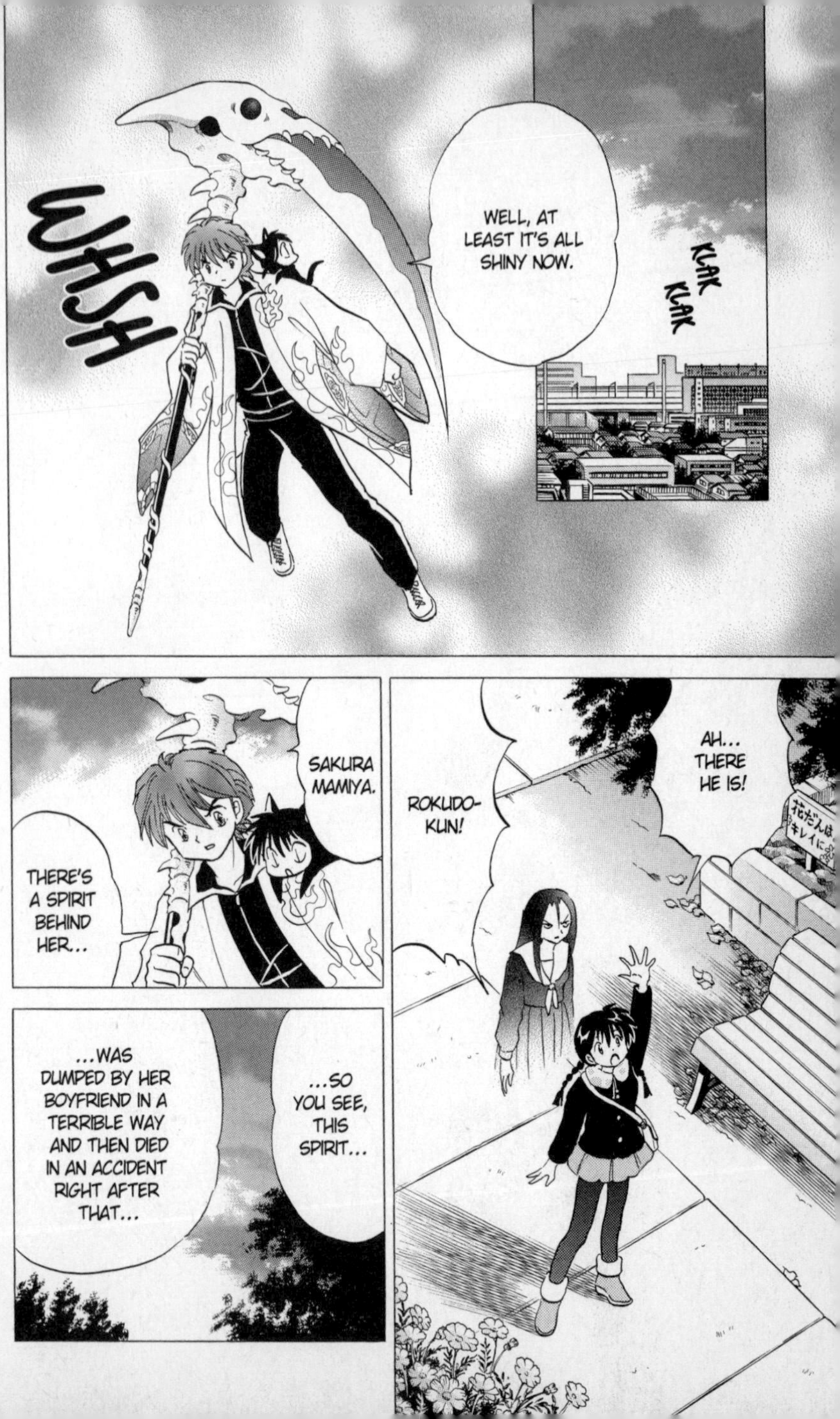
KLAK KLAK
WELL, AT LEAST IT'S ALL SHINY NOW.
WHSH
AH... THERE HE IS!
ROKUDO-KUN!
花だんは
キレイに
SAKURA MAMIYA.
THERE'S A SPIRIT BEHIND HER...
...SO YOU SEE, THIS SPIRIT...
...WAS DUMPED BY HER BOYFRIEND IN A TERRIBLE WAY AND THEN DIED IN AN ACCIDENT RIGHT AFTER THAT...

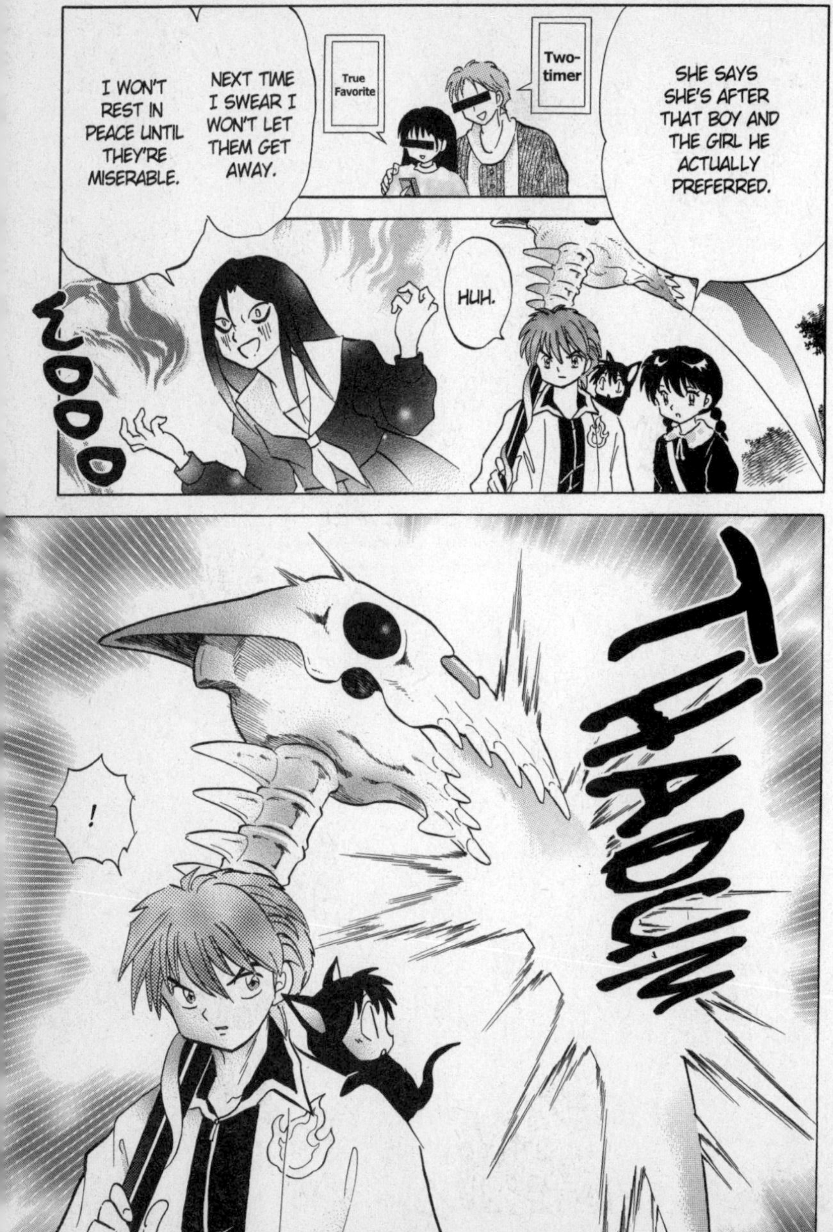
SHE SAYS SHE'S AFTER THAT BOY AND THE GIRL HE ACTUALLY PREFERRED.
Two-timer
True Favorite
NEXT TIME I SWEAR I WON'T LET THEM GET AWAY.
I WON'T REST IN PEACE UNTIL THEY'RE MISERABLE.
HUH.
WOOO
THADUN
!

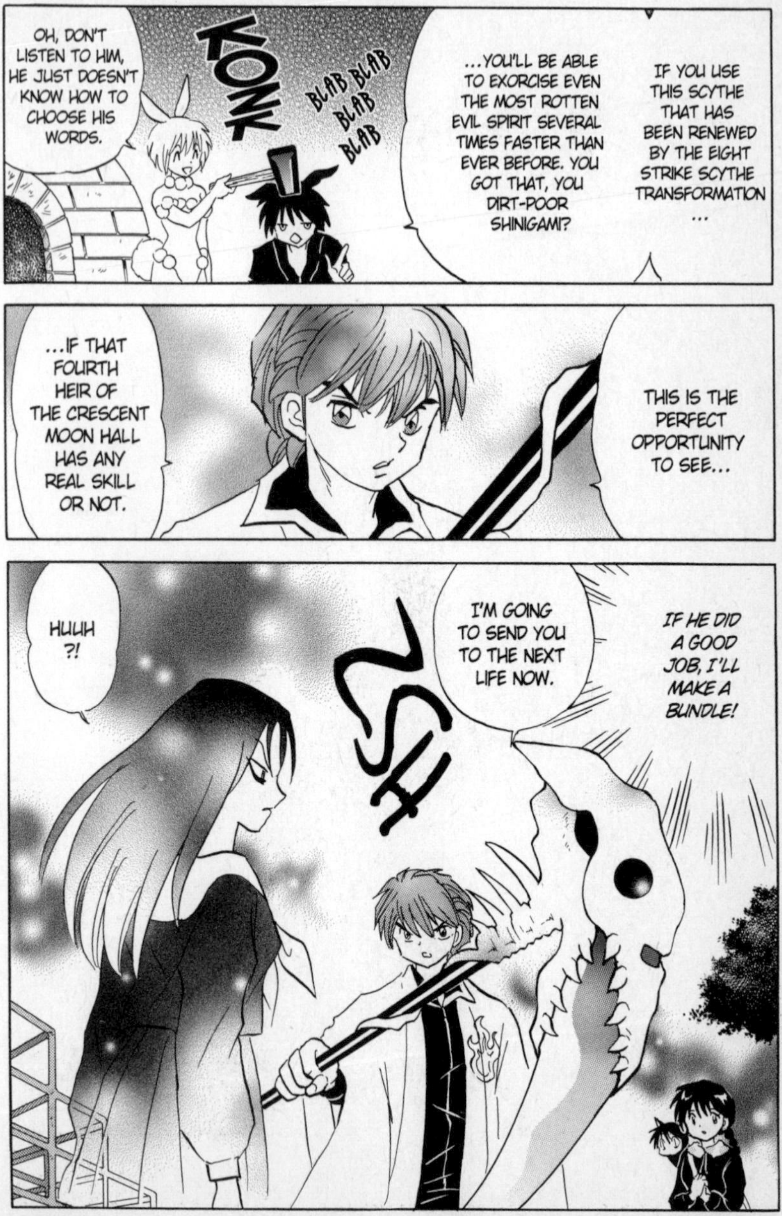
IF YOU USE THIS SCYTHE THAT HAS BEEN RENEWED BY THE EIGHT STRIKE SCYTHE TRANSFORMATION...
...YOU'LL BE ABLE TO EXORCISE EVEN THE MOST ROTTEN EVIL SPIRIT SEVERAL TIMES FASTER THAN EVER BEFORE. YOU GOT THAT, YOU DIRT-POOR SHINIGAMI?
BLAB BLAB BLAB BLAB
KONK
OH, DON'T LISTEN TO HIM, HE JUST DOESN'T KNOW HOW TO CHOOSE HIS WORDS.
THIS IS THE PERFECT OPPORTUNITY TO SEE...
...IF THAT FOURTH HEIR OF THE CRESCENT MOON HALL HAS ANY REAL SKILL OR NOT.
IF HE DID A GOOD JOB, I'LL MAKE A BUNDLE!
I'M GOING TO SEND YOU TO THE NEXT LIFE NOW.
HUUH ?!

CHAPTER 121: MY HANSEI

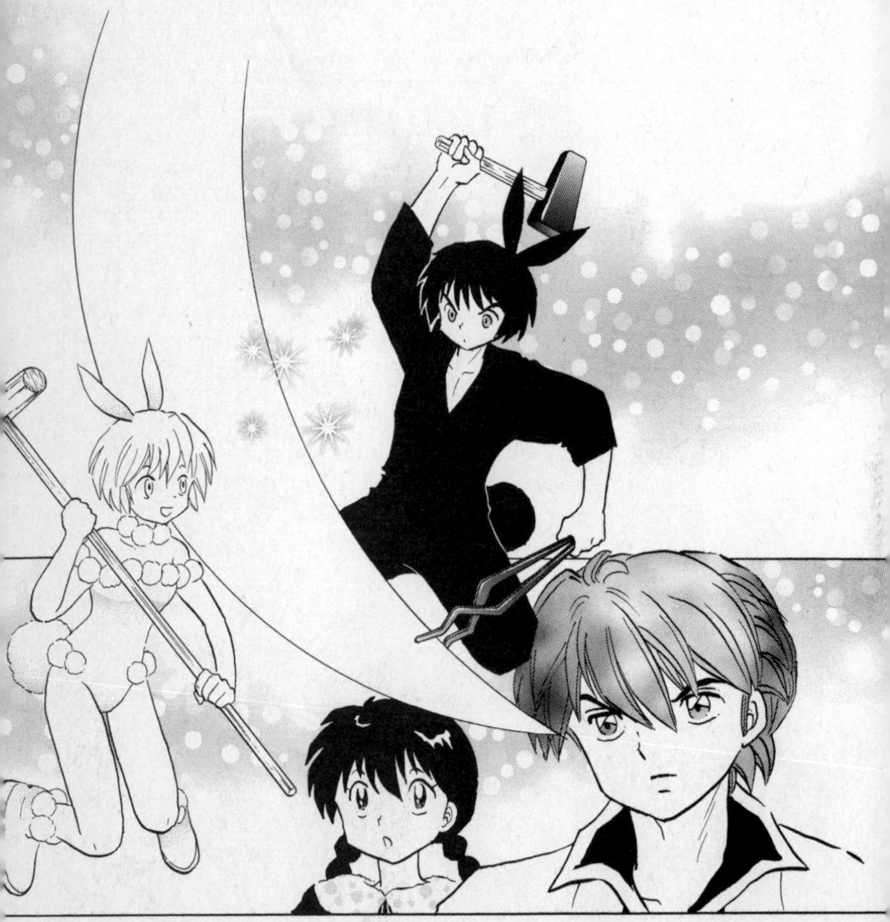

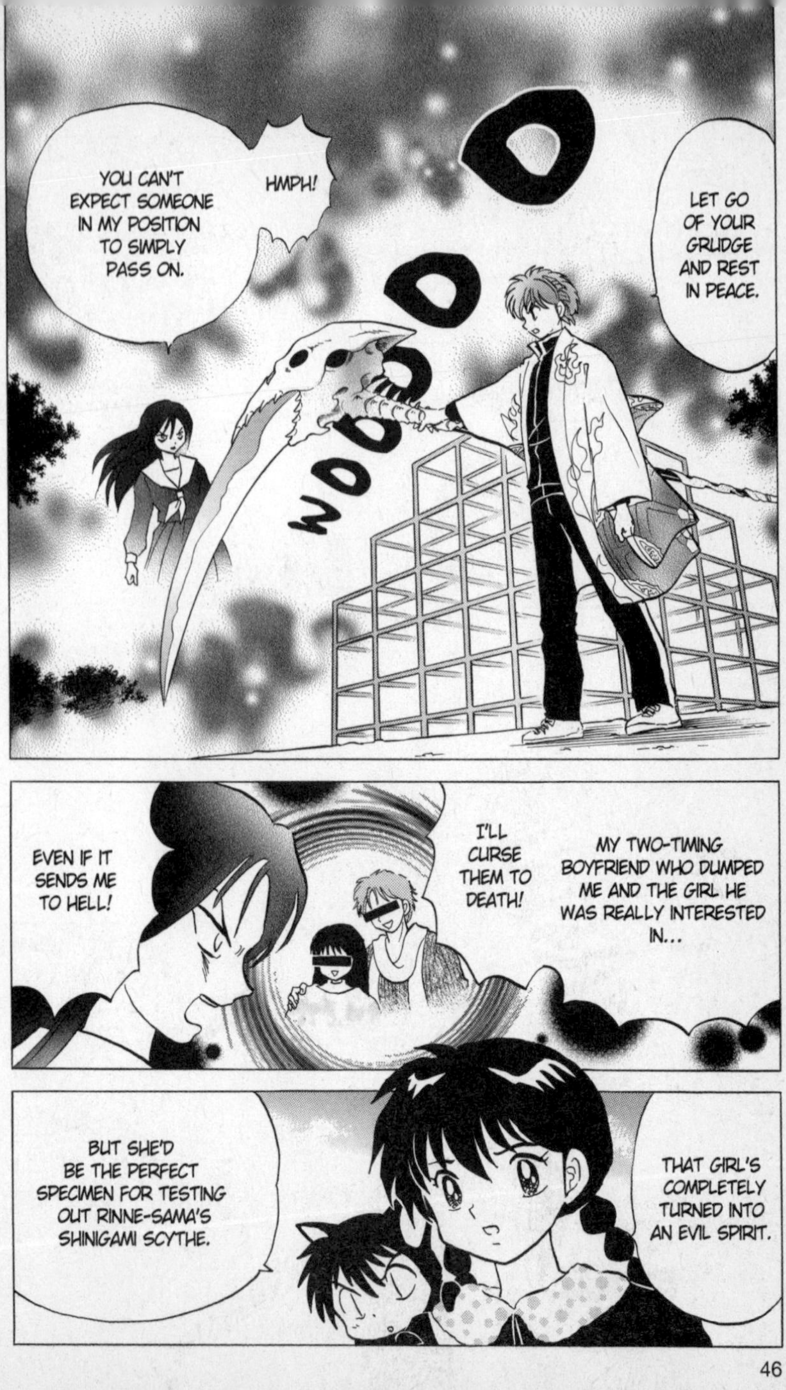
LET GO OF YOUR GRUDGE AND REST IN PEACE.
HMPH!
YOU CAN'T EXPECT SOMEONE IN MY POSITION TO SIMPLY PASS ON.
MY TWO-TIMING BOYFRIEND WHO DUMPED ME AND THE GIRL HE WAS REALLY INTERESTED IN...
I'LL CURSE THEM TO DEATH!
EVEN IF IT SENDS ME TO HELL!
THAT GIRL'S COMPLETELY TURNED INTO AN EVIL SPIRIT.
BUT SHE'D BE THE PERFECT SPECIMEN FOR TESTING OUT RINNE-SAMA'S SHINIGAMI SCYTHE.

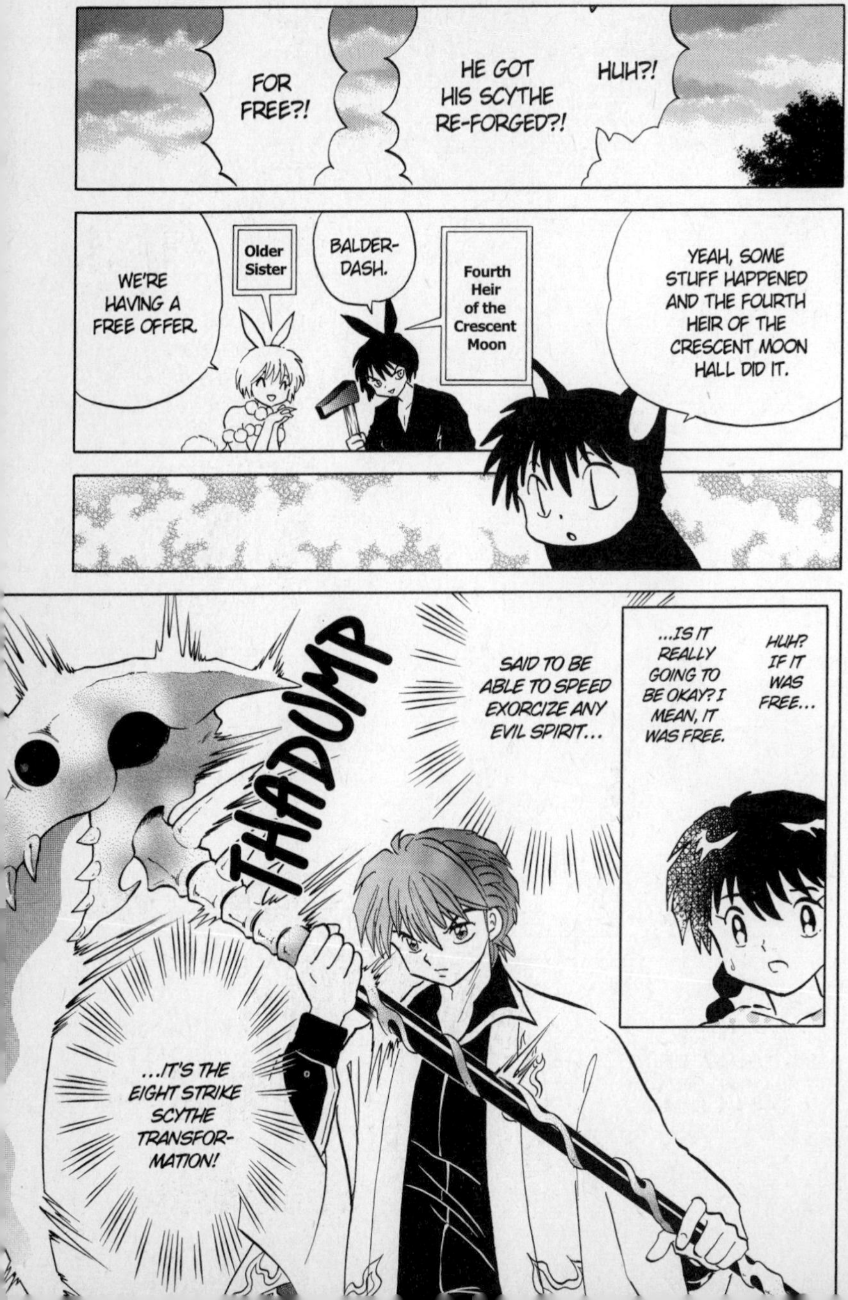
HUH?!
HE GOT HIS SCYTHE RE-FORGED?!
FOR FREE?!
YEAH, SOME STUFF HAPPENED AND THE FOURTH HEIR OF THE CRESCENT MOON HALL DID IT.
Fourth Heir of the Crescent Moon
BALDER-DASH.
Older Sister
WE'RE HAVING A FREE OFFER.
HUH? IF IT WAS FREE...
...IS IT REALLY GOING TO BE OKAY? I MEAN, IT WAS FREE.
SAID TO BE ABLE TO SPEED EXORCIZE ANY EVIL SPIRIT...
THADUMP
...IT'S THE EIGHT STRIKE SCYTHE TRANSFORMATION!

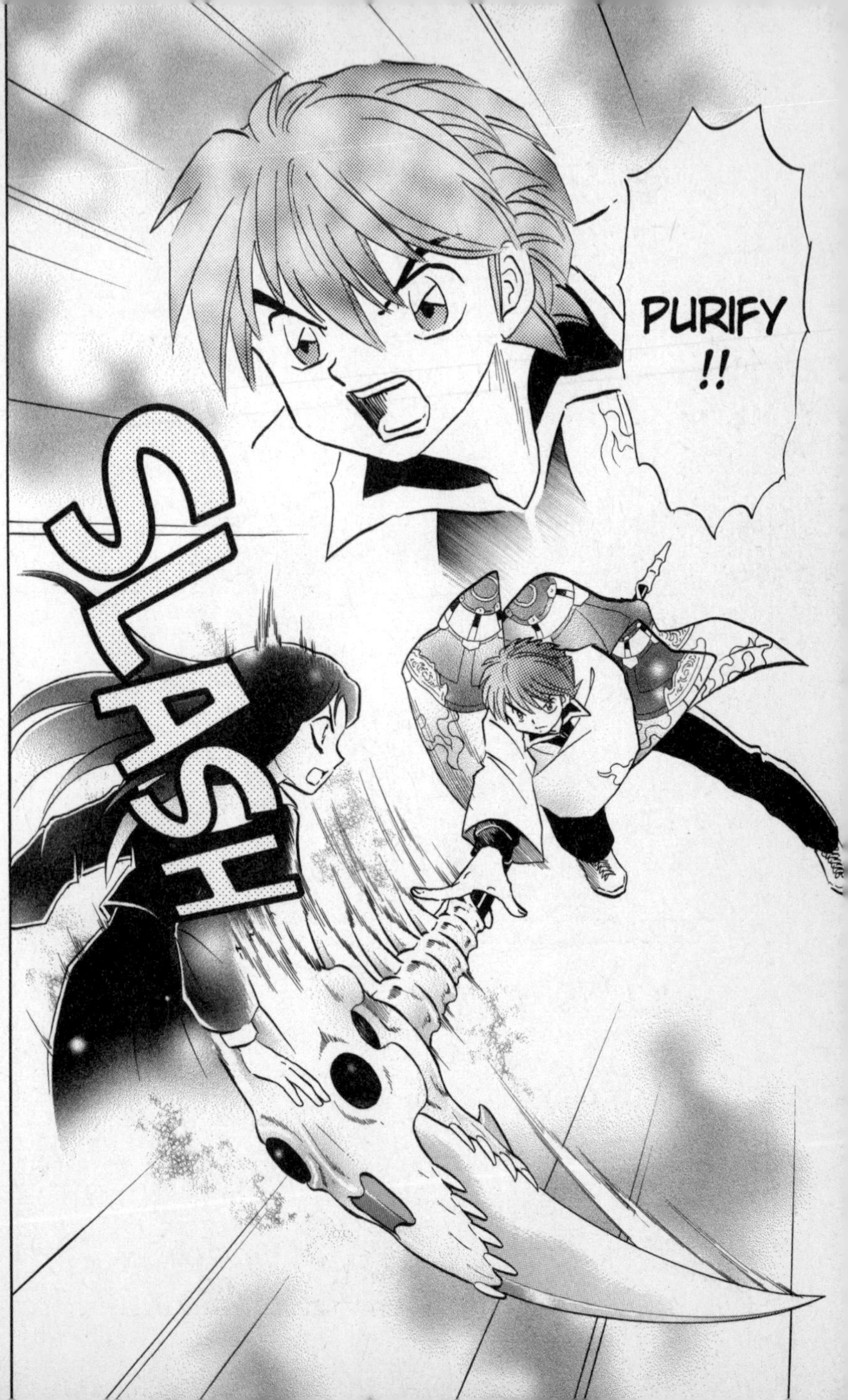
PURIFY !!
SLASH

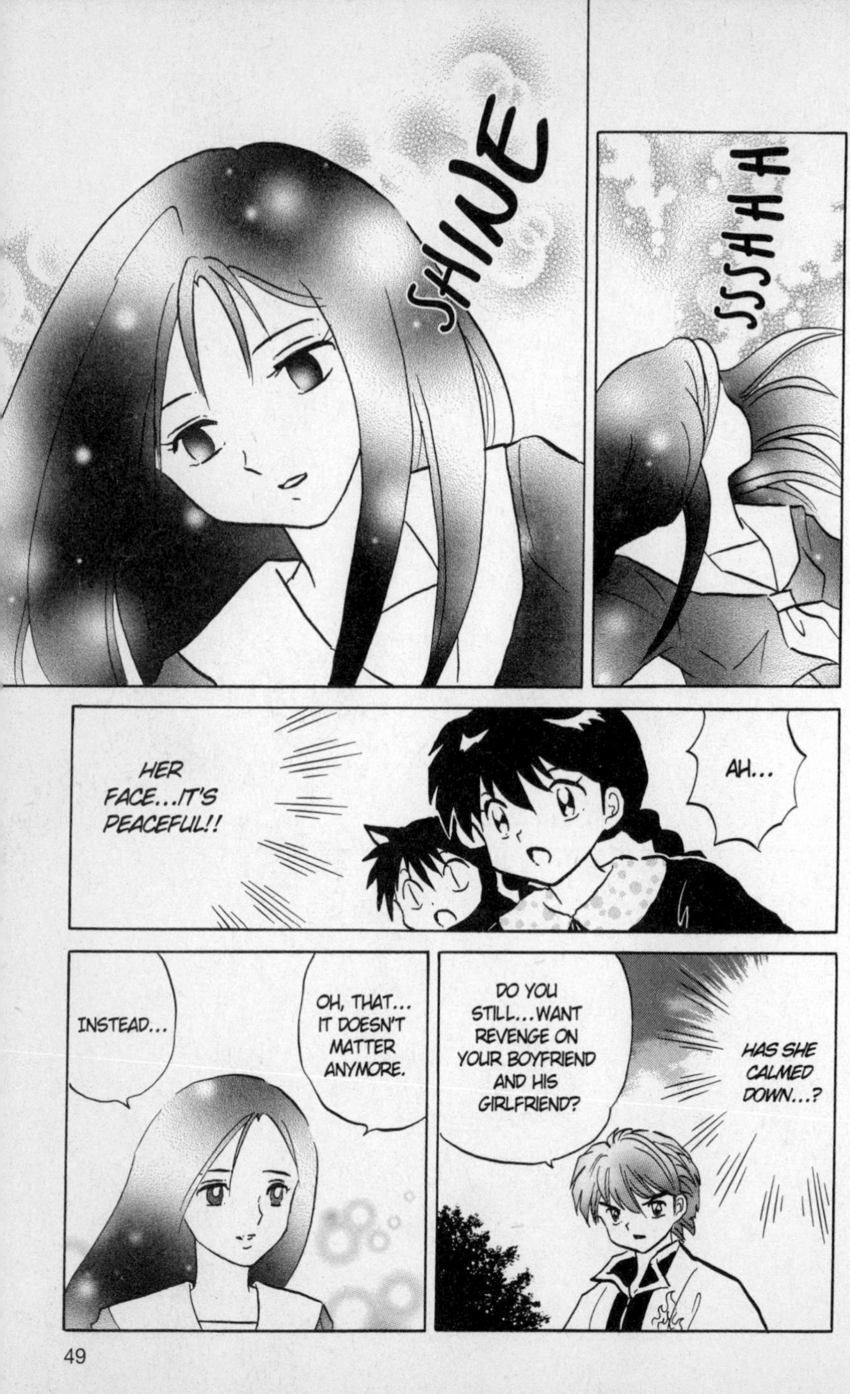
SSSHHH
SHINE
AH...
HER FACE...IT'S PEACEFUL!!
HAS SHE CALMED DOWN...?
DO YOU STILL...WANT REVENGE ON YOUR BOYFRIEND AND HIS GIRLFRIEND?
OH, THAT... IT DOESN'T MATTER ANYMORE.
INSTEAD...

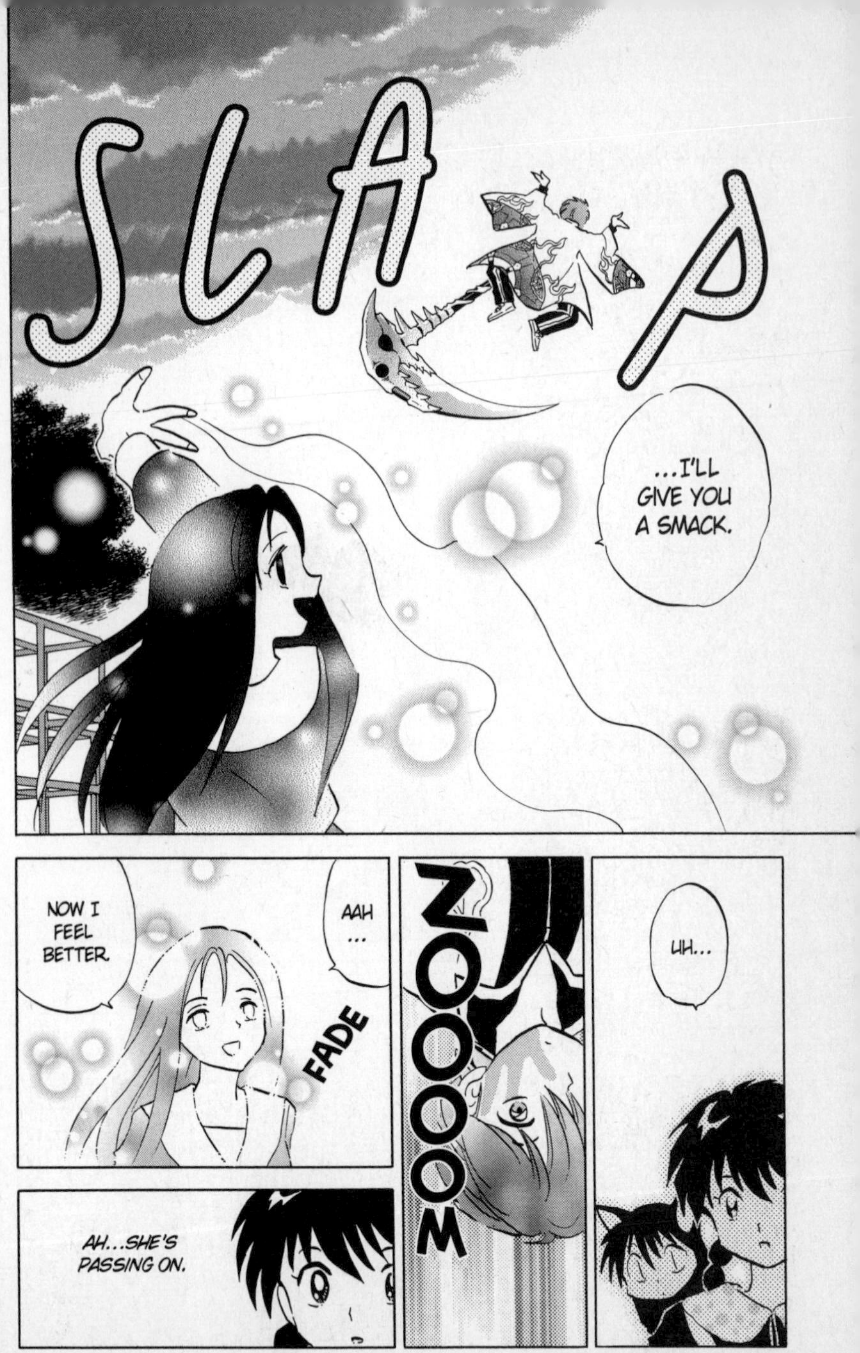
SLAP
...I'LL GIVE YOU A SMACK.
UH...
ZOOOOOM
AAH ...
NOW I FEEL BETTER.
FADE
AH...SHE'S PASSING ON.

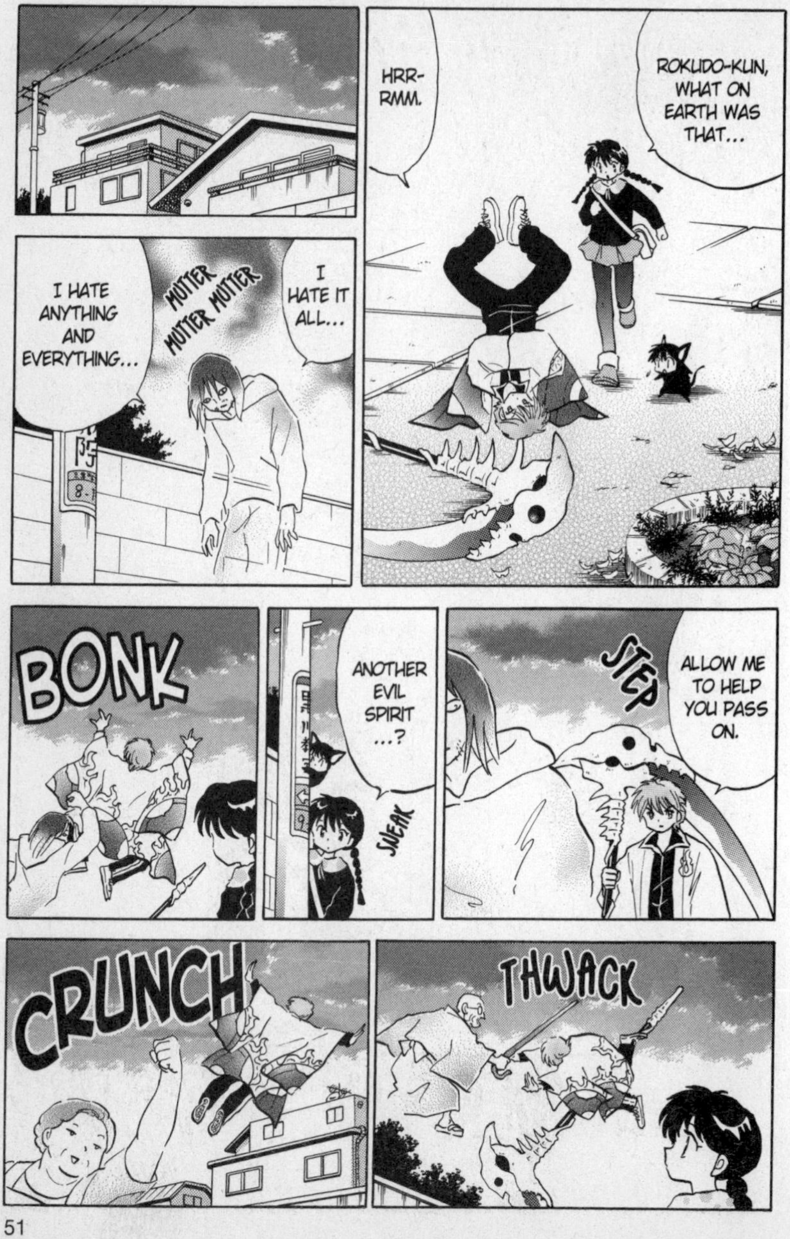
ROKUDO-KUN, WHAT ON EARTH WAS THAT...
HRR-RMM.
I HATE IT ALL...
MUTTER MUTTER MUTTER
I HATE ANYTHING AND EVERYTHING...
STEP
ALLOW ME TO HELP YOU PASS ON.
ANOTHER EVIL SPIRIT ...?
SNEAK
BONK
THWACK
CRUNCH

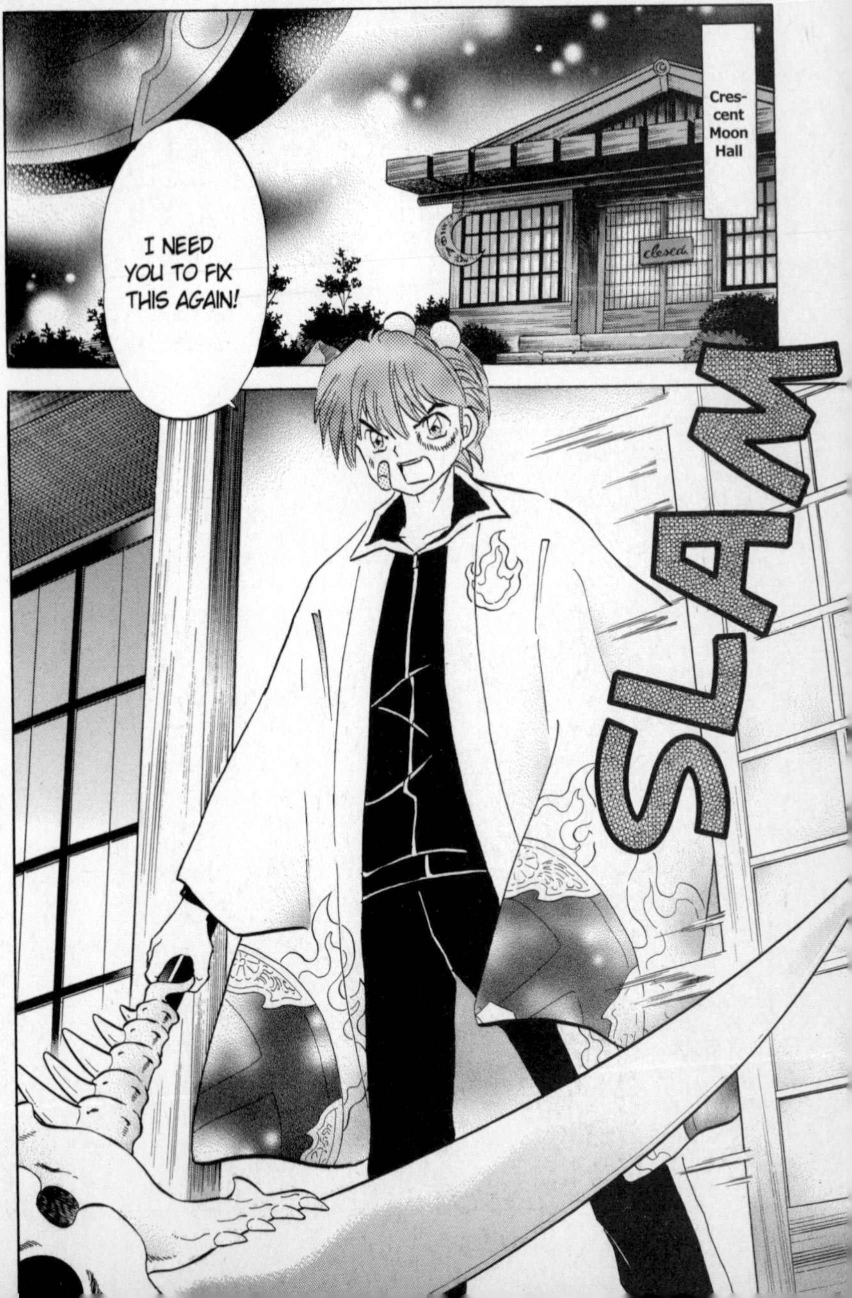
Cres-
cent
Moon
Hall
closed
I NEED YOU TO FIX THIS AGAIN!
SLAM

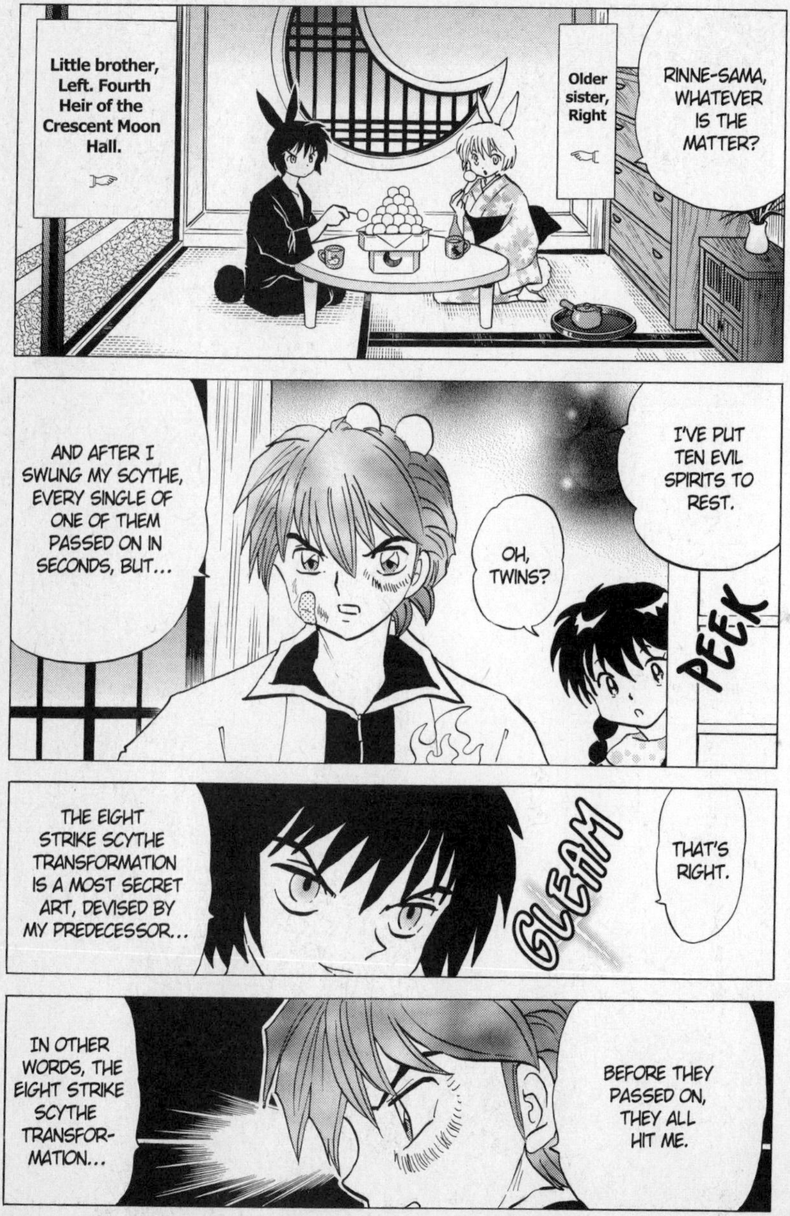
RINNE-SAMA, WHATEVER IS THE MATTER?
Older sister, Right
Little brother, Left. Fourth Heir of the Crescent Moon Hall.
I'VE PUT TEN EVIL SPIRITS TO REST.
PEEK
OH, TWINS?
AND AFTER I SWUNG MY SCYTHE, EVERY SINGLE OF ONE OF THEM PASSED ON IN SECONDS, BUT...
THAT'S RIGHT.
GLEAM
THE EIGHT STRIKE SCYTHE TRANSFORMATION IS A MOST SECRET ART, DEVISED BY MY PREDECESSOR...
BEFORE THEY PASSED ON, THEY ALL HIT ME.
IN OTHER WORDS, THE EIGHT STRIKE SCYTHE TRANSFOR-MATION...

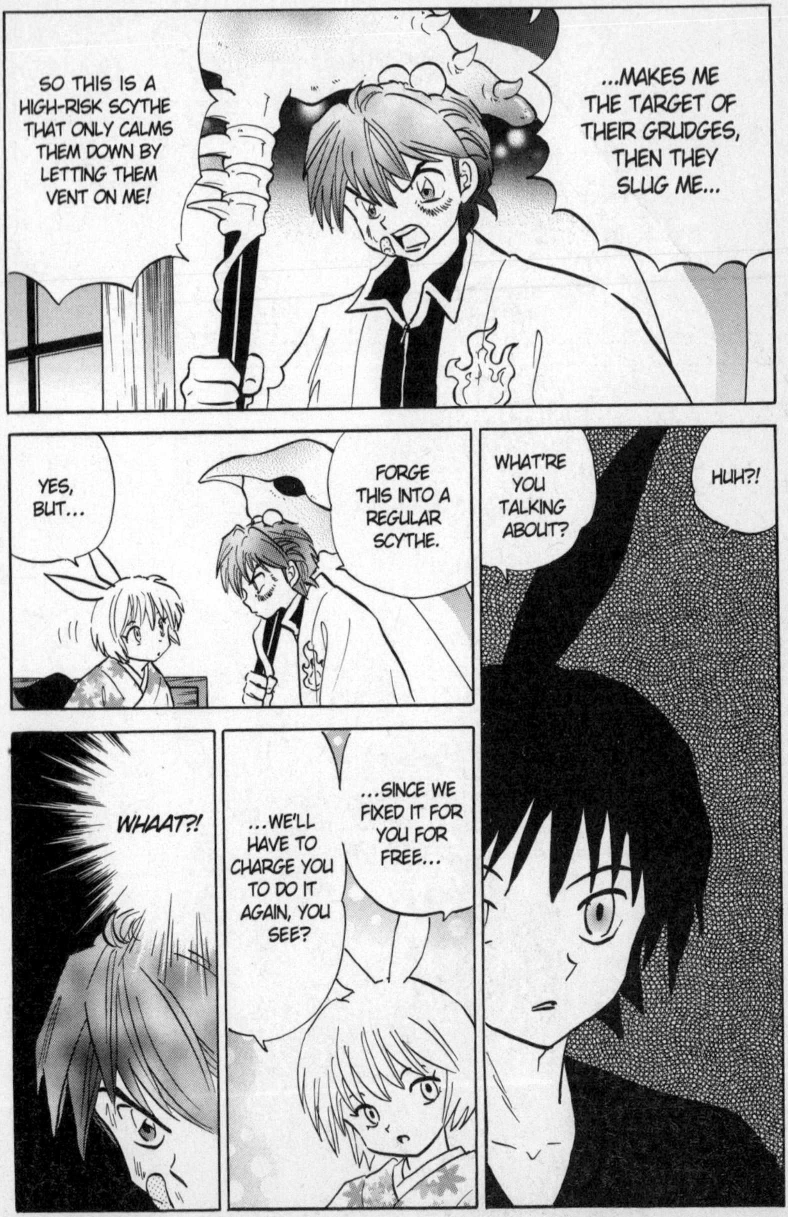
...MAKES ME THE TARGET OF THEIR GRUDGES, THEN THEY SLUG ME...
SO THIS IS A HIGH-RISK SCYTHE THAT ONLY CALMS THEM DOWN BY LETTING THEM VENT ON ME!
HUH?!
WHAT'RE YOU TALKING ABOUT?
FORGE THIS INTO A REGULAR SCYTHE.
YES, BUT...
...SINCE WE FIXED IT FOR YOU FOR FREE...
...WE'LL HAVE TO CHARGE YOU TO DO IT AGAIN, YOU SEE?
WHAAT?!

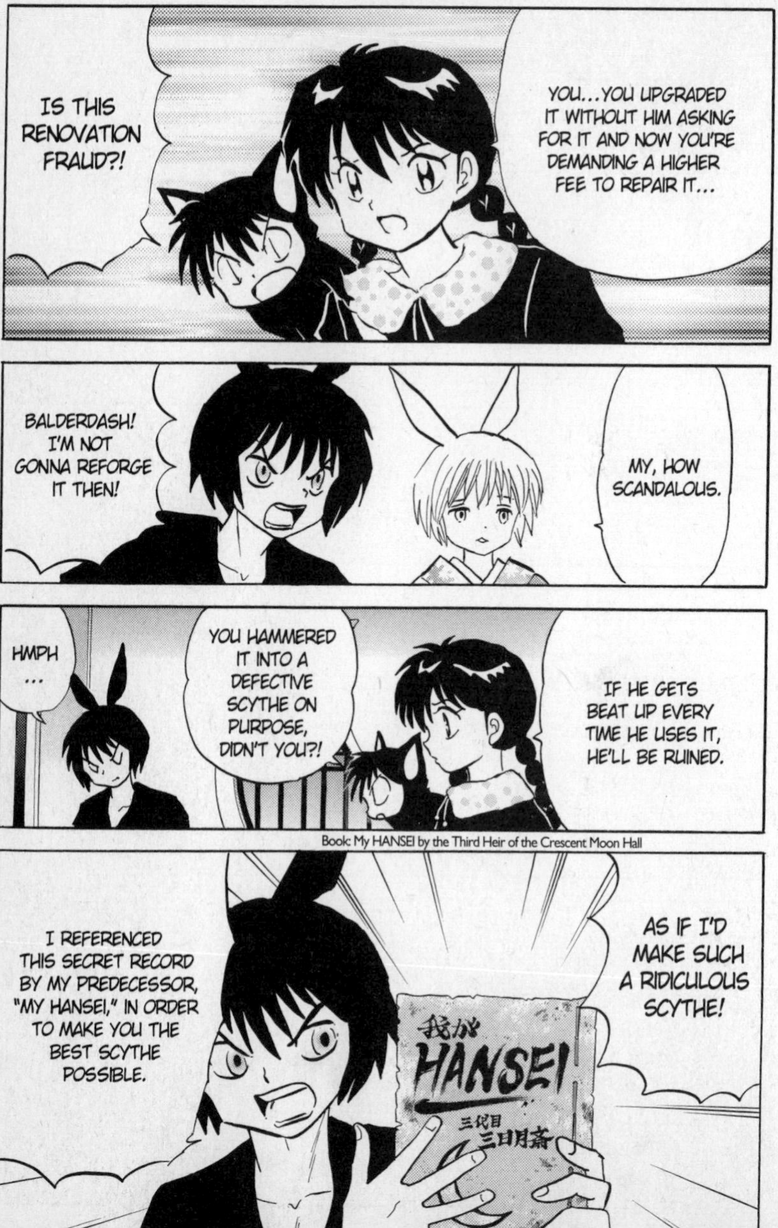
YOU…YOU UPGRADED IT WITHOUT HIM ASKING FOR IT AND NOW YOU'RE DEMANDING A HIGHER FEE TO REPAIR IT…
IS THIS RENOVATION FRAUD?!
MY, HOW SCANDALOUS.
BALDERDASH! I'M NOT GONNA REFORGE IT THEN!
IF HE GETS BEAT UP EVERY TIME HE USES IT, HE'LL BE RUINED.
YOU HAMMERED IT INTO A DEFECTIVE SCYTHE ON PURPOSE, DIDN'T YOU?!
HMPH …
Book: My HANSEI by the Third Heir of the Crescent Moon Hall
AS IF I'D MAKE SUCH A RIDICULOUS SCYTHE!
我が
HANSEI
三代目
三日月斎
I REFERENCED THIS SECRET RECORD BY MY PREDECESSOR, "MY HANSEI," IN ORDER TO MAKE YOU THE BEST SCYTHE POSSIBLE.

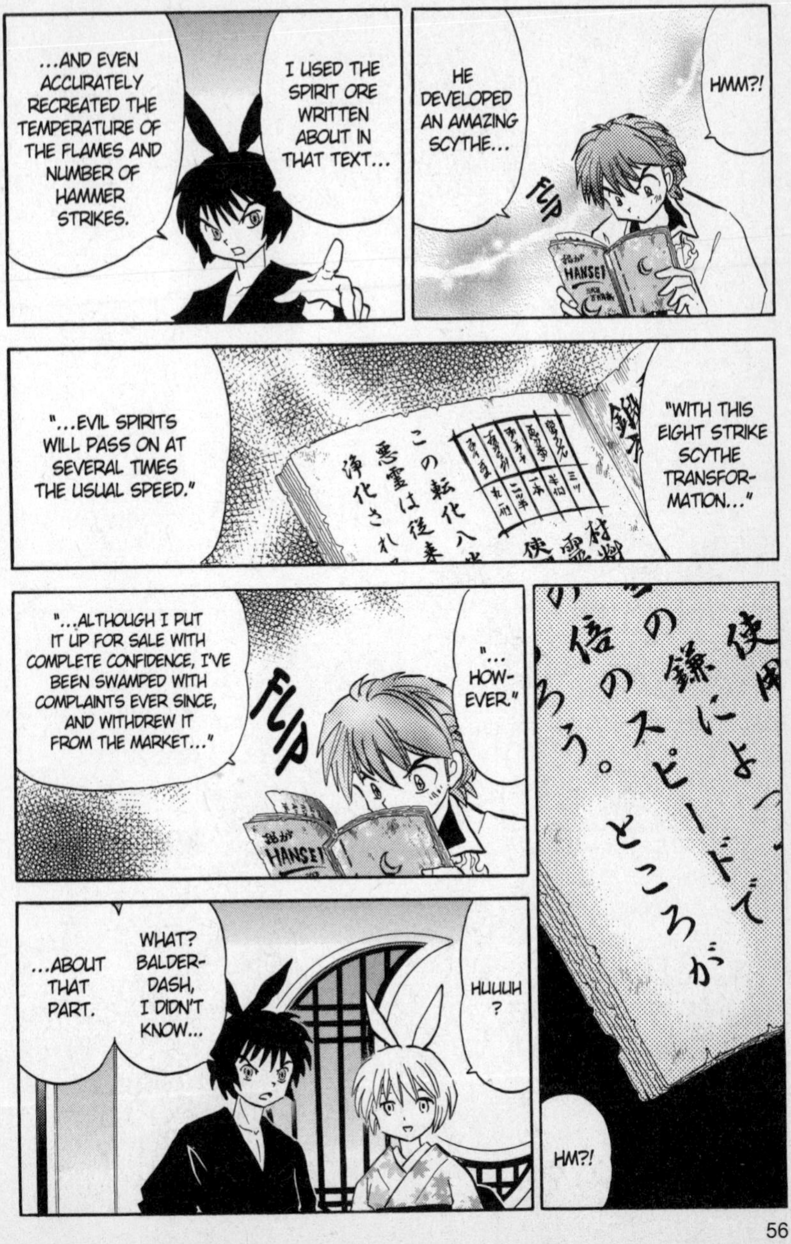
HMM?!
HE DEVELOPED AN AMAZING SCYTHE...
FLIP
I USED THE SPIRIT ORE WRITTEN ABOUT IN THAT TEXT...
...AND EVEN ACCURATELY RECREATED THE TEMPERATURE OF THE FLAMES AND NUMBER OF HAMMER STRIKES.
"WITH THIS EIGHT STRIKE SCYTHE TRANSFORMATION..."
"...EVIL SPIRITS WILL PASS ON AT SEVERAL TIMES THE USUAL SPEED."
HM?!
"...HOWEVER."
FLIP
"...ALTHOUGH I PUT IT UP FOR SALE WITH COMPLETE CONFIDENCE, I'VE BEEN SWAMPED WITH COMPLAINTS EVER SINCE, AND WITHDREW IT FROM THE MARKET..."
HUUUH?
WHAT? BALDERDASH, I DIDN'T KNOW...
...ABOUT THAT PART.

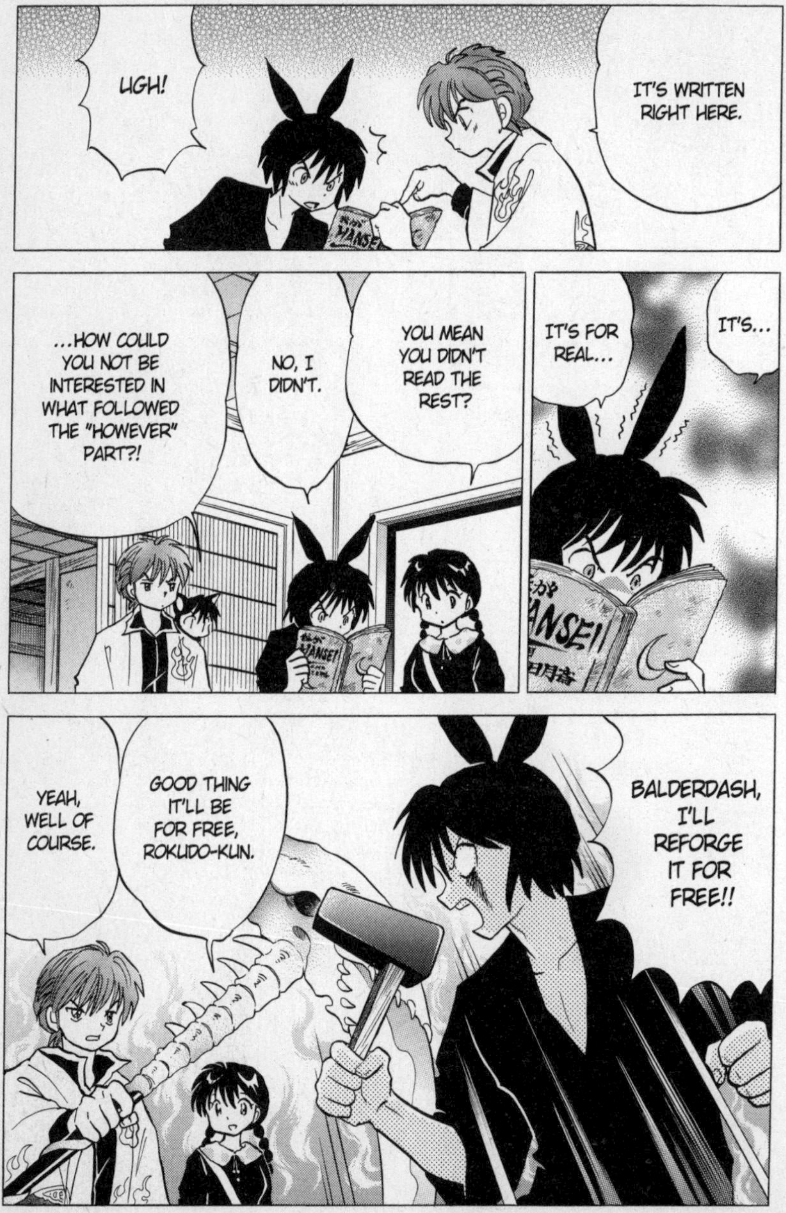
IT'S WRITTEN RIGHT HERE.
UGH!
IT'S...
IT'S FOR REAL...
YOU MEAN YOU DIDN'T READ THE REST?
NO, I DIDN'T.
...HOW COULD YOU NOT BE INTERESTED IN WHAT FOLLOWED THE "HOWEVER" PART?!
BALDERDASH, I'LL REFORGE IT FOR FREE!!
GOOD THING IT'LL BE FOR FREE, ROKUDO-KUN.
YEAH, WELL OF COURSE.

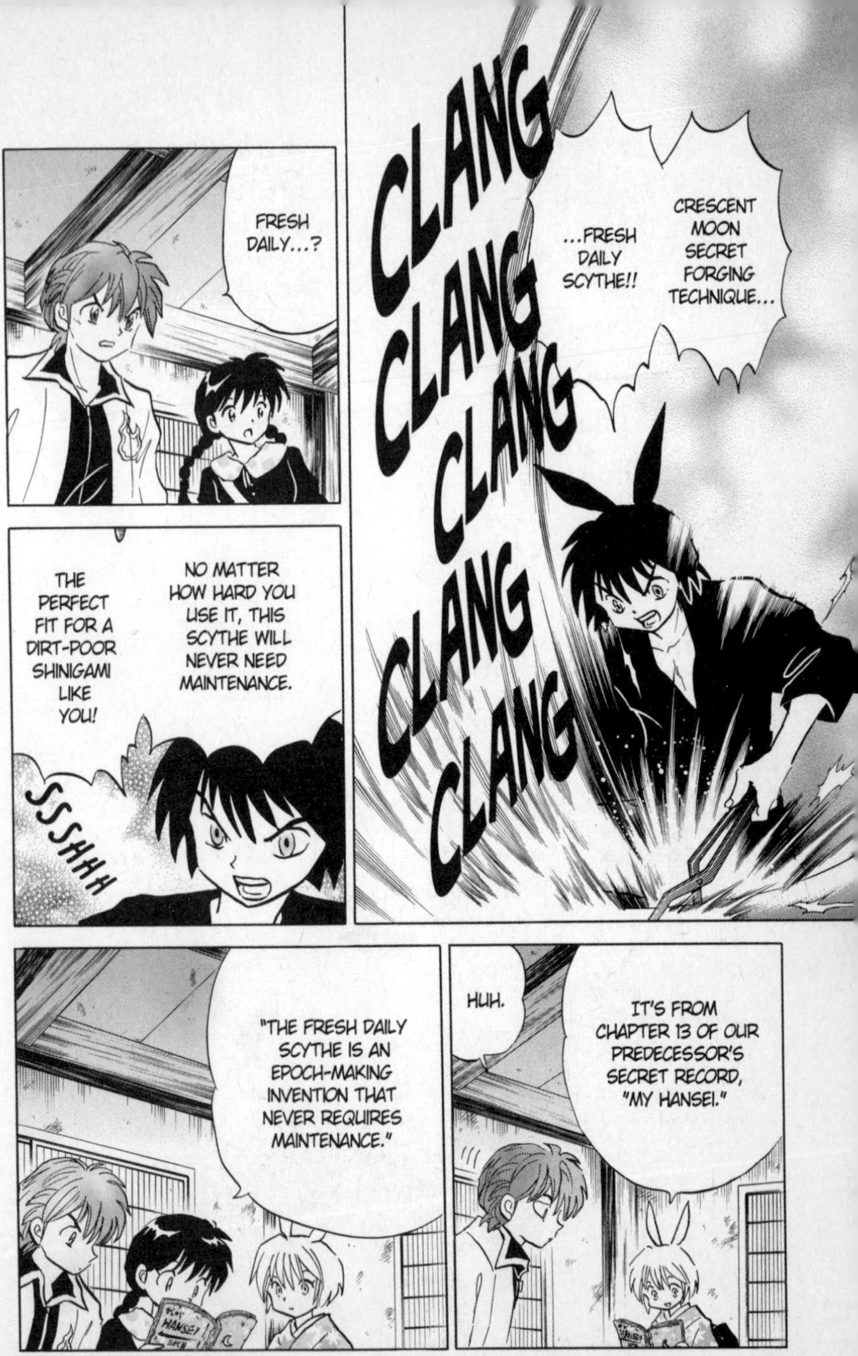
CRESCENT MOON SECRET FORGING TECHNIQUE...
...FRESH DAILY SCYTHE!!
CLANG CLANG CLANG CLANG CLANG
FRESH DAILY...?
NO MATTER HOW HARD YOU USE IT, THIS SCYTHE WILL NEVER NEED MAINTENANCE.
THE PERFECT FIT FOR A DIRT-POOR SHINIGAMI LIKE YOU!
SSSHHH
IT'S FROM CHAPTER 13 OF OUR PREDECESSOR'S SECRET RECORD, "MY HANSEI."
HUH.
"THE FRESH DAILY SCYTHE IS AN EPOCH-MAKING INVENTION THAT NEVER REQUIRES MAINTENANCE."

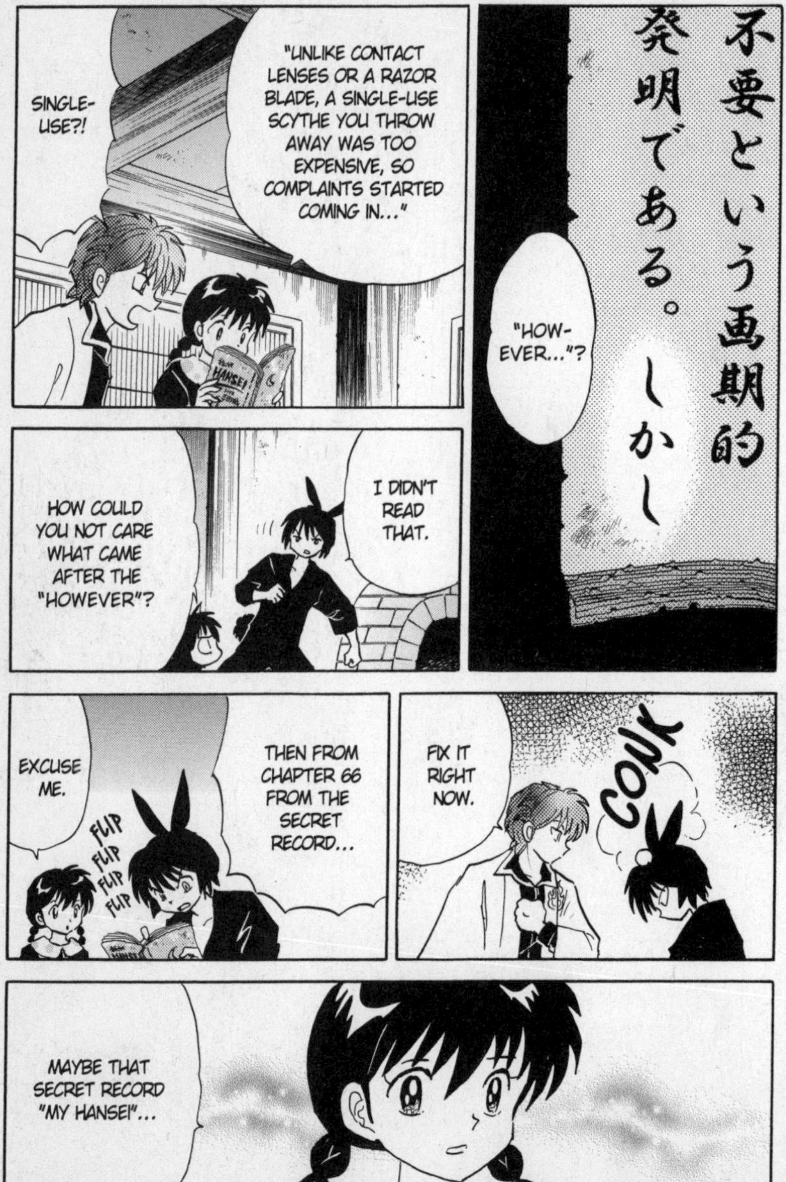

不要という画期的発明である。しかし
"HOW-EVER..."?
"UNLIKE CONTACT LENSES OR A RAZOR BLADE, A SINGLE-USE SCYTHE YOU THROW AWAY WAS TOO EXPENSIVE, SO COMPLAINTS STARTED COMING IN..."
SINGLE-USE?!
I DIDN'T READ THAT.
HOW COULD YOU NOT CARE WHAT CAME AFTER THE "HOWEVER"?
FIX IT RIGHT NOW.
COUK
THEN FROM CHAPTER 66 FROM THE SECRET RECORD...
EXCUSE ME.
FLIP FLIP FLIP FLIP
MAYBE THAT SECRET RECORD "MY HANSEI"...

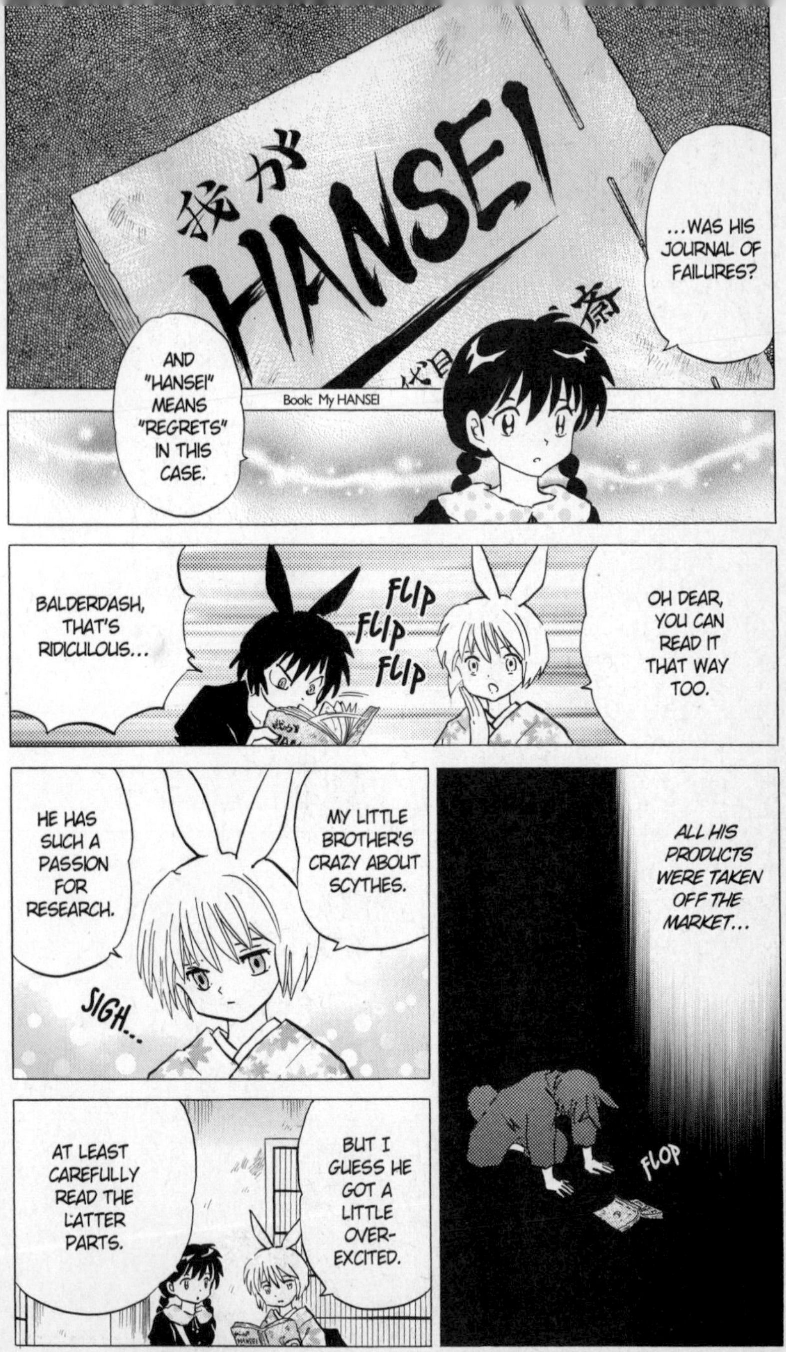
...WAS HIS JOURNAL OF FAILURES?
我が HANSEI
Book: My HANSEI
AND "HANSEI" MEANS "REGRETS" IN THIS CASE.
OH DEAR, YOU CAN READ IT THAT WAY TOO.
FLIP FLIP FLIP
BALDERDASH, THAT'S RIDICULOUS...
ALL HIS PRODUCTS WERE TAKEN OFF THE MARKET...
FLOP
MY LITTLE BROTHER'S CRAZY ABOUT SCYTHES.
HE HAS SUCH A PASSION FOR RESEARCH.
SIGH...
BUT I GUESS HE GOT A LITTLE OVER-EXCITED.
AT LEAST CAREFULLY READ THE LATTER PARTS.

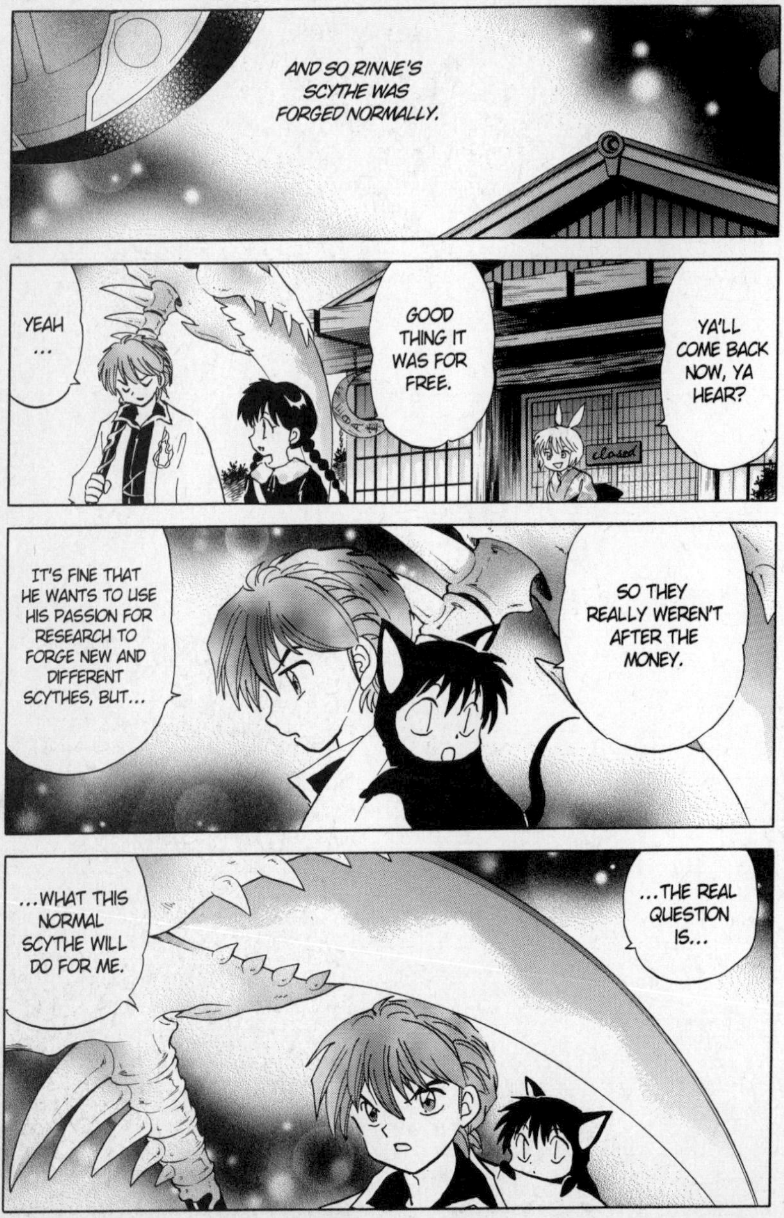
AND SO RINNE'S SCYTHE WAS FORGED NORMALLY.
YA'LL COME BACK NOW, YA HEAR?
GOOD THING IT WAS FOR FREE.
YEAH ...
closed
SO THEY REALLY WEREN'T AFTER THE MONEY.
IT'S FINE THAT HE WANTS TO USE HIS PASSION FOR RESEARCH TO FORGE NEW AND DIFFERENT SCYTHES, BUT...
...THE REAL QUESTION IS...
...WHAT THIS NORMAL SCYTHE WILL DO FOR ME.

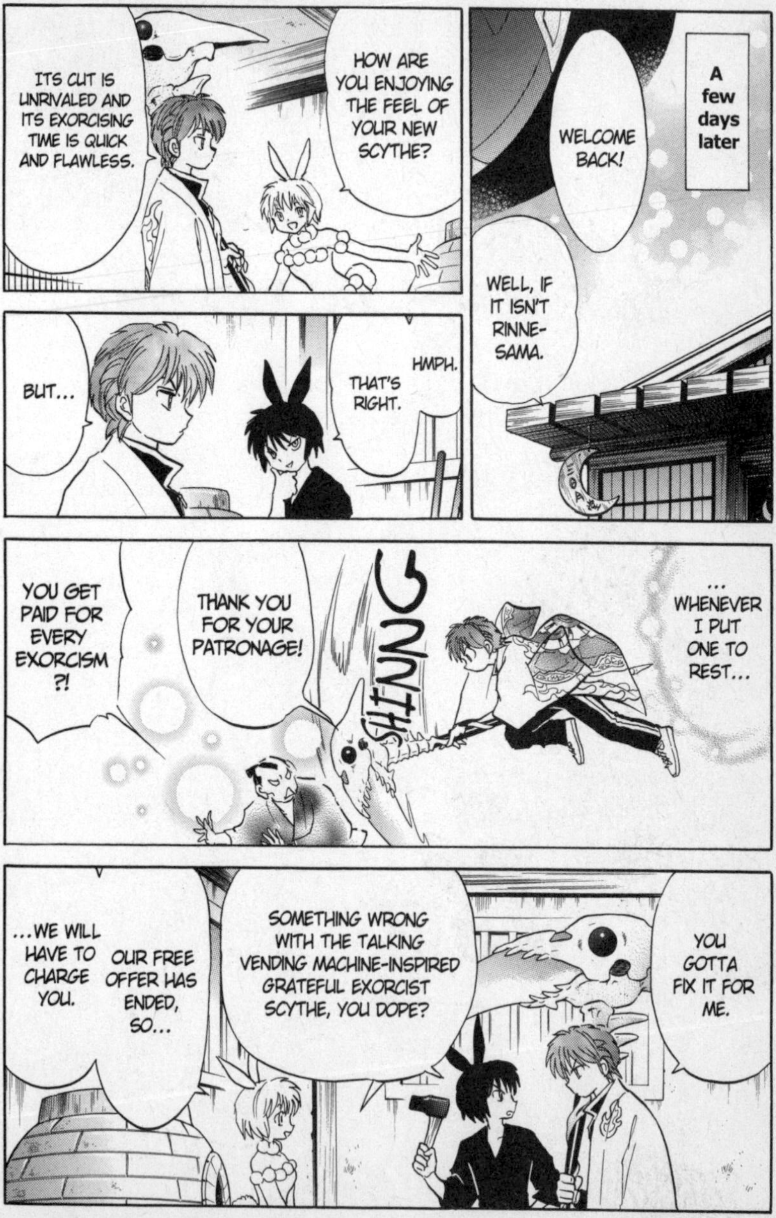
A few days later
WELCOME BACK!
WELL, IF IT ISN'T RINNE-SAMA.
HOW ARE YOU ENJOYING THE FEEL OF YOUR NEW SCYTHE?
ITS CUT IS UNRIVALED AND ITS EXORCISING TIME IS QUICK AND FLAWLESS.
HMPH.
THAT'S RIGHT.
BUT...
... WHENEVER I PUT ONE TO REST...
SHING
THANK YOU FOR YOUR PATRONAGE!
YOU GET PAID FOR EVERY EXORCISM ?!
YOU GOTTA FIX IT FOR ME.
SOMETHING WRONG WITH THE TALKING VENDING MACHINE-INSPIRED GRATEFUL EXORCIST SCYTHE, YOU DOPE?
OUR FREE OFFER HAS ENDED, SO...
...WE WILL HAVE TO CHARGE YOU.

CHAPTER 122:
CARE FOR SOME WAX?

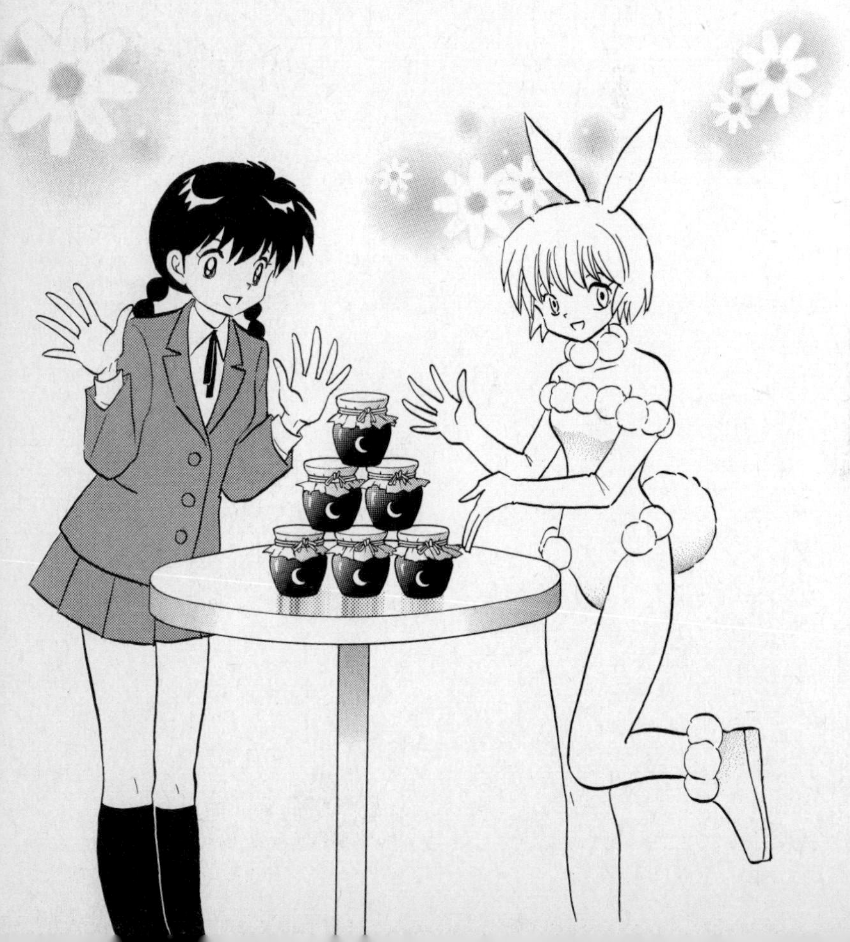

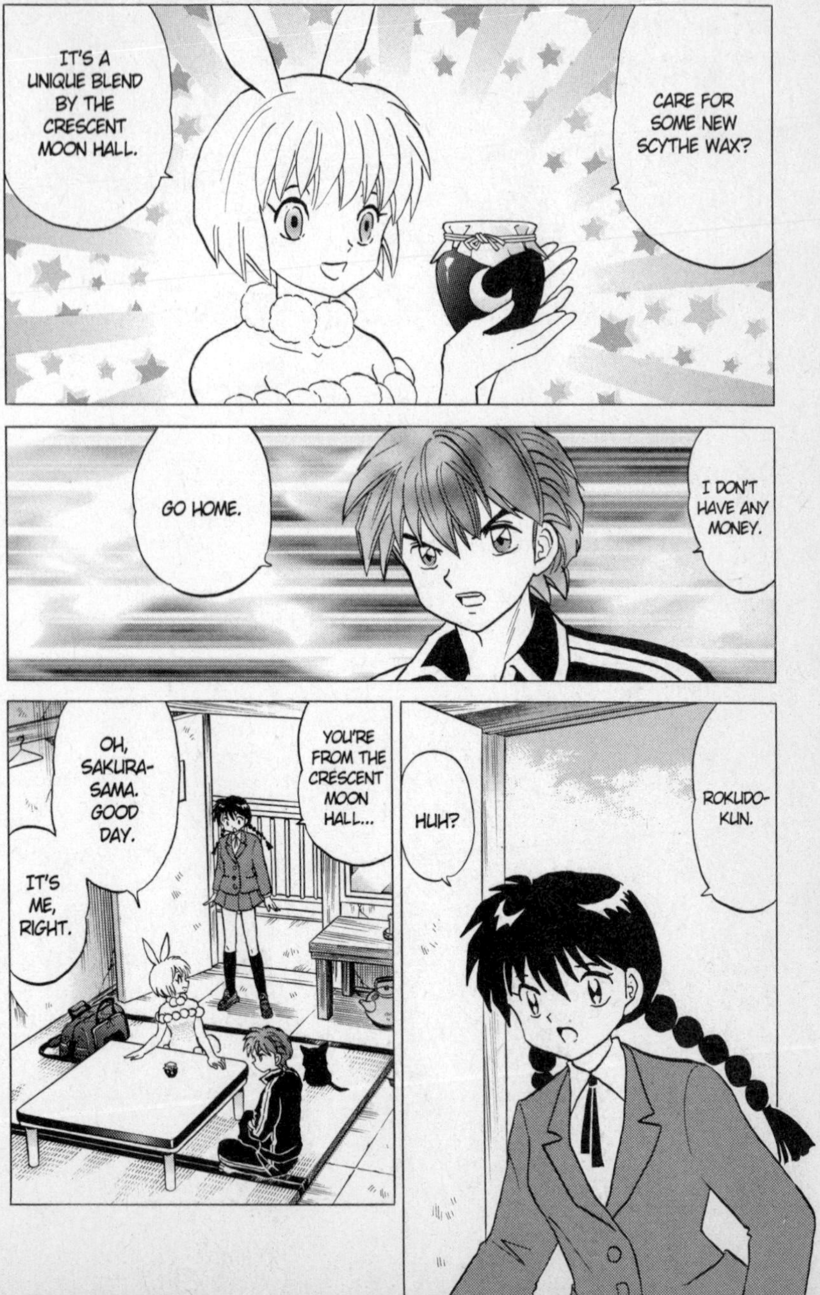
CARE FOR SOME NEW SCYTHE WAX?
IT'S A UNIQUE BLEND BY THE CRESCENT MOON HALL.
I DON'T HAVE ANY MONEY.
GO HOME.
ROKUDO-KUN.
HUH?
YOU'RE FROM THE CRESCENT MOON HALL...
OH, SAKURA-SAMA. GOOD DAY.
IT'S ME, RIGHT.

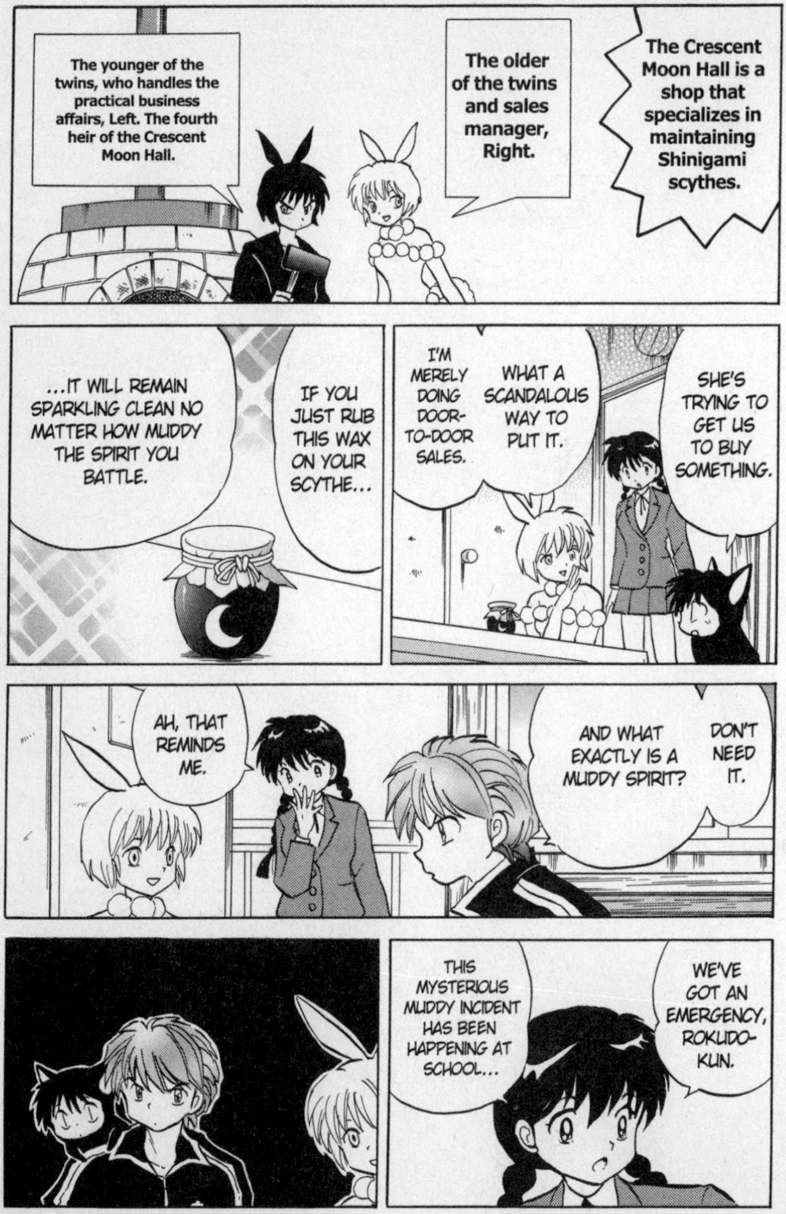

The Crescent Moon Hall is a shop that specializes in maintaining Shinigami scythes.
The older of the twins and sales manager, Right.
The younger of the twins, who handles the practical business affairs, Left. The fourth heir of the Crescent Moon Hall.
SHE'S TRYING TO GET US TO BUY SOMETHING.
WHAT A SCANDALOUS WAY TO PUT IT.
I'M MERELY DOING DOOR-TO-DOOR SALES.
IF YOU JUST RUB THIS WAX ON YOUR SCYTHE...
...IT WILL REMAIN SPARKLING CLEAN NO MATTER HOW MUDDY THE SPIRIT YOU BATTLE.
DON'T NEED IT.
AND WHAT EXACTLY IS A MUDDY SPIRIT?
AH, THAT REMINDS ME.
WE'VE GOT AN EMERGENCY, ROKUDO-KUN.
THIS MYSTERIOUS MUDDY INCIDENT HAS BEEN HAPPENING AT SCHOOL...

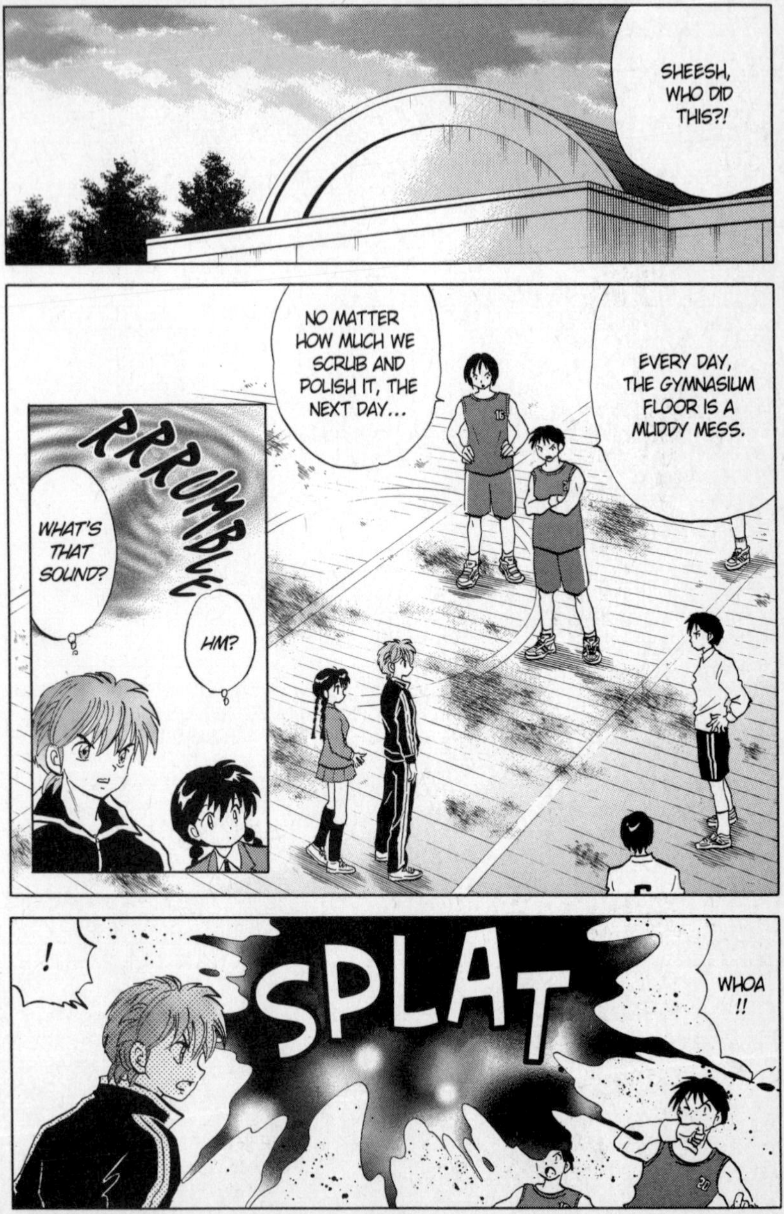
SHEESH, WHO DID THIS?!
EVERY DAY, THE GYMNASIUM FLOOR IS A MUDDY MESS.
NO MATTER HOW MUCH WE SCRUB AND POLISH IT, THE NEXT DAY...
RRRUMBLE
WHAT'S THAT SOUND?
HM?
WHOA!!
SPLAT
!

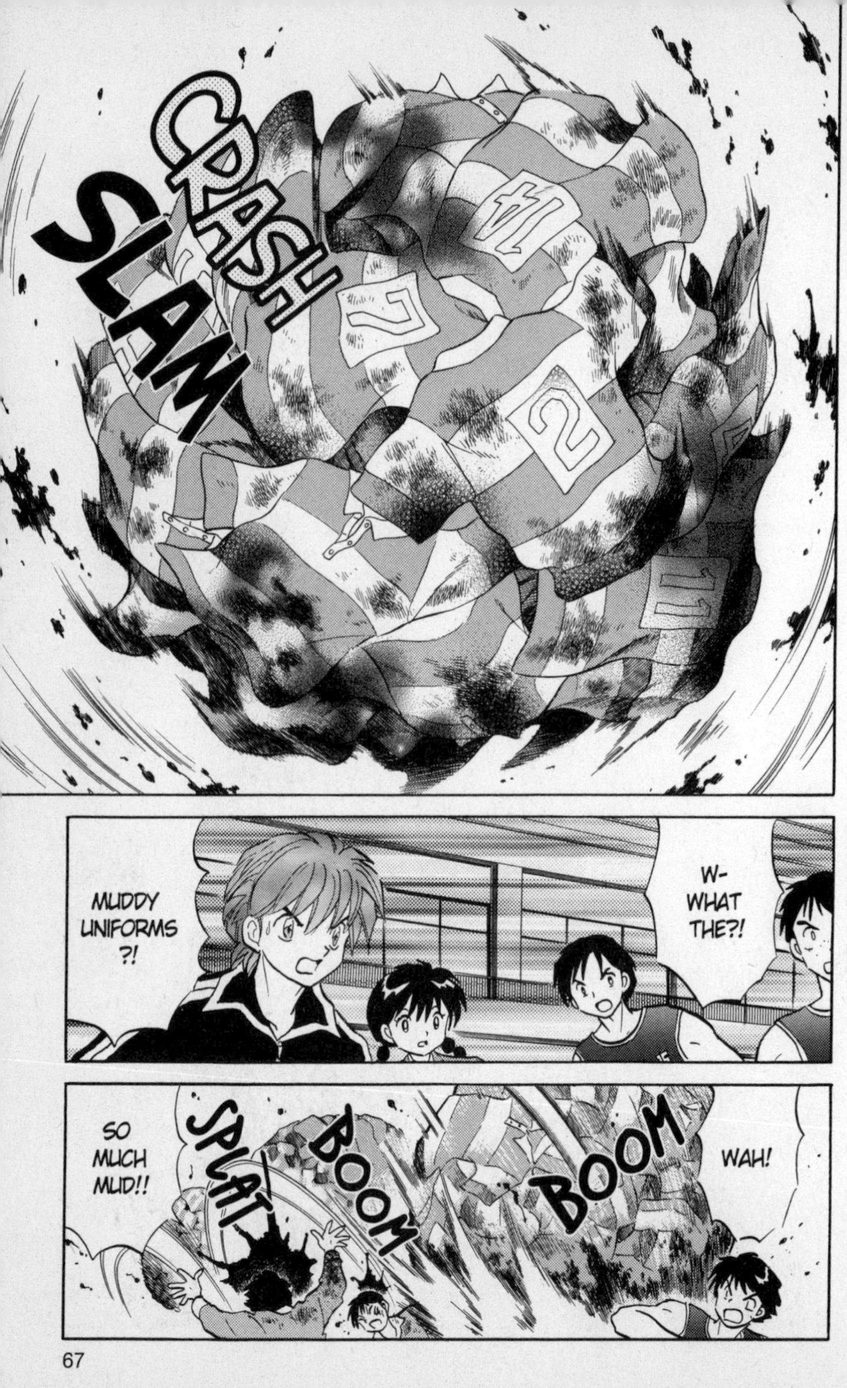
CRASH
SLAM
W- WHAT THE?!
MUDDY UNIFORMS ?!
BOOM
WAH!
BOOM
SPLAT
SO MUCH MUD!!

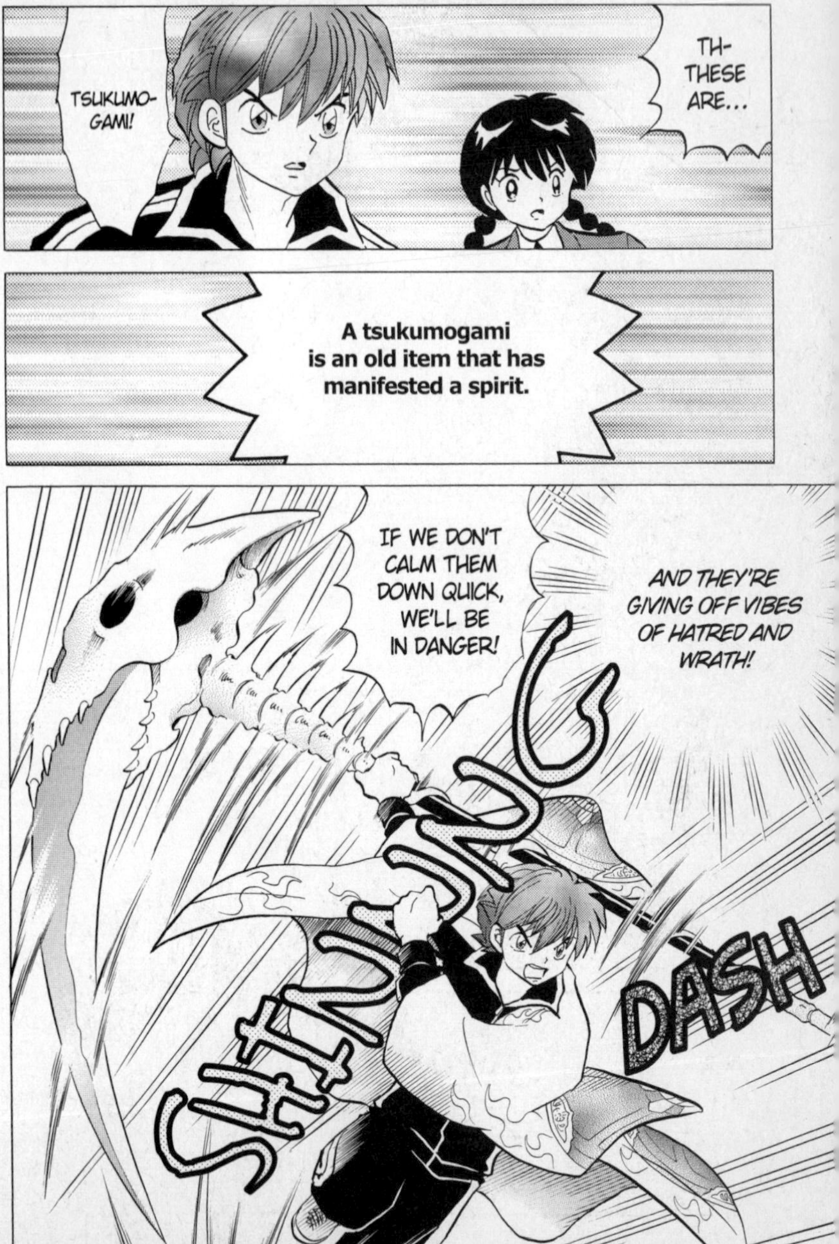
TH- THESE ARE...
TSUKUMO-GAMI!
A tsukumogami is an old item that has manifested a spirit.
AND THEY'RE GIVING OFF VIBES OF HATRED AND WRATH!
IF WE DON'T CALM THEM DOWN QUICK, WE'LL BE IN DANGER!
DASH

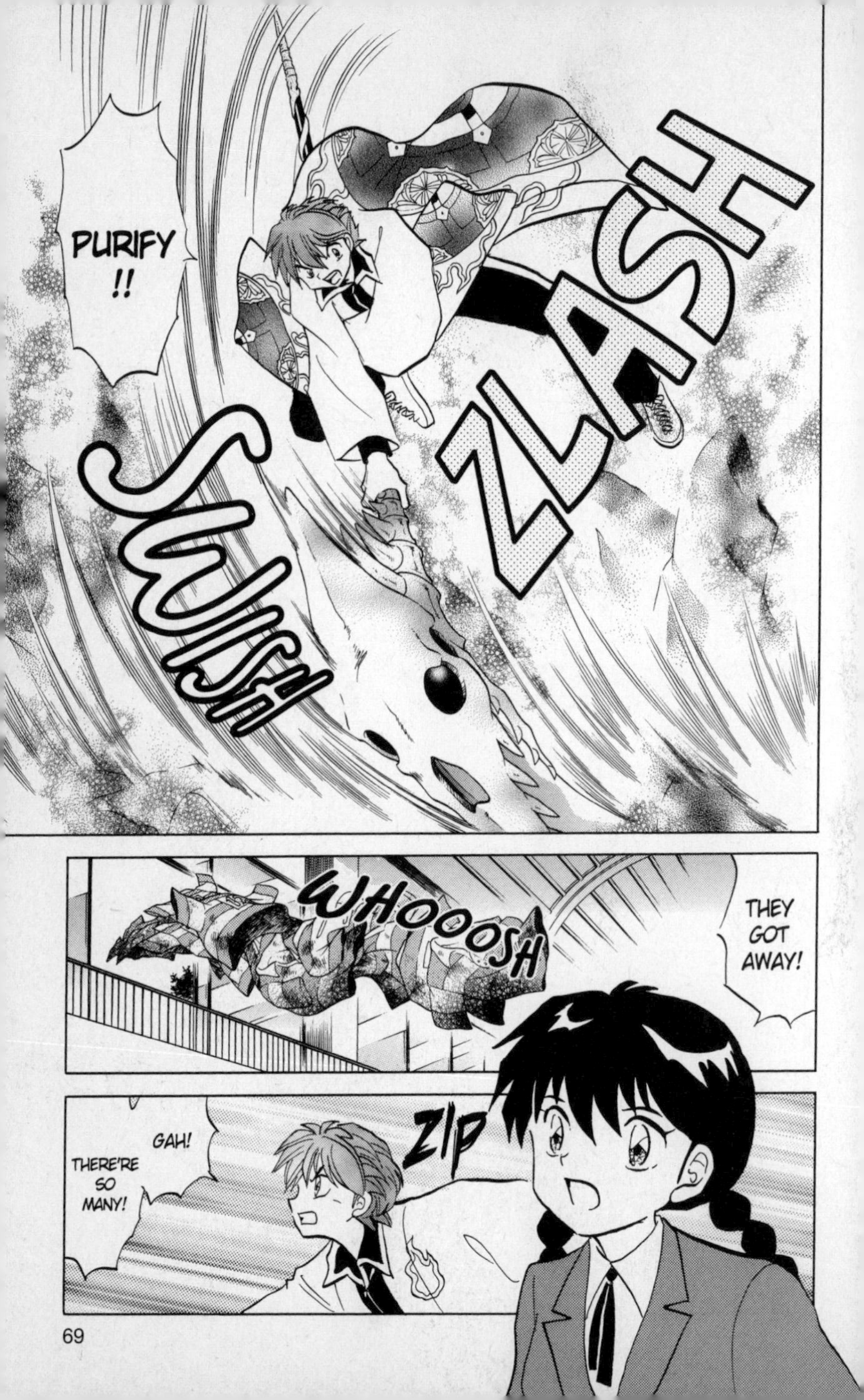
PURIFY !!
ZZASH
SWISH
WHOOOOSH
THEY GOT AWAY!
ZIP
GAH!
THERE'RE SO MANY!

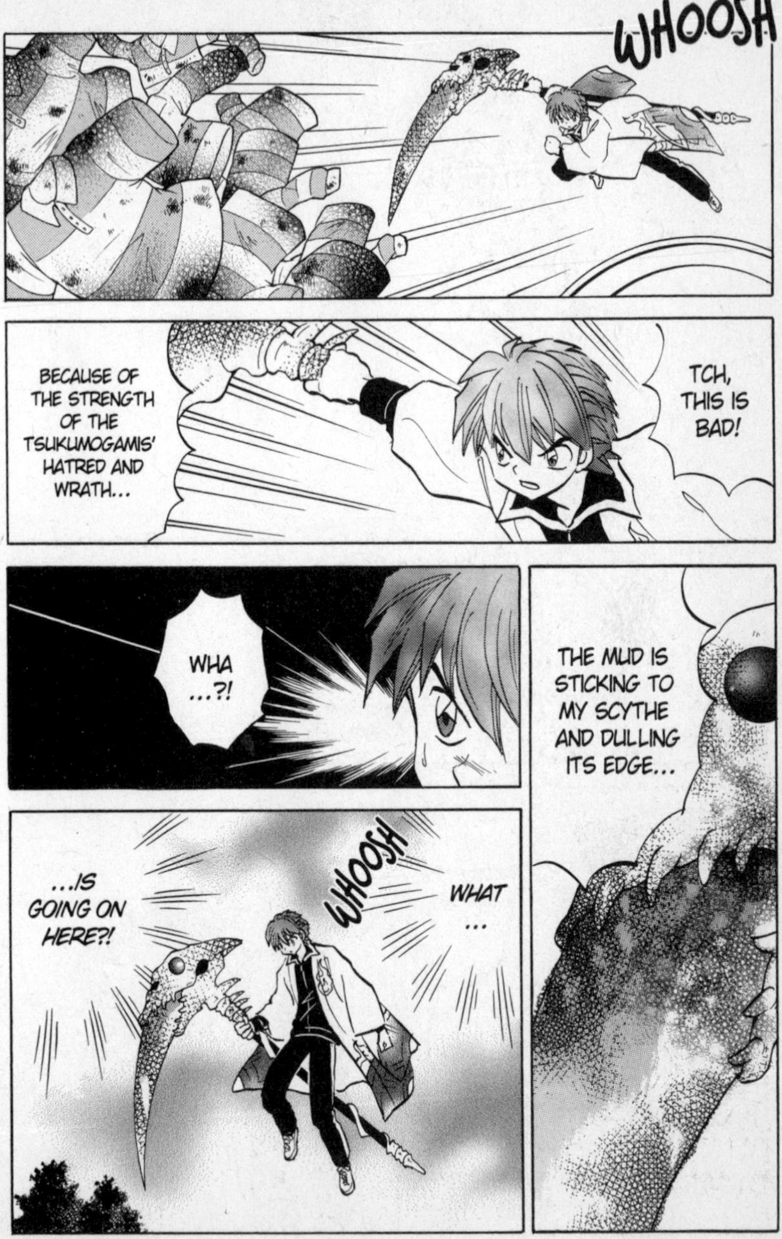
WHOOSH
TCH, THIS IS BAD!
BECAUSE OF THE STRENGTH OF THE TSUKUMOGAMIS' HATRED AND WRATH...
THE MUD IS STICKING TO MY SCYTHE AND DULLING ITS EDGE...
WHA ...?!
WHAT ...
WHOOSH
...IS GOING ON HERE?!

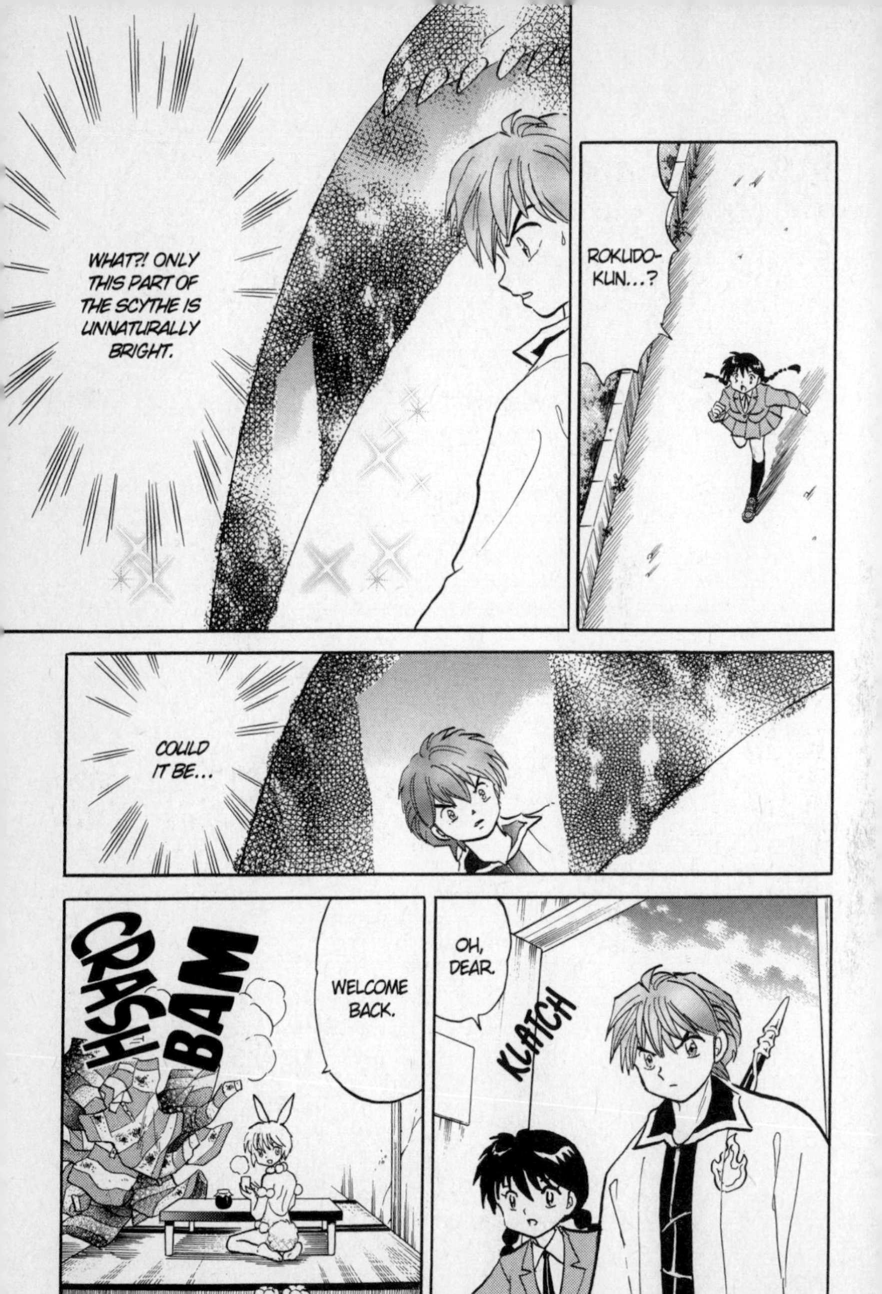
ROKUDO-KUN...?
WHAT?! ONLY THIS PART OF THE SCYTHE IS UNNATURALLY BRIGHT.
COULD IT BE...
OH, DEAR.
KLATCH
WELCOME BACK.
CRASH
BAM

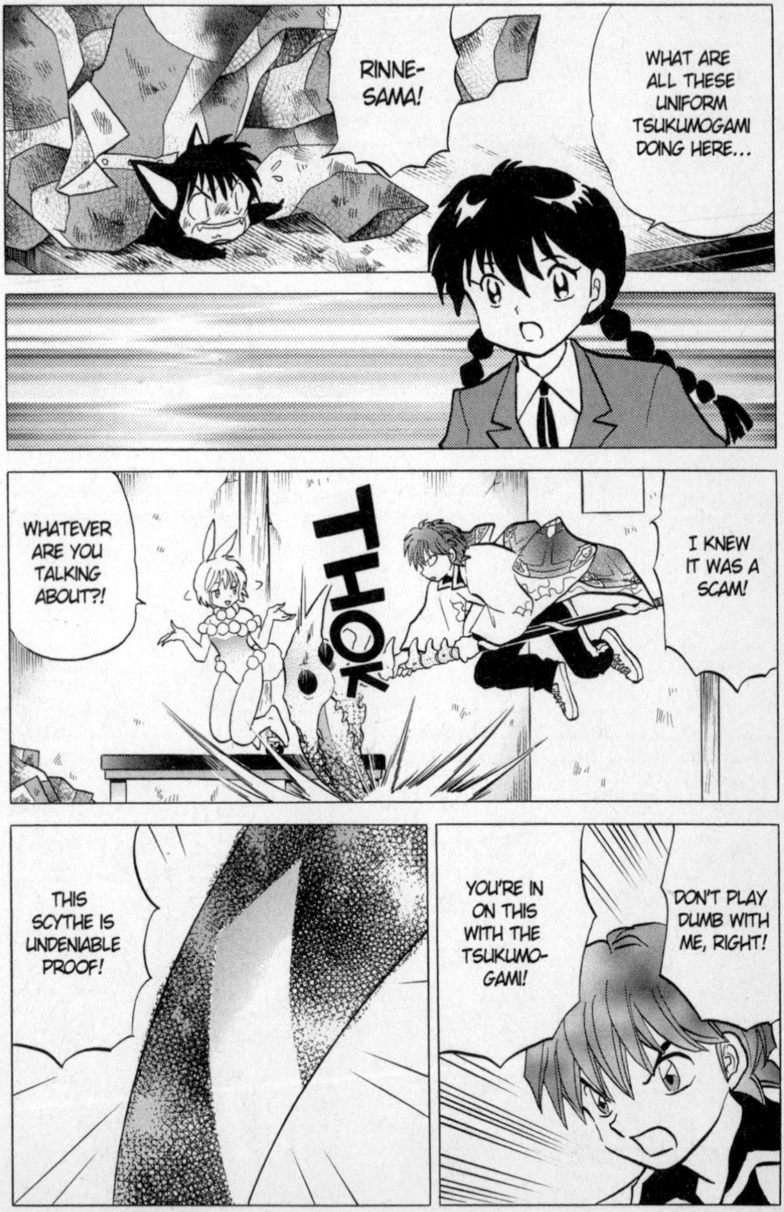
WHAT ARE ALL THESE UNIFORM TSUKUMOGAMI DOING HERE...
RINNE-SAMA!
I KNEW IT WAS A SCAM!
THOK
WHATEVER ARE YOU TALKING ABOUT?!
DON'T PLAY DUMB WITH ME, RIGHT!
YOU'RE IN ON THIS WITH THE TSUKUMO-GAMI!
THIS SCYTHE IS UNDENIABLE PROOF!

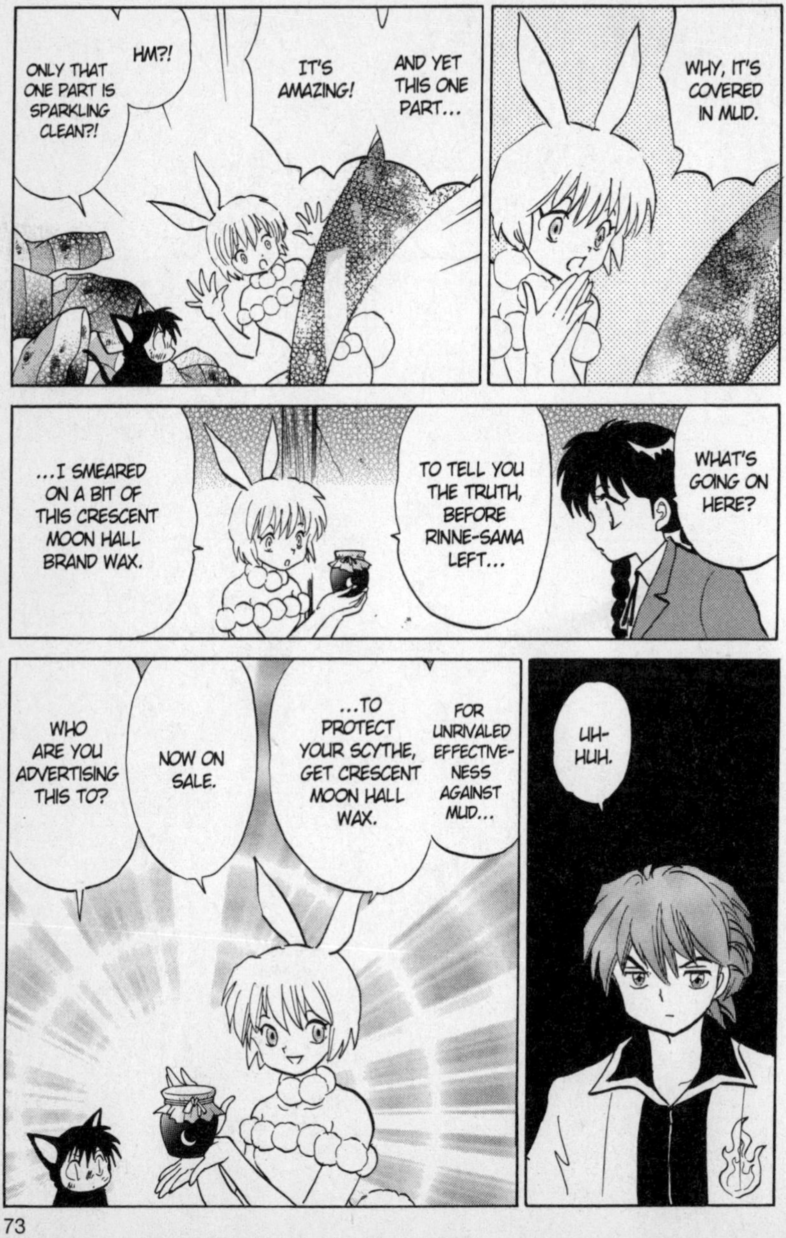
WHY, IT'S COVERED IN MUD.
AND YET THIS ONE PART...
IT'S AMAZING!
HM?!
ONLY THAT ONE PART IS SPARKLING CLEAN?!
WHAT'S GOING ON HERE?
TO TELL YOU THE TRUTH, BEFORE RINNE-SAMA LEFT...
...I SMEARED ON A BIT OF THIS CRESCENT MOON HALL BRAND WAX.
UH-HUH.
FOR UNRIVALED EFFECTIVE-NESS AGAINST MUD...
...TO PROTECT YOUR SCYTHE, GET CRESCENT MOON HALL WAX.
NOW ON SALE.
WHO ARE YOU ADVERTISING THIS TO?

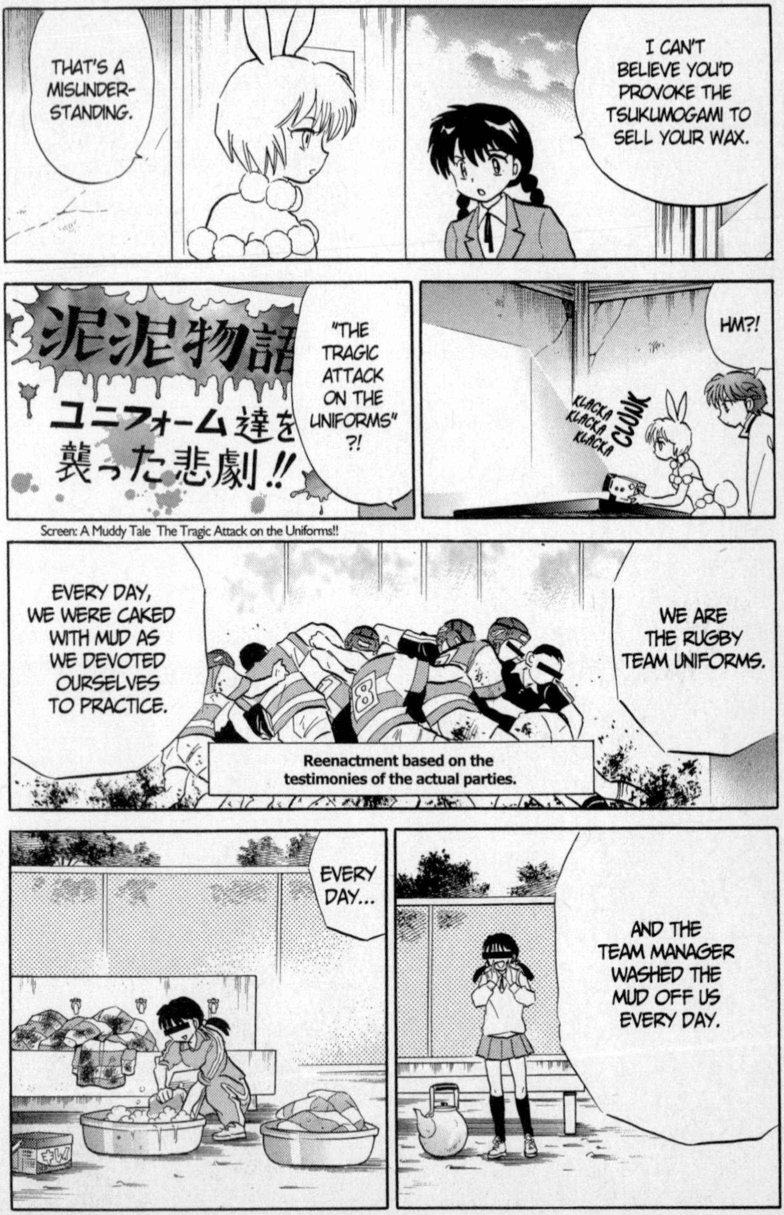
I CAN'T BELIEVE YOU'D PROVOKE THE TSUKUMOGAMI TO SELL YOUR WAX.
THAT'S A MISUNDER-STANDING.
HM?!
KLACKA KLACKA KLACKA
CLUNK
泥泥物語
ユニフォーム達を襲った悲劇!!
"THE TRAGIC ATTACK ON THE UNIFORMS"?!
Screen: A Muddy Tale The Tragic Attack on the Uniforms!!
WE ARE THE RUGBY TEAM UNIFORMS.
EVERY DAY, WE WERE CAKED WITH MUD AS WE DEVOTED OURSELVES TO PRACTICE.
Reenactment based on the testimonies of the actual parties.
AND THE TEAM MANAGER WASHED THE MUD OFF US EVERY DAY.
EVERY DAY...

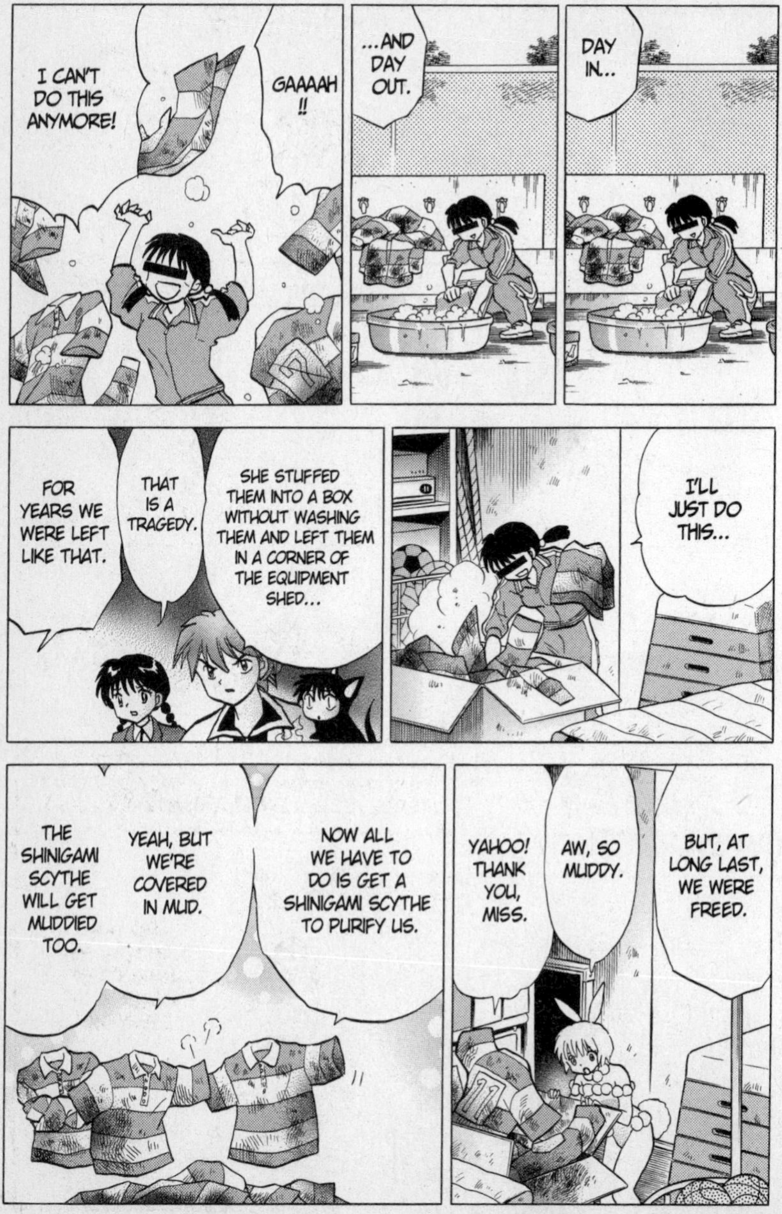
DAY IN...
...AND DAY OUT.
GAAAAH !!
I CAN'T DO THIS ANYMORE!
I'LL JUST DO THIS...
SHE STUFFED THEM INTO A BOX WITHOUT WASHING THEM AND LEFT THEM IN A CORNER OF THE EQUIPMENT SHED...
THAT IS A TRAGEDY.
FOR YEARS WE WERE LEFT LIKE THAT.
BUT, AT LONG LAST, WE WERE FREED.
AW, SO MUDDY.
YAHOO! THANK YOU, MISS.
NOW ALL WE HAVE TO DO IS GET A SHINIGAMI SCYTHE TO PURIFY US.
YEAH, BUT WE'RE COVERED IN MUD.
THE SHINIGAMI SCYTHE WILL GET MUDDIED TOO.

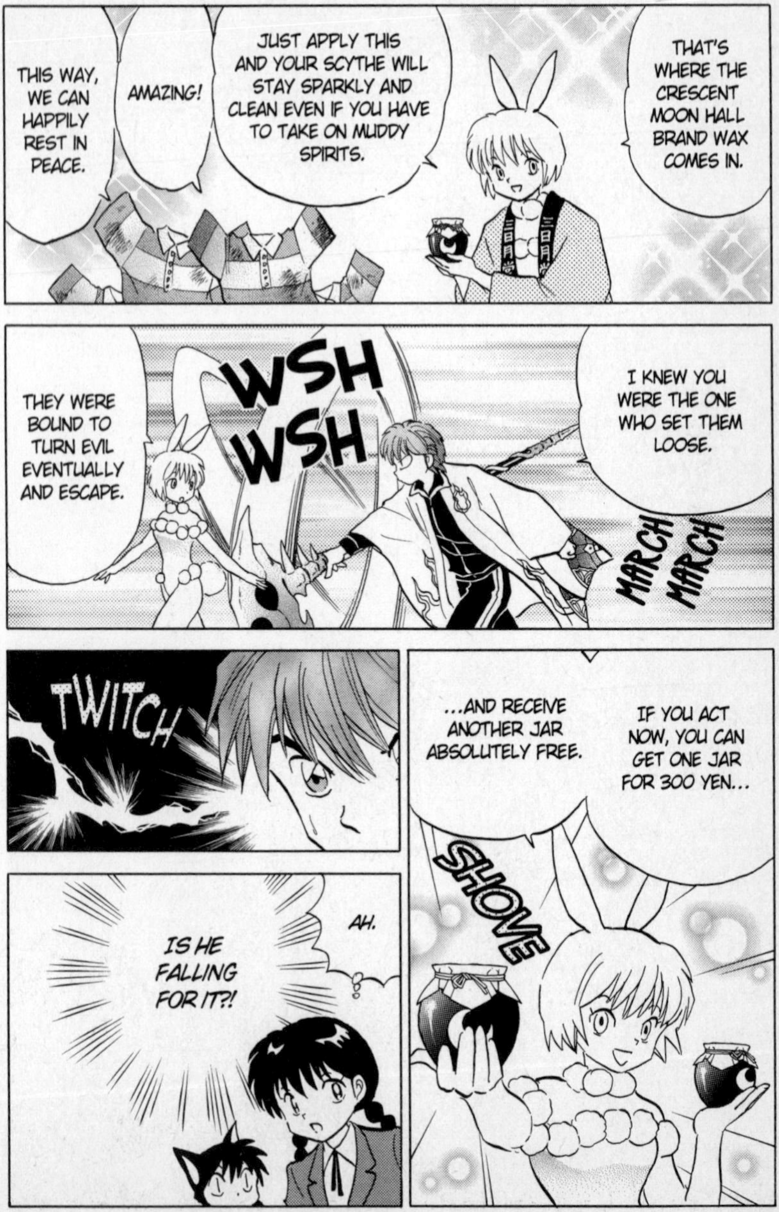
THAT'S WHERE THE CRESCENT MOON HALL BRAND WAX COMES IN.
JUST APPLY THIS AND YOUR SCYTHE WILL STAY SPARKLY AND CLEAN EVEN IF YOU HAVE TO TAKE ON MUDDY SPIRITS.
AMAZING!
THIS WAY, WE CAN HAPPILY REST IN PEACE.
I KNEW YOU WERE THE ONE WHO SET THEM LOOSE.
MARCH MARCH
WSH WSH
THEY WERE BOUND TO TURN EVIL EVENTUALLY AND ESCAPE.
IF YOU ACT NOW, YOU CAN GET ONE JAR FOR 300 YEN...
...AND RECEIVE ANOTHER JAR ABSOLUTELY FREE.
SHOVE
TWITCH
AH.
IS HE FALLING FOR IT?!

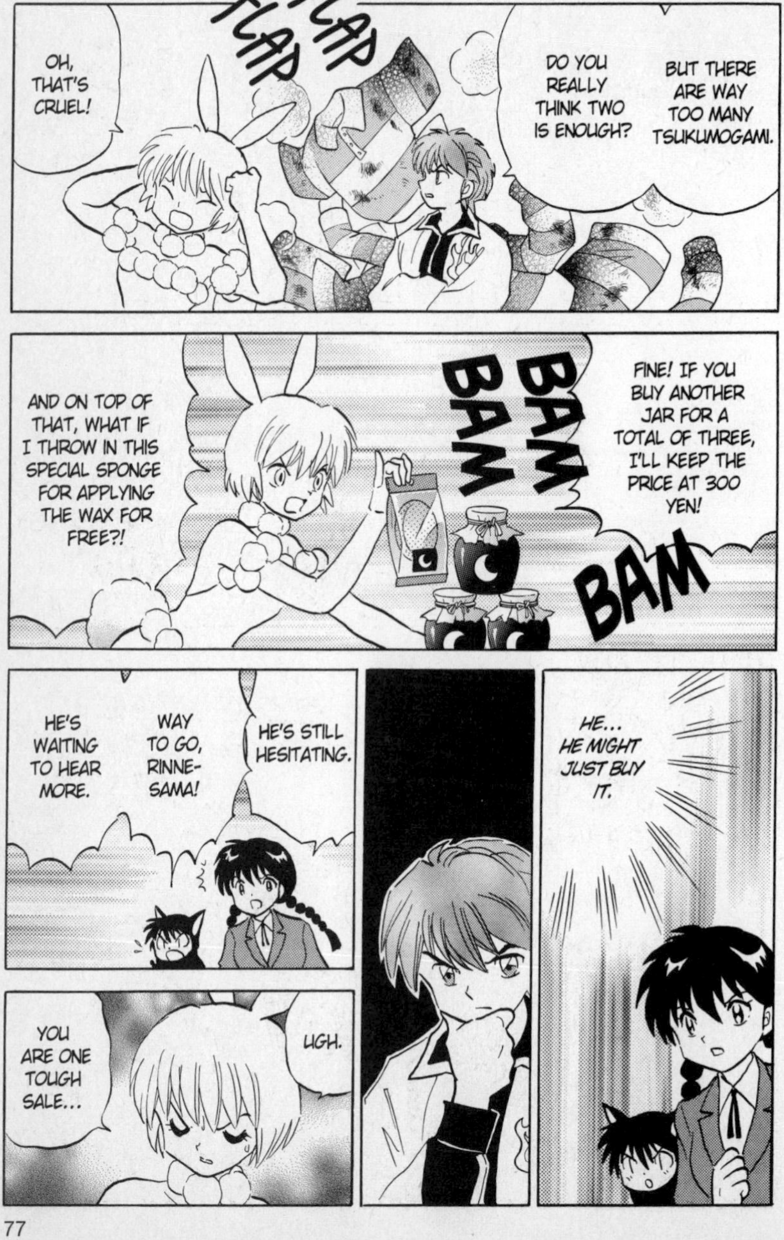
BUT THERE ARE WAY TOO MANY TSUKUMOGAMI.
DO YOU REALLY THINK TWO IS ENOUGH?
FLAP
FLAP
OH, THAT'S CRUEL!
FINE! IF YOU BUY ANOTHER JAR FOR A TOTAL OF THREE, I'LL KEEP THE PRICE AT 300 YEN!
BAM
BAM
BAM
AND ON TOP OF THAT, WHAT IF I THROW IN THIS SPECIAL SPONGE FOR APPLYING THE WAX FOR FREE?!
HE... HE MIGHT JUST BUY IT.
HE'S STILL HESITATING.
WAY TO GO, RINNE-SAMA!
HE'S WAITING TO HEAR MORE.
UGH.
YOU ARE ONE TOUGH SALE...

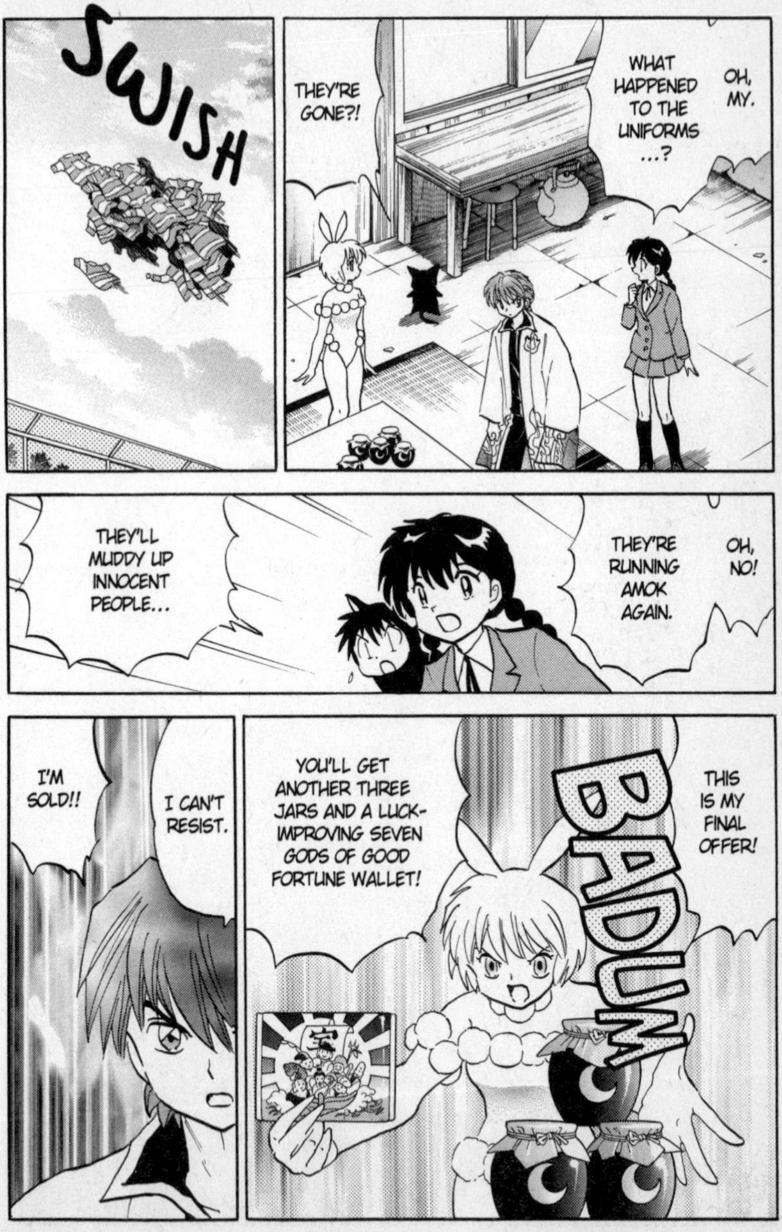
OH, MY.
WHAT HAPPENED TO THE UNIFORMS ...?
THEY'RE GONE?!
SWISH
OH, NO!
THEY'RE RUNNING AMOK AGAIN.
THEY'LL MUDDY UP INNOCENT PEOPLE...
THIS IS MY FINAL OFFER!
BADUM
YOU'LL GET ANOTHER THREE JARS AND A LUCK-IMPROVING SEVEN GODS OF GOOD FORTUNE WALLET!
I CAN'T RESIST.
I'M SOLD!!

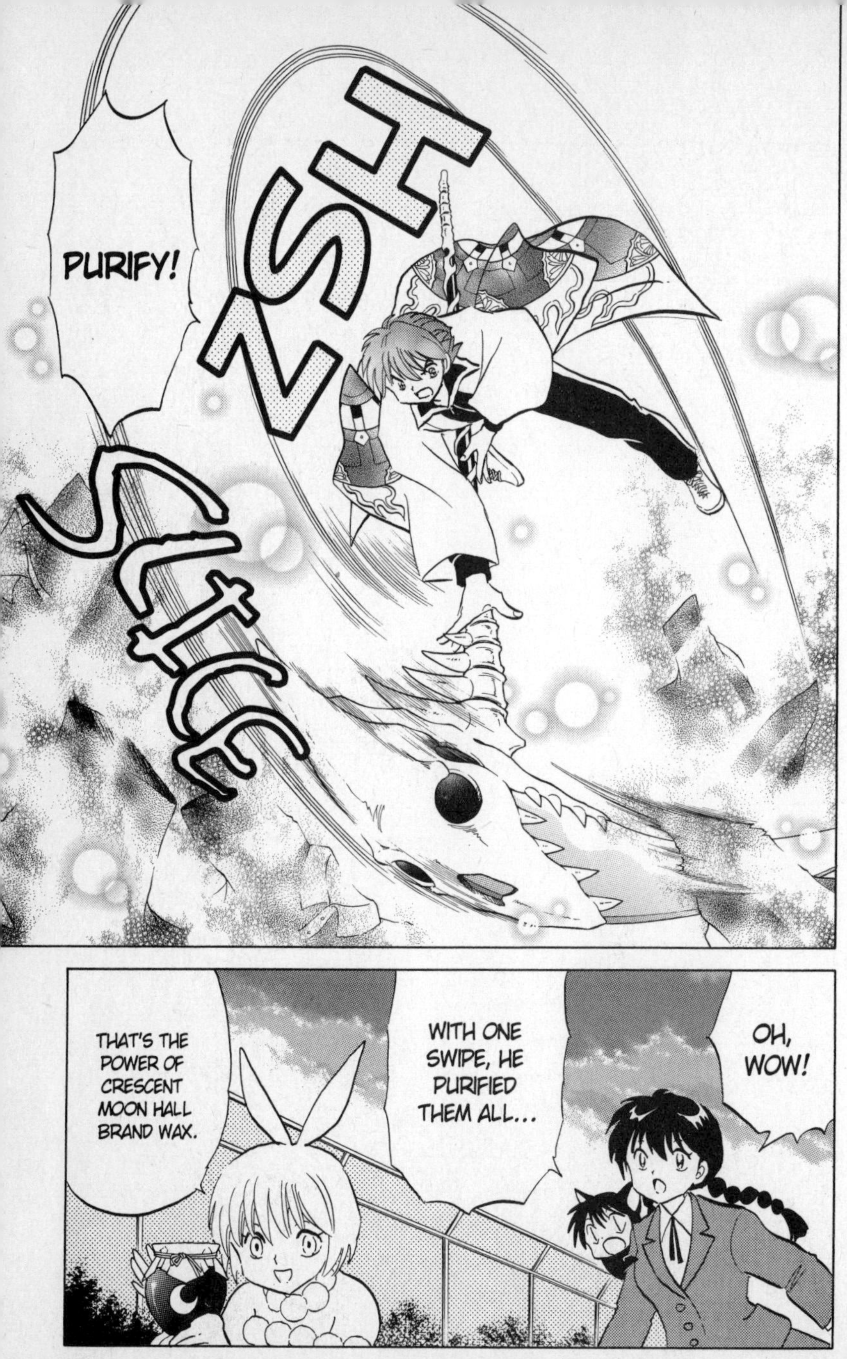
ZZSH
PURIFY!
SLICE
OH, WOW!
WITH ONE SWIPE, HE PURIFIED THEM ALL...
THAT'S THE POWER OF CRESCENT MOON HALL BRAND WAX.

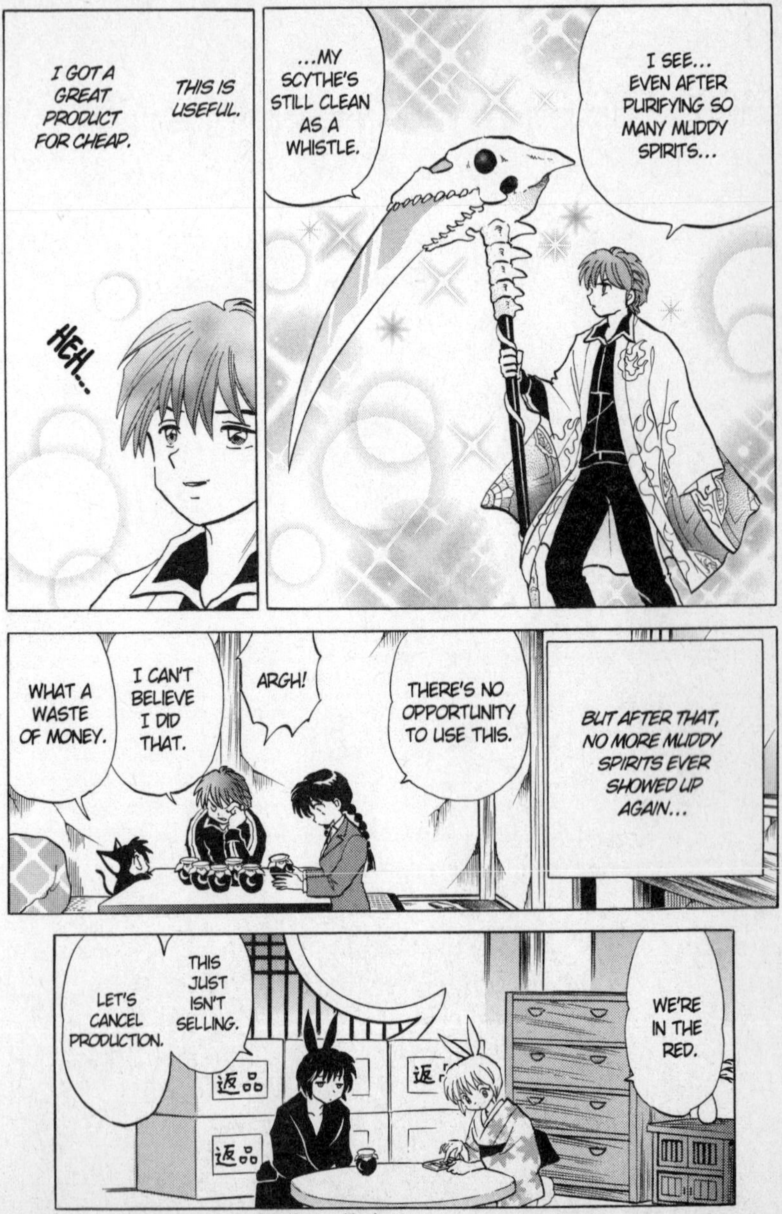
I SEE... EVEN AFTER PURIFYING SO MANY MUDDY SPIRITS...
...MY SCYTHE'S STILL CLEAN AS A WHISTLE.
THIS IS USEFUL.
I GOT A GREAT PRODUCT FOR CHEAP.
HEH...
BUT AFTER THAT, NO MORE MUDDY SPIRITS EVER SHOWED UP AGAIN...
THERE'S NO OPPORTUNITY TO USE THIS.
ARGH!
I CAN'T BELIEVE I DID THAT.
WHAT A WASTE OF MONEY.
WE'RE IN THE RED.
THIS JUST ISN'T SELLING.
LET'S CANCEL PRODUCTION.
返品
返品

Boxes: Return to Manufacturer

CHAPTER 123: FALSELY ACCUSED

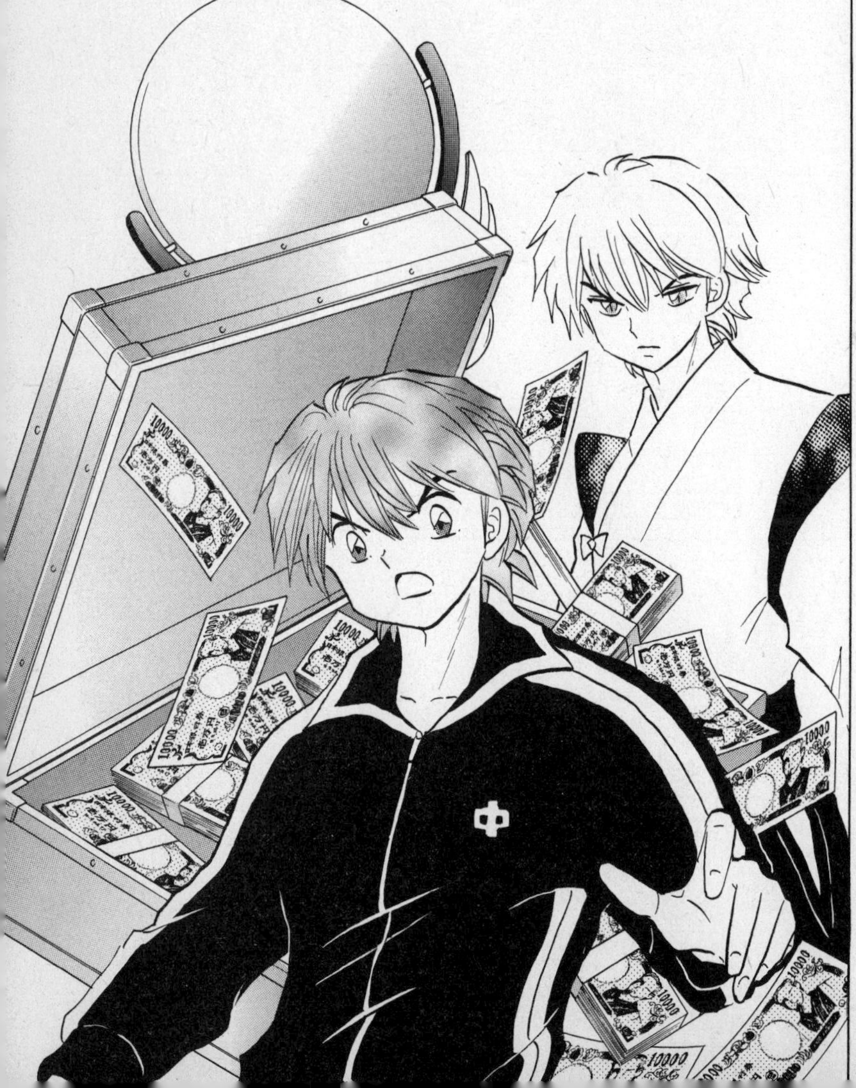

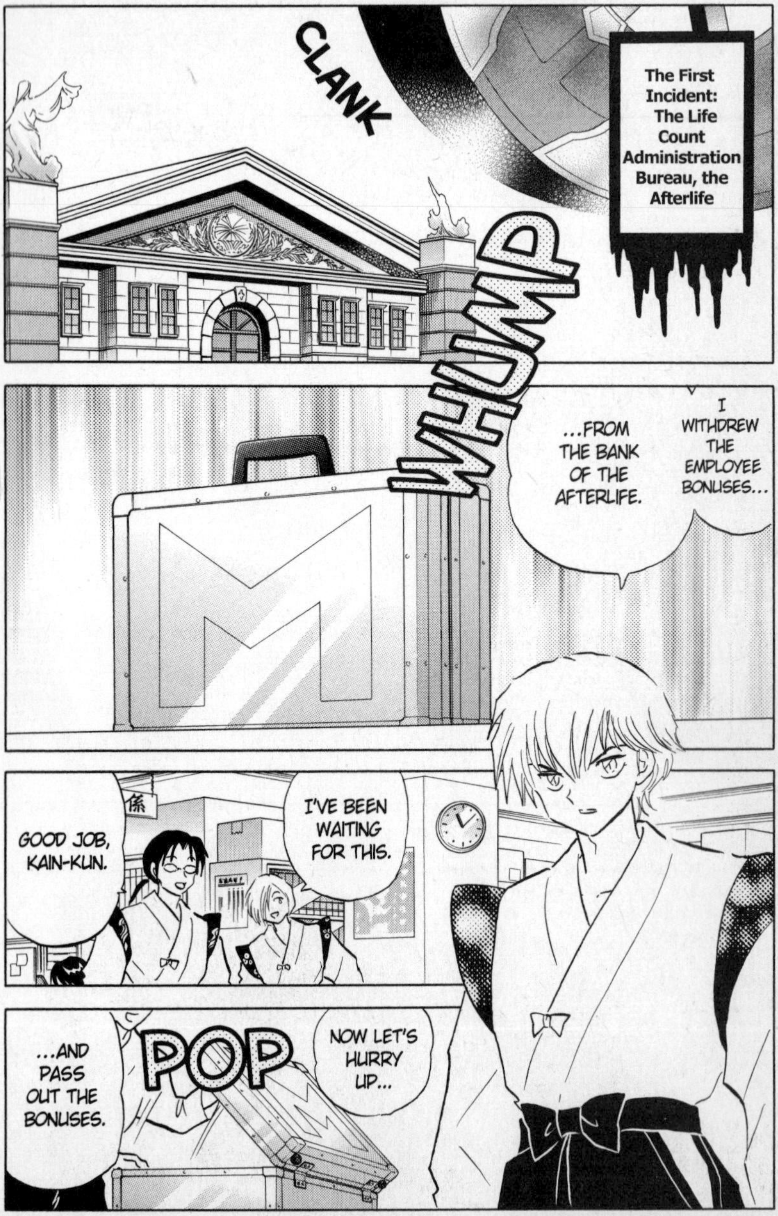
The First Incident: The Life Count Administration Bureau, the Afterlife
CLANK
WHUMP
I WITHDREW THE EMPLOYEE BONUSES...
...FROM THE BANK OF THE AFTERLIFE.
I'VE BEEN WAITING FOR THIS.
GOOD JOB, KAIN-KUN.
NOW LET'S HURRY UP...
POP
...AND PASS OUT THE BONUSES.

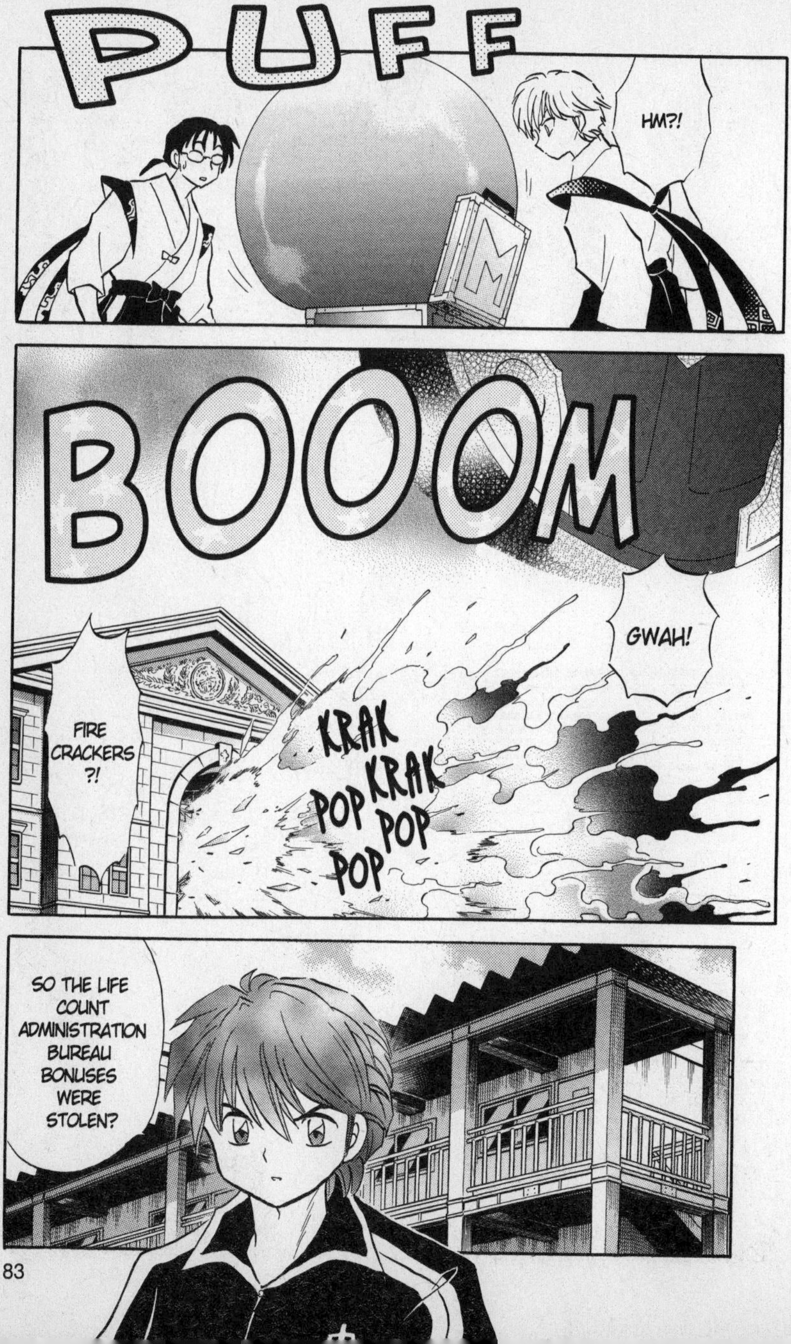
PUFF
HM?!
BOOOM
GWAH!
KRAK KRAK
POP POP POP
FIRE CRACKERS ?!
SO THE LIFE COUNT ADMINISTRATION BUREAU BONUSES WERE STOLEN?

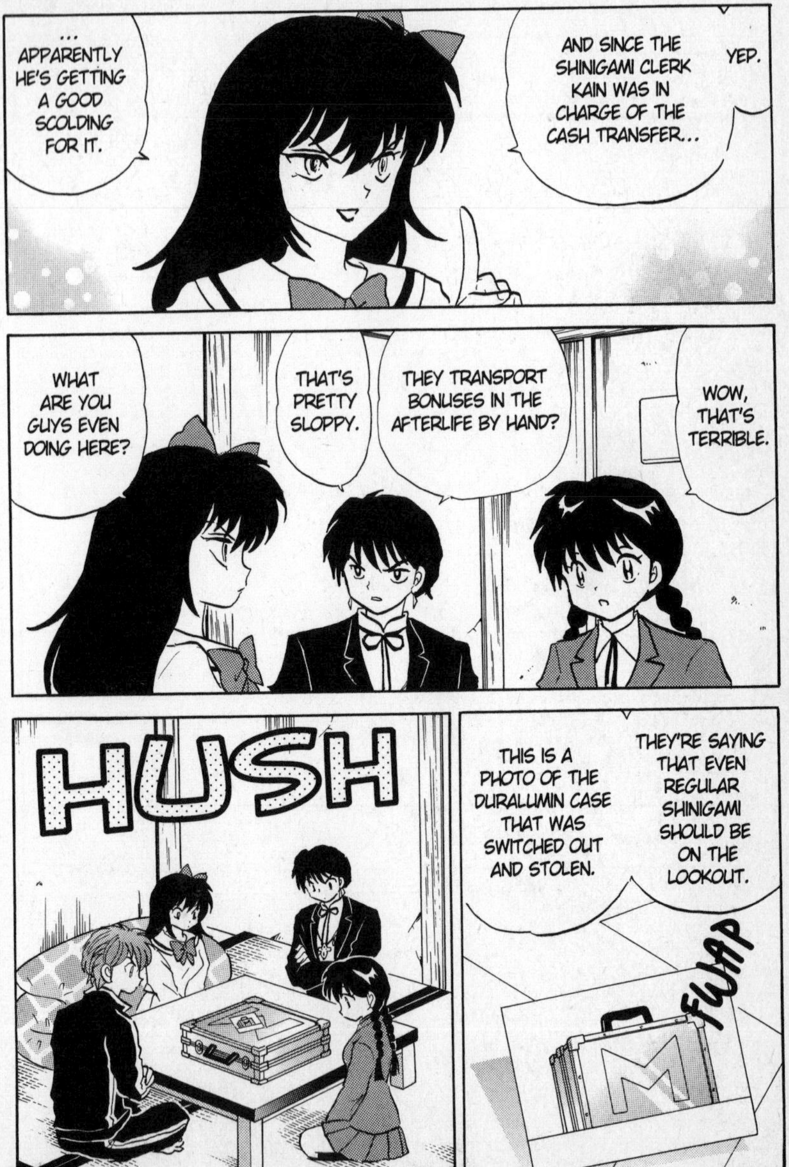

YEP.
AND SINCE THE SHINIGAMI CLERK KAIN WAS IN CHARGE OF THE CASH TRANSFER...
... APPARENTLY HE'S GETTING A GOOD SCOLDING FOR IT.
WOW, THAT'S TERRIBLE.
THEY TRANSPORT BONUSES IN THE AFTERLIFE BY HAND?
THAT'S PRETTY SLOPPY.
WHAT ARE YOU GUYS EVEN DOING HERE?
THEY'RE SAYING THAT EVEN REGULAR SHINIGAMI SHOULD BE ON THE LOOKOUT.
THIS IS A PHOTO OF THE DURALUMIN CASE THAT WAS SWITCHED OUT AND STOLEN.
FWAP
HUSH

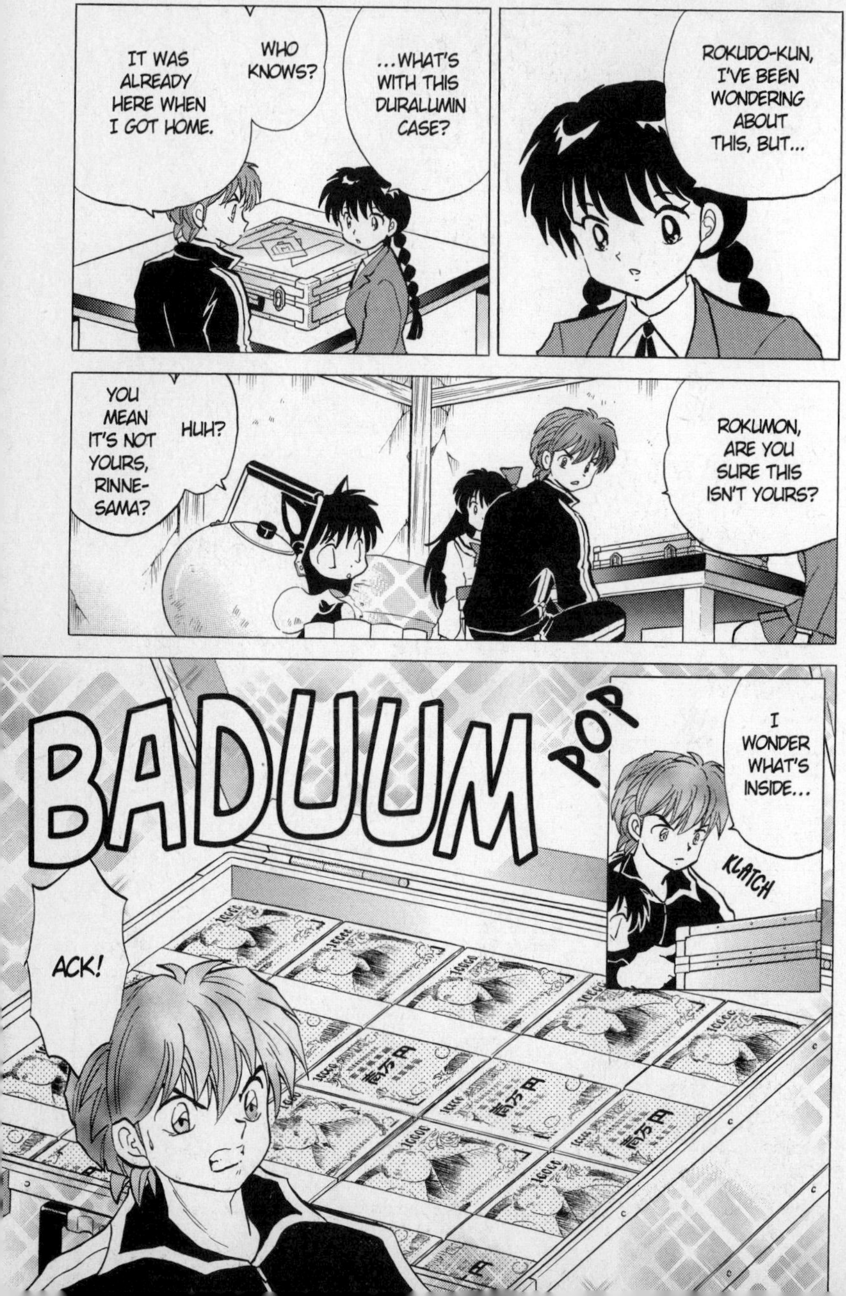
ROKUDO-KUN, I'VE BEEN WONDERING ABOUT THIS, BUT...
...WHAT'S WITH THIS DURALUMIN CASE?
WHO KNOWS?
IT WAS ALREADY HERE WHEN I GOT HOME.
ROKUMON, ARE YOU SURE THIS ISN'T YOURS?
HUH?
YOU MEAN IT'S NOT YOURS, RINNE-SAMA?
I WONDER WHAT'S INSIDE...
KLATCH
POP
BADUUM
ACK!

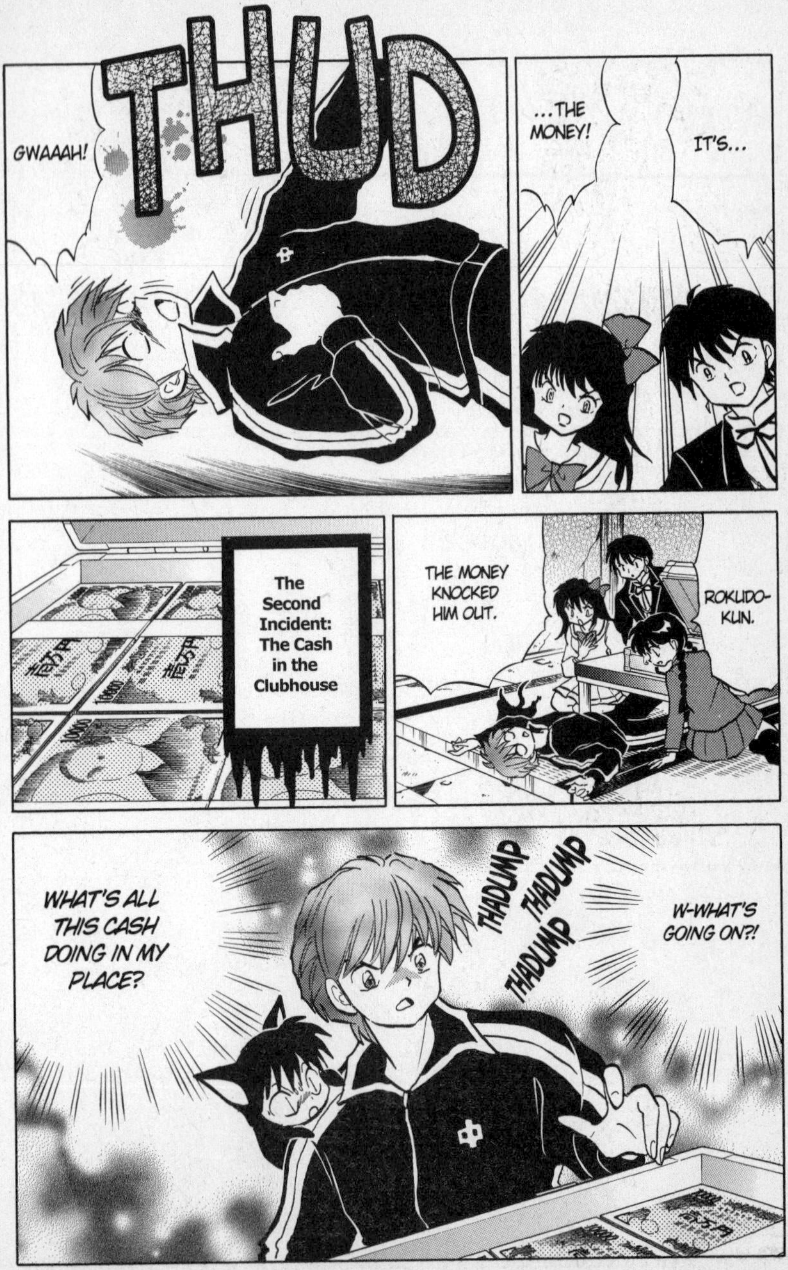
IT'S...
...THE MONEY!
THUD
GWAAAH!
ROKUDO-KUN.
THE MONEY KNOCKED HIM OUT.
The Second Incident: The Cash in the Clubhouse
W-WHAT'S GOING ON?!
THADUMP THADUMP THADUMP
WHAT'S ALL THIS CASH DOING IN MY PLACE?

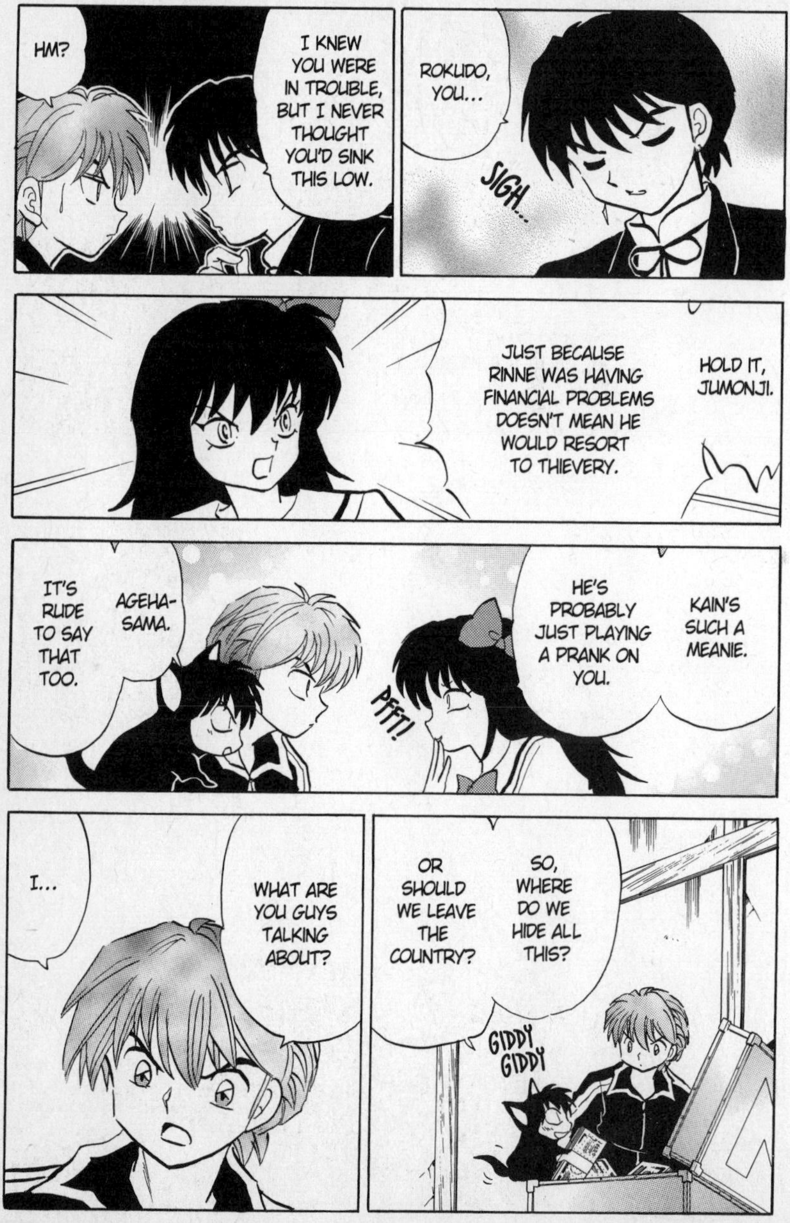
ROKUDO, YOU...
SIGH...
I KNEW YOU WERE IN TROUBLE, BUT I NEVER THOUGHT YOU'D SINK THIS LOW.
HM?
HOLD IT, JUMONJI.
JUST BECAUSE RINNE WAS HAVING FINANCIAL PROBLEMS DOESN'T MEAN HE WOULD RESORT TO THIEVERY.
KAIN'S SUCH A MEANIE.
HE'S PROBABLY JUST PLAYING A PRANK ON YOU.
PFFT!
AGEHA-SAMA.
IT'S RUDE TO SAY THAT TOO.
SO, WHERE DO WE HIDE ALL THIS?
OR SHOULD WE LEAVE THE COUNTRY?
GIDDY GIDDY
WHAT ARE YOU GUYS TALKING ABOUT?
I...

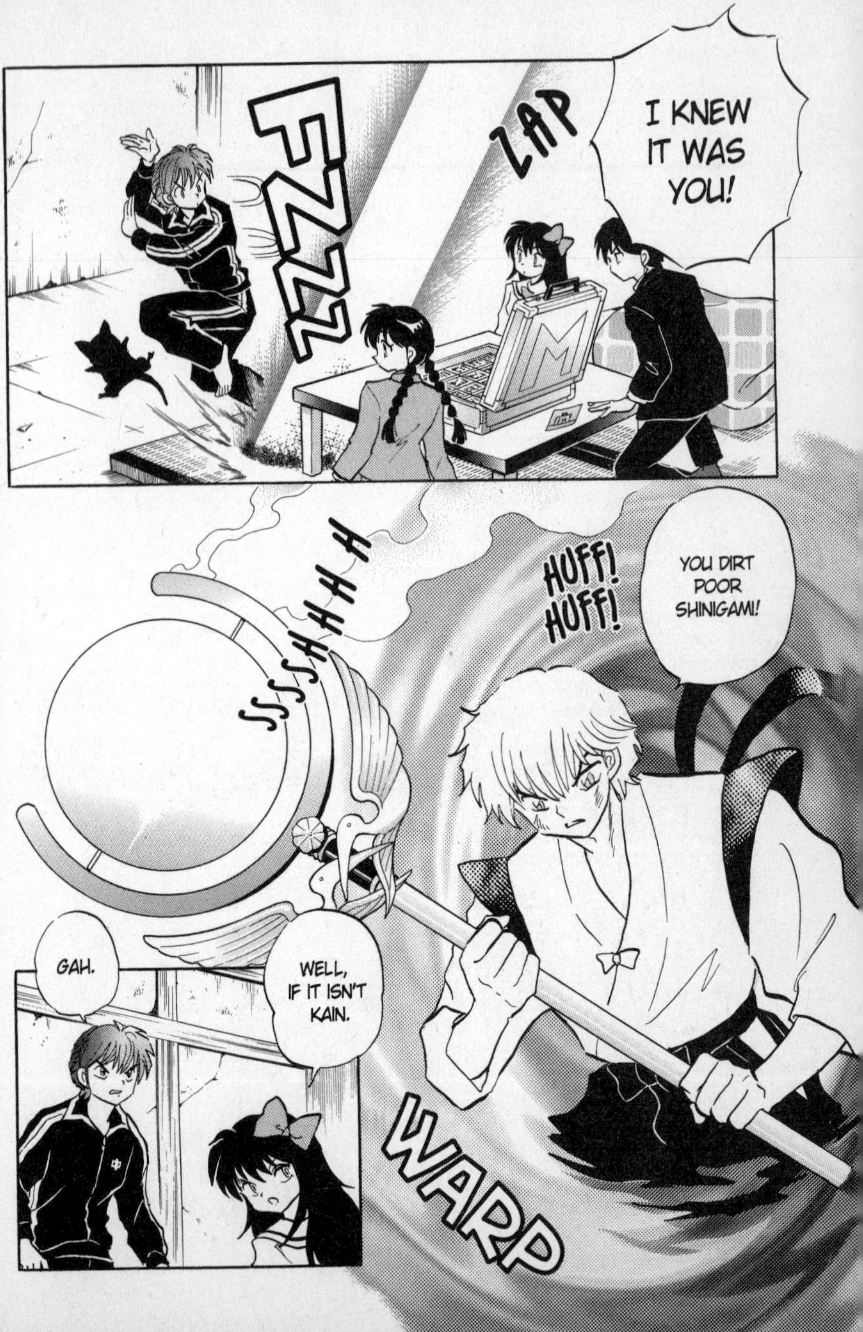
I KNEW IT WAS YOU!
ZAP
FZZZZ
YOU DIRT POOR SHINIGAMI!
HUFF! HUFF!
JSSSHHHHH
WARP
WELL, IF IT ISN'T KAIN.
GAH.

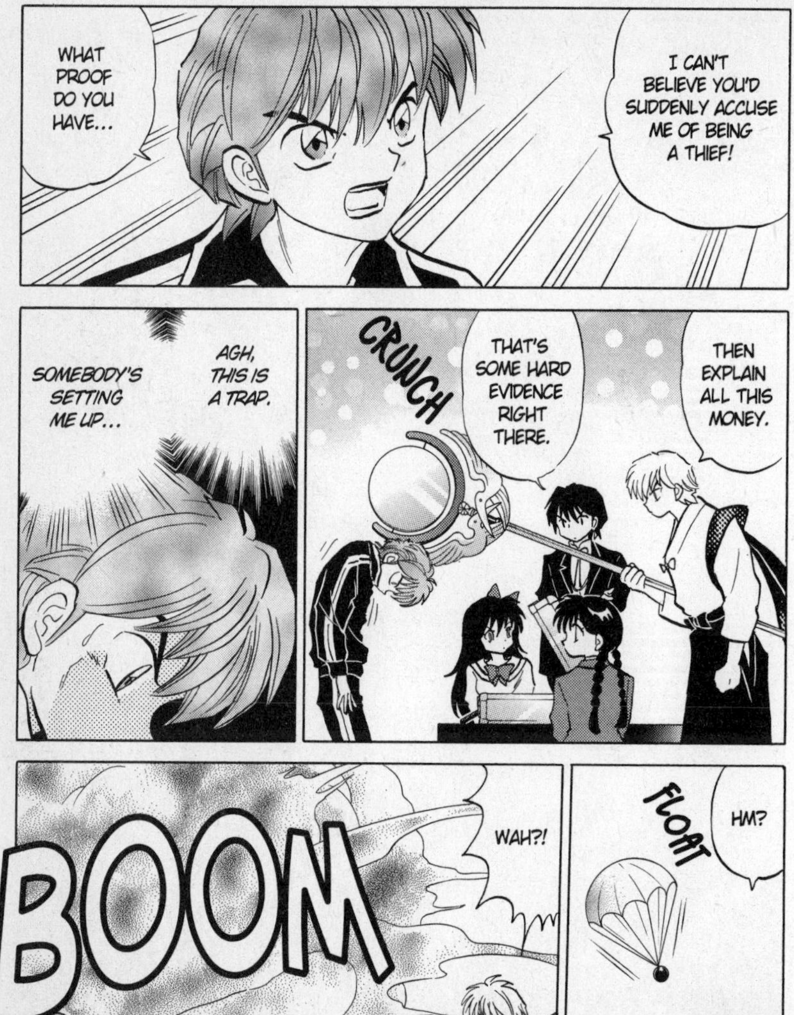
I CAN'T BELIEVE YOU'D SUDDENLY ACCUSE ME OF BEING A THIEF!
WHAT PROOF DO YOU HAVE...
THEN EXPLAIN ALL THIS MONEY.
THAT'S SOME HARD EVIDENCE RIGHT THERE.
CRUNCH
AGH, THIS IS A TRAP.
SOMEBODY'S SETTING ME UP...
HM?
FLOAT
WAH?!
BOOM

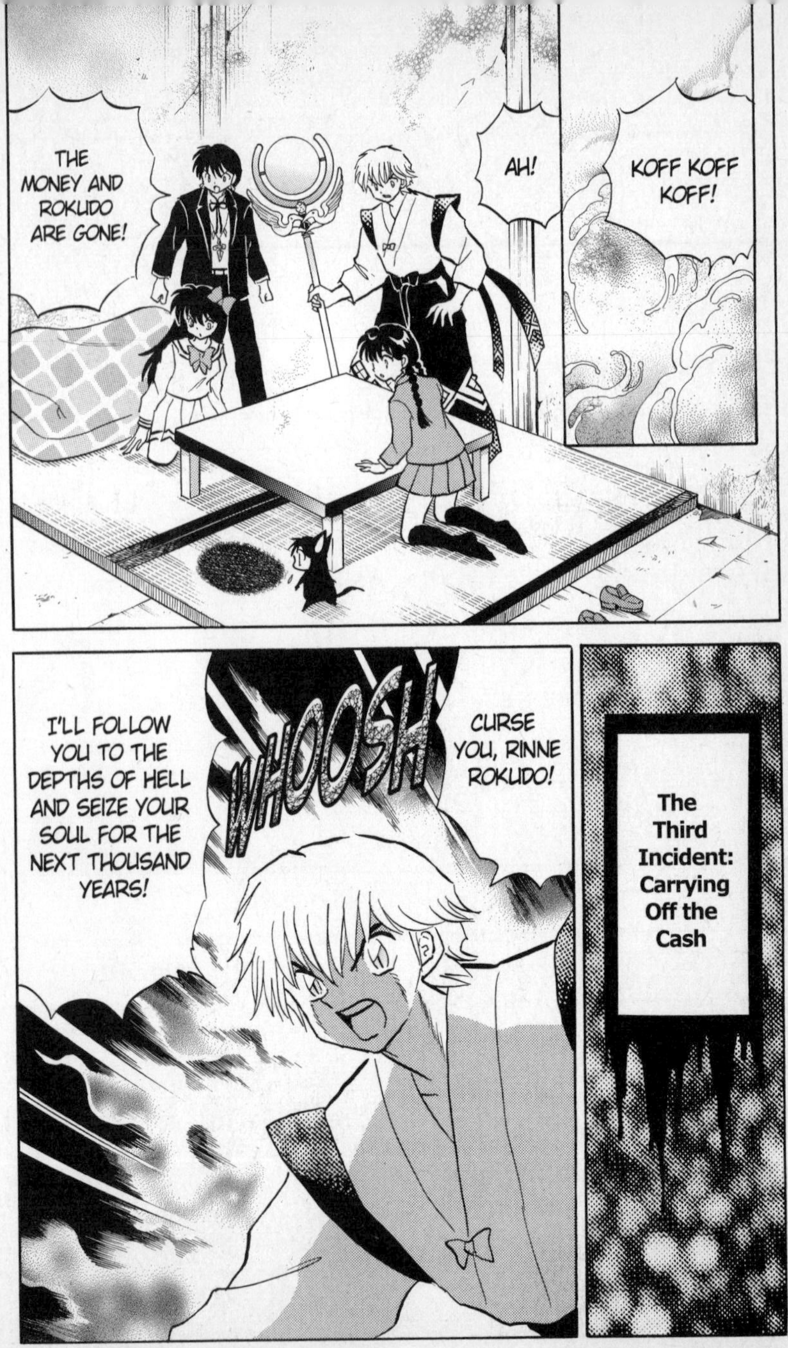
KOFF KOFF KOFF!
AH!
THE MONEY AND ROKUDO ARE GONE!
The Third Incident: Carrying Off the Cash
CURSE YOU, RINNE ROKUDO!
WHOOSH
I'LL FOLLOW YOU TO THE DEPTHS OF HELL AND SEIZE YOUR SOUL FOR THE NEXT THOUSAND YEARS!

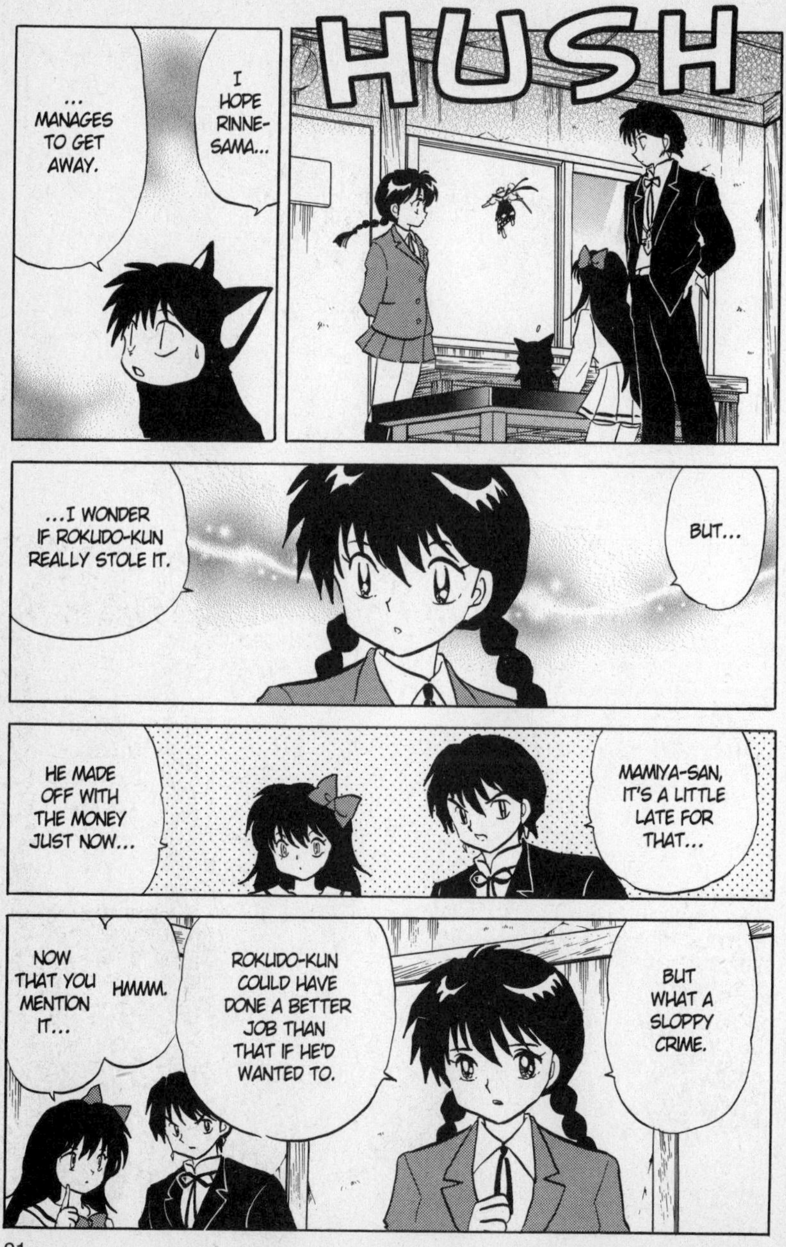
HUSH
I HOPE RINNE-SAMA...
...MANAGES TO GET AWAY.
BUT...
...I WONDER IF ROKUDO-KUN REALLY STOLE IT.
MAMIYA-SAN, IT'S A LITTLE LATE FOR THAT...
HE MADE OFF WITH THE MONEY JUST NOW...
BUT WHAT A SLOPPY CRIME.
ROKUDO-KUN COULD HAVE DONE A BETTER JOB THAN THAT IF HE'D WANTED TO.
HMMM.
NOW THAT YOU MENTION IT...

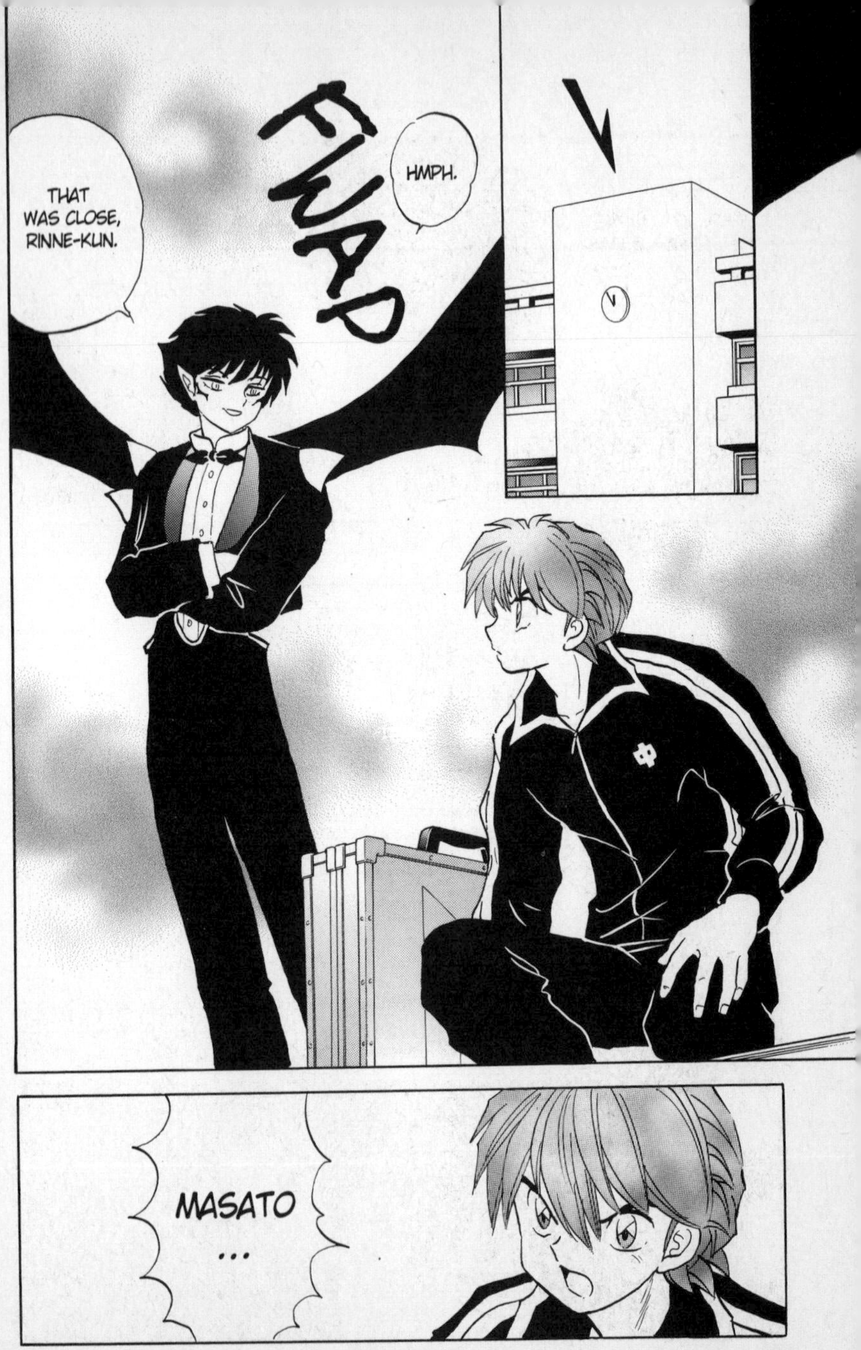
HMPH.
FWAP
THAT WAS CLOSE, RINNE-KUN.
MASATO ...

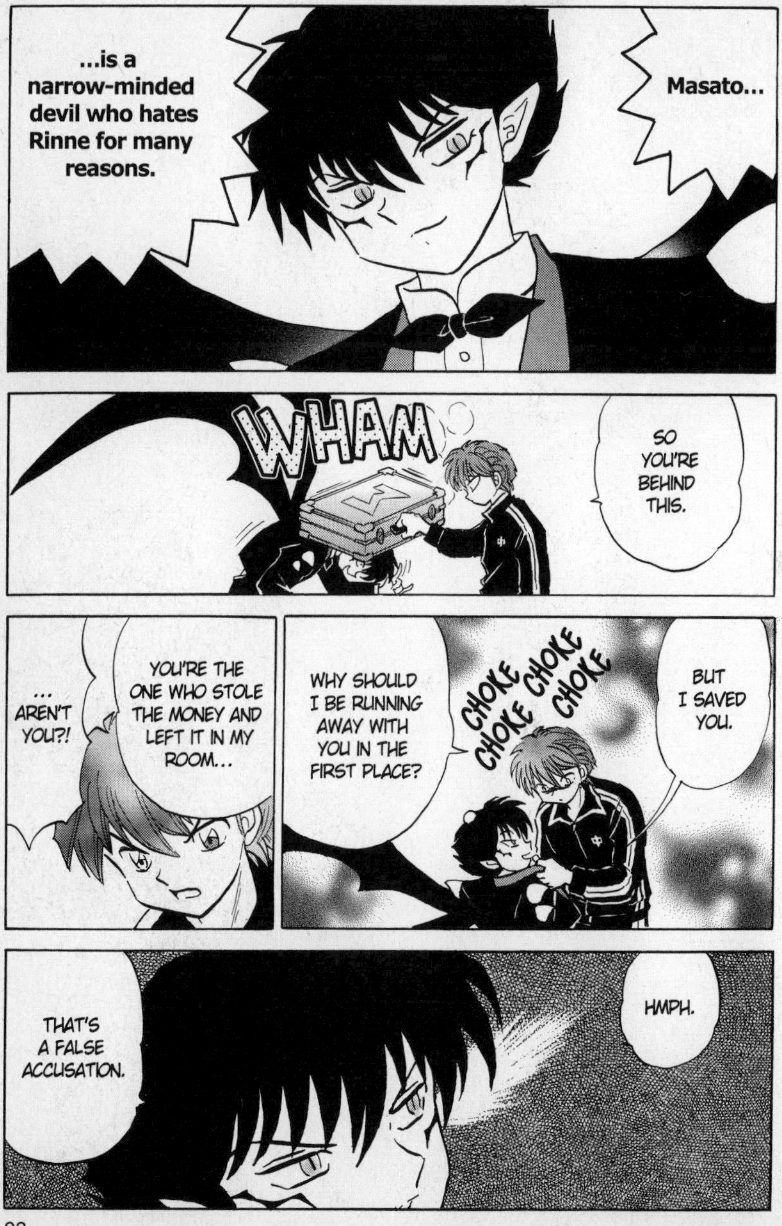
Masato...
...is a narrow-minded devil who hates Rinne for many reasons.
WHAM
SO YOU'RE BEHIND THIS.
BUT I SAVED YOU.
CHOKE CHOKE CHOKE CHOKE
WHY SHOULD I BE RUNNING AWAY WITH YOU IN THE FIRST PLACE?
YOU'RE THE ONE WHO STOLE THE MONEY AND LEFT IT IN MY ROOM...
...AREN'T YOU?!
HMPH.
THAT'S A FALSE ACCUSATION.

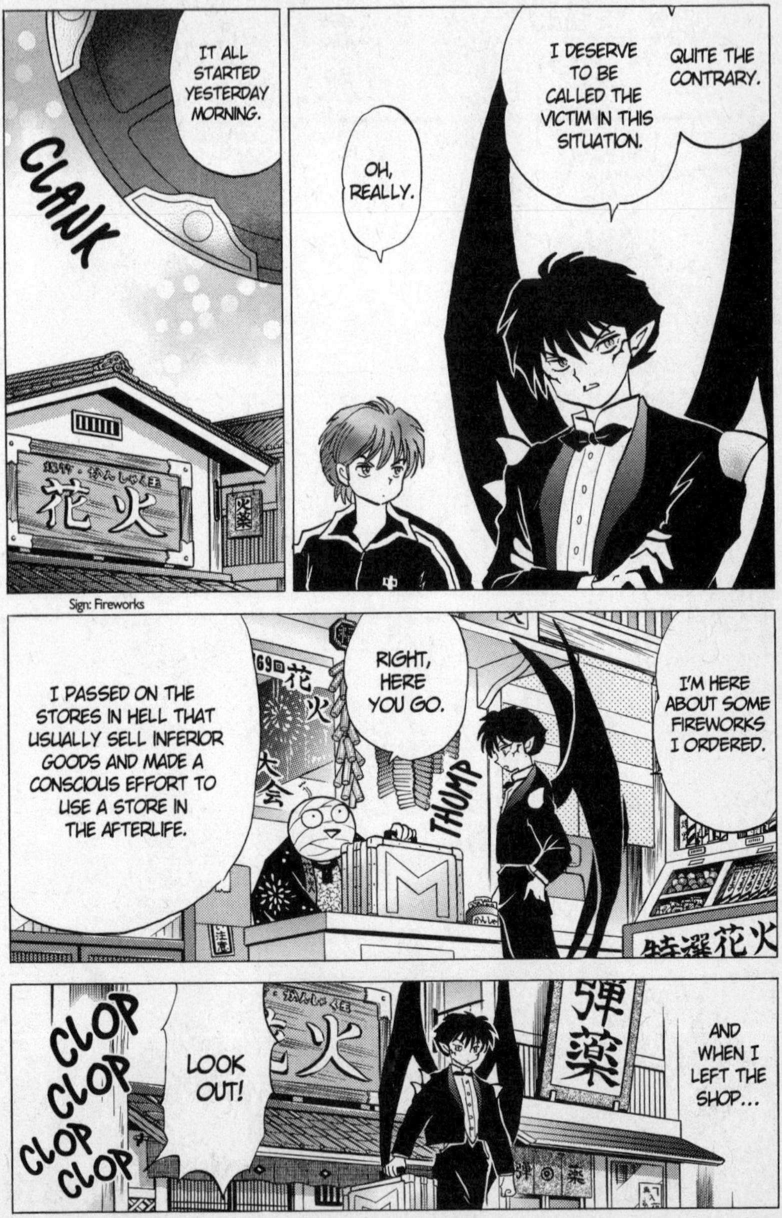
QUITE THE CONTRARY.
I DESERVE TO BE CALLED THE VICTIM IN THIS SITUATION.
OH, REALLY.
IT ALL STARTED YESTERDAY MORNING.
CLANK
花火
I'M HERE ABOUT SOME FIREWORKS I ORDERED.
RIGHT, HERE YOU GO.
THUMP
I PASSED ON THE STORES IN HELL THAT USUALLY SELL INFERIOR GOODS AND MADE A CONSCIOUS EFFORT TO USE A STORE IN THE AFTERLIFE.
特選花火
AND WHEN I LEFT THE SHOP...
弾薬
LOOK OUT!
CLOP CLOP CLOP CLOP CLOP
Sign: Fireworks

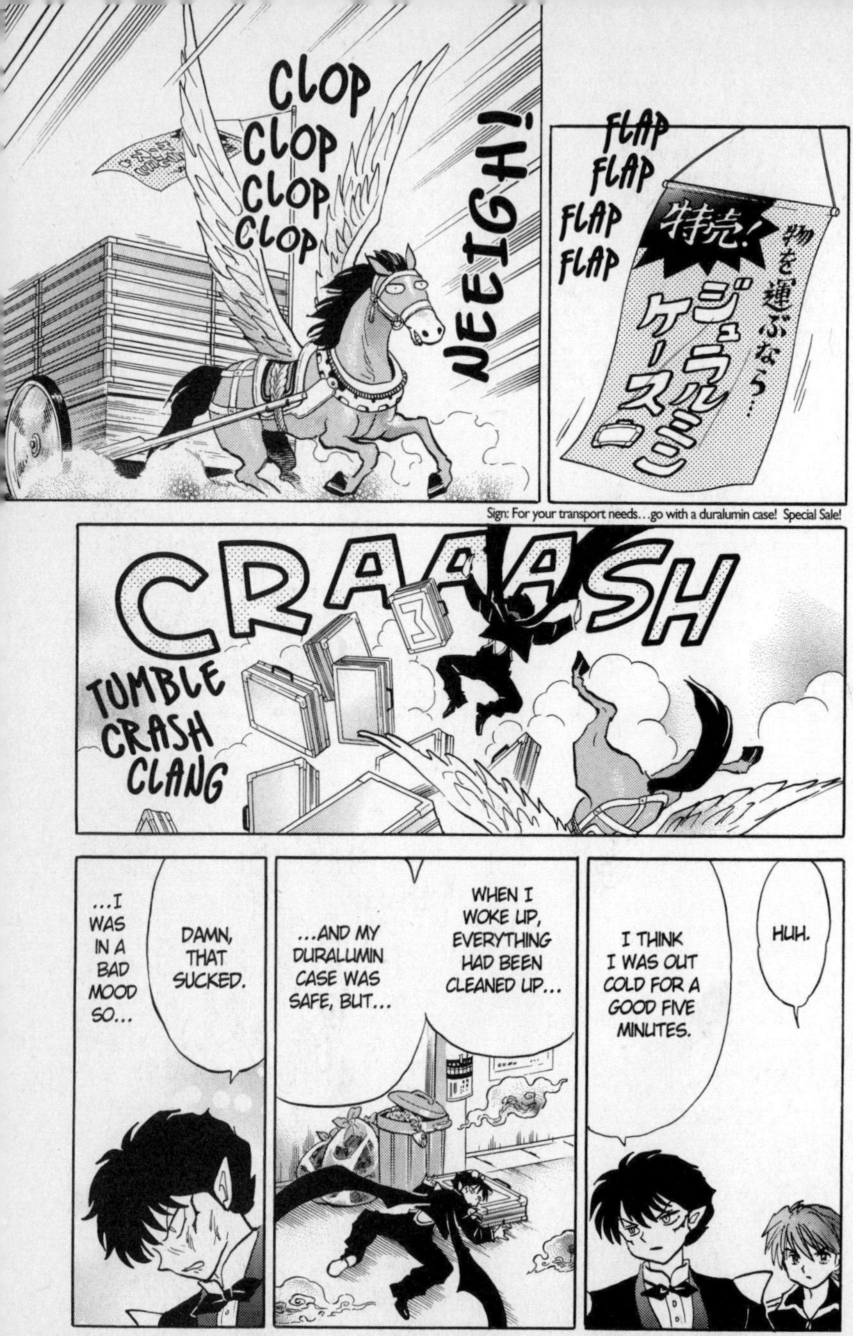
FLAP
FLAP
FLAP
FLAP
特売!
物を運ぶなら…
ジュラルミンケース
CLOP
CLOP
CLOP
CLOP
NEEIGH!
CRAAASH
TUMBLE
CRASH
CLANG
HUH.
I THINK I WAS OUT COLD FOR A GOOD FIVE MINUTES.
WHEN I WOKE UP, EVERYTHING HAD BEEN CLEANED UP…
…AND MY DURALUMIN CASE WAS SAFE, BUT…
DAMN, THAT SUCKED.
…I WAS IN A BAD MOOD SO…

Sign: For your transport needs…go with a duralumin case! Special Sale!

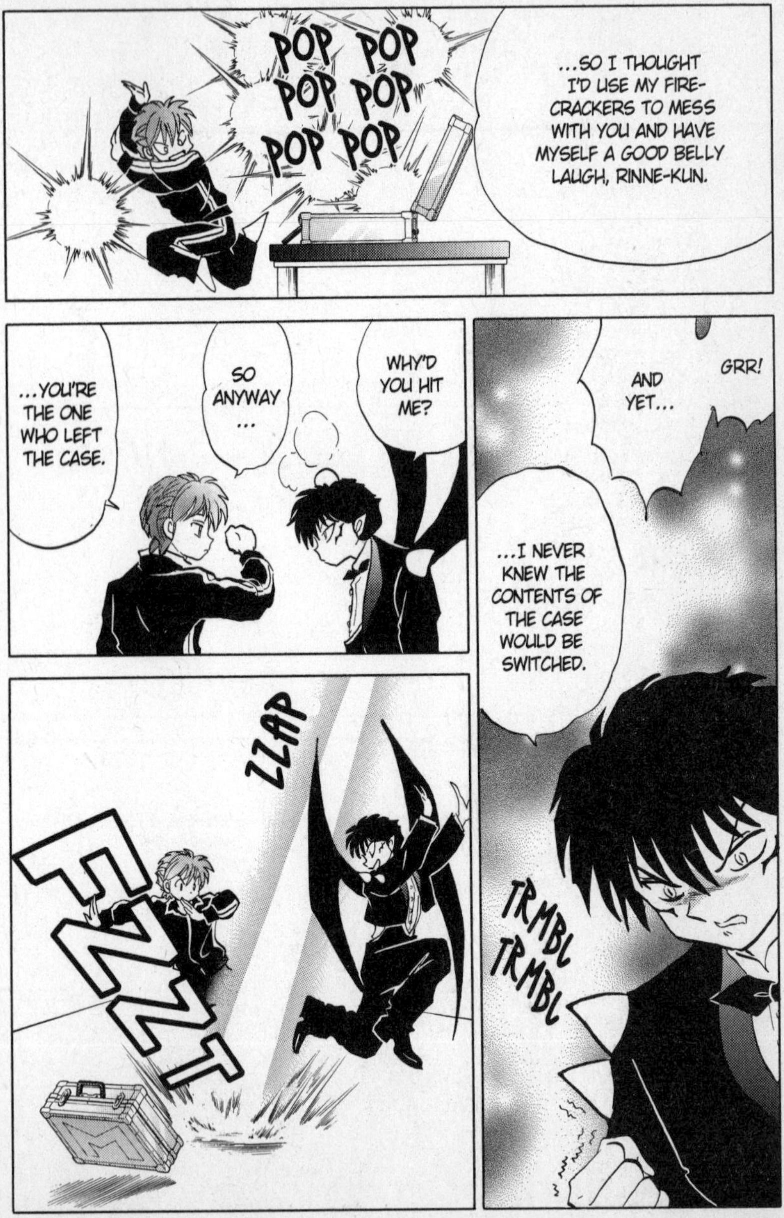
...SO I THOUGHT I'D USE MY FIRE-CRACKERS TO MESS WITH YOU AND HAVE MYSELF A GOOD BELLY LAUGH, RINNE-KUN.
POP POP POP POP POP POP
GRR!
AND YET...
...I NEVER KNEW THE CONTENTS OF THE CASE WOULD BE SWITCHED.
TRMBL TRMBL
WHY'D YOU HIT ME?
SO ANYWAY...
...YOU'RE THE ONE WHO LEFT THE CASE.
ZZAP
FZZT

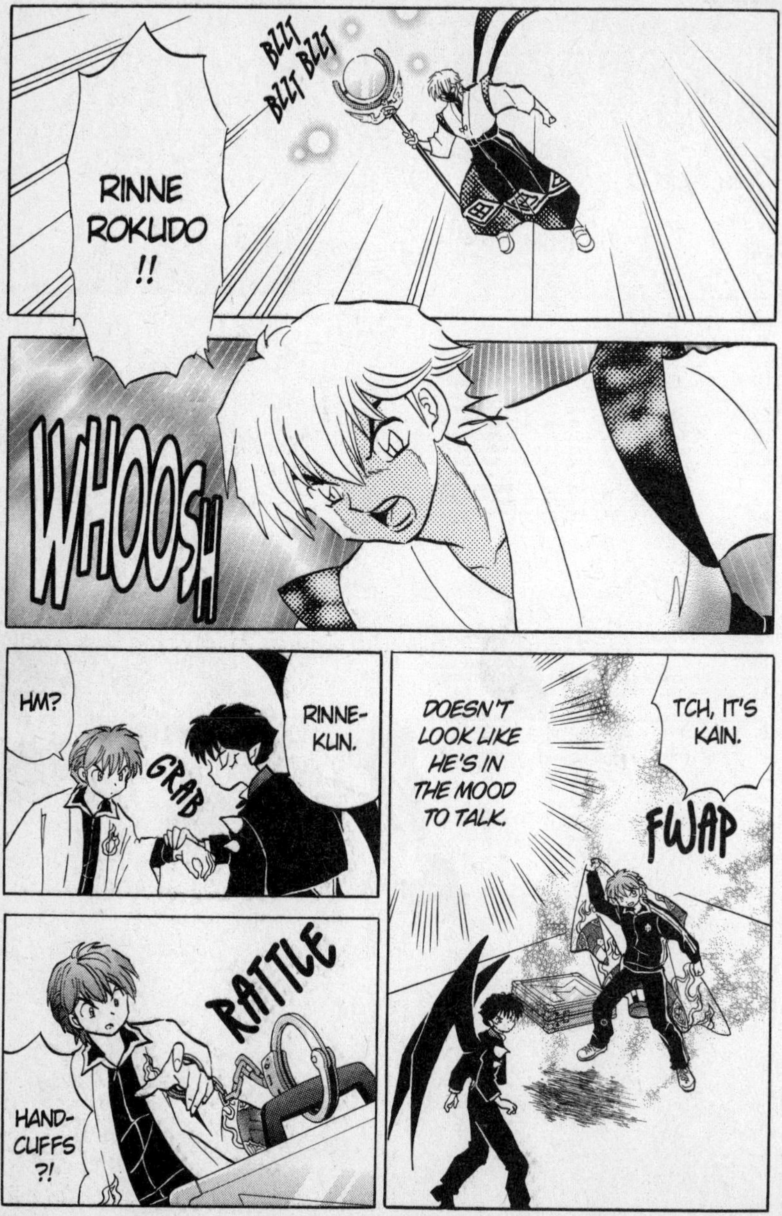
BZZT BZZT BZZT
RINNE ROKUDO !!
WHOOSH
TCH, IT'S KAIN.
DOESN'T LOOK LIKE HE'S IN THE MOOD TO TALK.
FWAP
RINNE-KUN.
HM?
GRAB
RATTLE
HAND-CUFFS ?!

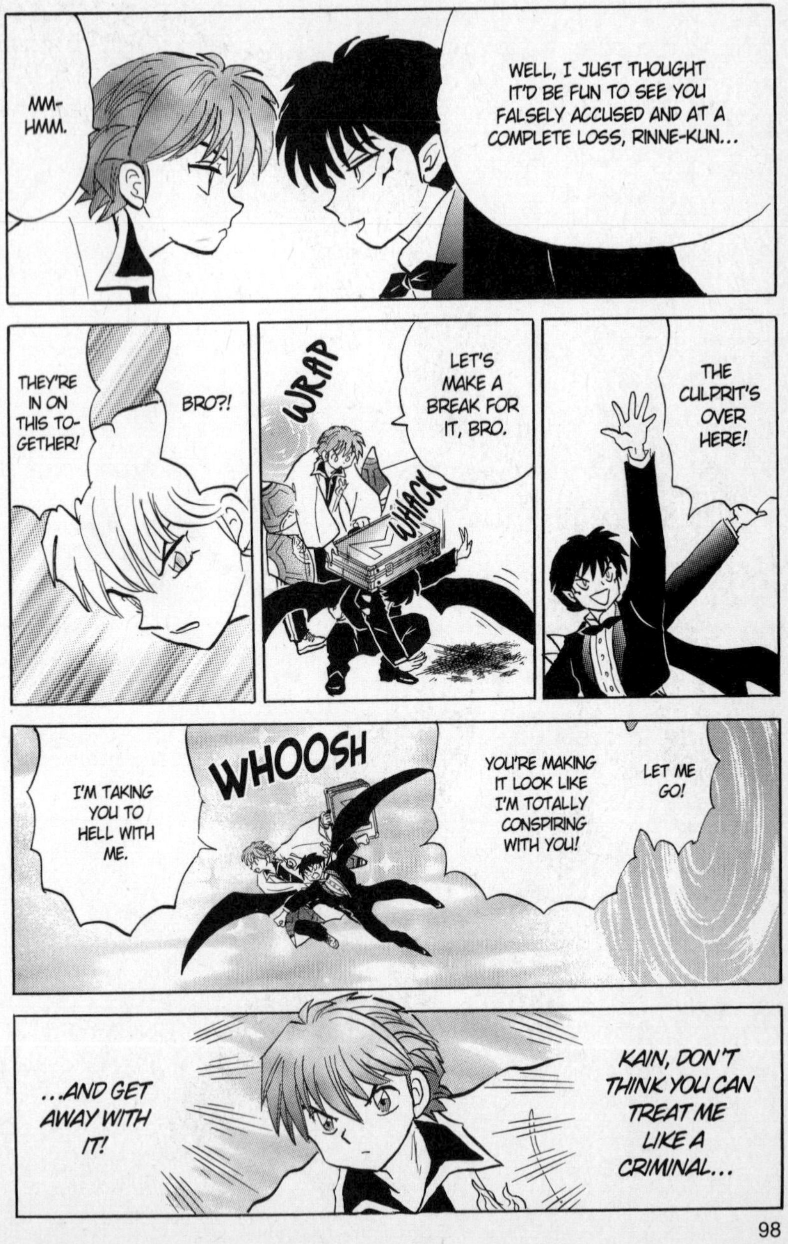
WELL, I JUST THOUGHT IT'D BE FUN TO SEE YOU FALSELY ACCUSED AND AT A COMPLETE LOSS, RINNE-KUN...
MM-HMM.
THE CULPRIT'S OVER HERE!
LET'S MAKE A BREAK FOR IT, BRO.
WRAP
WHACK
BRO?!
THEY'RE IN ON THIS TO-GETHER!
LET ME GO!
YOU'RE MAKING IT LOOK LIKE I'M TOTALLY CONSPIRING WITH YOU!
WHOOSH
I'M TAKING YOU TO HELL WITH ME.
KAIN, DON'T THINK YOU CAN TREAT ME LIKE A CRIMINAL...
...AND GET AWAY WITH IT!

CHAPTER 124: THE TRAGEDY OF M

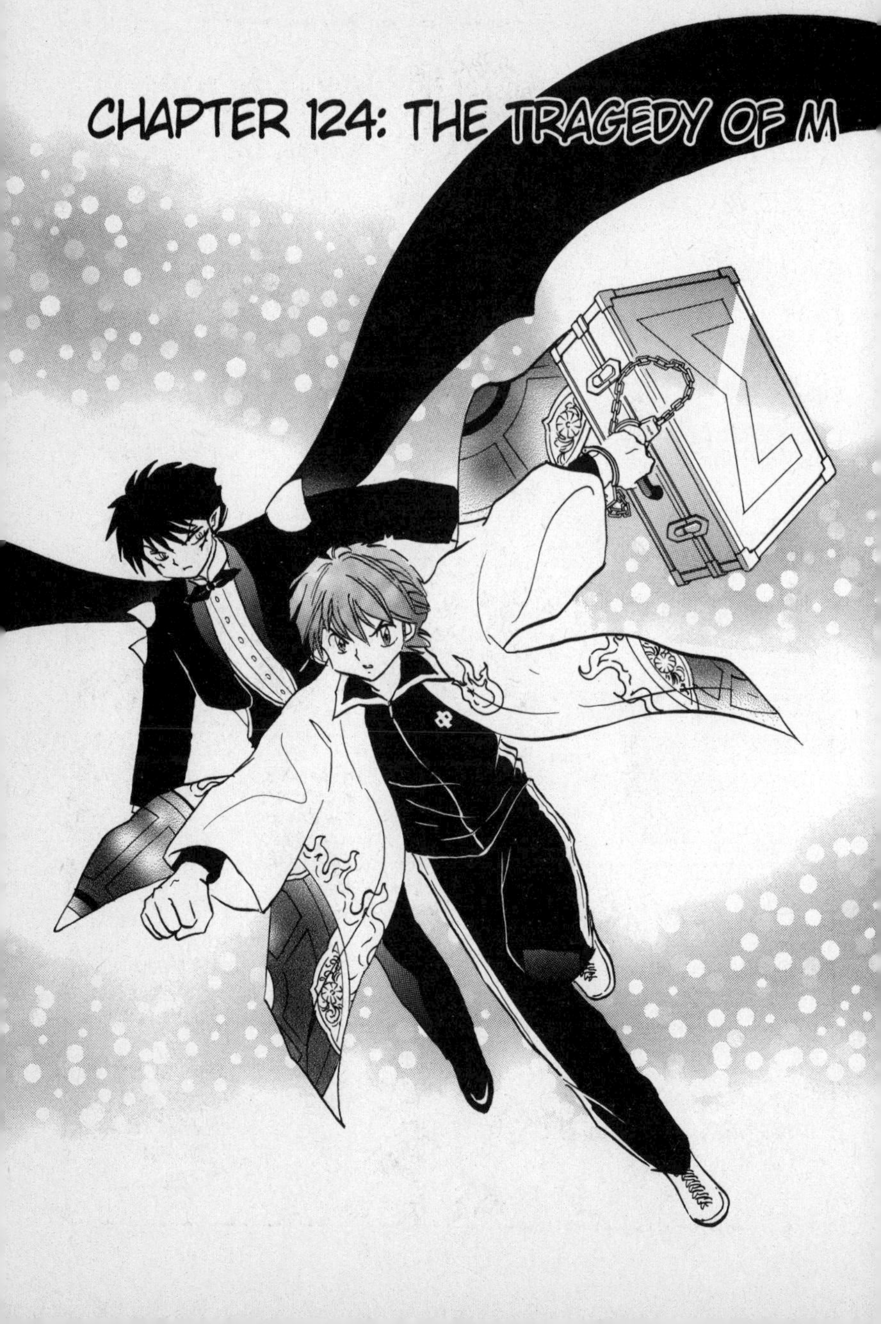

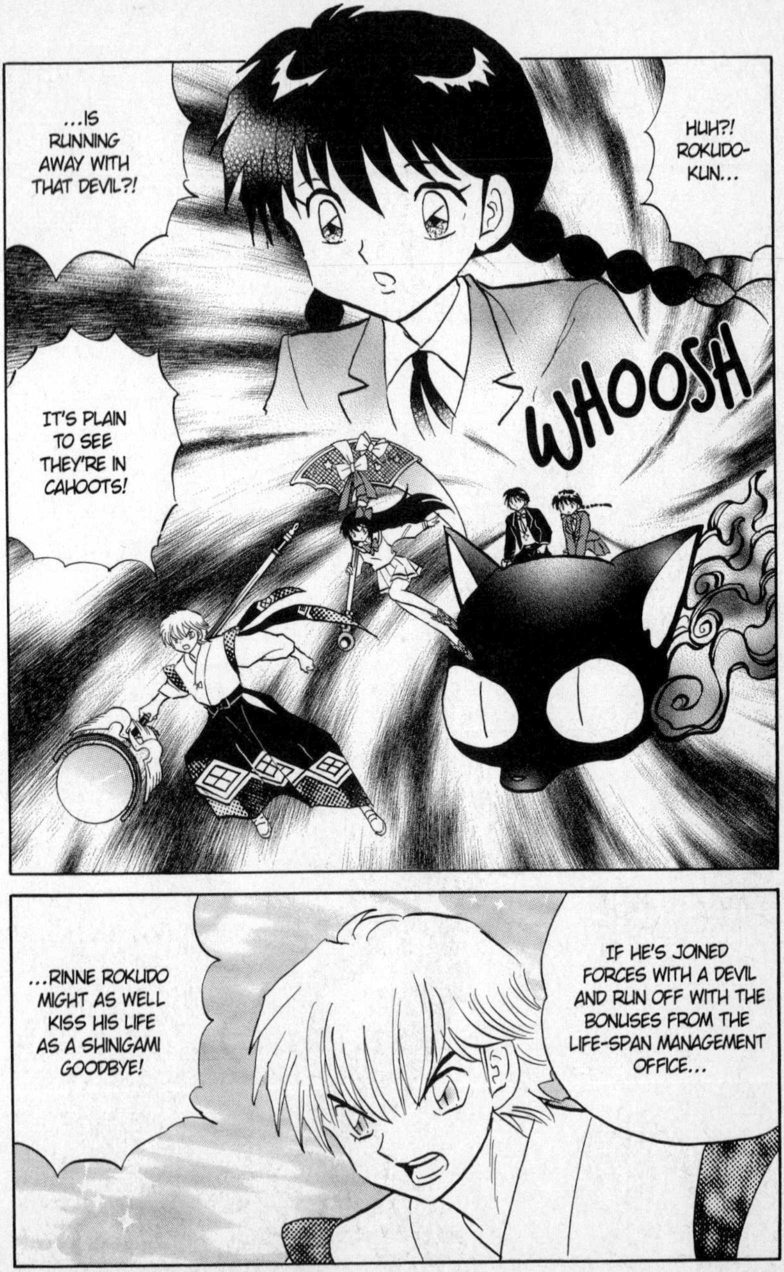
HUH?! ROKUDO-KUN...
WHOOSH
...IS RUNNING AWAY WITH THAT DEVIL?!
IT'S PLAIN TO SEE THEY'RE IN CAHOOTS!
IF HE'S JOINED FORCES WITH A DEVIL AND RUN OFF WITH THE BONUSES FROM THE LIFE-SPAN MANAGEMENT OFFICE...
...RINNE ROKUDO MIGHT AS WELL KISS HIS LIFE AS A SHINIGAMI GOODBYE!

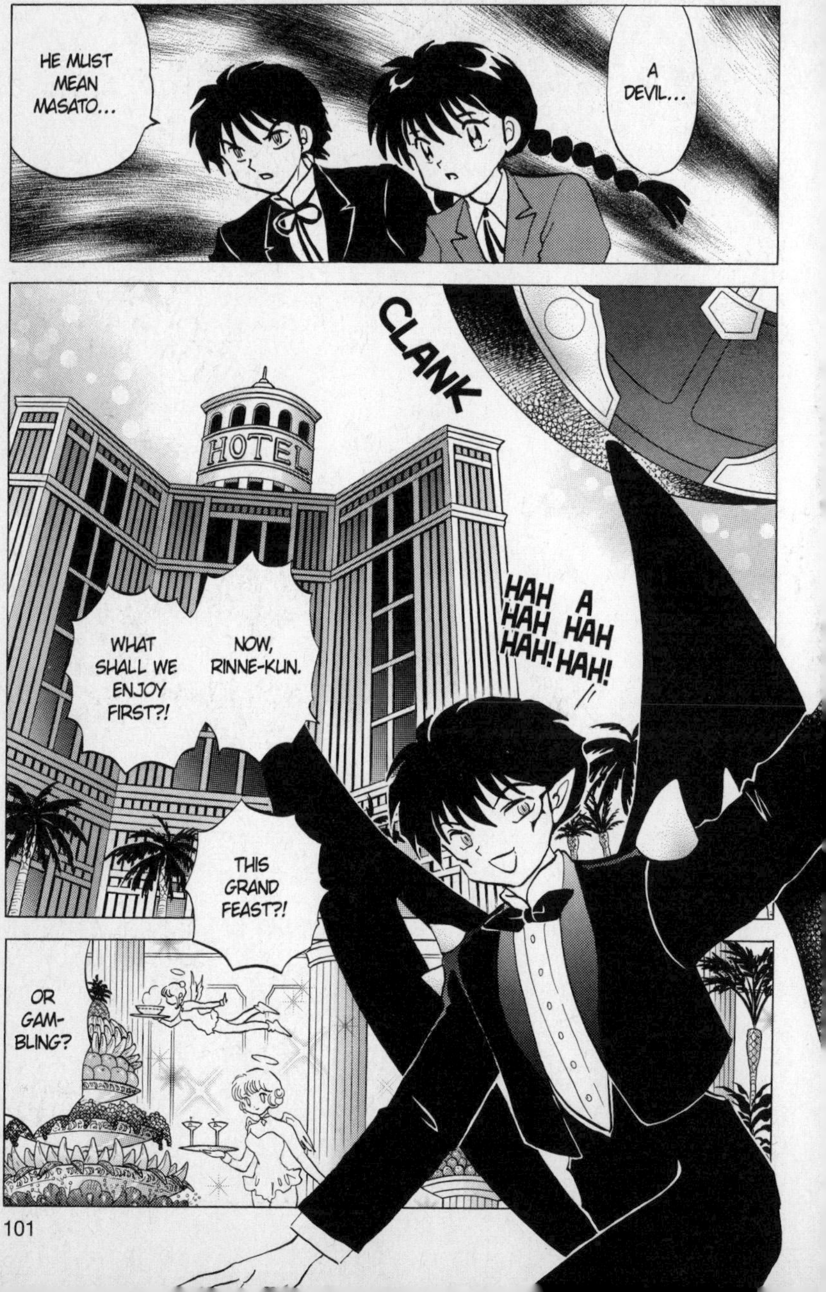
A DEVIL...
HE MUST MEAN MASATO...
CLANK
HAH HAH HAH! A HAH HAH!
NOW, RINNE-KUN.
WHAT SHALL WE ENJOY FIRST?!
THIS GRAND FEAST?!
OR GAMBLING?
HOTEL

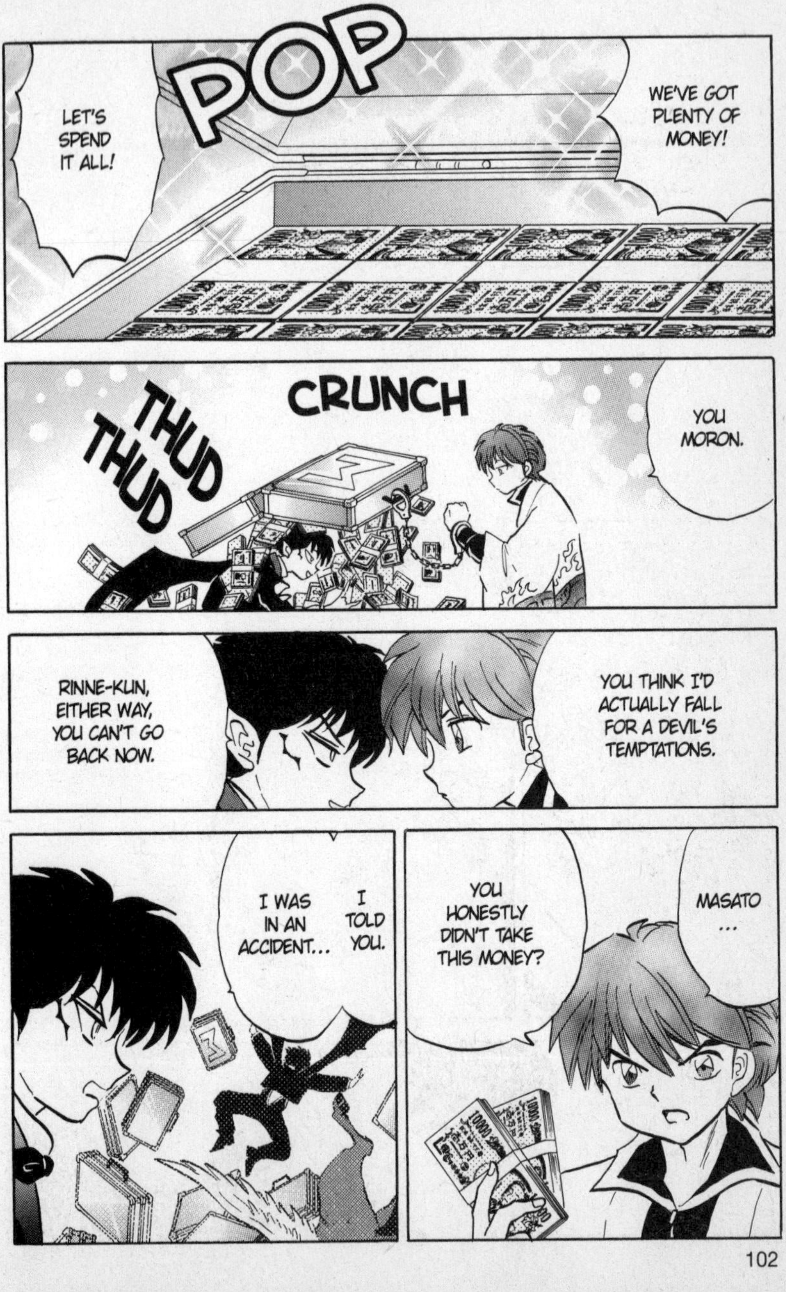
WE'VE GOT PLENTY OF MONEY!
POP
LET'S SPEND IT ALL!
YOU MORON.
CRUNCH
THUD THUD
YOU THINK I'D ACTUALLY FALL FOR A DEVIL'S TEMPTATIONS.
RINNE-KUN, EITHER WAY, YOU CAN'T GO BACK NOW.
MASATO ...
YOU HONESTLY DIDN'T TAKE THIS MONEY?
I TOLD YOU.
I WAS IN AN ACCIDENT...

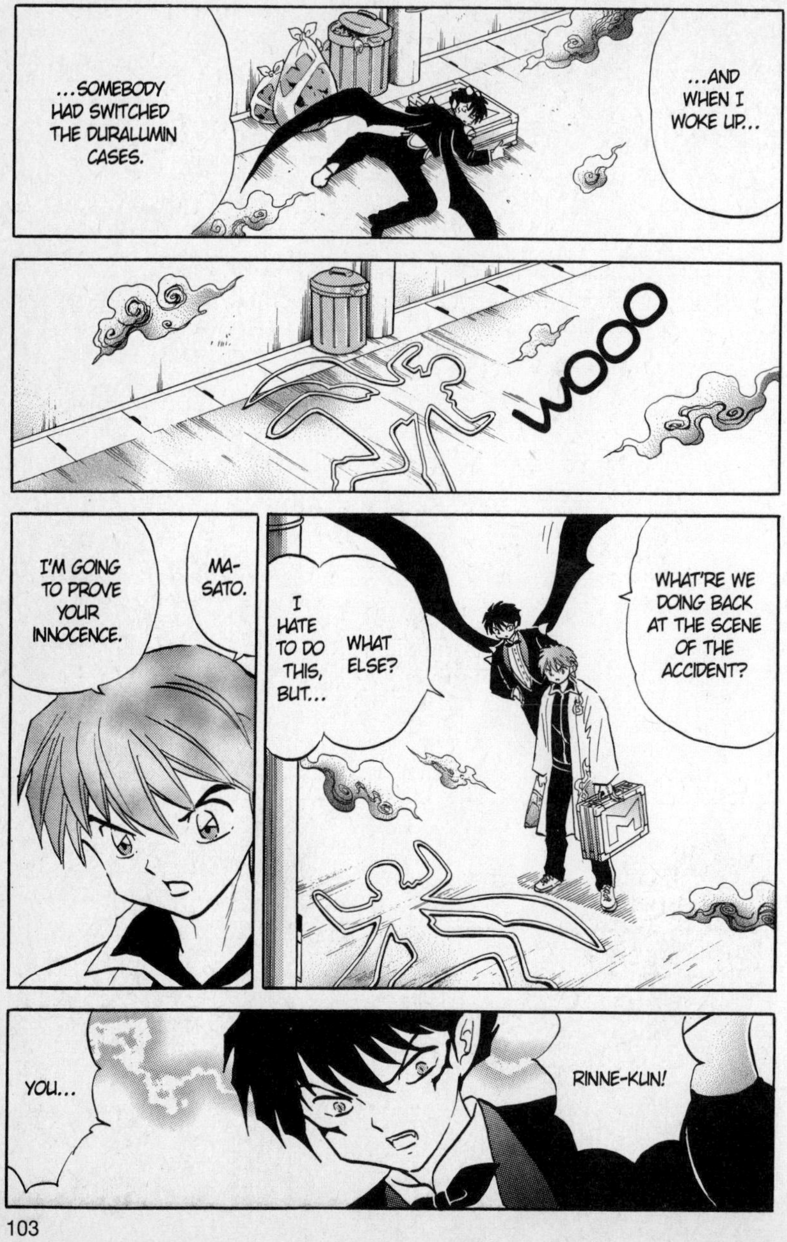
...AND WHEN I WOKE UP...
...SOMEBODY HAD SWITCHED THE DURALUMIN CASES.
WOOO
WHAT'RE WE DOING BACK AT THE SCENE OF THE ACCIDENT?
WHAT ELSE?
I HATE TO DO THIS, BUT...
MA-SATO.
I'M GOING TO PROVE YOUR INNOCENCE.
RINNE-KUN!
YOU...

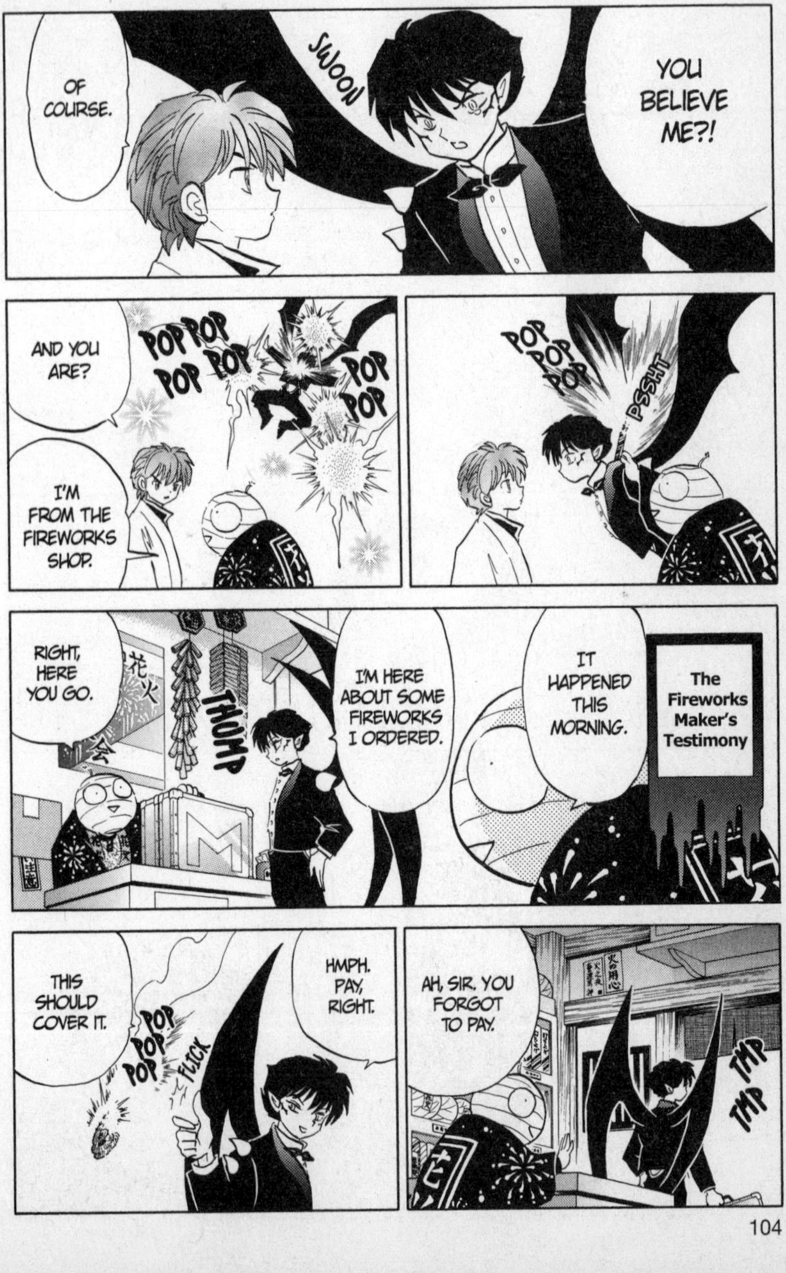
YOU BELIEVE ME?!
SWOON
OF COURSE.
POP POP POP
PSSHT
POP POP
POP POP
POP POP
AND YOU ARE?
I'M FROM THE FIREWORKS SHOP.
The Fireworks Maker's Testimony
IT HAPPENED THIS MORNING.
I'M HERE ABOUT SOME FIREWORKS I ORDERED.
THUMP
RIGHT, HERE YOU GO.
TMP TMP
AH, SIR. YOU FORGOT TO PAY.
HMPH. PAY, RIGHT.
FLICK
POP POP POP
THIS SHOULD COVER IT.

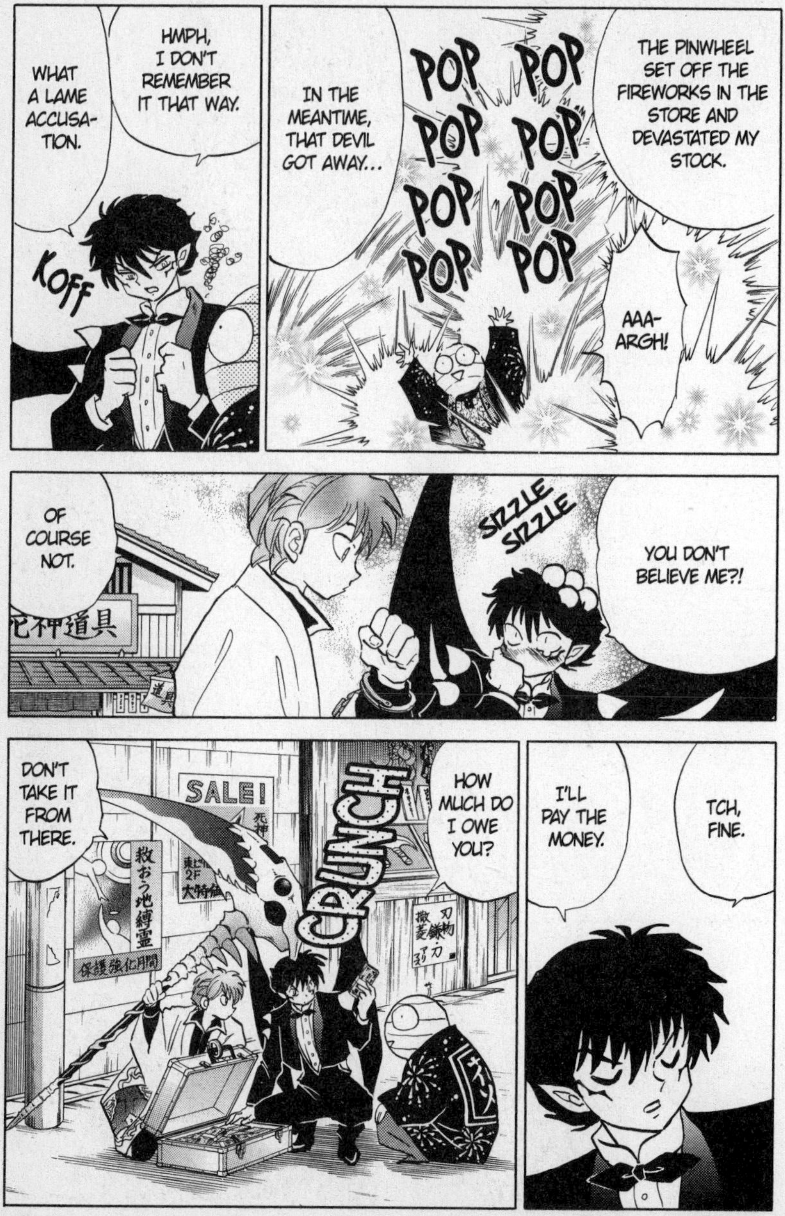
THE PINWHEEL SET OFF THE FIREWORKS IN THE STORE AND DEVASTATED MY STOCK.
POP POP POP POP POP POP POP POP
AAA-ARGH!
IN THE MEANTIME, THAT DEVIL GOT AWAY...
HMPH, I DON'T REMEMBER IT THAT WAY.
KOFF
WHAT A LAME ACCUSA-TION.
YOU DON'T BELIEVE ME?!
SIZZLE SIZZLE
OF COURSE NOT.
TCH, FINE.
I'LL PAY THE MONEY.
HOW MUCH DO I OWE YOU?
CRUNCH
SALE!
DON'T TAKE IT FROM THERE.

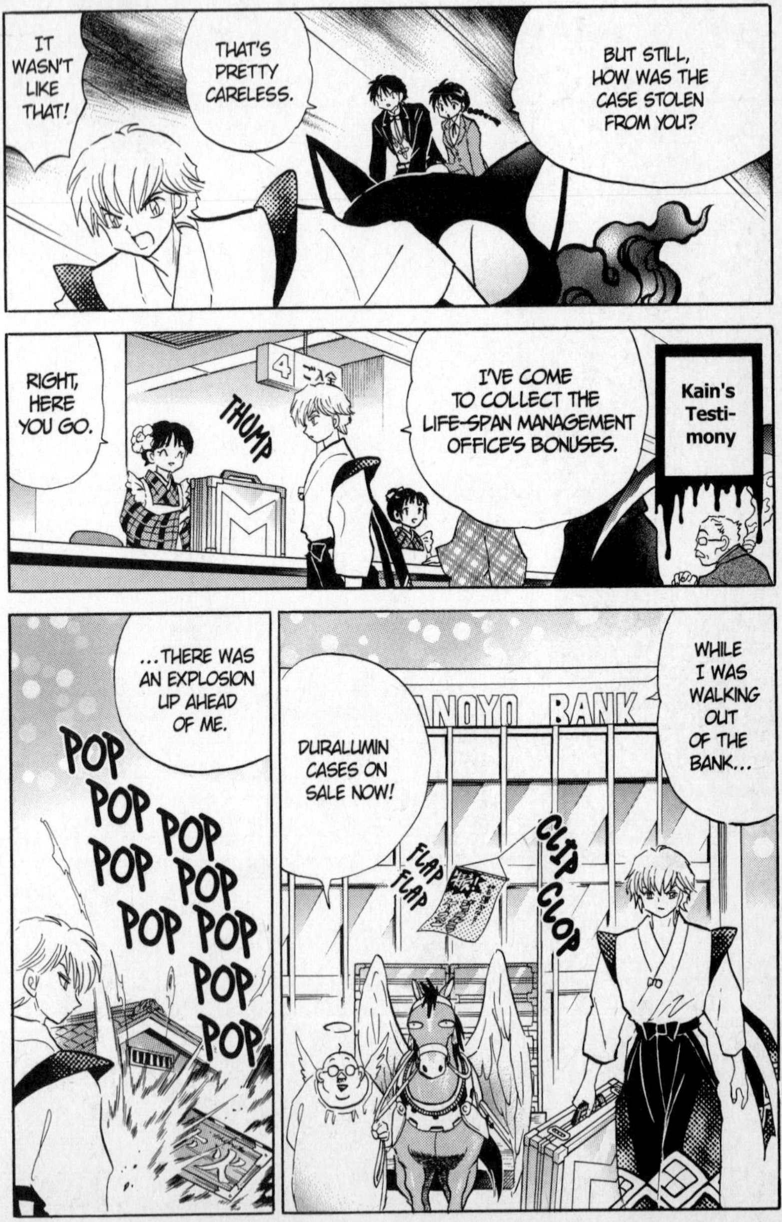
BUT STILL, HOW WAS THE CASE STOLEN FROM YOU?
THAT'S PRETTY CARELESS.
IT WASN'T LIKE THAT!
Kain's Testimony
I'VE COME TO COLLECT THE LIFE-SPAN MANAGEMENT OFFICE'S BONUSES.
THUMP
RIGHT, HERE YOU GO.
WHILE I WAS WALKING OUT OF THE BANK...
ANOYO BANK
CLIP CLOP
FLAP FLAP
DURALUMIN CASES ON SALE NOW!
...THERE WAS AN EXPLOSION UP AHEAD OF ME.
POP POP POP POP POP POP POP POP POP POP POP

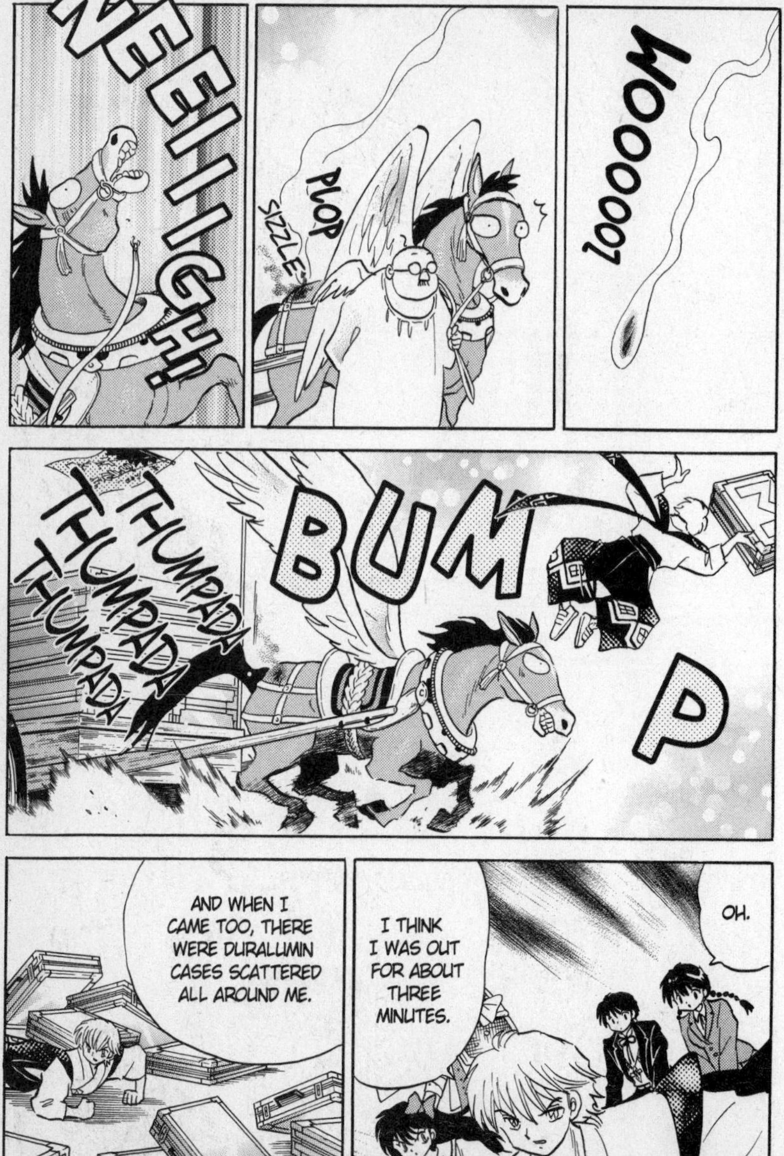
WOOOOO!
PLOP
SIZZLE
NEEIIIGH!
BUMP
THUMPADA
THUMPADA
THUMPADA
OH.
I THINK I WAS OUT FOR ABOUT THREE MINUTES.
AND WHEN I CAME TOO, THERE WERE DURALUMIN CASES SCATTERED ALL AROUND ME.

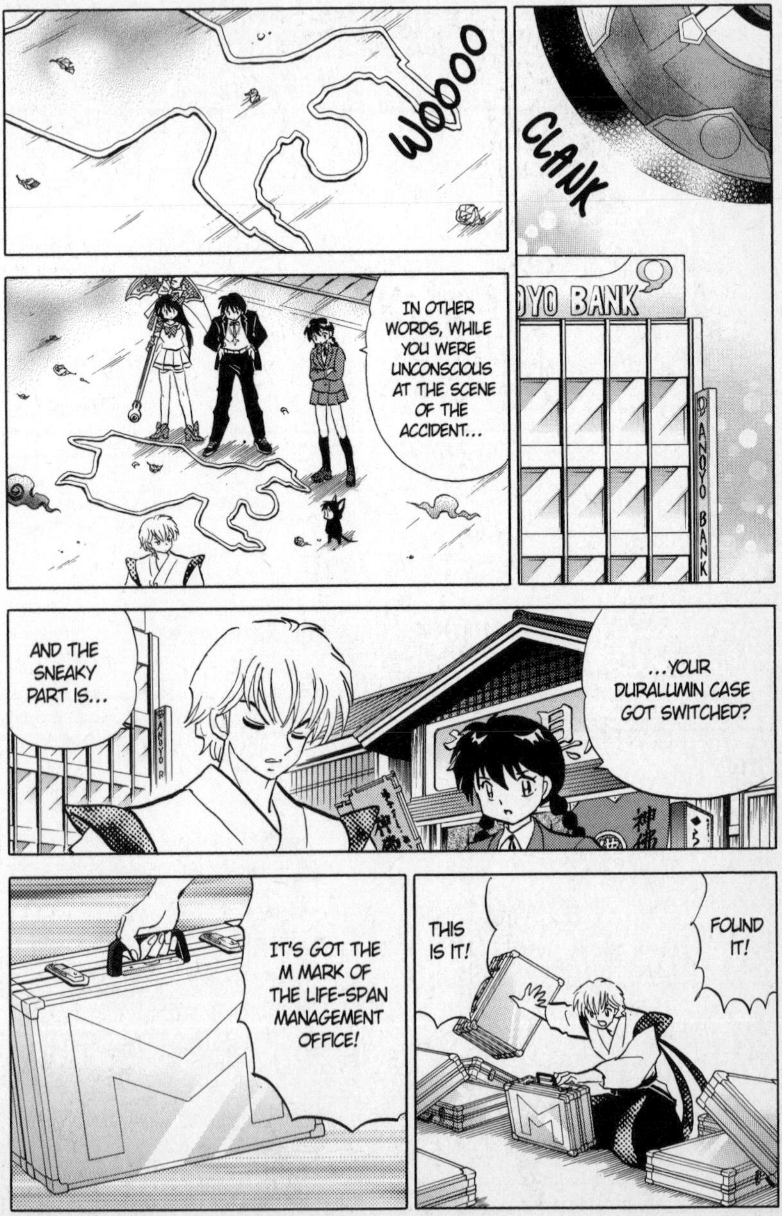
CLANK
OYO BANK
ANOYO BANK
WOOOO
IN OTHER WORDS, WHILE YOU WERE UNCONSCIOUS AT THE SCENE OF THE ACCIDENT...
...YOUR DURALUMIN CASE GOT SWITCHED?
AND THE SNEAKY PART IS...
FOUND IT!
THIS IS IT!
IT'S GOT THE M MARK OF THE LIFE-SPAN MANAGEMENT OFFICE!

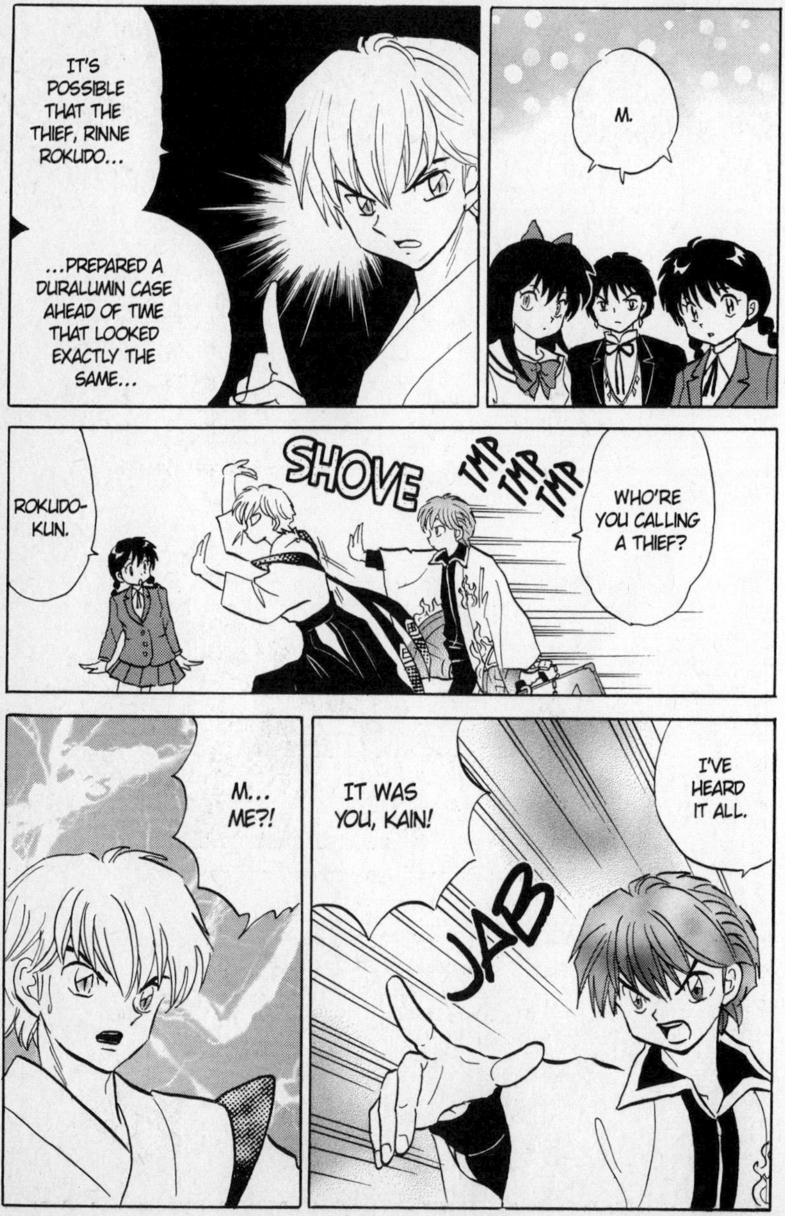
M.
IT'S POSSIBLE THAT THE THIEF, RINNE ROKUDO...
...PREPARED A DURALUMIN CASE AHEAD OF TIME THAT LOOKED EXACTLY THE SAME...
WHO'RE YOU CALLING A THIEF?
TMP TMP TMP
SHOVE
ROKUDO-KUN.
I'VE HEARD IT ALL.
JAB
IT WAS YOU, KAIN!
M... ME?!

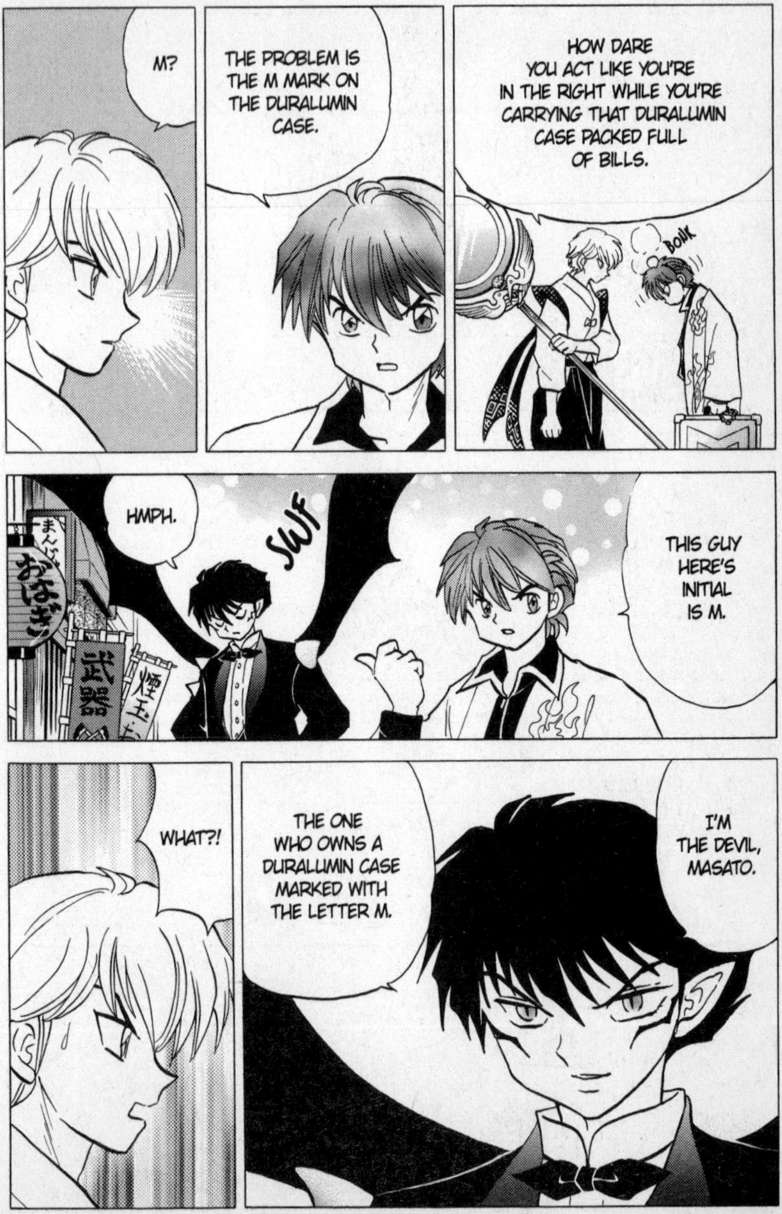
HOW DARE YOU ACT LIKE YOU'RE IN THE RIGHT WHILE YOU'RE CARRYING THAT DURALUMIN CASE PACKED FULL OF BILLS.
BONK
THE PROBLEM IS THE M MARK ON THE DURALUMIN CASE.
M?
THIS GUY HERE'S INITIAL IS M.
SWF
HMPH.
おはぎ
武器
I'M THE DEVIL, MASATO.
THE ONE WHO OWNS A DURALUMIN CASE MARKED WITH THE LETTER M.
WHAT?!

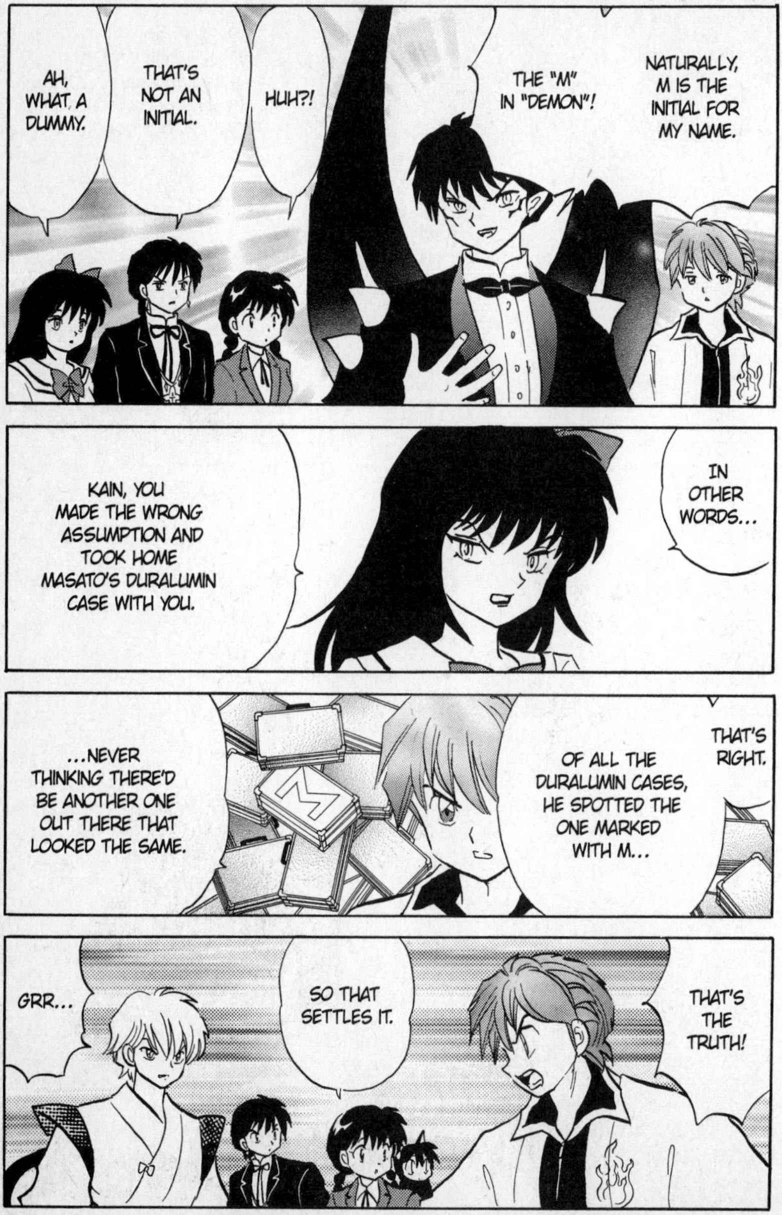
NATURALLY, M IS THE INITIAL FOR MY NAME.
THE "M" IN "DEMON"!
HUH?!
THAT'S NOT AN INITIAL.
AH, WHAT A DUMMY.
IN OTHER WORDS...
KAIN, YOU MADE THE WRONG ASSUMPTION AND TOOK HOME MASATO'S DURALUMIN CASE WITH YOU.
THAT'S RIGHT.
OF ALL THE DURALUMIN CASES, HE SPOTTED THE ONE MARKED WITH M...
...NEVER THINKING THERE'D BE ANOTHER ONE OUT THERE THAT LOOKED THE SAME.
THAT'S THE TRUTH!
SO THAT SETTLES IT.
GRR...

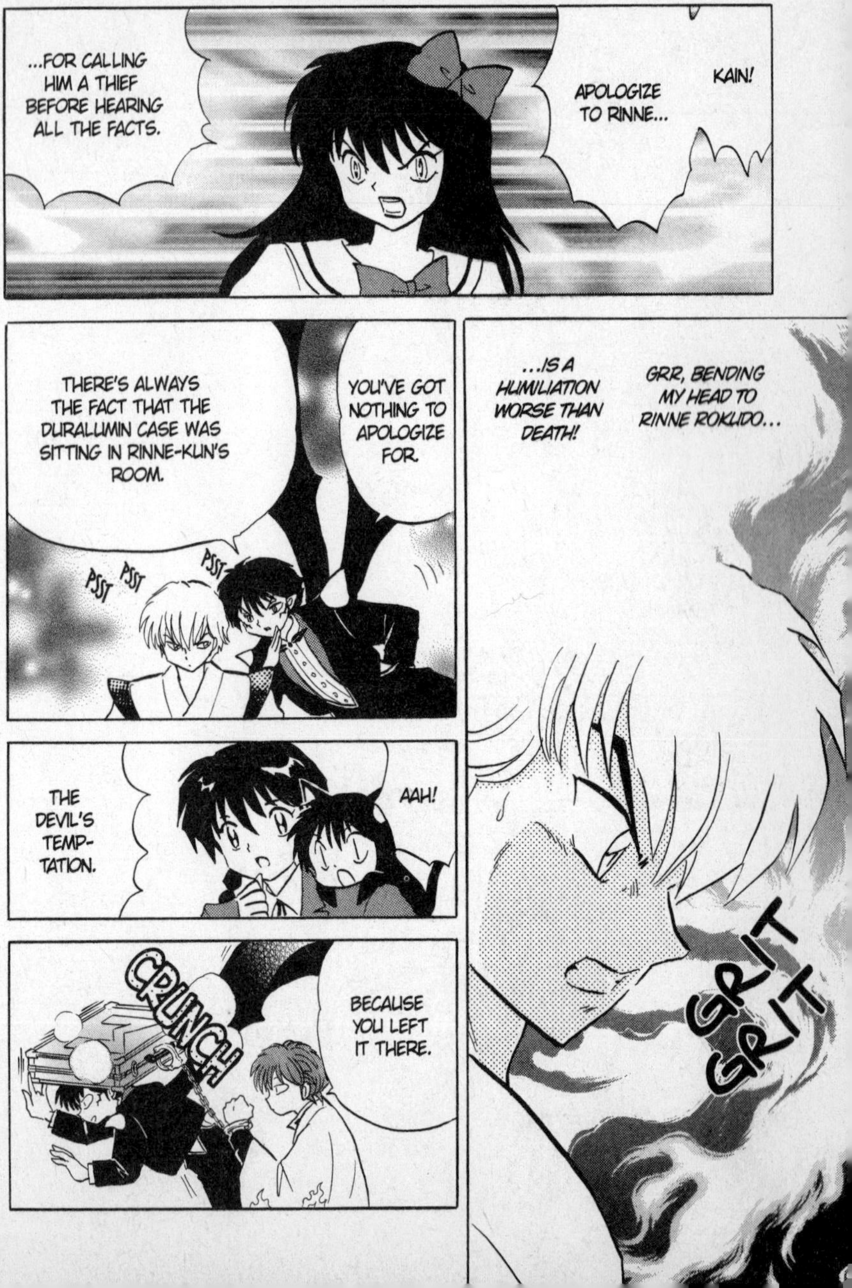
KAIN!
APOLOGIZE TO RINNE...
...FOR CALLING HIM A THIEF BEFORE HEARING ALL THE FACTS.
GRR, BENDING MY HEAD TO RINNE ROKUDO...
...IS A HUMILIATION WORSE THAN DEATH!
GRIT GRIT
YOU'VE GOT NOTHING TO APOLOGIZE FOR.
THERE'S ALWAYS THE FACT THAT THE DURALUMIN CASE WAS SITTING IN RINNE-KUN'S ROOM.
PSSST PSST PSST
AAH!
THE DEVIL'S TEMP-TATION.
BECAUSE YOU LEFT IT THERE.
CRUNCH

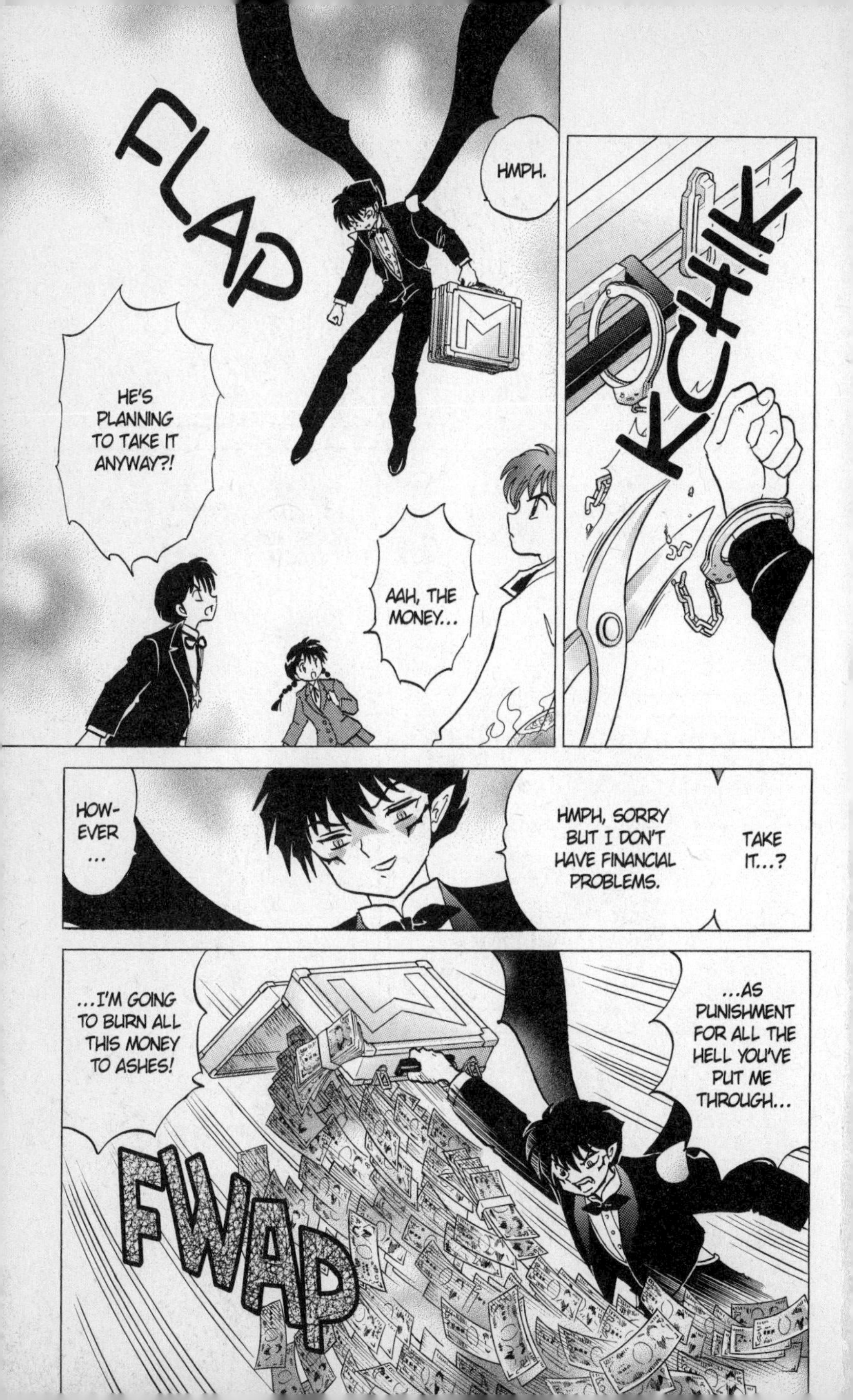
CHIK
HMPH.
FLAP
HE'S PLANNING TO TAKE IT ANYWAY?!
AAH, THE MONEY...
TAKE IT...?
HMPH, SORRY BUT I DON'T HAVE FINANCIAL PROBLEMS.
HOW-EVER...
...AS PUNISHMENT FOR ALL THE HELL YOU'VE PUT ME THROUGH...
...I'M GOING TO BURN ALL THIS MONEY TO ASHES!
FWAP

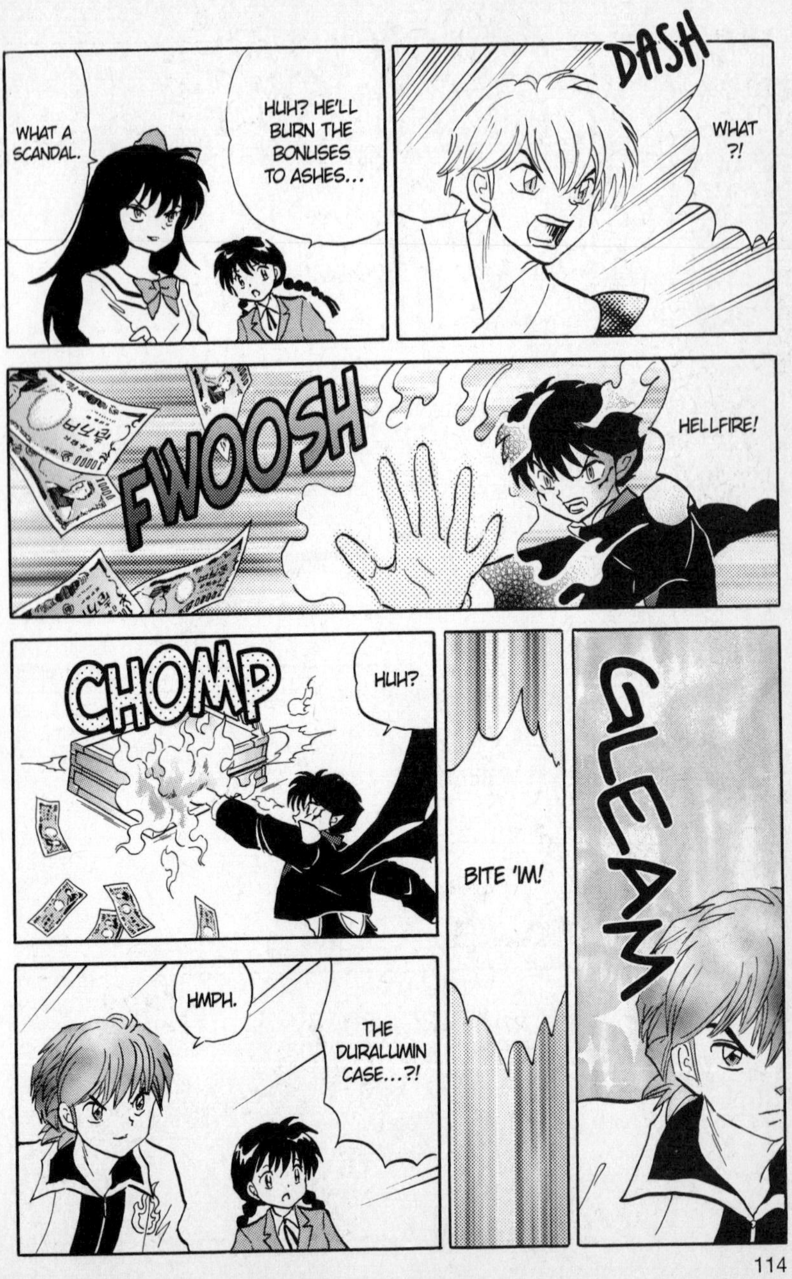
DASH
WHAT ?!
HUH? HE'LL BURN THE BONUSES TO ASHES...
WHAT A SCANDAL.
HELLFIRE!
FWOOSH
GLEAM
BITE 'IM!
HUH?
CHOMP
THE DURALUMIN CASE...?!
HMPH.

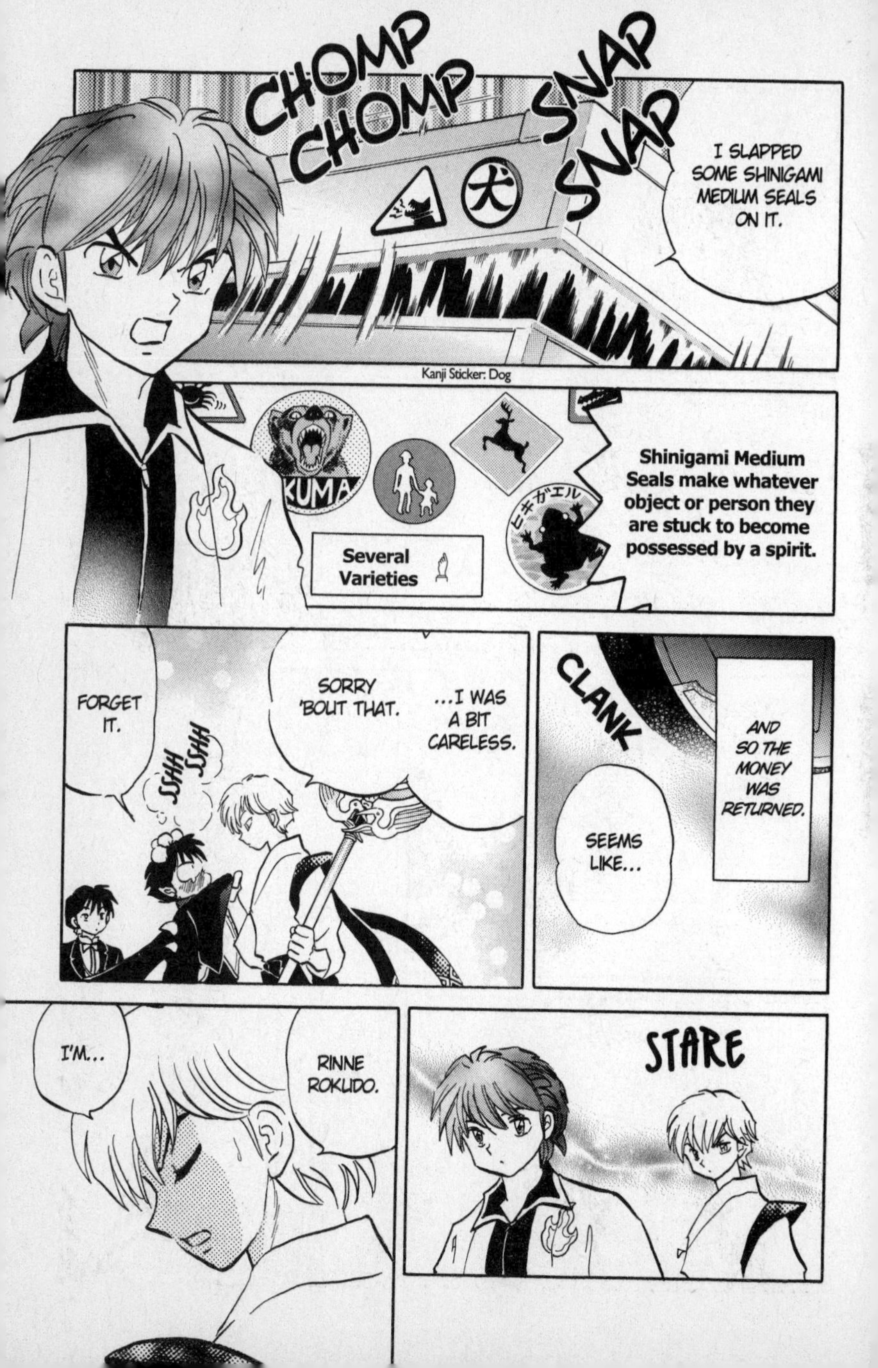
CHOMP CHOMP
SNAP SNAP
I SLAPPED SOME SHINIGAMI MEDIUM SEALS ON IT.
Kanji Sticker: Dog
Shinigami Medium Seals make whatever object or person they are stuck to become possessed by a spirit.
KUMA
ヒキガエル
Several Varieties
AND SO THE MONEY WAS RETURNED.
CLANK
SEEMS LIKE...
...I WAS A BIT CARELESS.
SORRY 'BOUT THAT.
FORGET IT.
SSHH SSHH
STARE
RINNE ROKUDO.
I'M...

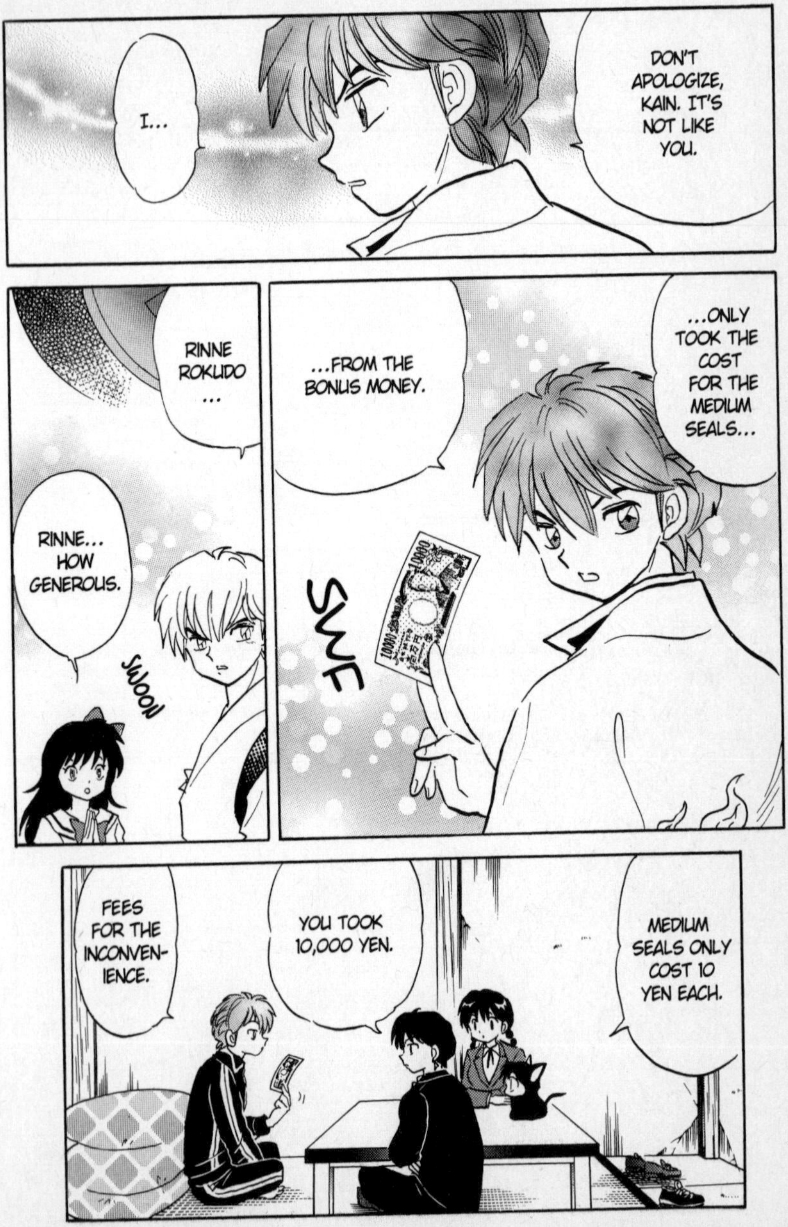
DON'T APOLOGIZE, KAIN. IT'S NOT LIKE YOU.
I...
...ONLY TOOK THE COST FOR THE MEDIUM SEALS...
...FROM THE BONUS MONEY.
SWF
RINNE ROKUDO ...
RINNE... HOW GENEROUS.
SWOON
MEDIUM SEALS ONLY COST 10 YEN EACH.
YOU TOOK 10,000 YEN.
FEES FOR THE INCONVEN-IENCE.

CHAPTER 125: THE DESSERT SPIRIT

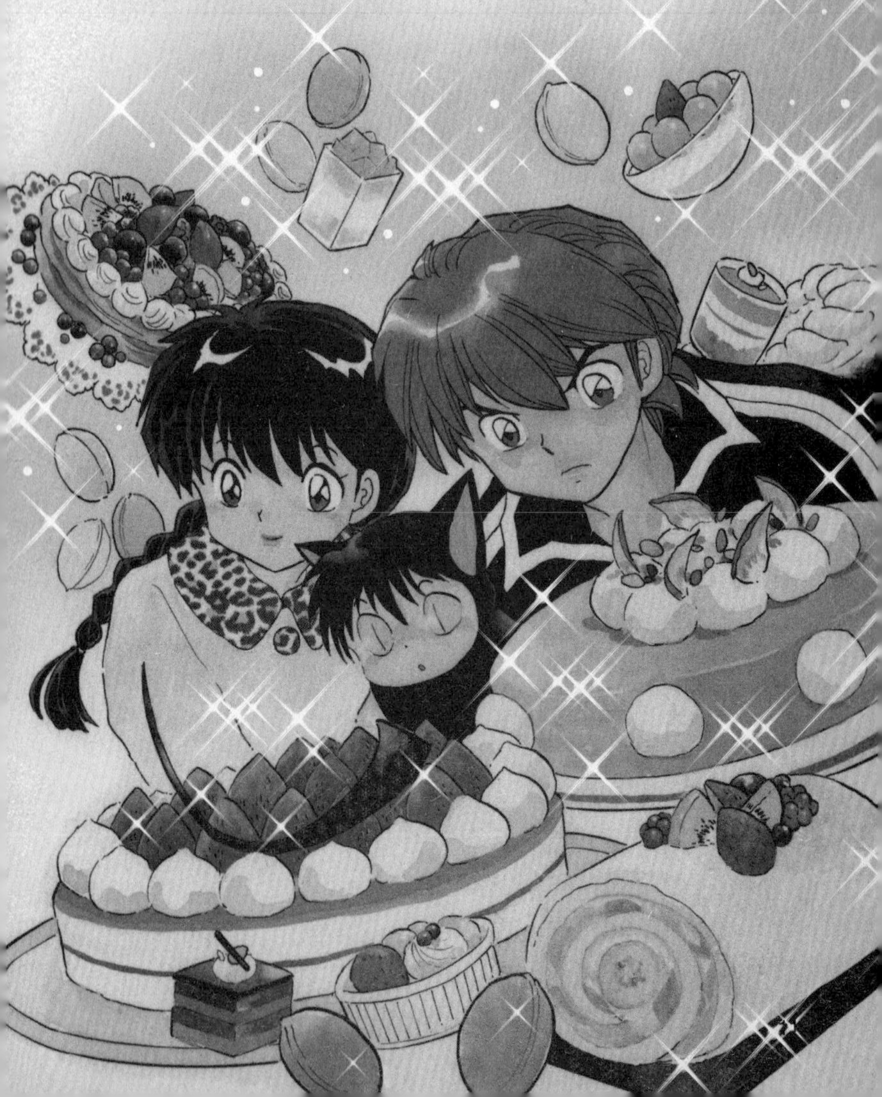

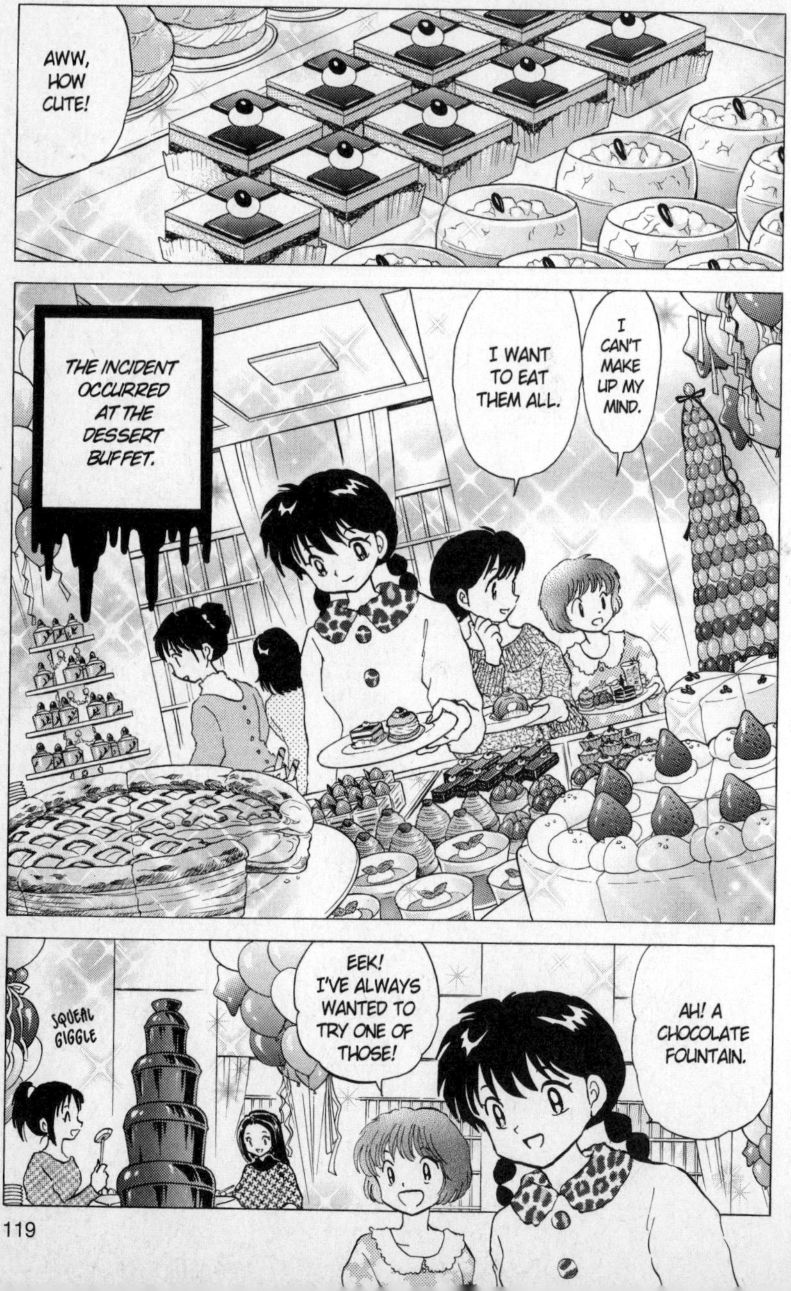
AWW, HOW CUTE!
I CAN'T MAKE UP MY MIND.
I WANT TO EAT THEM ALL.
THE INCIDENT OCCURRED AT THE DESSERT BUFFET.
AH! A CHOCOLATE FOUNTAIN.
EEK! I'VE ALWAYS WANTED TO TRY ONE OF THOSE!
SQUEAL GIGGLE

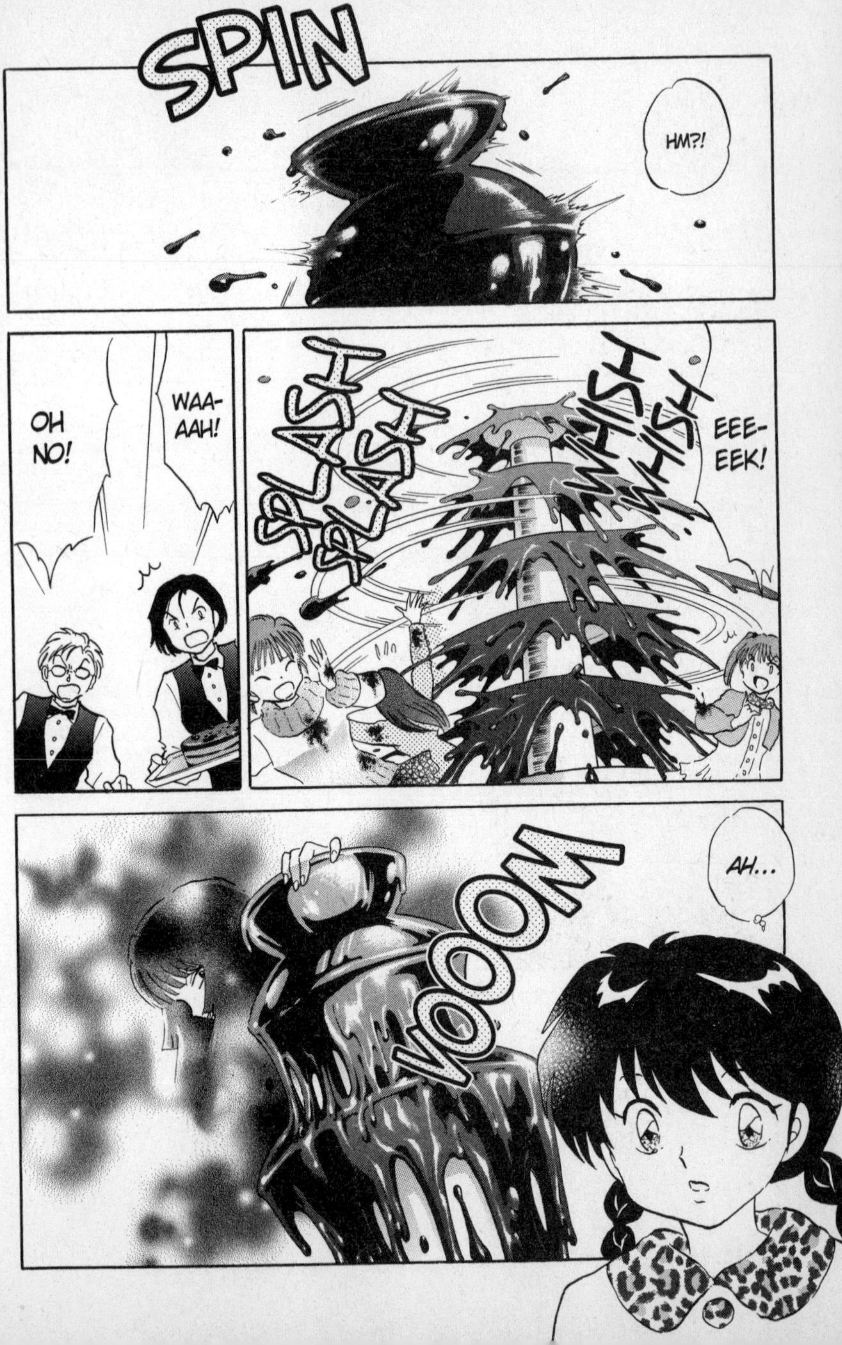
SPIN
HM?!
EEE-EEK!
WHISH
WHISH
SPLASH
SPLASH
WAA-AAH!
OH NO!
AH...
VOOOOM

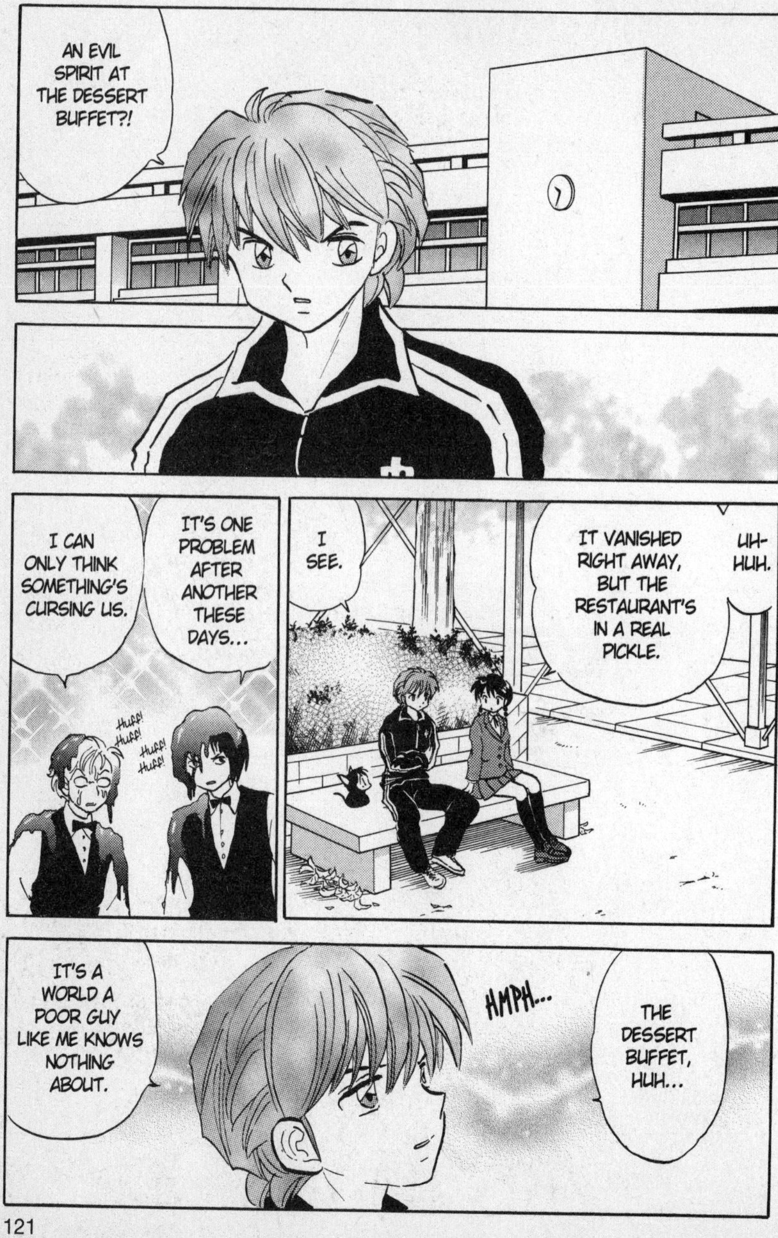
AN EVIL SPIRIT AT THE DESSERT BUFFET?!
UH-HUH.
IT VANISHED RIGHT AWAY, BUT THE RESTAURANT'S IN A REAL PICKLE.
I SEE.
IT'S ONE PROBLEM AFTER ANOTHER THESE DAYS...
I CAN ONLY THINK SOMETHING'S CURSING US.
Huff! Huff!
Huff! Huff!
THE DESSERT BUFFET, HUH...
HMPH...
IT'S A WORLD A POOR GUY LIKE ME KNOWS NOTHING ABOUT.

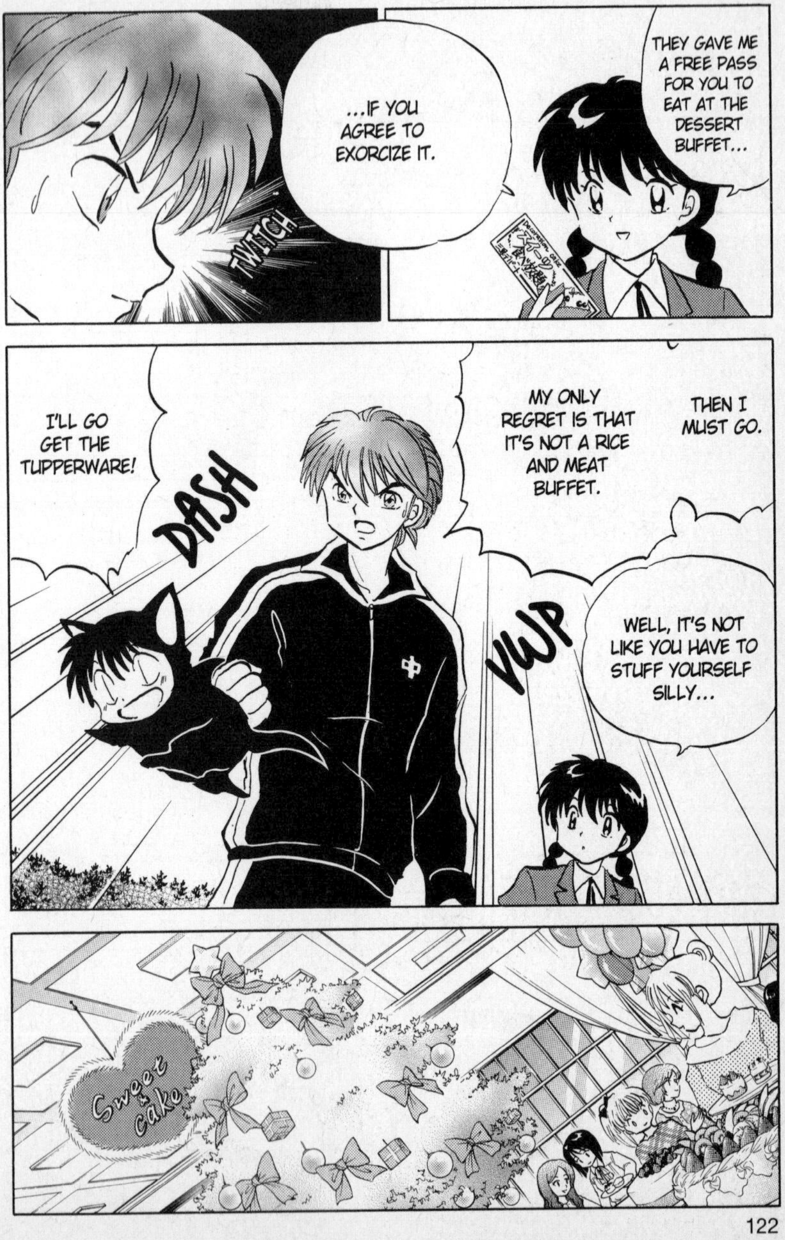
THEY GAVE ME A FREE PASS FOR YOU TO EAT AT THE DESSERT BUFFET...
...IF YOU AGREE TO EXORCIZE IT.
TWITCH
THEN I MUST GO.
MY ONLY REGRET IS THAT IT'S NOT A RICE AND MEAT BUFFET.
I'LL GO GET THE TUPPERWARE!
DASH
VUP
WELL, IT'S NOT LIKE YOU HAVE TO STUFF YOURSELF SILLY...
Sweet & cake

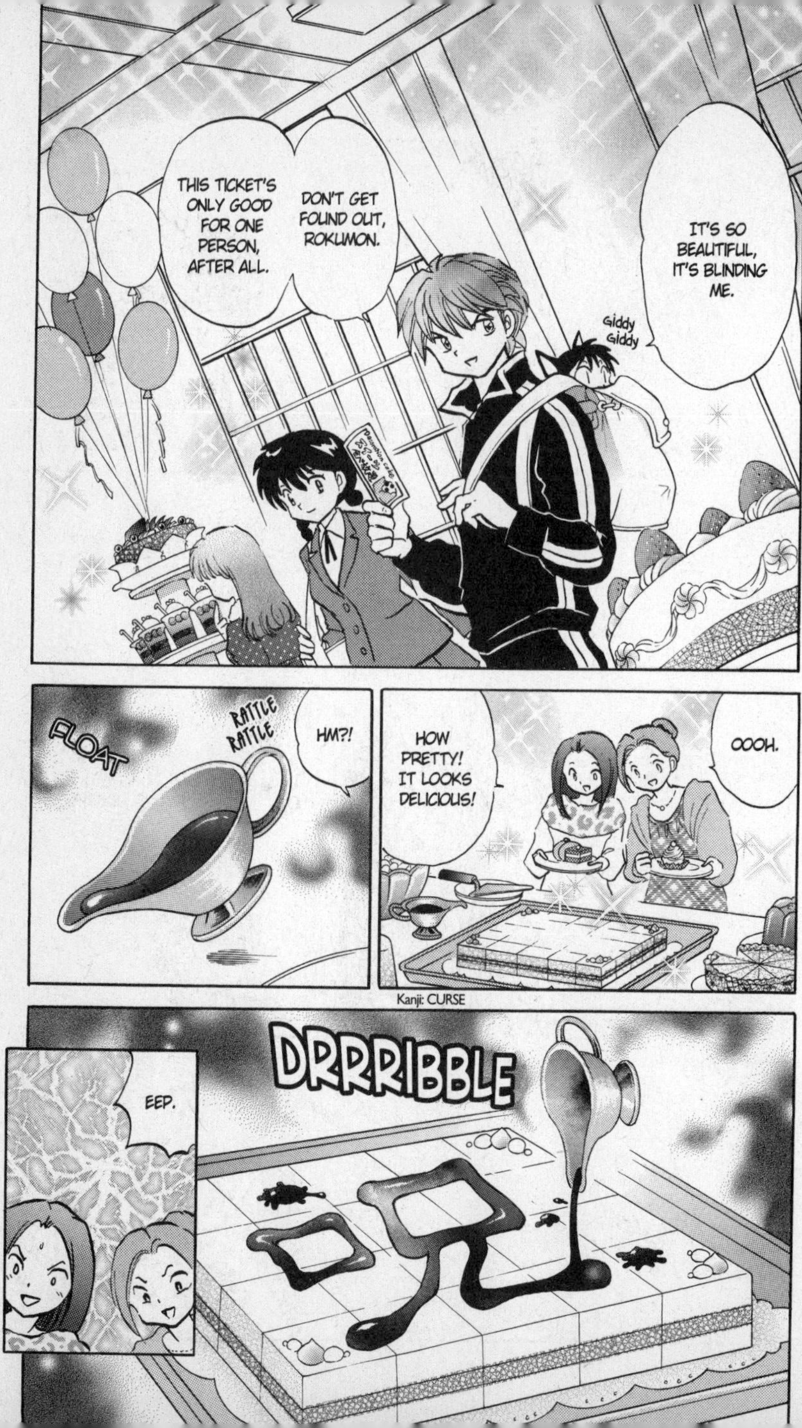
IT'S SO BEAUTIFUL, IT'S BLINDING ME.
Giddy Giddy
DON'T GET FOUND OUT, ROKUMON.
THIS TICKET'S ONLY GOOD FOR ONE PERSON, AFTER ALL.
OOOH.
HOW PRETTY! IT LOOKS DELICIOUS!
HM?!
RATTLE RATTLE
FLOAT
Kanji: CURSE
DRRRIBBLE
EEP.

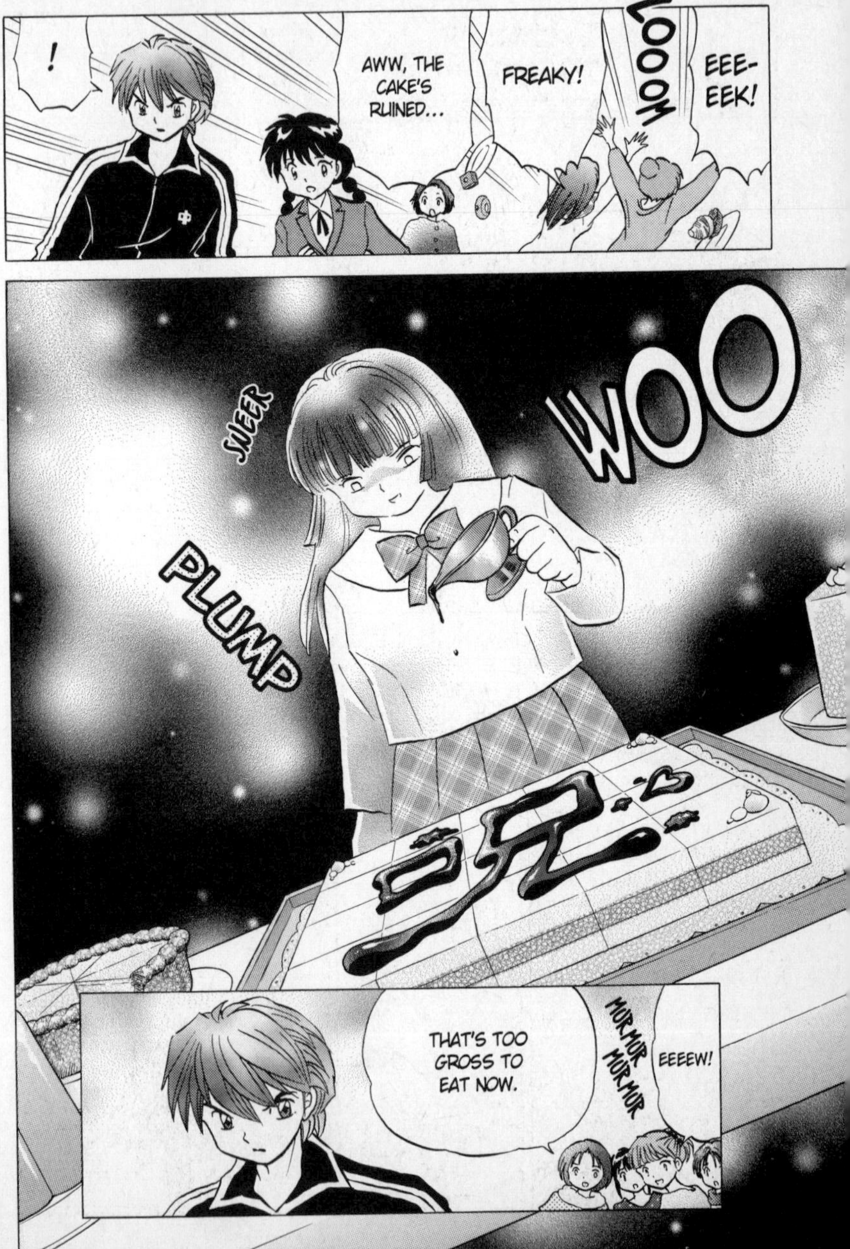
EEE-EEK!
LOOOM
FREAKY!
AWW, THE CAKE'S RUINED...
!
WOO
SNEER
PLUMP
EEEEW!
MUR MUR MUR MUR
THAT'S TOO GROSS TO EAT NOW.

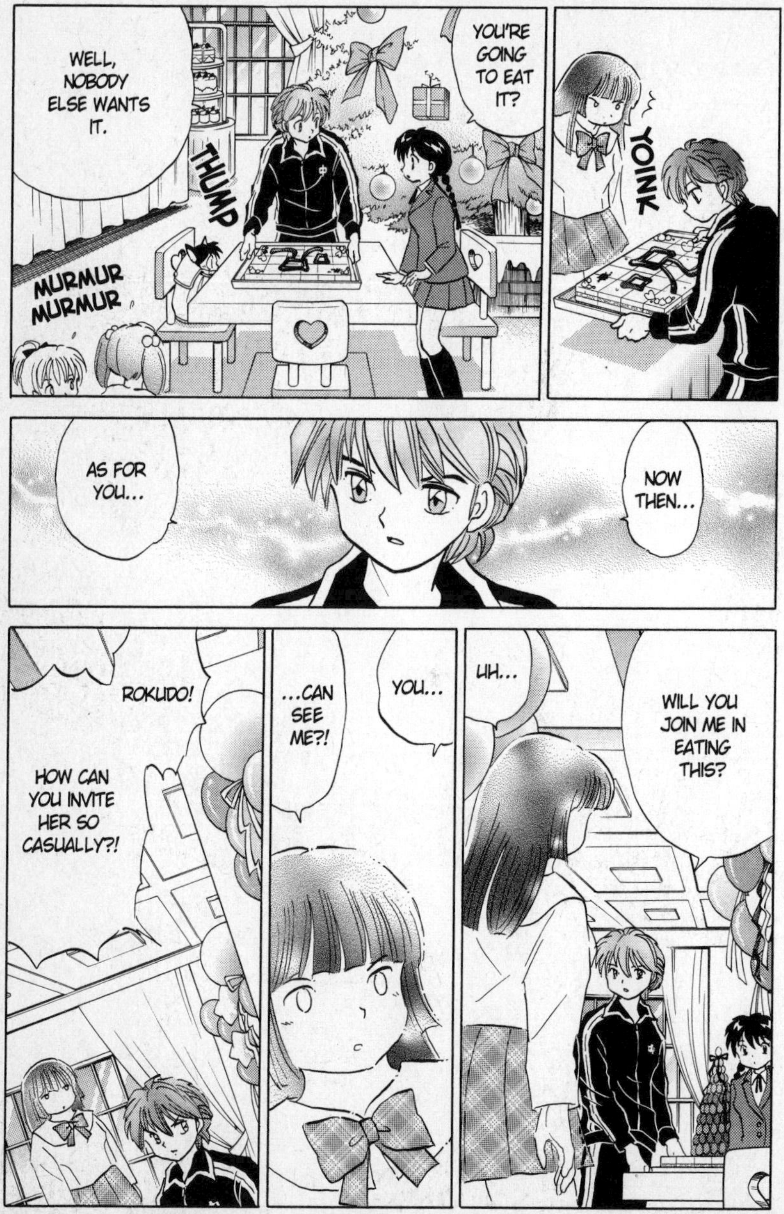
YOINK
YOU'RE GOING TO EAT IT?
WELL, NOBODY ELSE WANTS IT.
THUMP
MURMUR MURMUR
NOW THEN...
AS FOR YOU...
UH...
WILL YOU JOIN ME IN EATING THIS?
YOU...
...CAN SEE ME?!
ROKUDO!
HOW CAN YOU INVITE HER SO CASUALLY?!

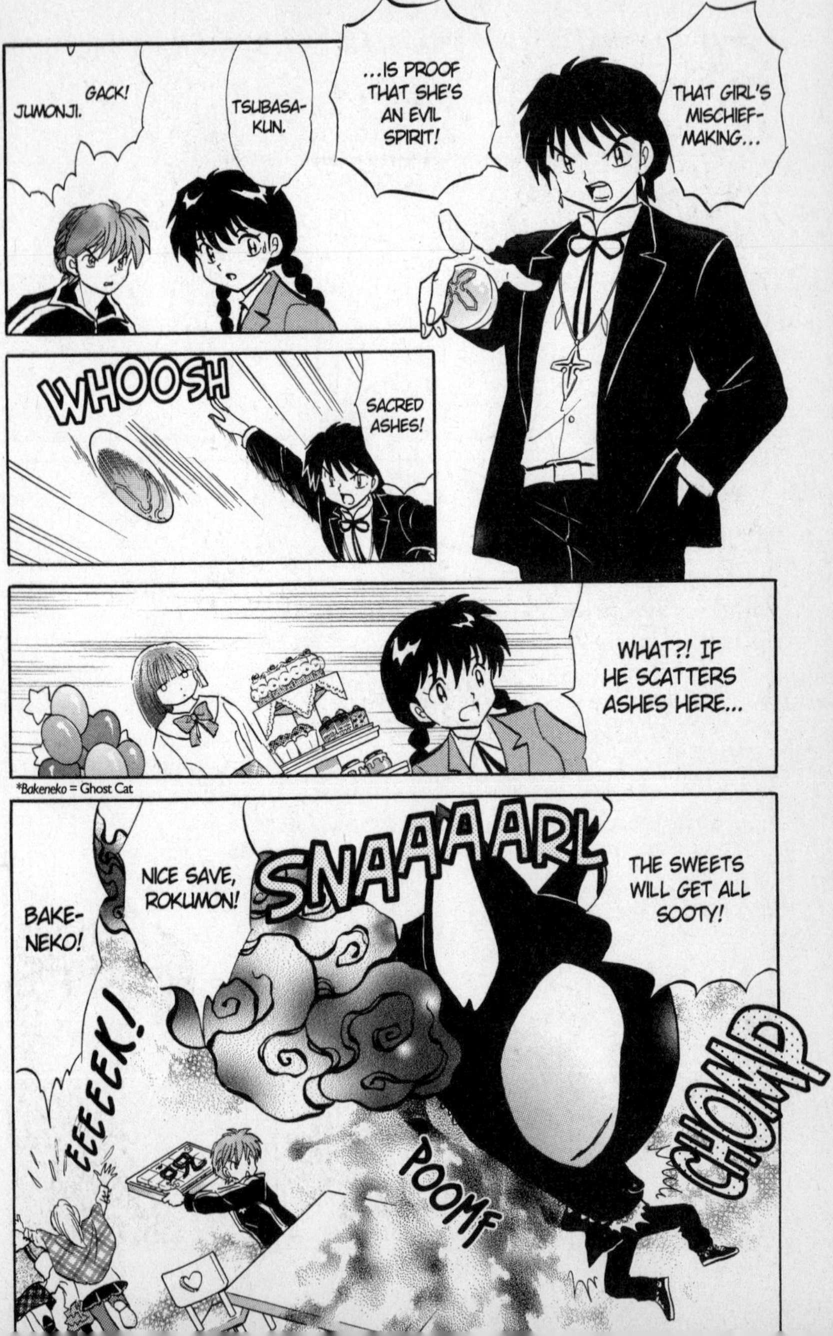
THAT GIRL'S MISCHIEF-MAKING...
...IS PROOF THAT SHE'S AN EVIL SPIRIT!
TSUBASA-KUN.
GACK!
JUMONJI.
SACRED ASHES!
WHOOSH
WHAT?! IF HE SCATTERS ASHES HERE...
THE SWEETS WILL GET ALL SOOTY!
SNAAAAARL
NICE SAVE, ROKUMON!
BAKE-NEKO!
CHOMP
POOMF
EEEEEK!

*Bakeneko = Ghost Cat

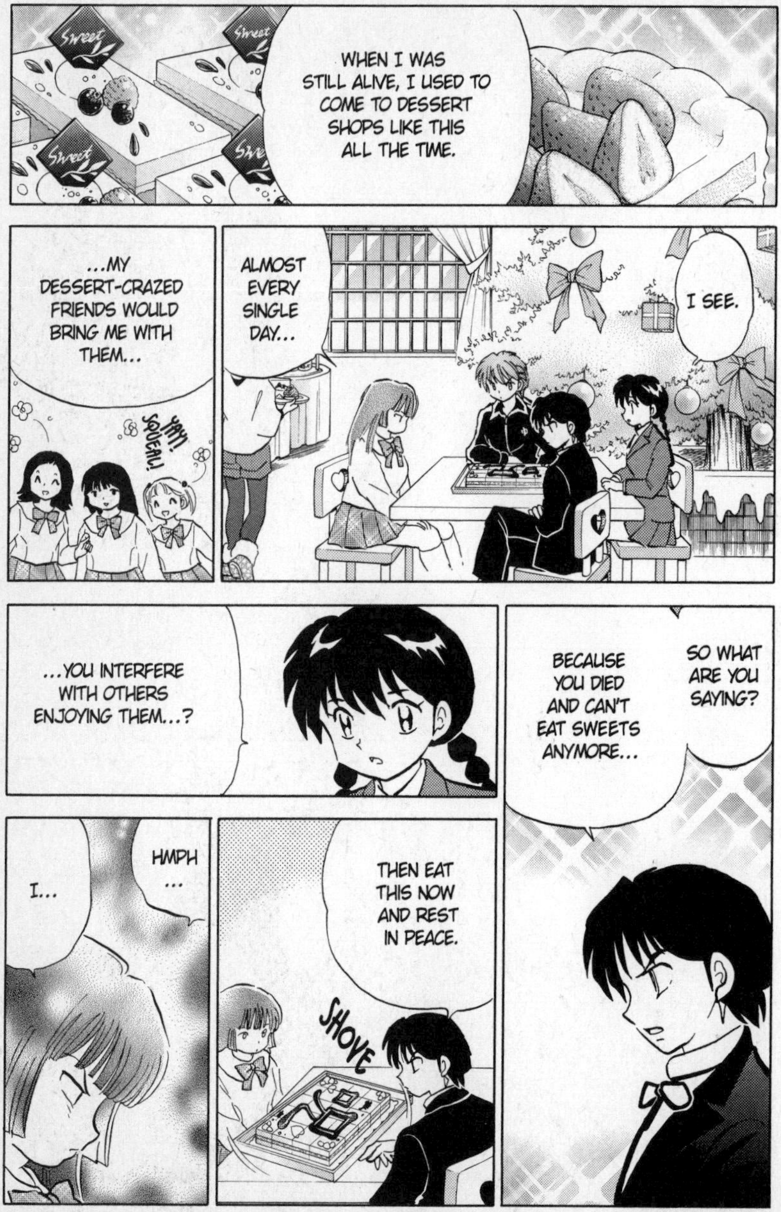
WHEN I WAS STILL ALIVE, I USED TO COME TO DESSERT SHOPS LIKE THIS ALL THE TIME.
I SEE.
ALMOST EVERY SINGLE DAY...
...MY DESSERT-CRAZED FRIENDS WOULD BRING ME WITH THEM...
YAY! SQUEAL!
SO WHAT ARE YOU SAYING?
BECAUSE YOU DIED AND CAN'T EAT SWEETS ANYMORE...
...YOU INTERFERE WITH OTHERS ENJOYING THEM...?
THEN EAT THIS NOW AND REST IN PEACE.
SHOVE
HMPH ...
I...

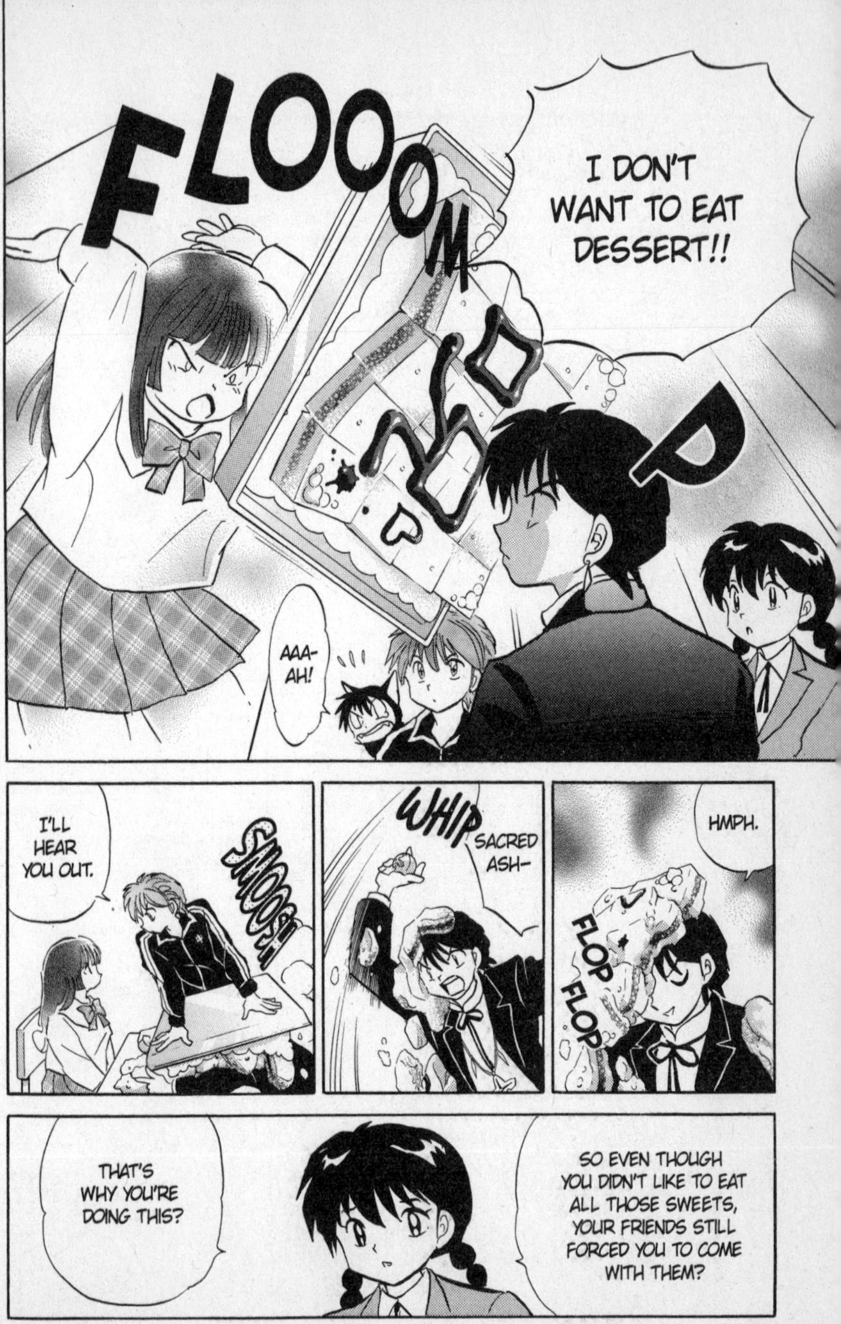
I DON'T WANT TO EAT DESSERT!!
FLOOOM
AAA-AH!
HMPH.
FLOP FLOP
WHIP
SACRED ASH-
SWOOSH
I'LL HEAR YOU OUT.
SO EVEN THOUGH YOU DIDN'T LIKE TO EAT ALL THOSE SWEETS, YOUR FRIENDS STILL FORCED YOU TO COME WITH THEM?
THAT'S WHY YOU'RE DOING THIS?

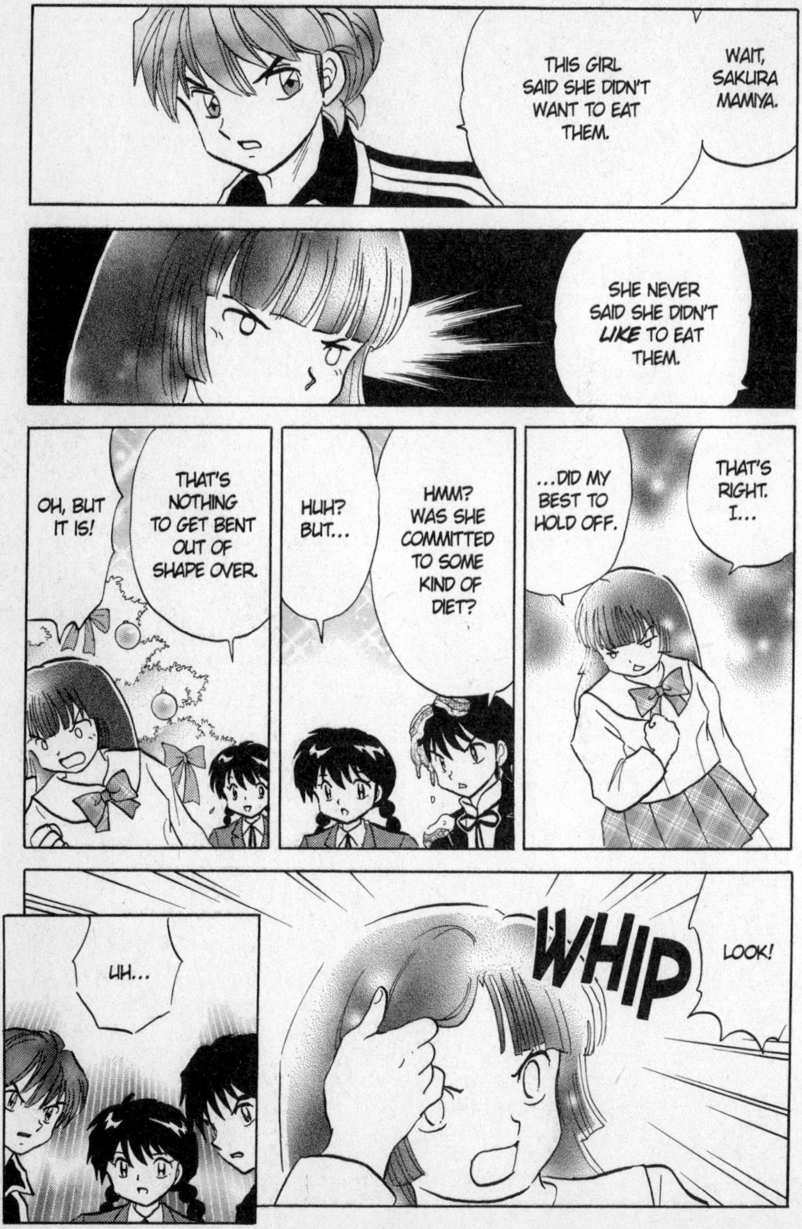
WAIT, SAKURA MAMIYA.
THIS GIRL SAID SHE DIDN'T WANT TO EAT THEM.
SHE NEVER SAID SHE DIDN'T *LIKE* TO EAT THEM.
THAT'S RIGHT. I...
...DID MY BEST TO HOLD OFF.
HMM? WAS SHE COMMITTED TO SOME KIND OF DIET?
HUH? BUT...
THAT'S NOTHING TO GET BENT OUT OF SHAPE OVER.
OH, BUT IT IS!
LOOK!
WHIP
UH...

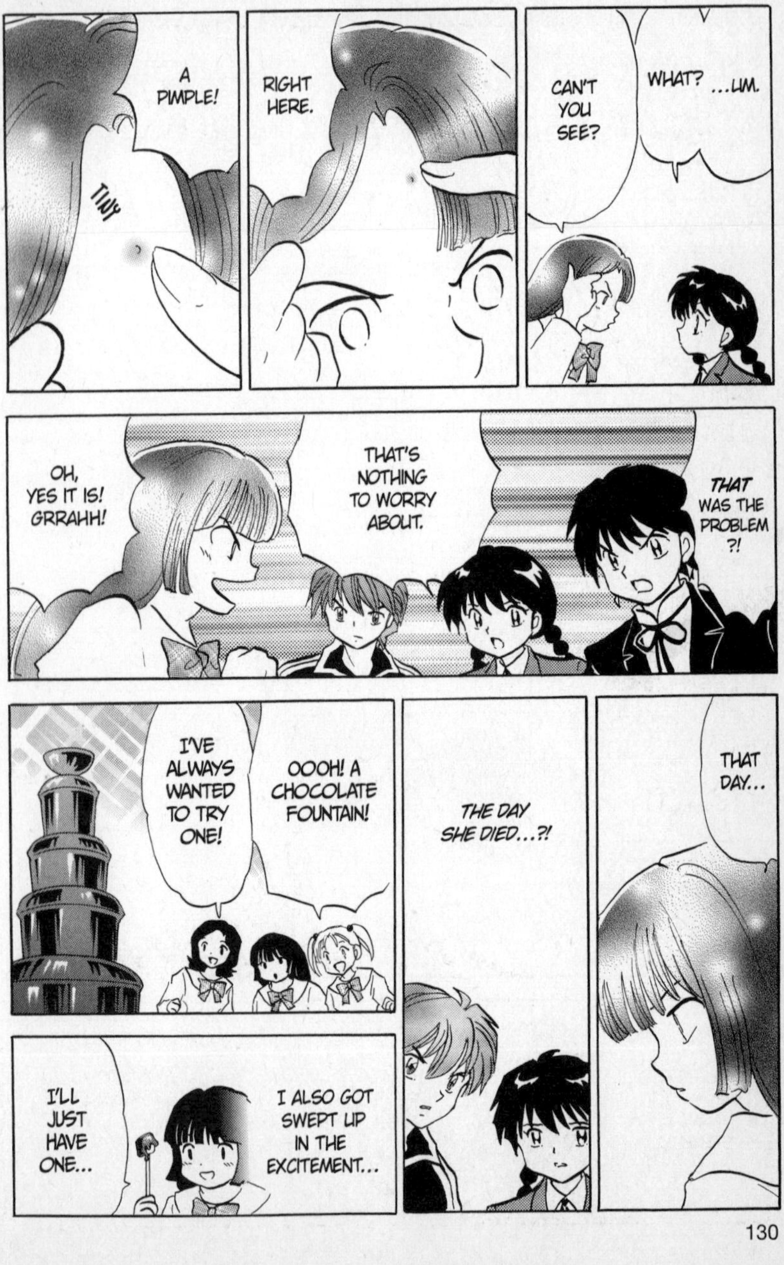
WHAT? ...UM.
CAN'T YOU SEE?
RIGHT HERE.
A PIMPLE!
TINY
THAT WAS THE PROBLEM ?!
THAT'S NOTHING TO WORRY ABOUT.
OH, YES IT IS! GRRAHH!
THAT DAY...
THE DAY SHE DIED...?!
OOOH! A CHOCOLATE FOUNTAIN!
I'VE ALWAYS WANTED TO TRY ONE!
I ALSO GOT SWEPT UP IN THE EXCITEMENT...
I'LL JUST HAVE ONE...

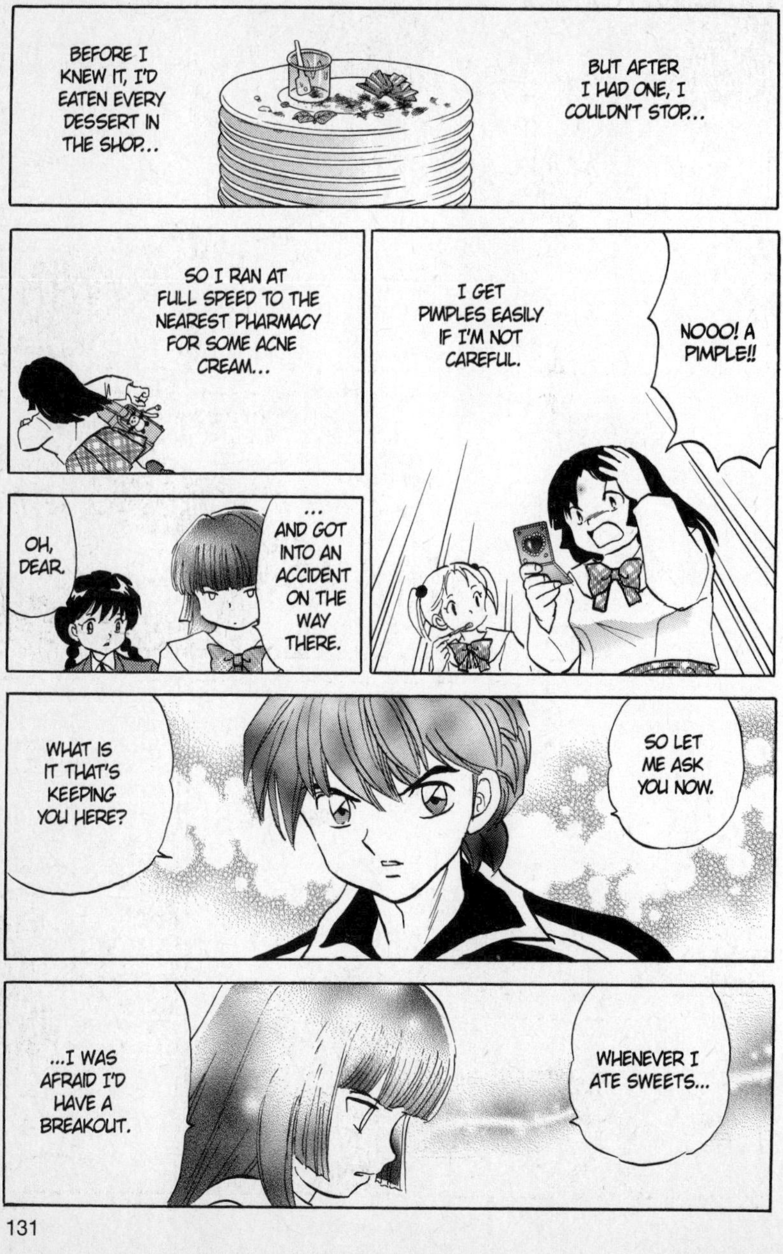
BUT AFTER I HAD ONE, I COULDN'T STOP...
BEFORE I KNEW IT, I'D EATEN EVERY DESSERT IN THE SHOP...
NOOO! A PIMPLE!!
I GET PIMPLES EASILY IF I'M NOT CAREFUL.
SO I RAN AT FULL SPEED TO THE NEAREST PHARMACY FOR SOME ACNE CREAM...
...AND GOT INTO AN ACCIDENT ON THE WAY THERE.
OH, DEAR.
SO LET ME ASK YOU NOW.
WHAT IS IT THAT'S KEEPING YOU HERE?
WHENEVER I ATE SWEETS...
...I WAS AFRAID I'D HAVE A BREAKOUT.

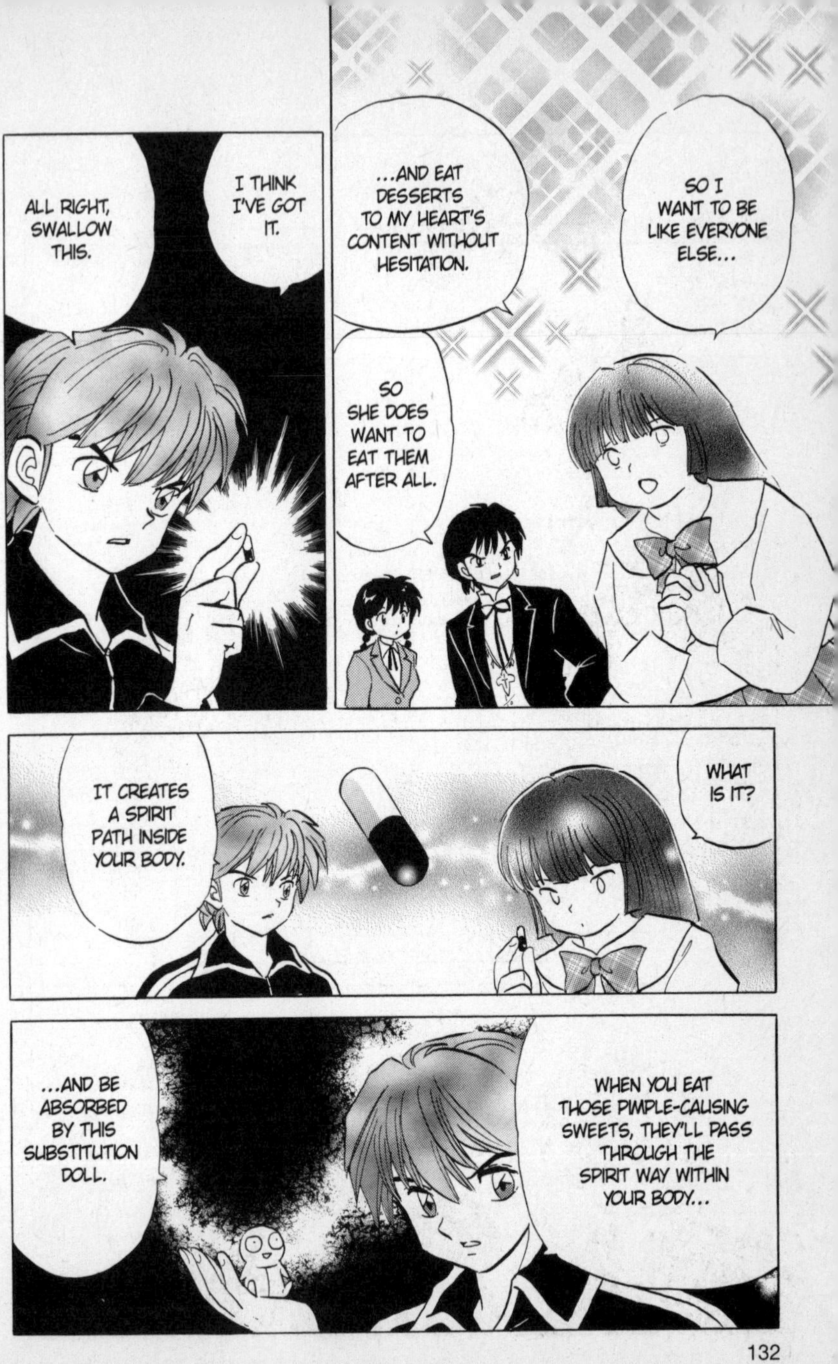
SO I WANT TO BE LIKE EVERYONE ELSE...
...AND EAT DESSERTS TO MY HEART'S CONTENT WITHOUT HESITATION.
SO SHE DOES WANT TO EAT THEM AFTER ALL.
I THINK I'VE GOT IT.
ALL RIGHT, SWALLOW THIS.
WHAT IS IT?
IT CREATES A SPIRIT PATH INSIDE YOUR BODY.
WHEN YOU EAT THOSE PIMPLE-CAUSING SWEETS, THEY'LL PASS THROUGH THE SPIRIT WAY WITHIN YOUR BODY...
...AND BE ABSORBED BY THIS SUBSTITUTION DOLL.

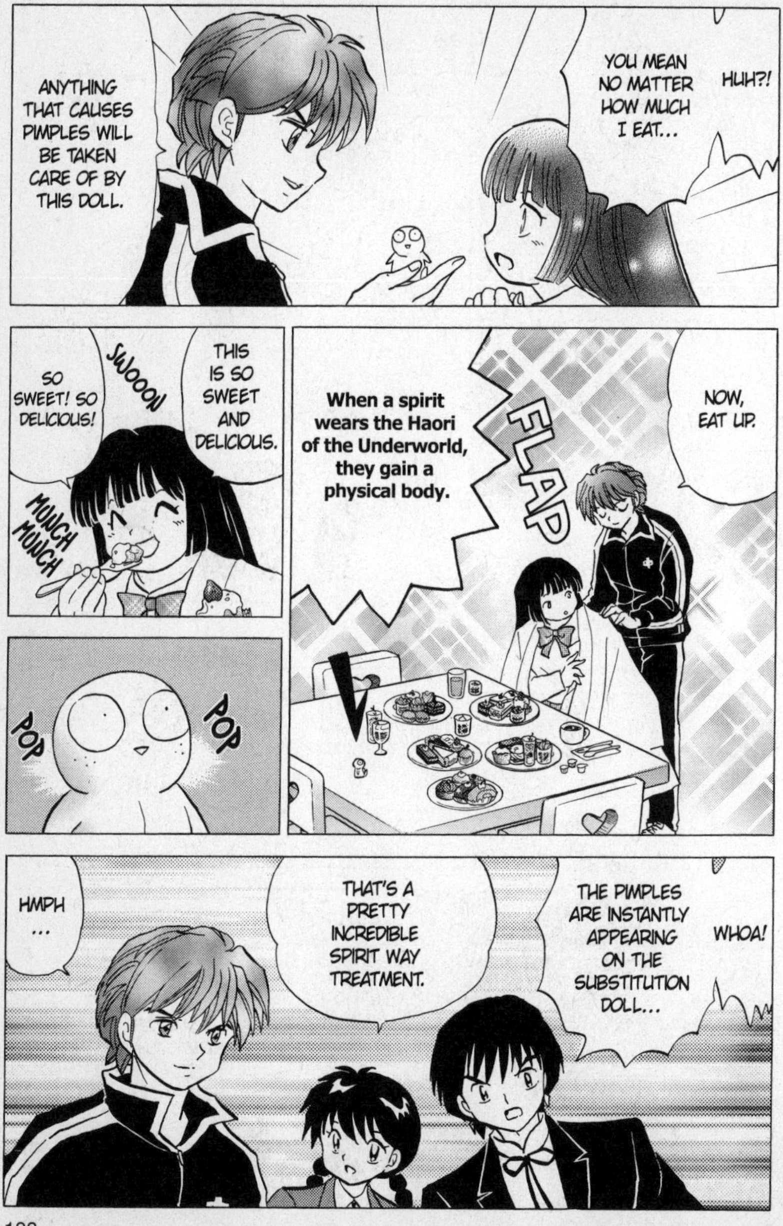
HUH?!
YOU MEAN NO MATTER HOW MUCH I EAT...
ANYTHING THAT CAUSES PIMPLES WILL BE TAKEN CARE OF BY THIS DOLL.
NOW, EAT UP.
FLAP
When a spirit wears the Haori of the Underworld, they gain a physical body.
THIS IS SO SWEET AND DELICIOUS.
SWOOON
SO SWEET! SO DELICIOUS!
MUNCH MUNCH
POP
POP
WHOA!
THE PIMPLES ARE INSTANTLY APPEARING ON THE SUBSTITUTION DOLL...
THAT'S A PRETTY INCREDIBLE SPIRIT WAY TREATMENT.
HMPH ...

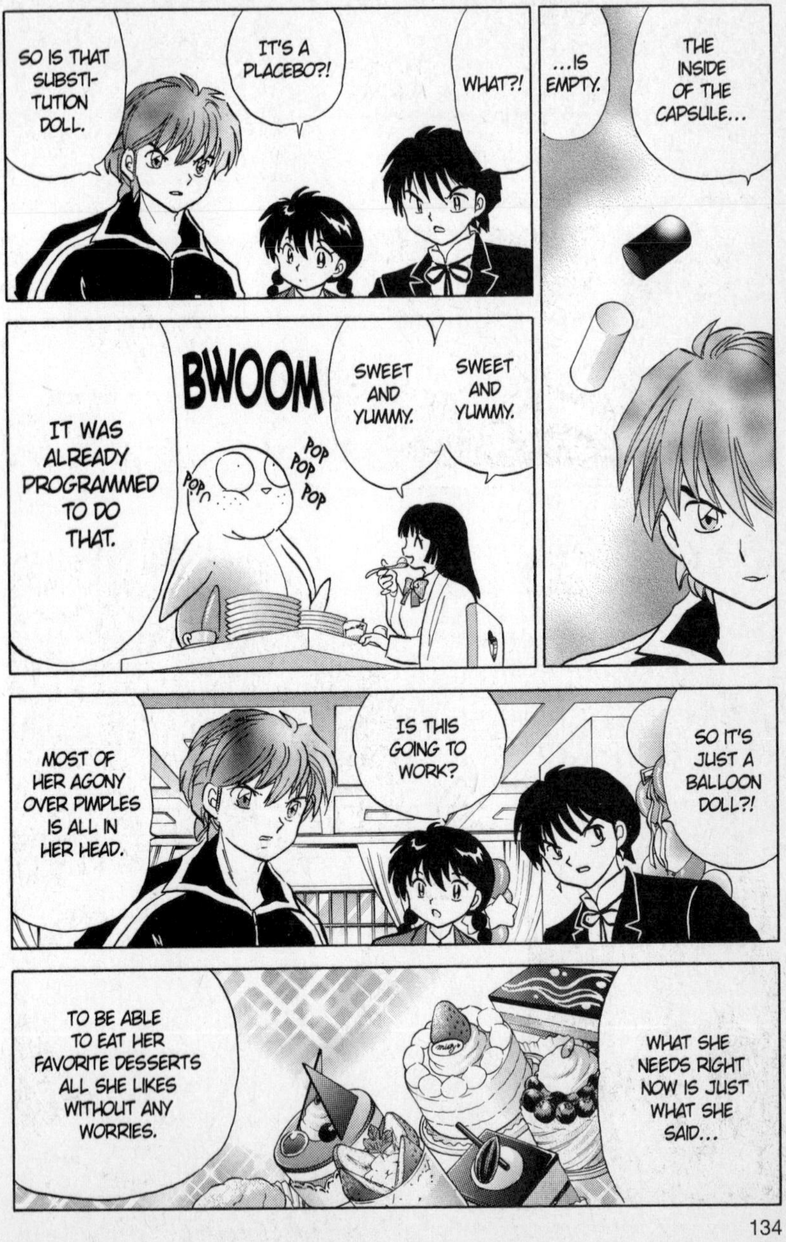
THE INSIDE OF THE CAPSULE...
...IS EMPTY.
WHAT?!
IT'S A PLACEBO?!
SO IS THAT SUBSTITUTION DOLL.
SWEET AND YUMMY.
SWEET AND YUMMY.
BWOOM
POP POP POP POP
IT WAS ALREADY PROGRAMMED TO DO THAT.
SO IT'S JUST A BALLOON DOLL?!
IS THIS GOING TO WORK?
MOST OF HER AGONY OVER PIMPLES IS ALL IN HER HEAD.
WHAT SHE NEEDS RIGHT NOW IS JUST WHAT SHE SAID...
TO BE ABLE TO EAT HER FAVORITE DESSERTS ALL SHE LIKES WITHOUT ANY WORRIES.

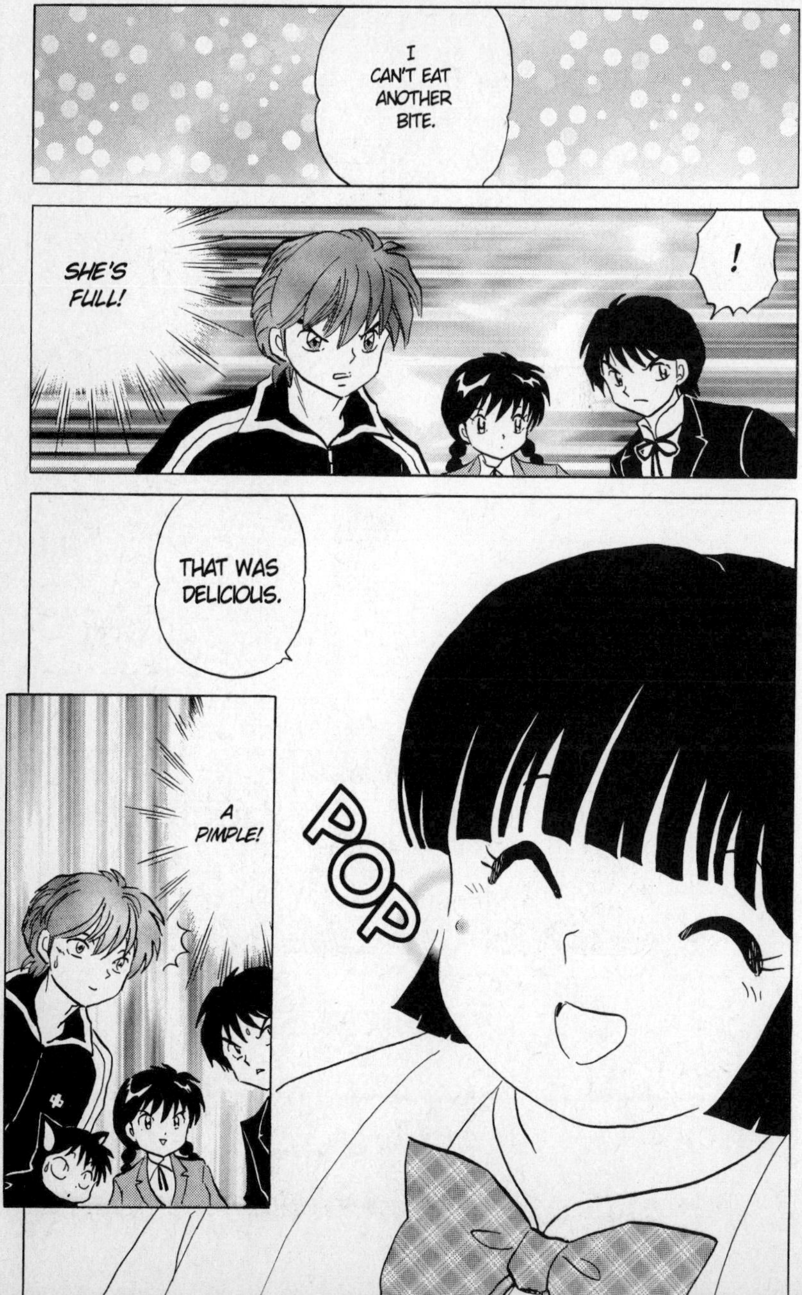
I CAN'T EAT ANOTHER BITE.
!
SHE'S FULL!
THAT WAS DELICIOUS.
POP
A PIMPLE!

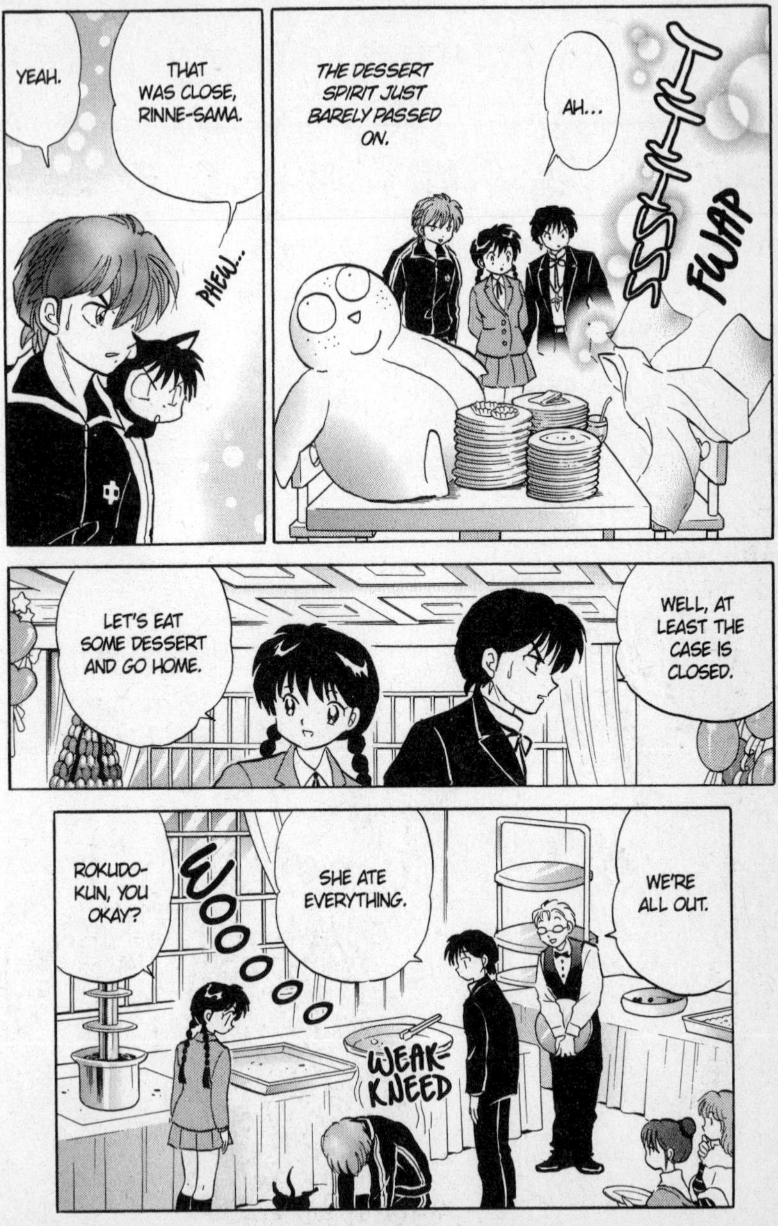
AH...
SSSHHHH
FWAP
THE DESSERT SPIRIT JUST BARELY PASSED ON.
THAT WAS CLOSE, RINNE-SAMA.
PHEW...
YEAH.
WELL, AT LEAST THE CASE IS CLOSED.
LET'S EAT SOME DESSERT AND GO HOME.
WE'RE ALL OUT.
SHE ATE EVERYTHING.
WOOOOOO
WEAK-KNEED
ROKUDO-KUN, YOU OKAY?

CHAPTER 126: THE TASTY TESTER

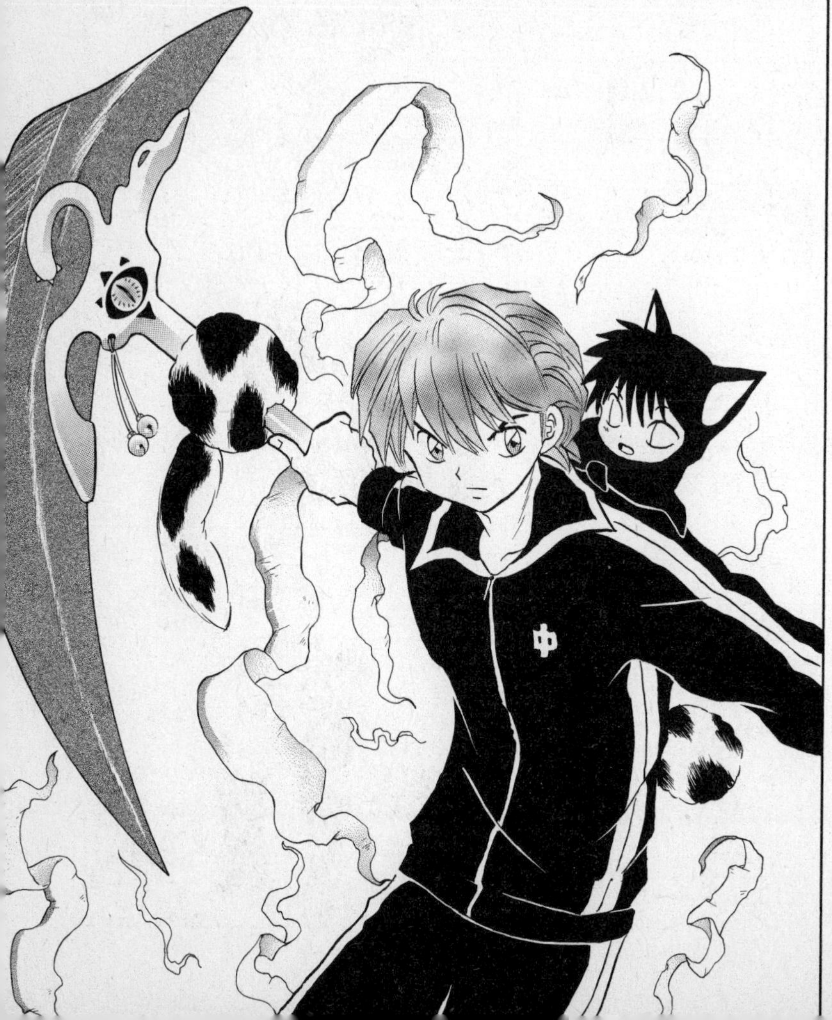

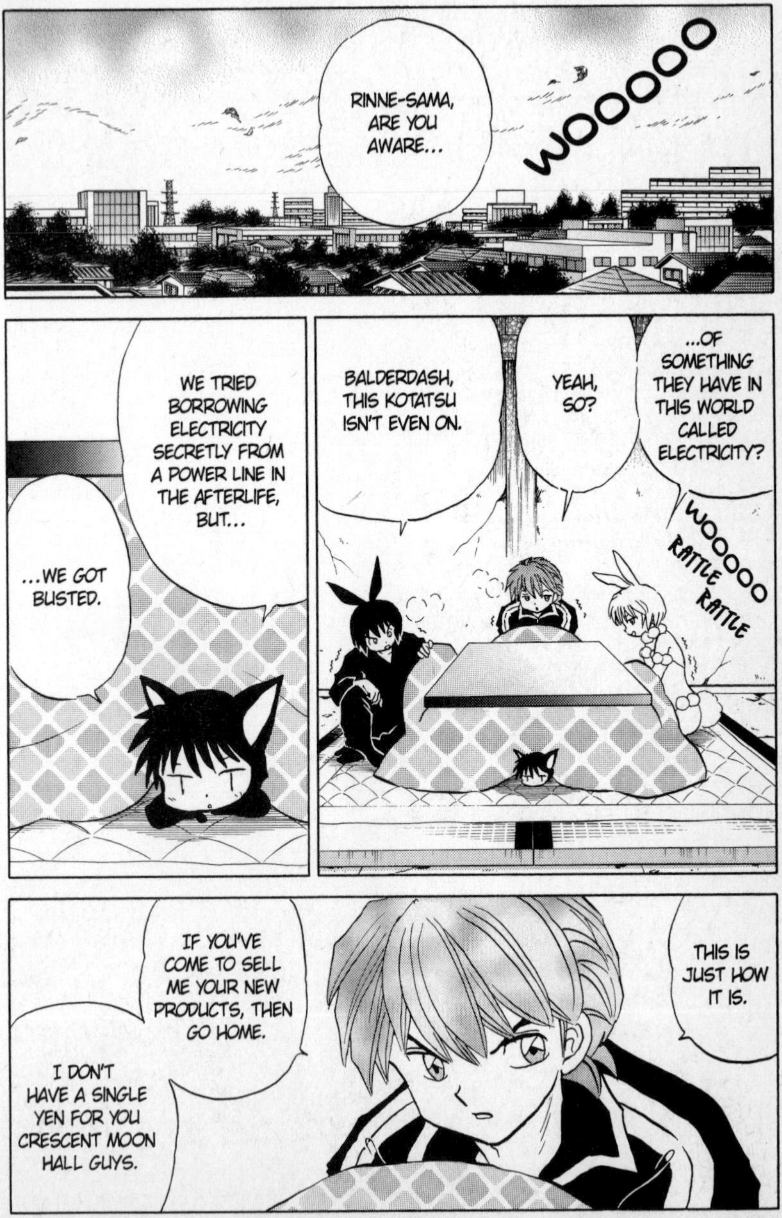
WOOOOO
RINNE-SAMA, ARE YOU AWARE...
...OF SOMETHING THEY HAVE IN THIS WORLD CALLED ELECTRICITY?
WOOOOO
RATTLE RATTLE
YEAH, SO?
BALDERDASH, THIS KOTATSU ISN'T EVEN ON.
WE TRIED BORROWING ELECTRICITY SECRETLY FROM A POWER LINE IN THE AFTERLIFE, BUT...
...WE GOT BUSTED.
THIS IS JUST HOW IT IS.
IF YOU'VE COME TO SELL ME YOUR NEW PRODUCTS, THEN GO HOME.
I DON'T HAVE A SINGLE YEN FOR YOU CRESCENT MOON HALL GUYS.

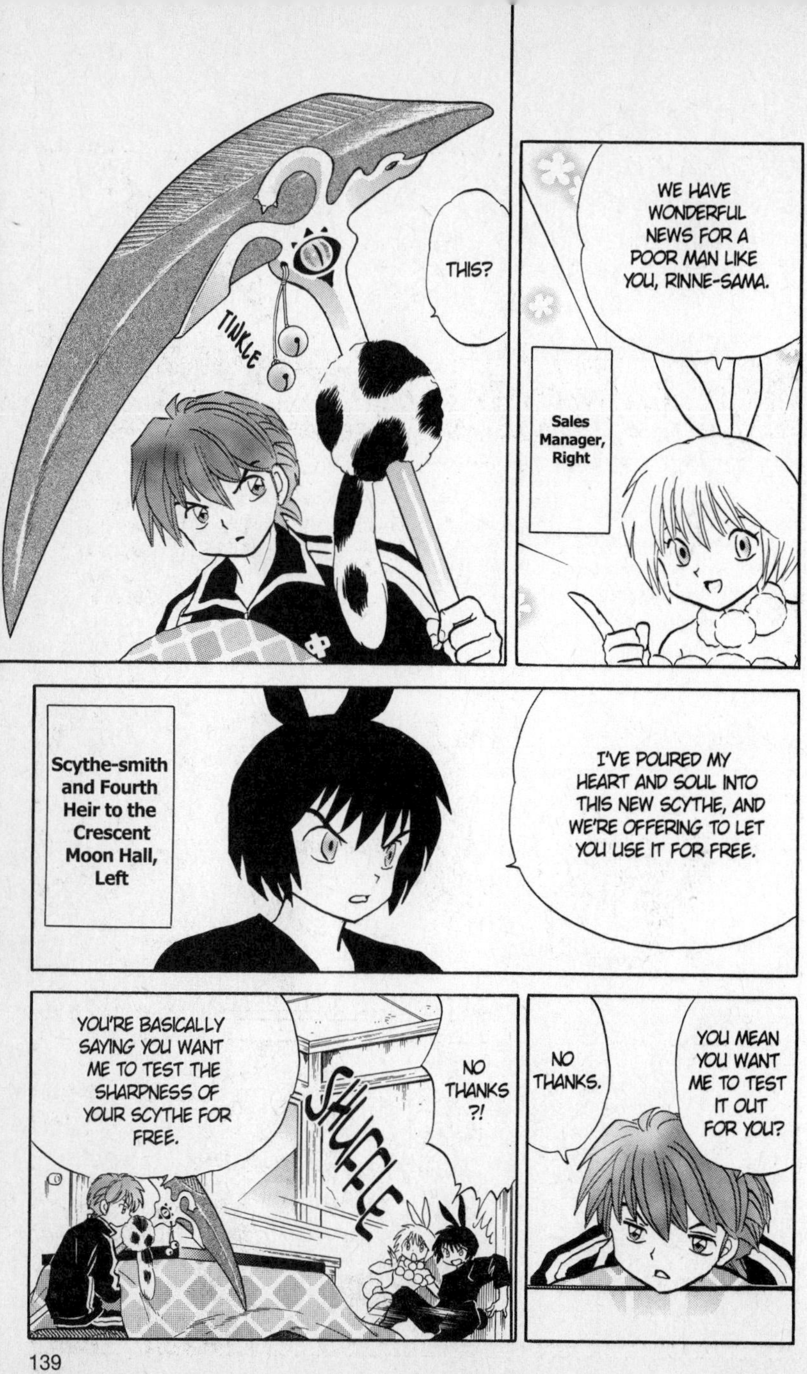
WE HAVE WONDERFUL NEWS FOR A POOR MAN LIKE YOU, RINNE-SAMA.
Sales Manager, Right
THIS?
TINKLE
I'VE POURED MY HEART AND SOUL INTO THIS NEW SCYTHE, AND WE'RE OFFERING TO LET YOU USE IT FOR FREE.
Scythe-smith and Fourth Heir to the Crescent Moon Hall, Left
YOU MEAN YOU WANT ME TO TEST IT OUT FOR YOU?
NO THANKS.
NO THANKS ?!
SHUFFLE
YOU'RE BASICALLY SAYING YOU WANT ME TO TEST THE SHARPNESS OF YOUR SCYTHE FOR FREE.

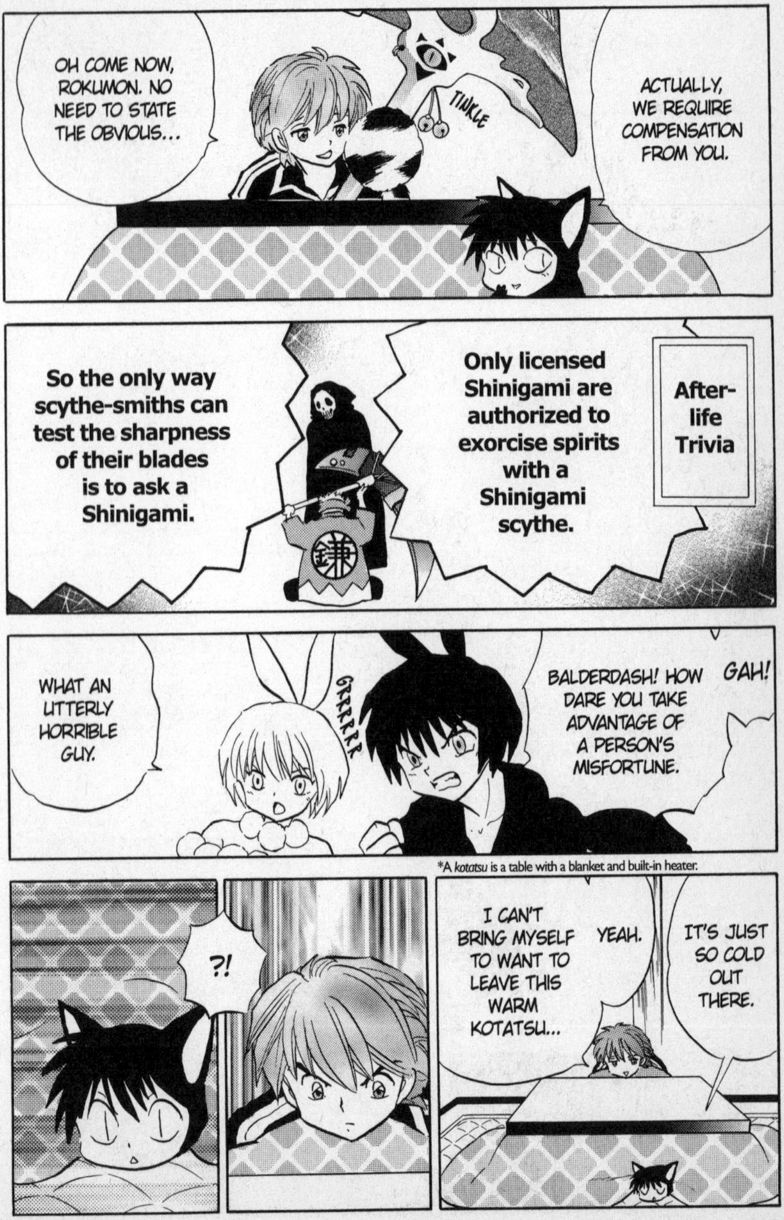
ACTUALLY, WE REQUIRE COMPENSATION FROM YOU.
TINKLE
OH COME NOW, ROKUMON. NO NEED TO STATE THE OBVIOUS...
After-life Trivia
Only licensed Shinigami are authorized to exorcise spirits with a Shinigami scythe.
So the only way scythe-smiths can test the sharpness of their blades is to ask a Shinigami.
GAH!
BALDERDASH! HOW DARE YOU TAKE ADVANTAGE OF A PERSON'S MISFORTUNE.
GRRRRRR
WHAT AN UTTERLY HORRIBLE GUY.
*A *kotatsu* is a table with a blanket and built-in heater.
IT'S JUST SO COLD OUT THERE.
YEAH.
I CAN'T BRING MYSELF TO WANT TO LEAVE THIS WARM KOTATSU...
?!

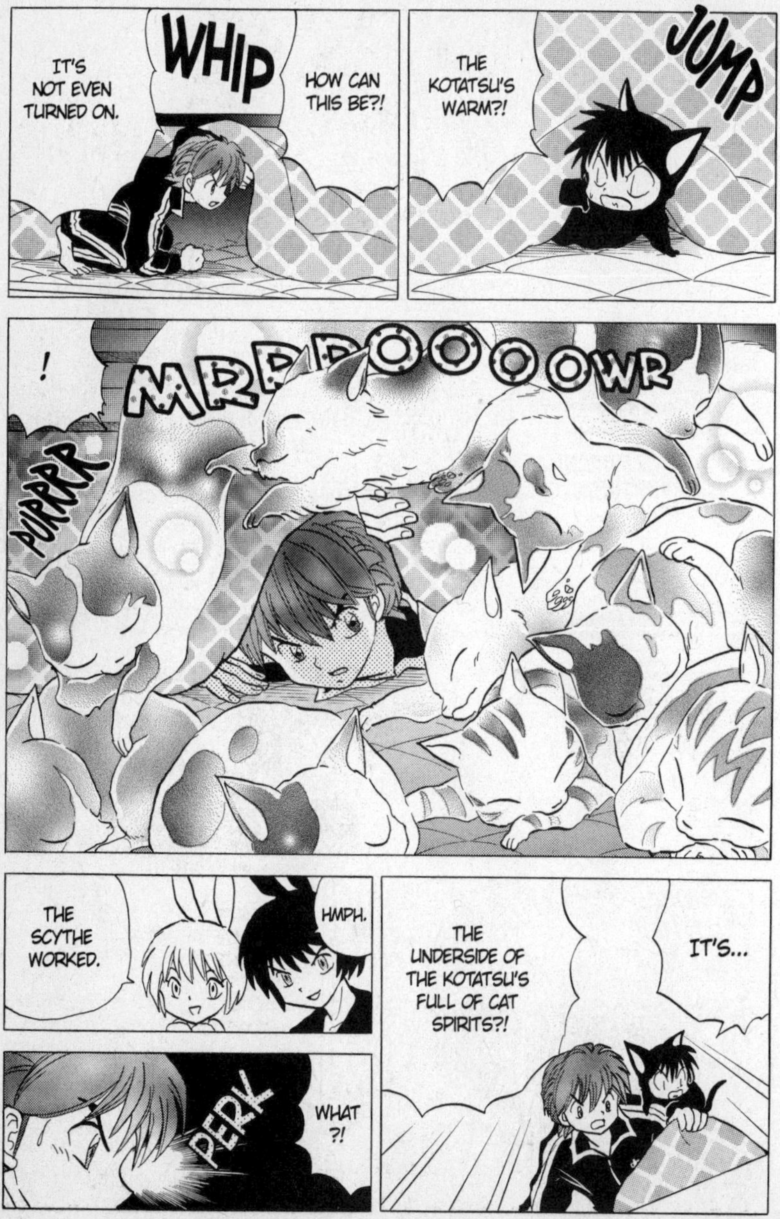

THE KOTATSU'S WARM?!
JUMP
HOW CAN THIS BE?!
WHIP
IT'S NOT EVEN TURNED ON.
MRRROOOOOWR
!
PURRRR
IT'S...
THE UNDERSIDE OF THE KOTATSU'S FULL OF CAT SPIRITS?!
HMPH.
THE SCYTHE WORKED.
WHAT ?!
PERK

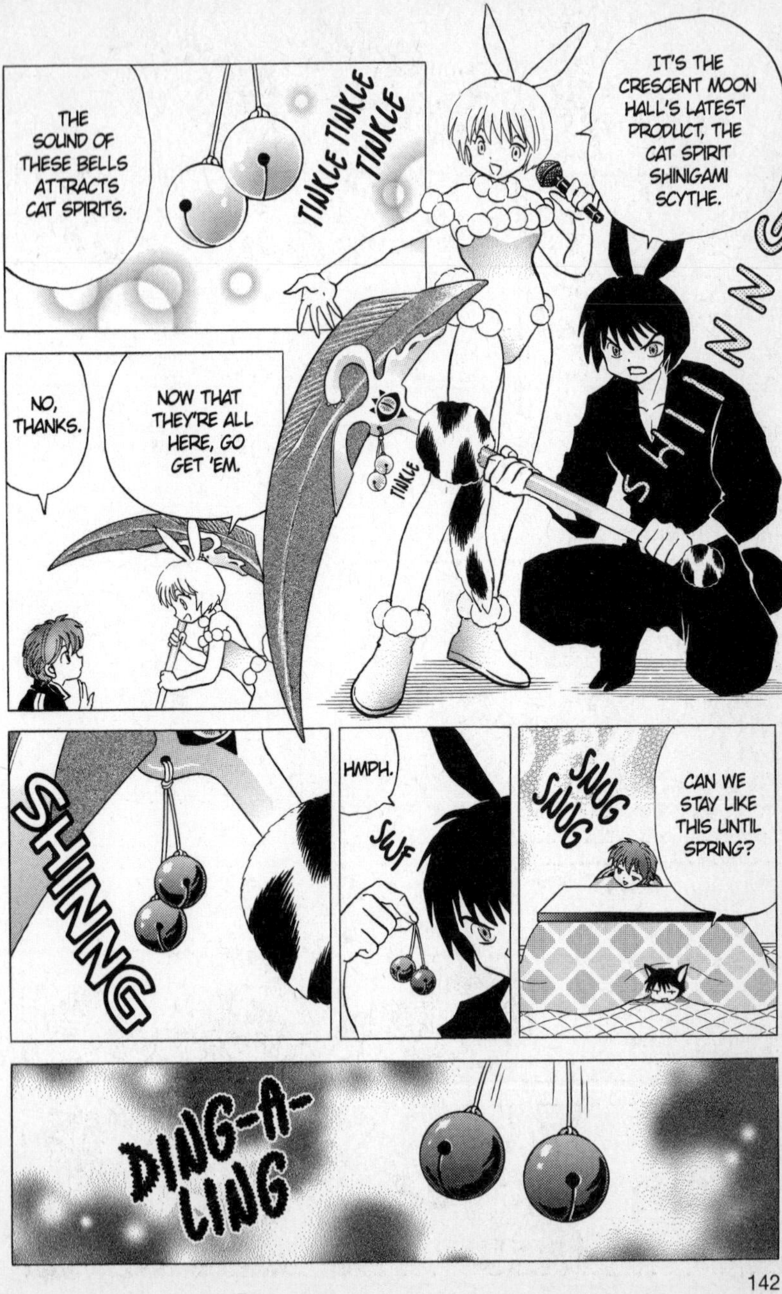
IT'S THE CRESCENT MOON HALL'S LATEST PRODUCT, THE CAT SPIRIT SHINIGAMI SCYTHE.
SHIIING
TINKLE
THE SOUND OF THESE BELLS ATTRACTS CAT SPIRITS.
TINKLE TINKLE TINKLE
NOW THAT THEY'RE ALL HERE, GO GET 'EM.
NO, THANKS.
SNUG SNUG
CAN WE STAY LIKE THIS UNTIL SPRING?
HMPH.
SWF
SHINING
DING-A-LING

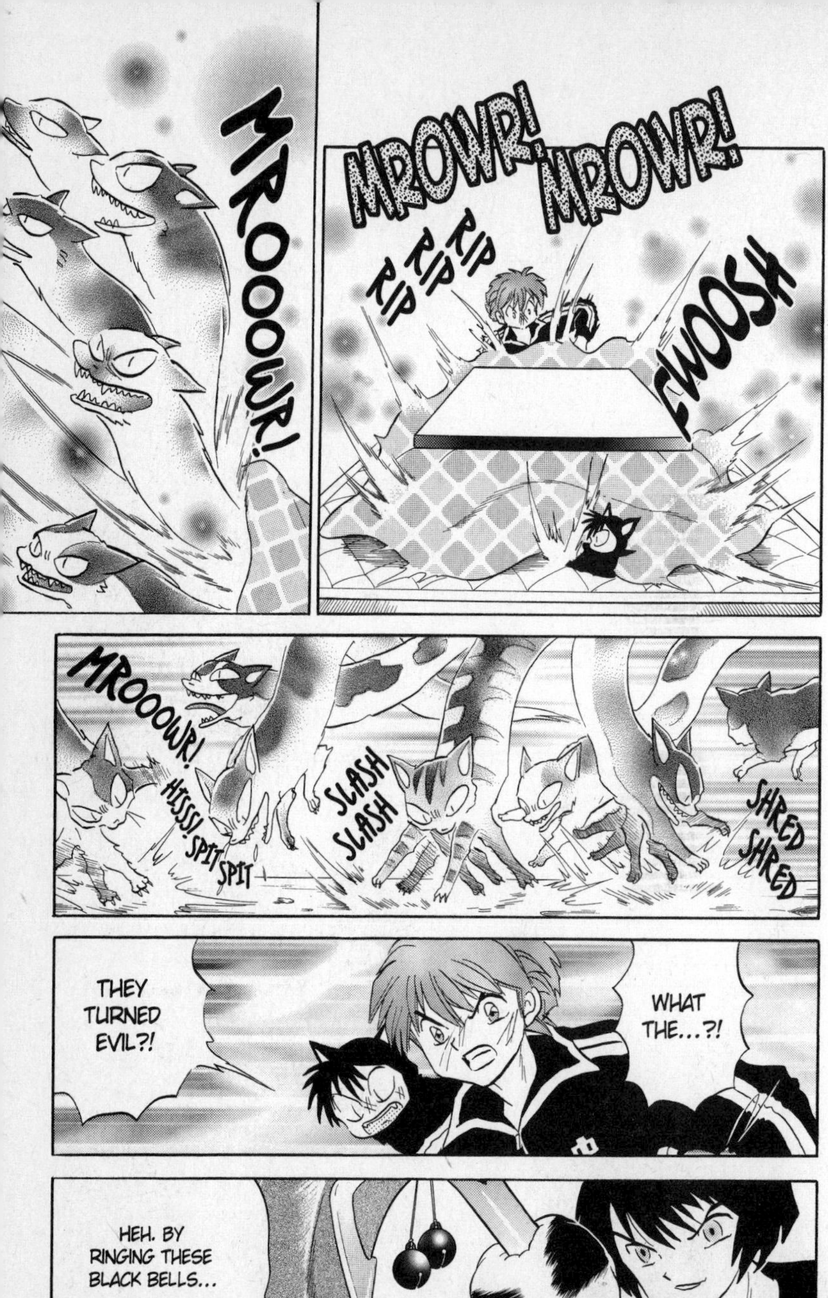
MROWR! MROWR!
RIP RIP RIP
FWOOSH
MROOOWR!
SHRED SHRED
SLASH SLASH
HISSS! SPIT SPIT
MROOOWR!
WHAT THE...?!
THEY TURNED EVIL?!
HEH. BY RINGING THESE BLACK BELLS...

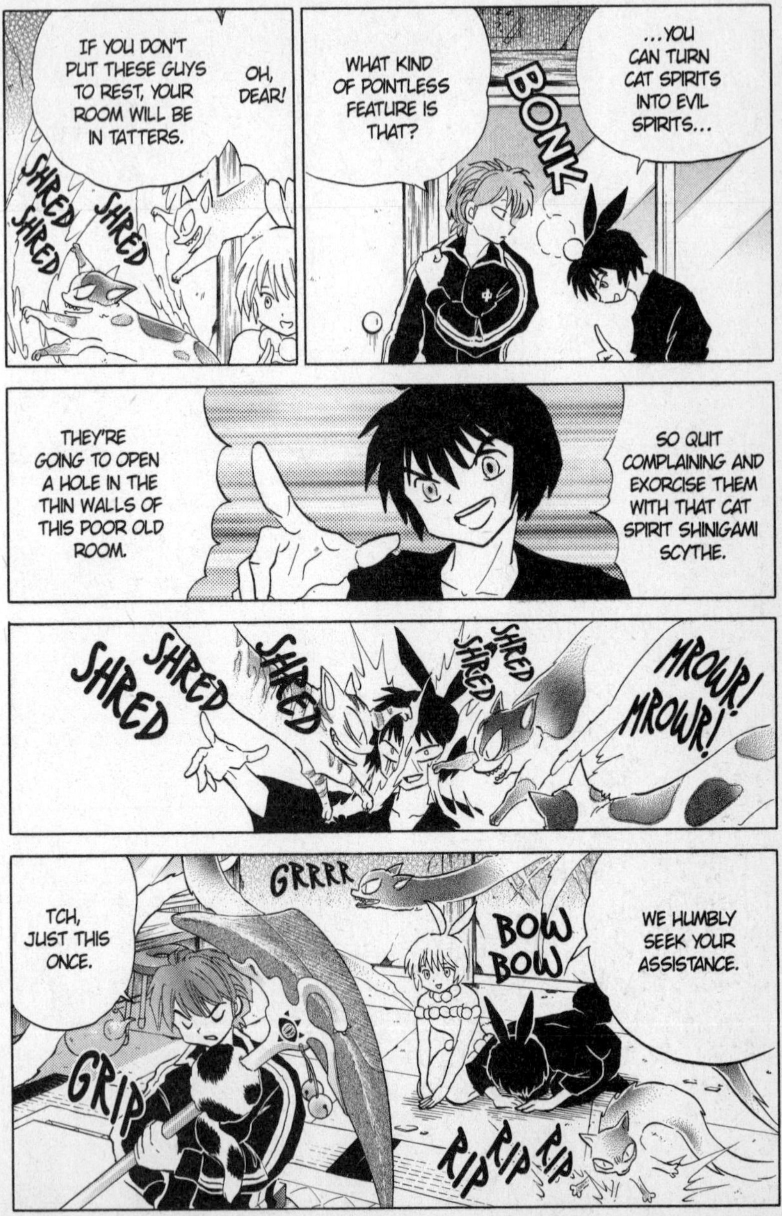
...YOU CAN TURN CAT SPIRITS INTO EVIL SPIRITS...
BONK
WHAT KIND OF POINTLESS FEATURE IS THAT?
OH, DEAR!
IF YOU DON'T PUT THESE GUYS TO REST, YOUR ROOM WILL BE IN TATTERS.
SHRED
SHRED SHRED
SO QUIT COMPLAINING AND EXORCISE THEM WITH THAT CAT SPIRIT SHINIGAMI SCYTHE.
THEY'RE GOING TO OPEN A HOLE IN THE THIN WALLS OF THIS POOR OLD ROOM.
MROWR! MROWR!
SHRED SHRED
SHRED
SHRED SHRED
WE HUMBLY SEEK YOUR ASSISTANCE.
BOW BOW
RIP RIP RIP
GRRRR
TCH, JUST THIS ONCE.
GRIP

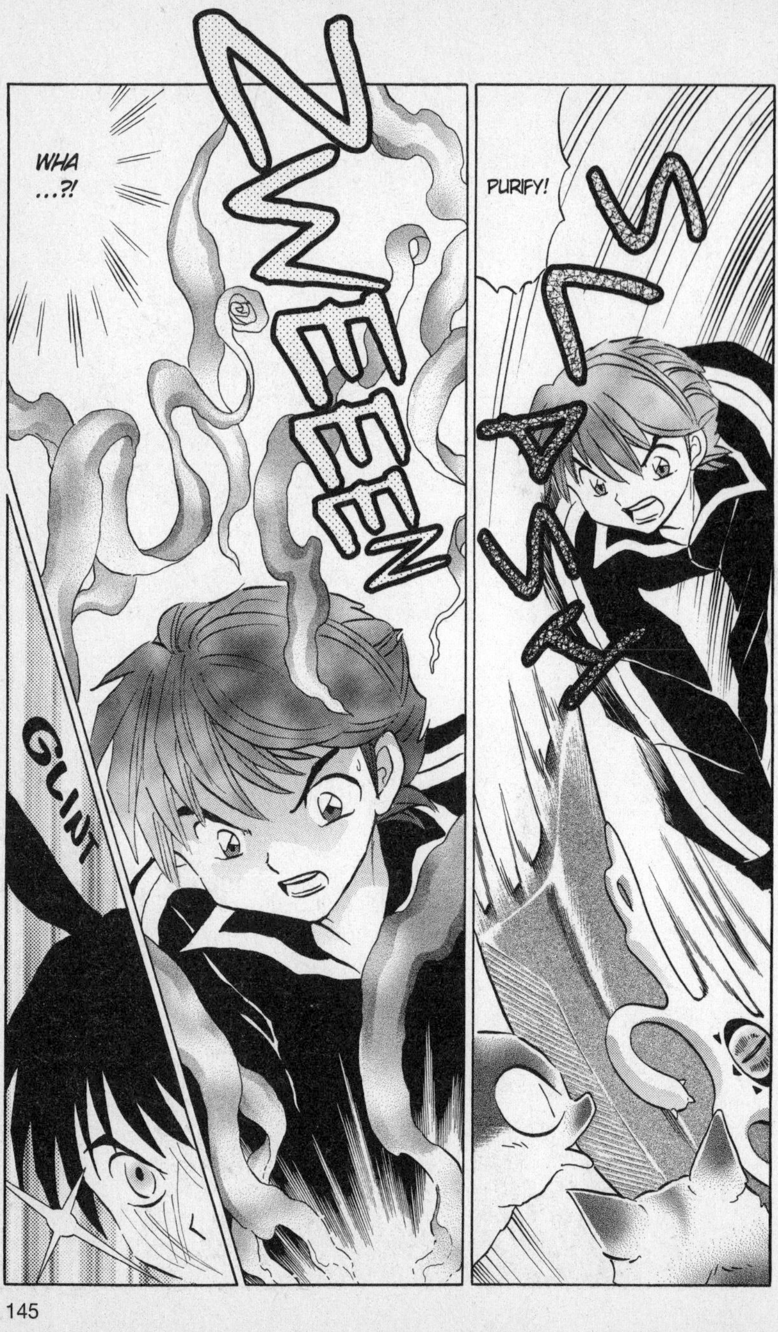
PURIFY!
SLASH
ZWEEEN
WHA ...?!
GLINT

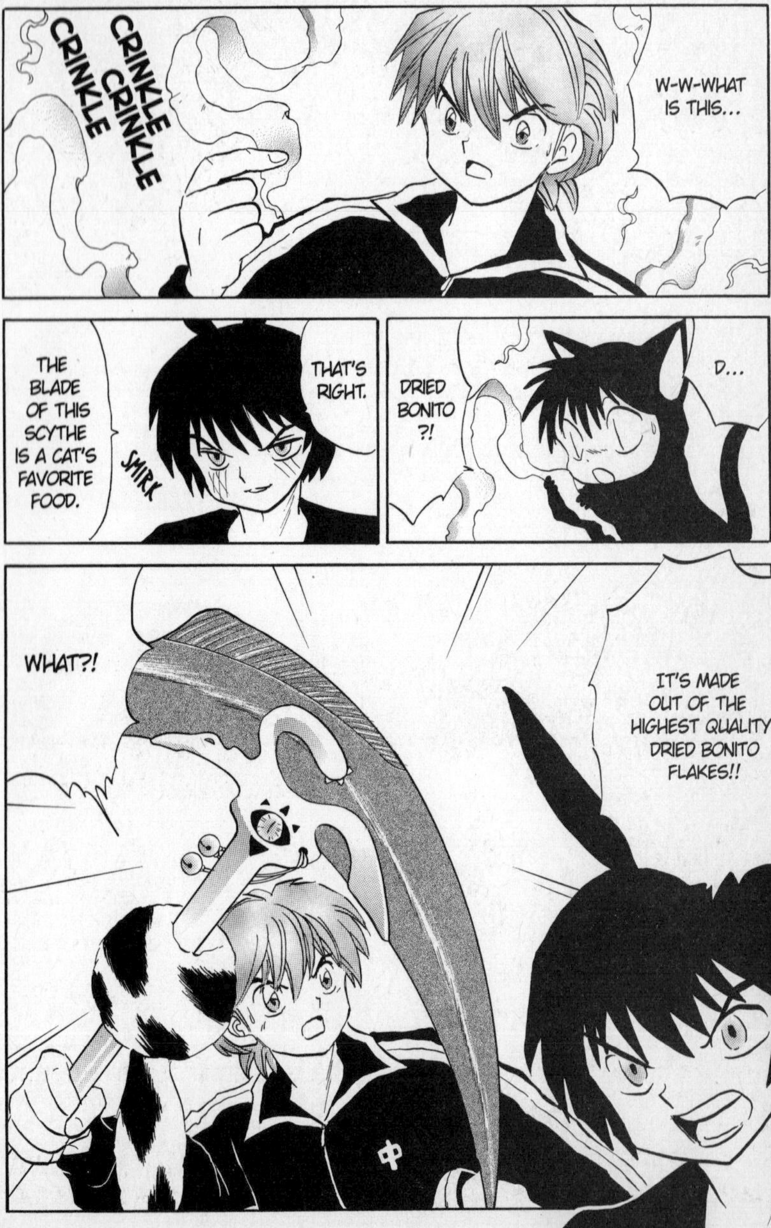
W-W-WHAT IS THIS...
CRINKLE CRINKLE CRINKLE
D...
DRIED BONITO ?!
THAT'S RIGHT.
THE BLADE OF THIS SCYTHE IS A CAT'S FAVORITE FOOD.
SMIRK
IT'S MADE OUT OF THE HIGHEST QUALITY DRIED BONITO FLAKES!!
WHAT?!

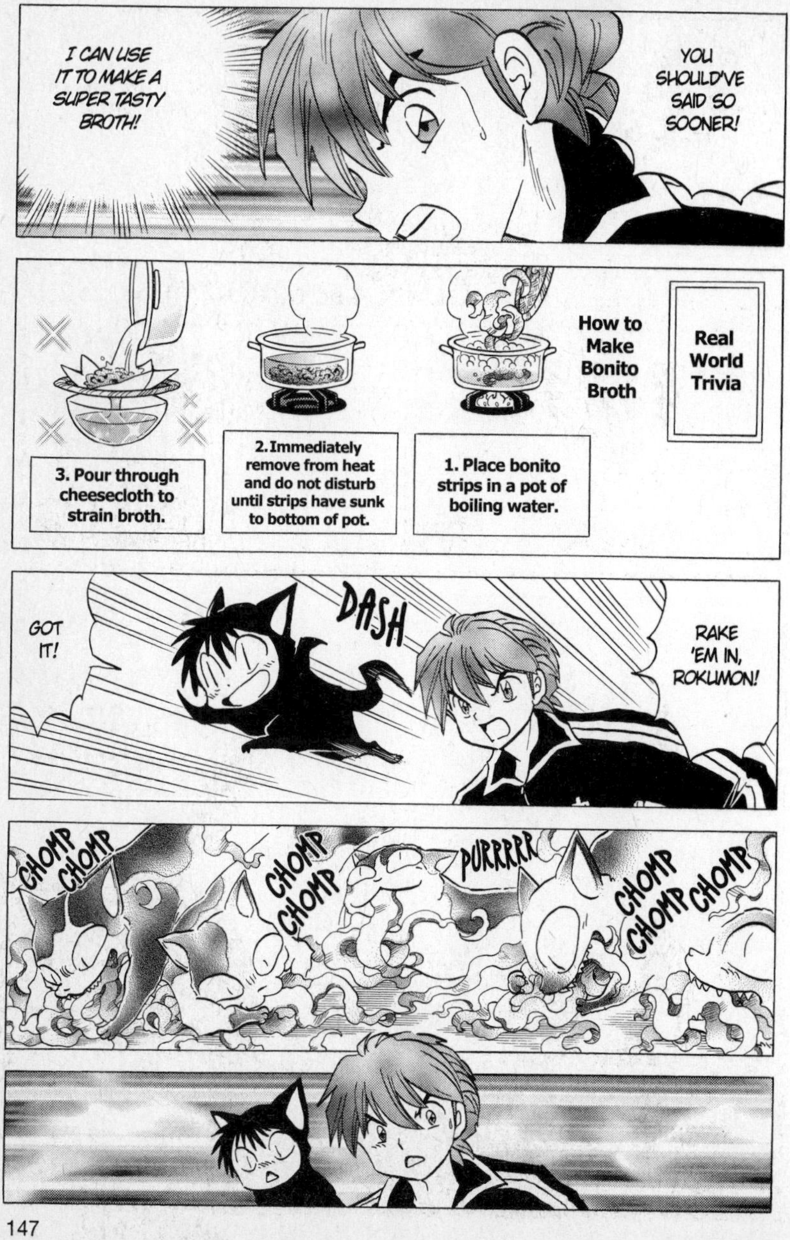
YOU SHOULD'VE SAID SO SOONER!
I CAN USE IT TO MAKE A SUPER TASTY BROTH!
Real World Trivia
How to Make Bonito Broth
1. Place bonito strips in a pot of boiling water.
2. Immediately remove from heat and do not disturb until strips have sunk to bottom of pot.
3. Pour through cheesecloth to strain broth.
RAKE 'EM IN, ROKUMON!
DASH
GOT IT!
CHOMP
CHOMP CHOMP
PURRRRR
CHOMP CHOMP
CHOMP CHOMP

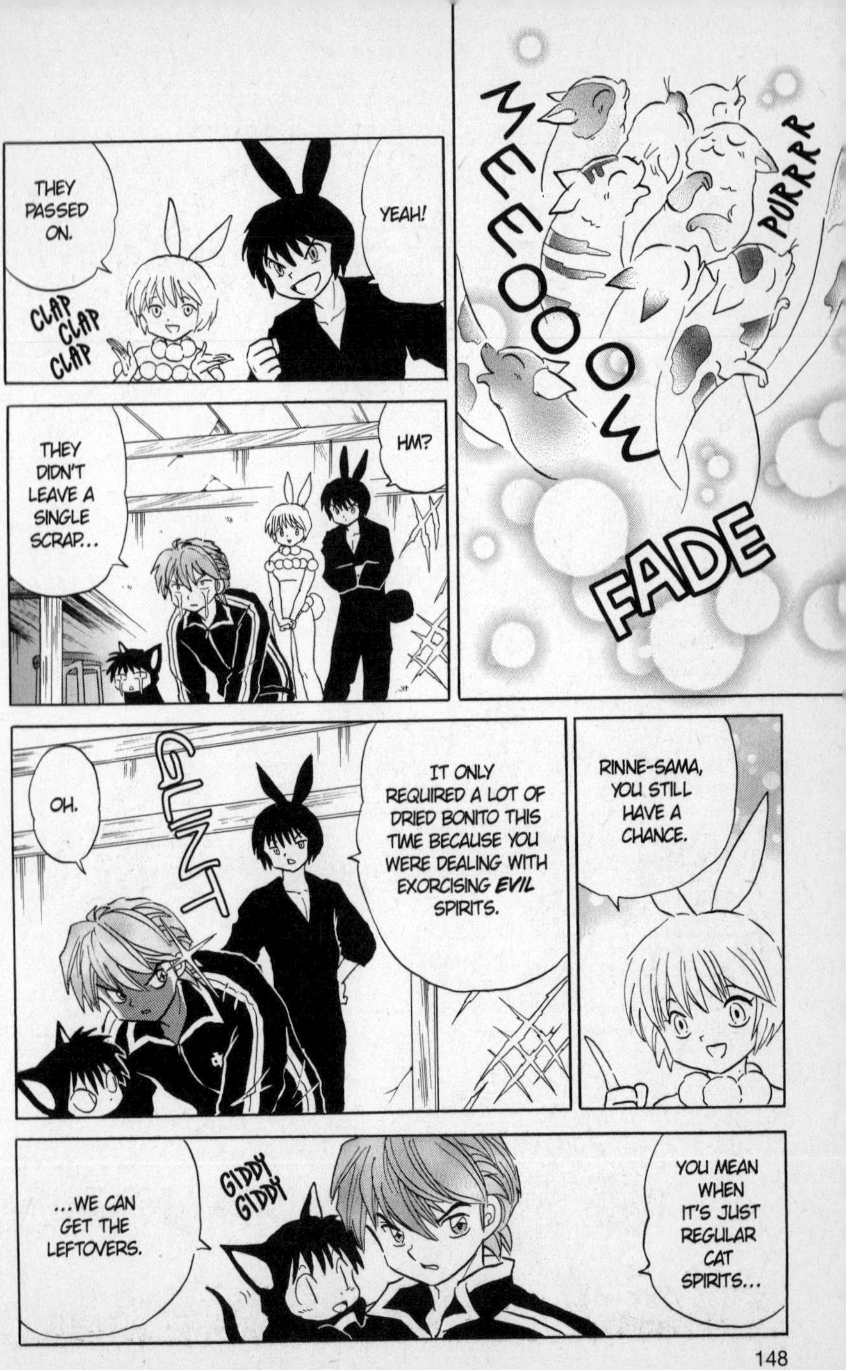
PURRRR
MEEOOOW
FADE
YEAH!
THEY PASSED ON.
CLAP CLAP CLAP
HM?
THEY DIDN'T LEAVE A SINGLE SCRAP...
RINNE-SAMA, YOU STILL HAVE A CHANCE.
IT ONLY REQUIRED A LOT OF DRIED BONITO THIS TIME BECAUSE YOU WERE DEALING WITH EXORCISING *EVIL* SPIRITS.
GLINT
OH.
YOU MEAN WHEN IT'S JUST REGULAR CAT SPIRITS...
GIDDY GIDDY
...WE CAN GET THE LEFTOVERS.

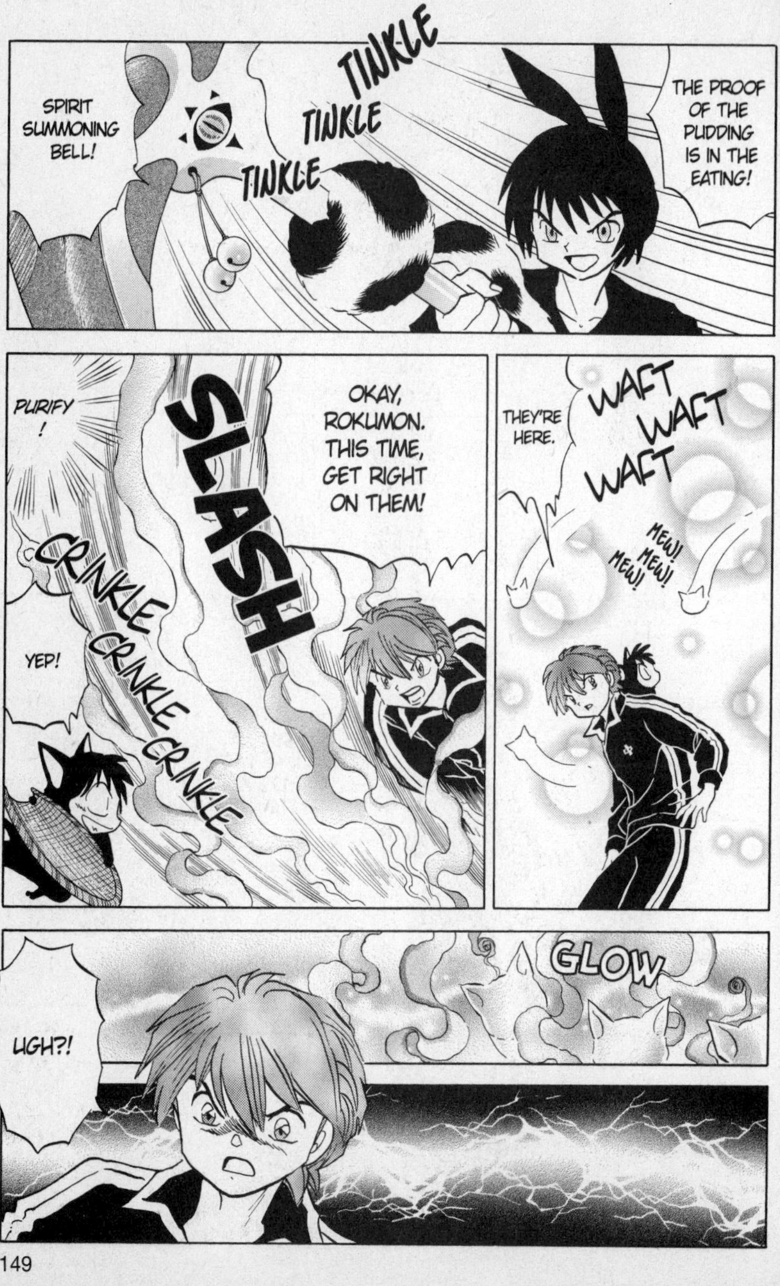
THE PROOF OF THE PUDDING IS IN THE EATING!
TINKLE
TINKLE
TINKLE
SPIRIT SUMMONING BELL!
THEY'RE HERE.
WAFT WAFT WAFT
MEW! MEW! MEW!
OKAY, ROKUMON. THIS TIME, GET RIGHT ON THEM!
SLASH
PURIFY!
CRINKLE CRINKLE CRINKLE
YEP!
GLOW
UGH?!

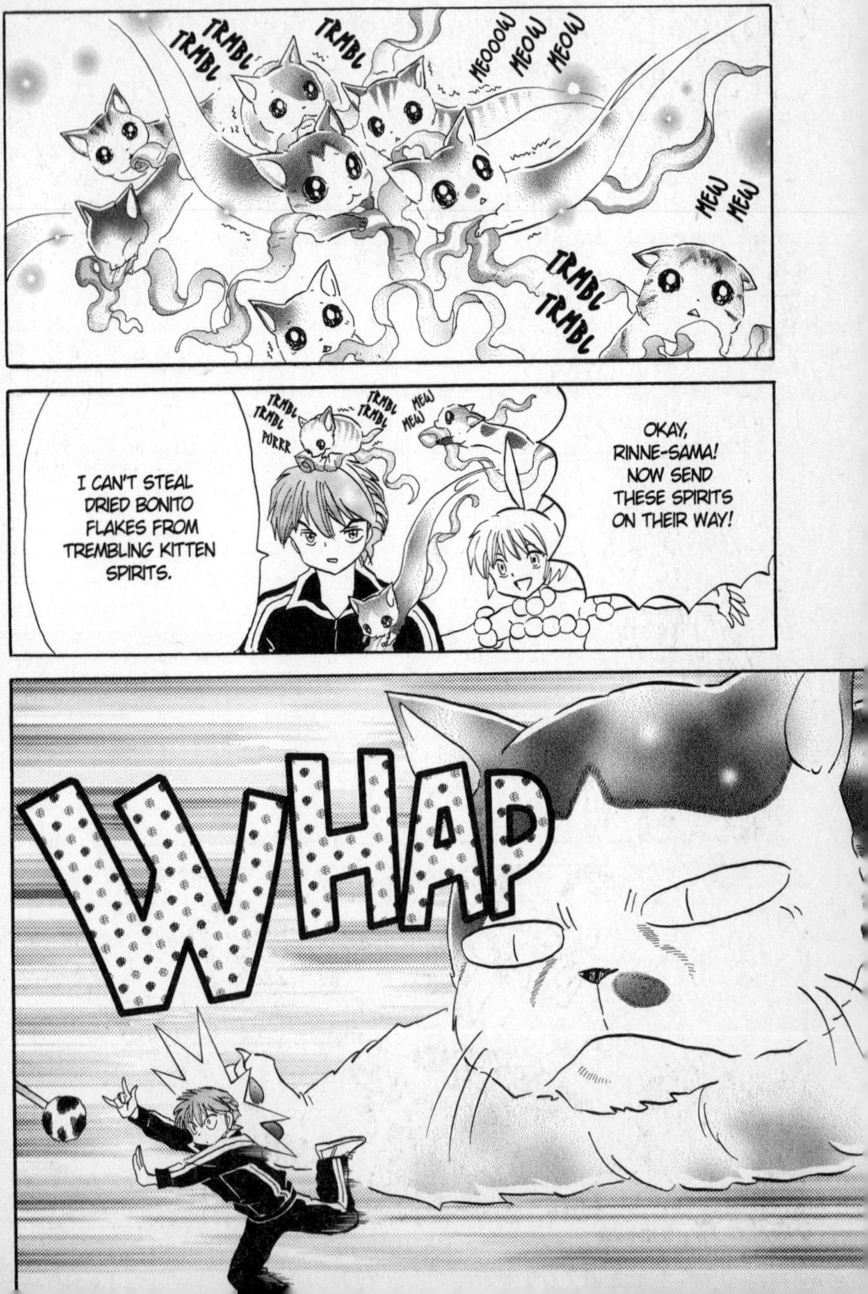
MEW MEW
MEOOOW MEOW MEOW
TRMBL
TRMBL TRMBL
TRMBL TRMBL
OKAY, RINNE-SAMA! NOW SEND THESE SPIRITS ON THEIR WAY!
MEW MEW
TRMBL TRMBL
TRMBL TRMBL PURRR
I CAN'T STEAL DRIED BONITO FLAKES FROM TREMBLING KITTEN SPIRITS.
WHAP

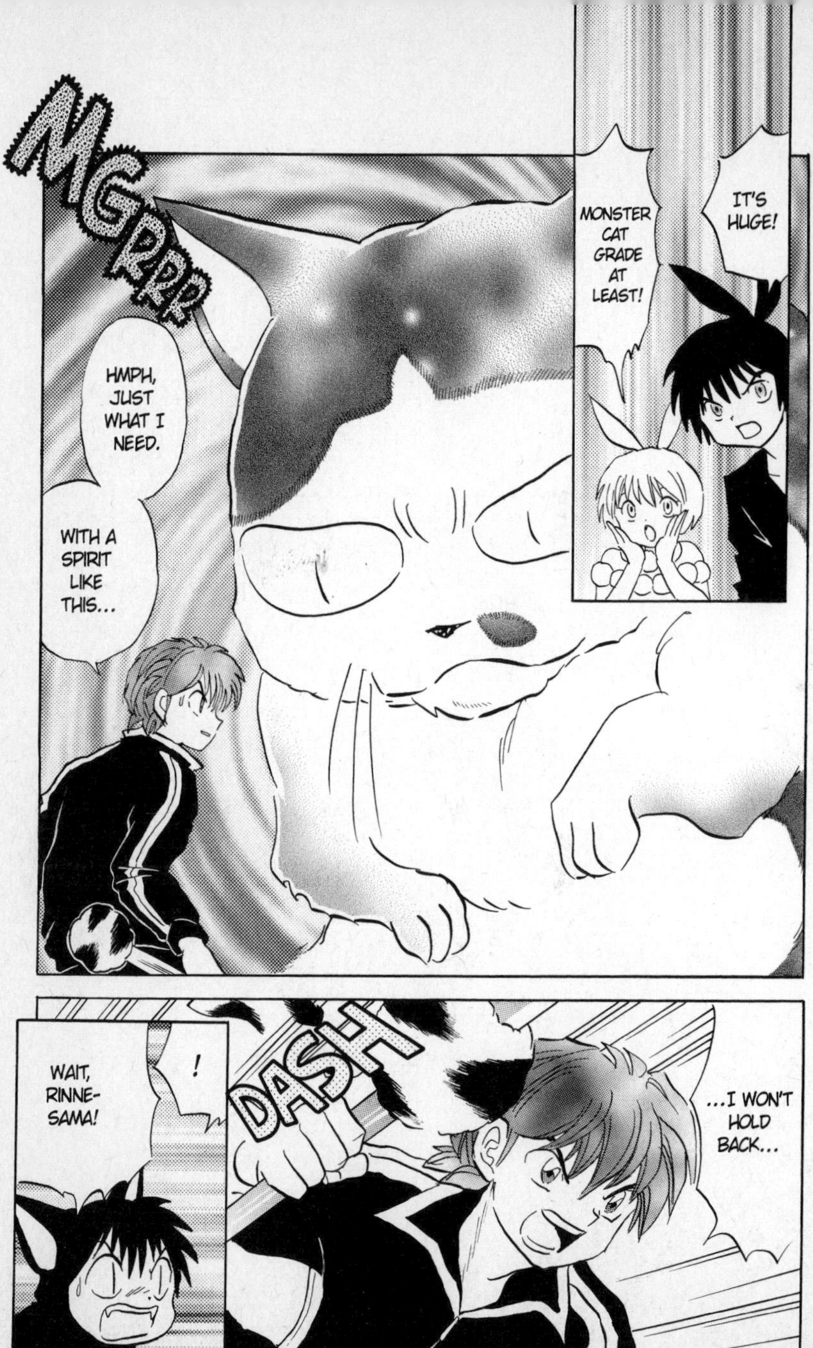
IT'S HUGE!
MONSTER CAT GRADE AT LEAST!
MGRRR
HMPH, JUST WHAT I NEED.
WITH A SPIRIT LIKE THIS...
...I WON'T HOLD BACK...
DASH
!
WAIT, RINNE-SAMA!

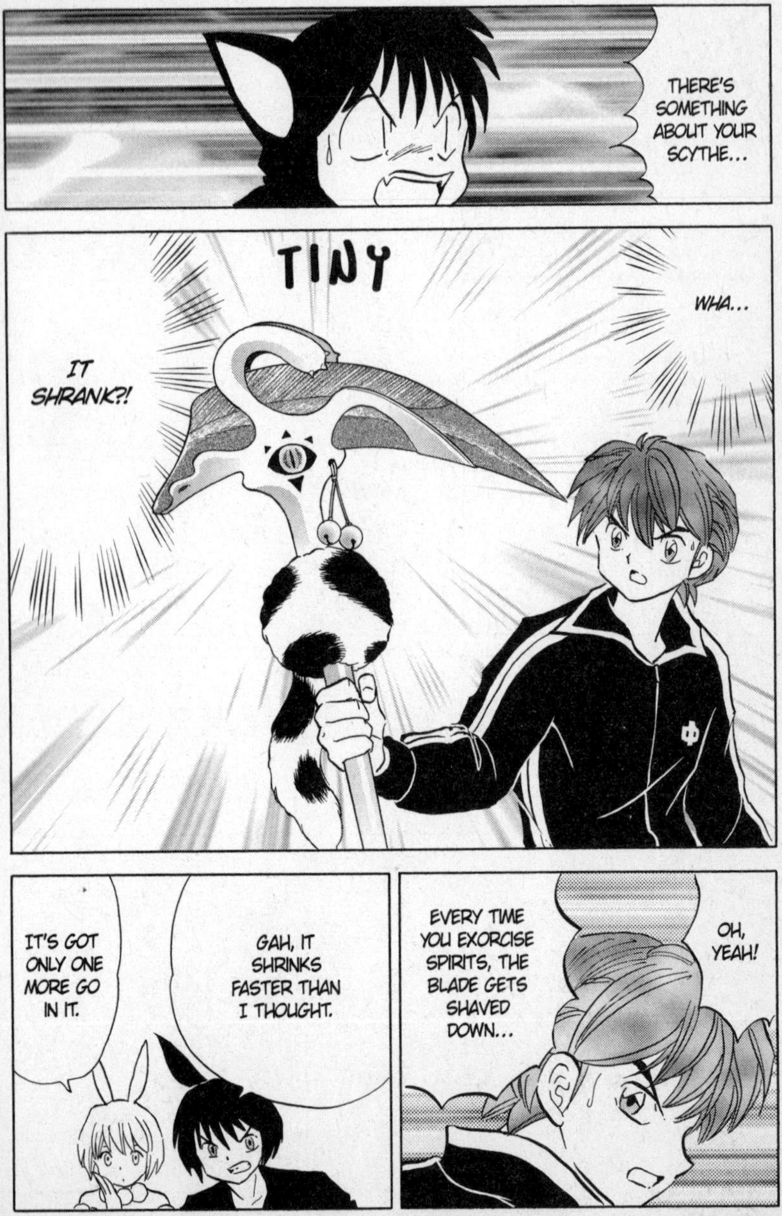
THERE'S SOMETHING ABOUT YOUR SCYTHE...
TINY
WHA...
IT SHRANK?!
OH, YEAH!
EVERY TIME YOU EXORCISE SPIRITS, THE BLADE GETS SHAVED DOWN...
GAH, IT SHRINKS FASTER THAN I THOUGHT.
IT'S GOT ONLY ONE MORE GO IN IT.

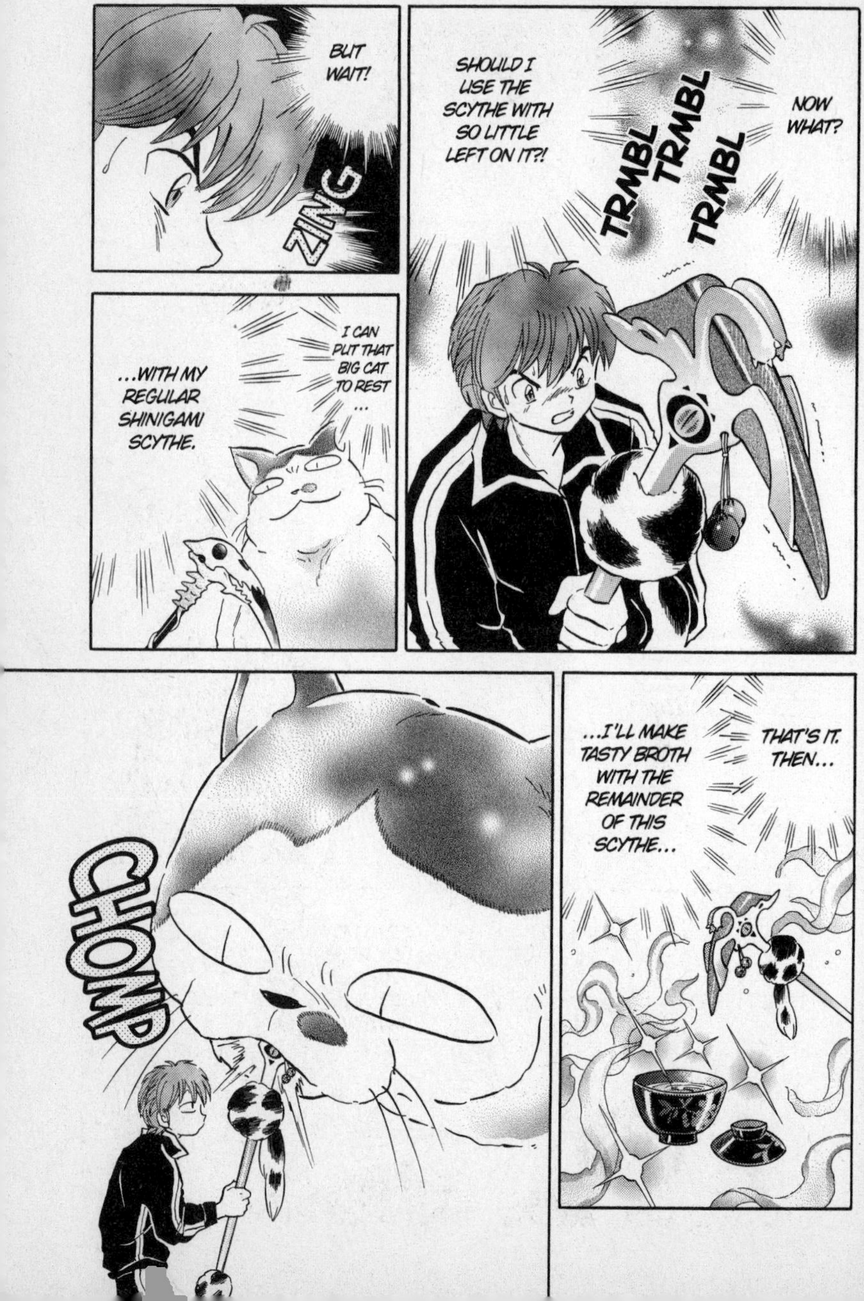
NOW WHAT?
TRMBL TRMBL TRMBL
SHOULD I USE THE SCYTHE WITH SO LITTLE LEFT ON IT?!
BUT WAIT!
ZING
I CAN PUT THAT BIG CAT TO REST...
...WITH MY REGULAR SHINIGAMI SCYTHE.
THAT'S IT. THEN...
...I'LL MAKE TASTY BROTH WITH THE REMAINDER OF THIS SCYTHE...
CHOMP

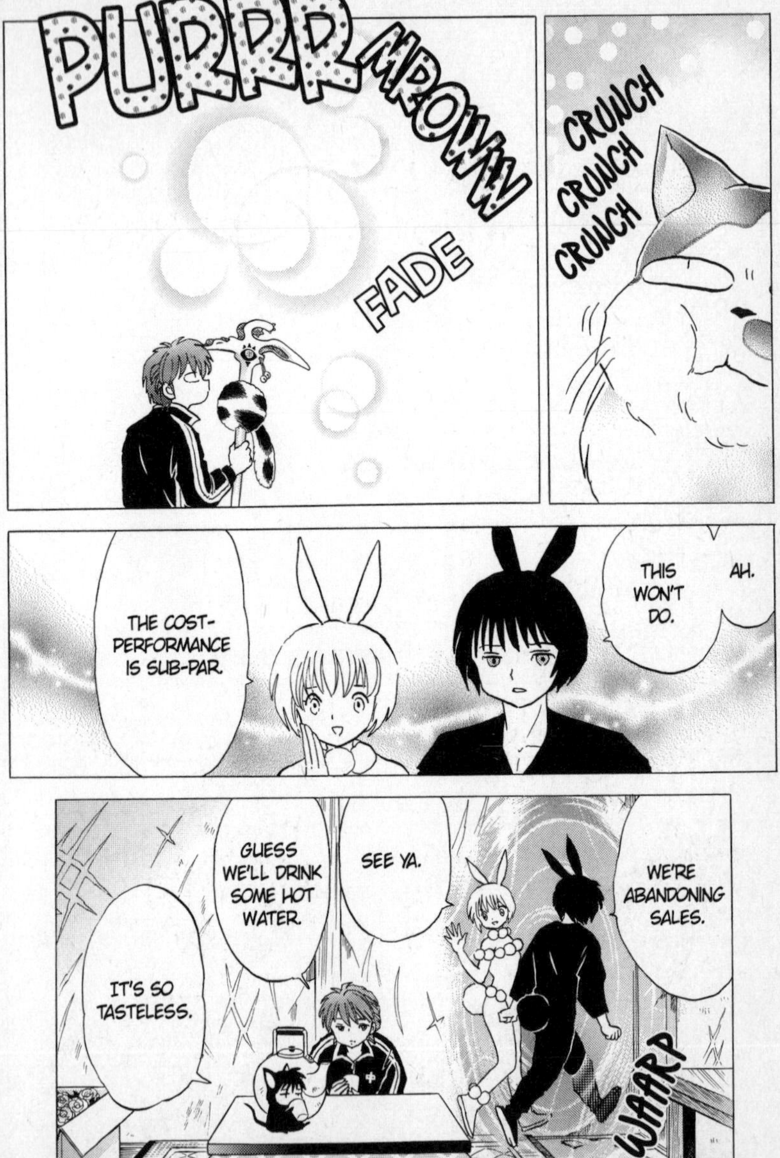
CRUNCH CRUNCH CRUNCH
PURRR
MROWW
FADE
AH.
THIS WON'T DO.
THE COST-PERFORMANCE IS SUB-PAR.
WE'RE ABANDONING SALES.
SEE YA.
GUESS WE'LL DRINK SOME HOT WATER.
IT'S SO TASTELESS.
WARRP

CHAPTER 127:
THE CHRISTMAS INCIDENT

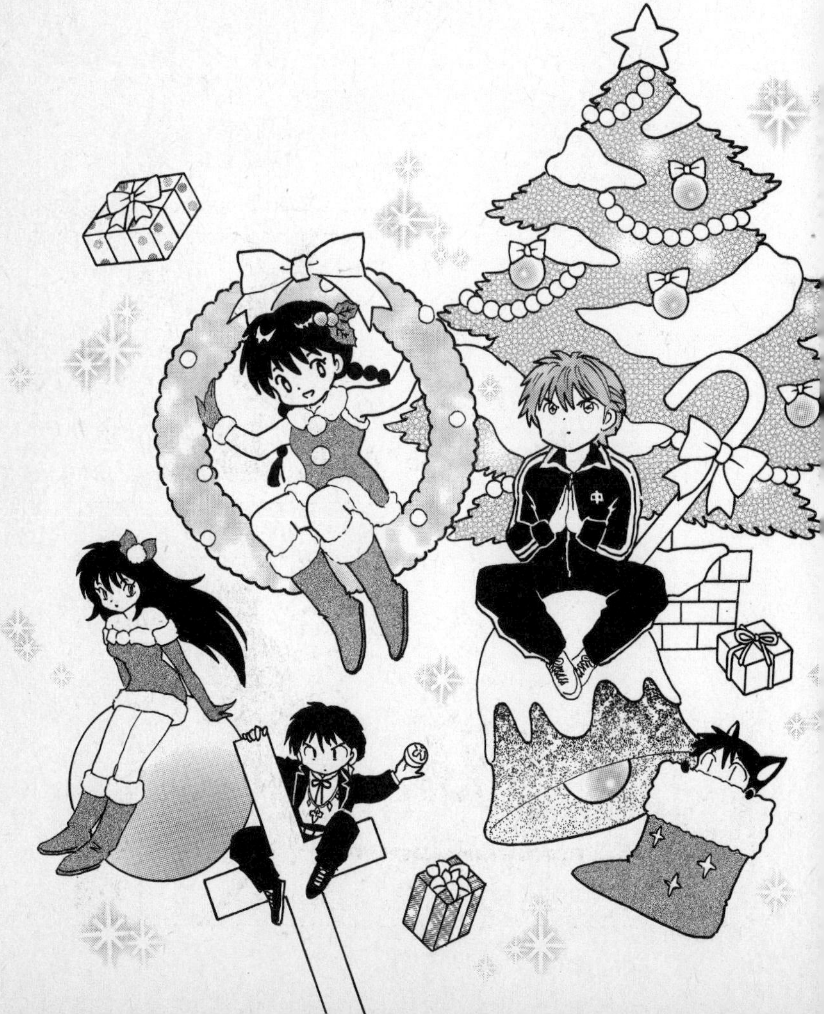

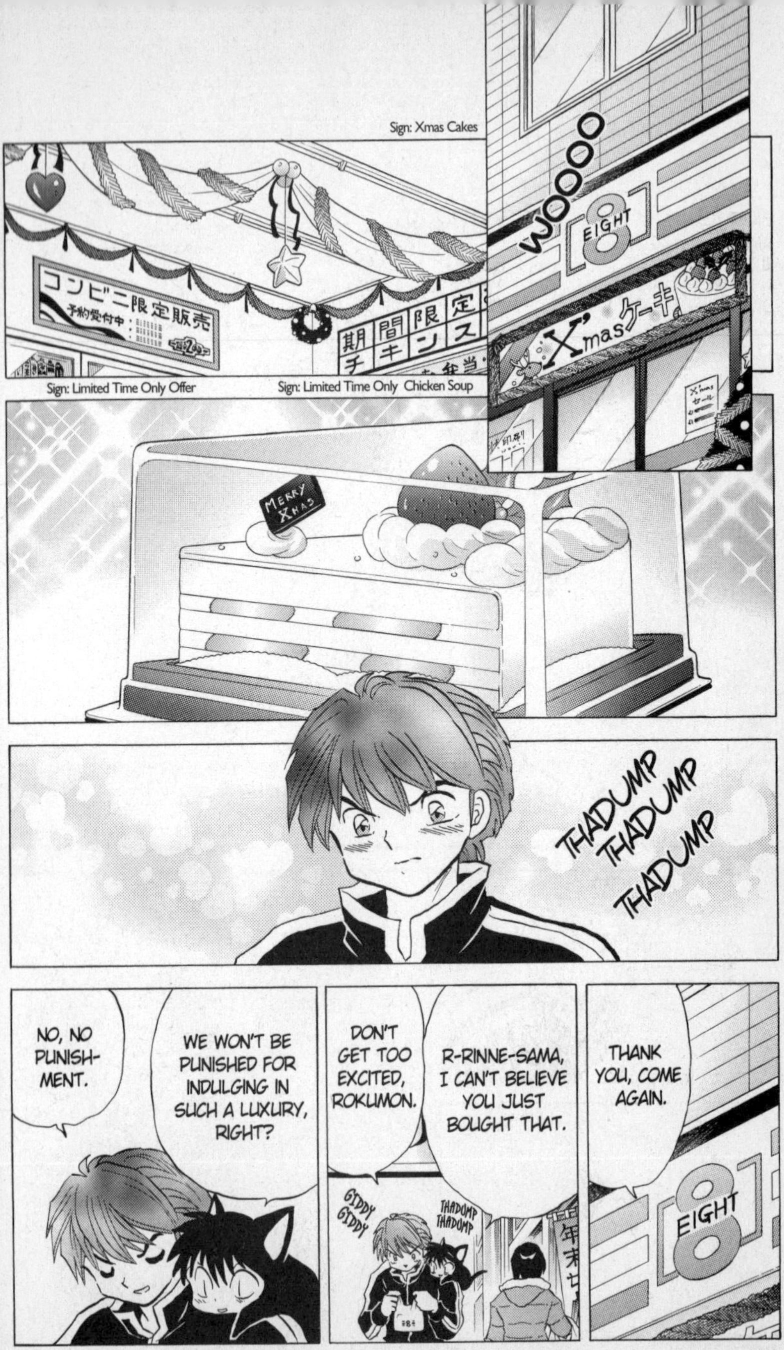
WOOOO
EIGHT
X'mas ケーキ
Sign: Xmas Cakes
コンビニ限定販売
予約受付中
Sign: Limited Time Only Offer
期間限定
Sign: Limited Time Only Chicken Soup
MERRY X'MAS
THADUMP THADUMP THADUMP
THANK YOU, COME AGAIN.
EIGHT
R-RINNE-SAMA, I CAN'T BELIEVE YOU JUST BOUGHT THAT.
DON'T GET TOO EXCITED, ROKUMON.
GIDDY GIDDY
THADUMP THADUMP
WE WON'T BE PUNISHED FOR INDULGING IN SUCH A LUXURY, RIGHT?
NO, NO PUNISHMENT.

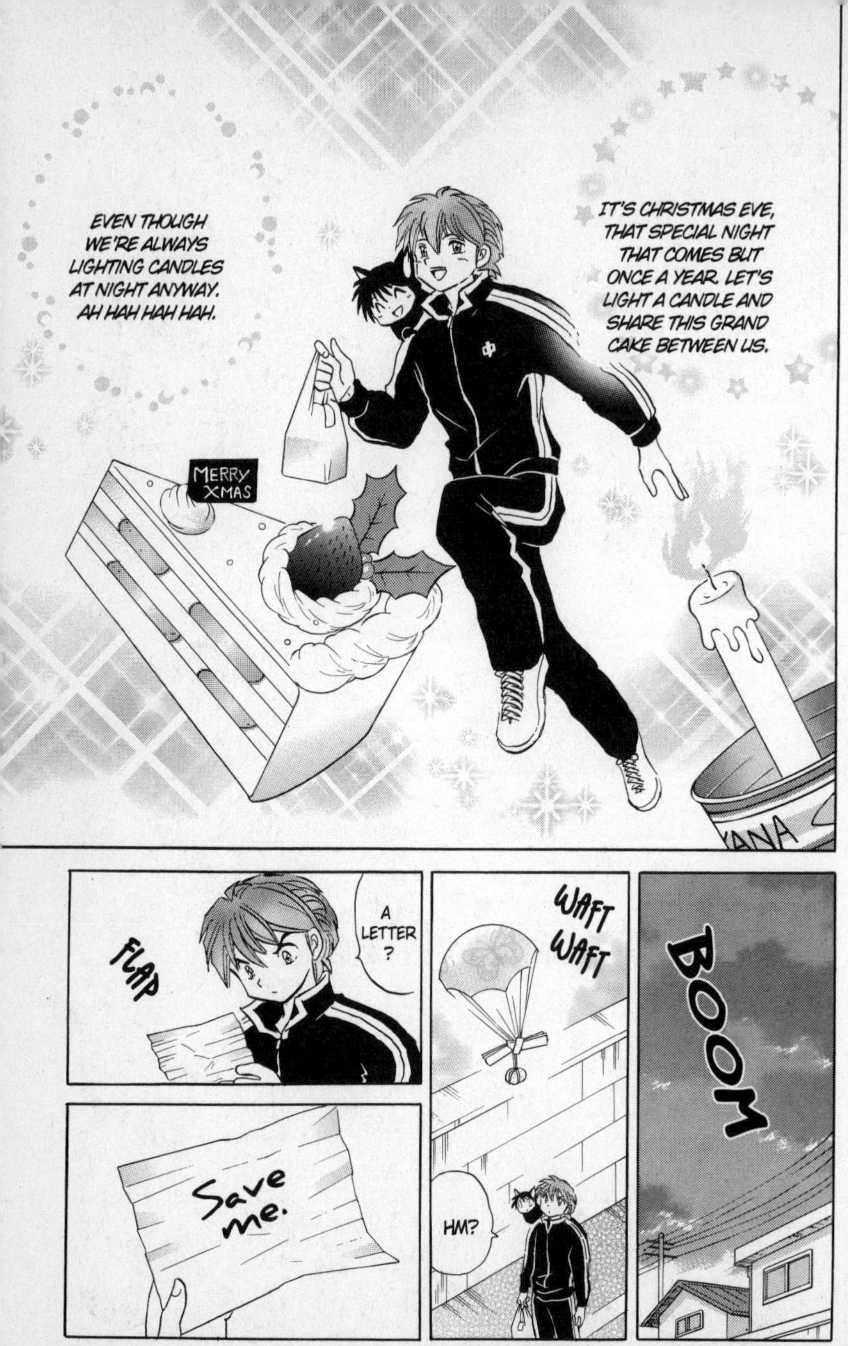
IT'S CHRISTMAS EVE, THAT SPECIAL NIGHT THAT COMES BUT ONCE A YEAR. LET'S LIGHT A CANDLE AND SHARE THIS GRAND CAKE BETWEEN US.
EVEN THOUGH WE'RE ALWAYS LIGHTING CANDLES AT NIGHT ANYWAY. AH HAH HAH HAH.
MERRY XMAS
BOOM
WAFT WAFT
HM?
A LETTER?
FLAP
Save me.

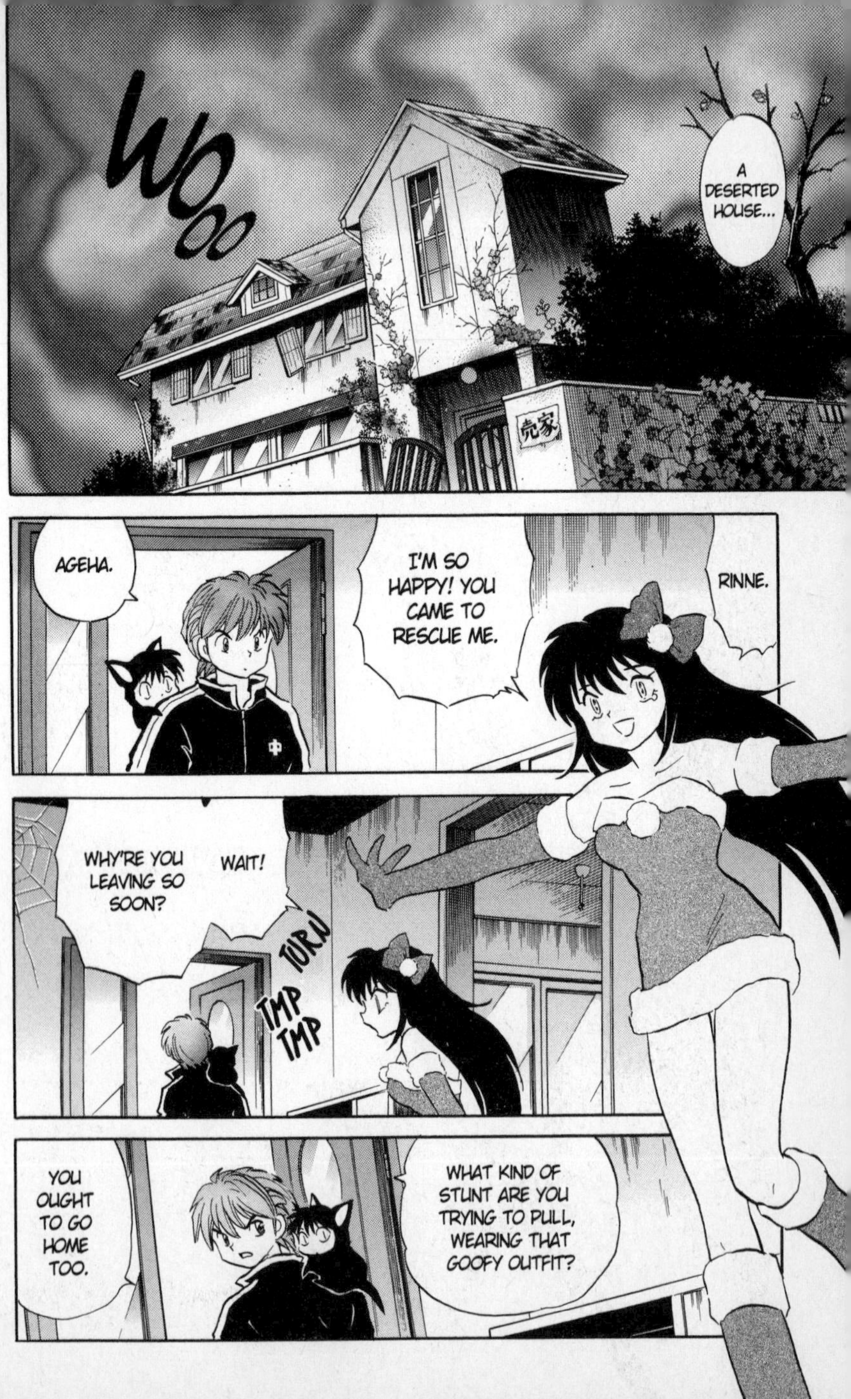
A DESERTED HOUSE...
WOOO
売家
RINNE.
I'M SO HAPPY! YOU CAME TO RESCUE ME.
AGEHA.
WAIT!
WHY'RE YOU LEAVING SO SOON?
TORU
TMP TMP
WHAT KIND OF STUNT ARE YOU TRYING TO PULL, WEARING THAT GOOFY OUTFIT?
YOU OUGHT TO GO HOME TOO.

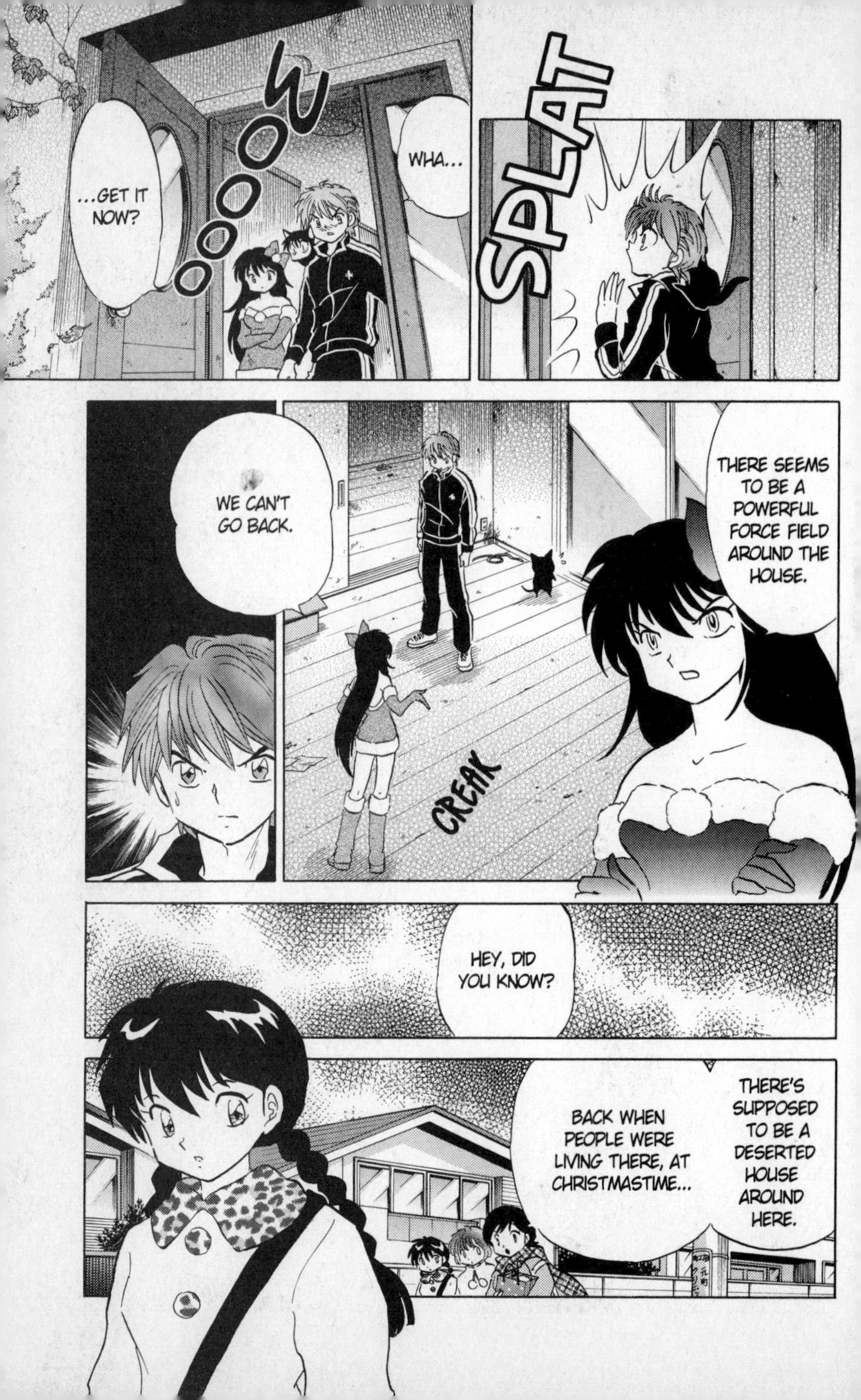
SPLAT
WHA...
WOOOO
...GET IT NOW?
THERE SEEMS TO BE A POWERFUL FORCE FIELD AROUND THE HOUSE.
CREAK
WE CAN'T GO BACK.
HEY, DID YOU KNOW?
THERE'S SUPPOSED TO BE A DESERTED HOUSE AROUND HERE.
BACK WHEN PEOPLE WERE LIVING THERE, AT CHRISTMASTIME...

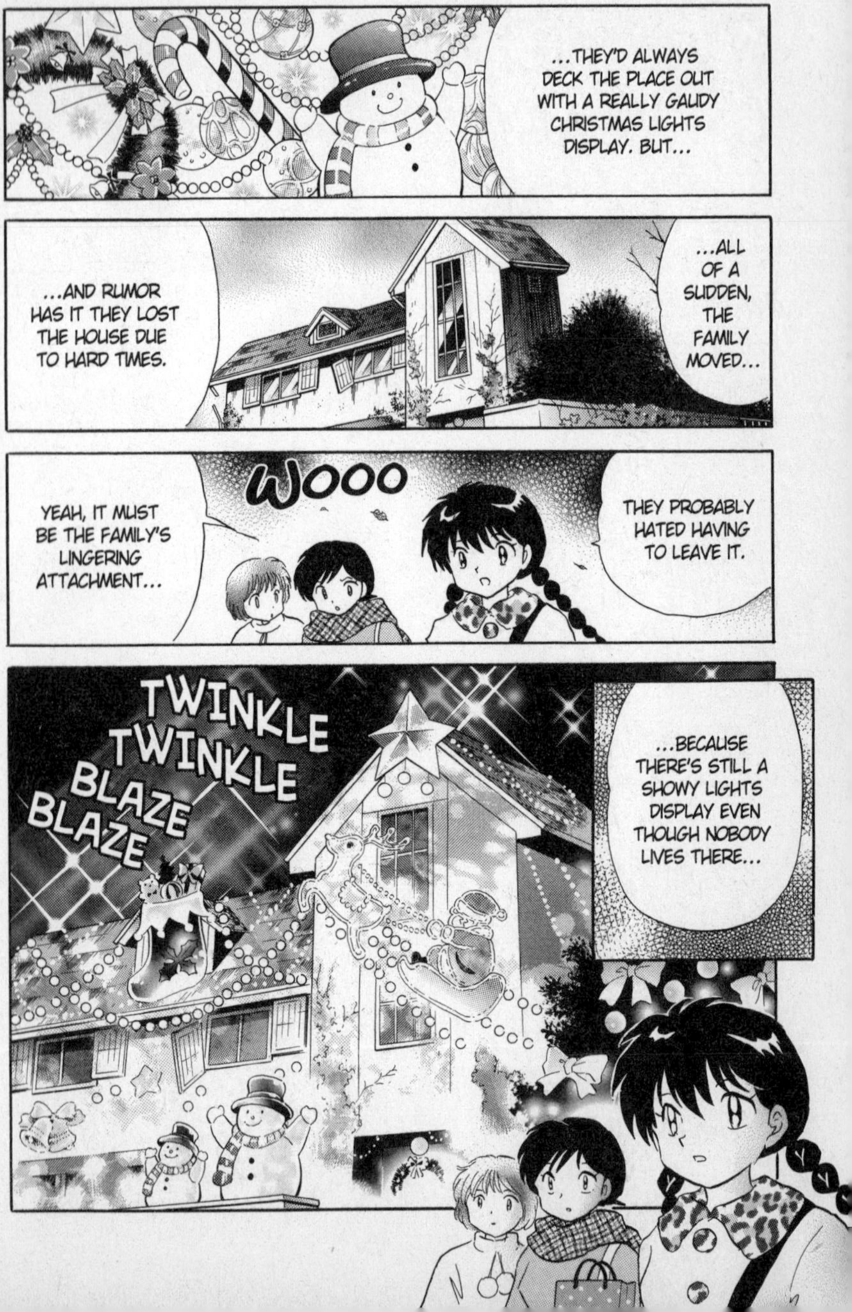
...THEY'D ALWAYS DECK THE PLACE OUT WITH A REALLY GAUDY CHRISTMAS LIGHTS DISPLAY. BUT...
...ALL OF A SUDDEN, THE FAMILY MOVED...
...AND RUMOR HAS IT THEY LOST THE HOUSE DUE TO HARD TIMES.
THEY PROBABLY HATED HAVING TO LEAVE IT.
WOOO
YEAH, IT MUST BE THE FAMILY'S LINGERING ATTACHMENT...
...BECAUSE THERE'S STILL A SHOWY LIGHTS DISPLAY EVEN THOUGH NOBODY LIVES THERE...
TWINKLE TWINKLE
BLAZE BLAZE

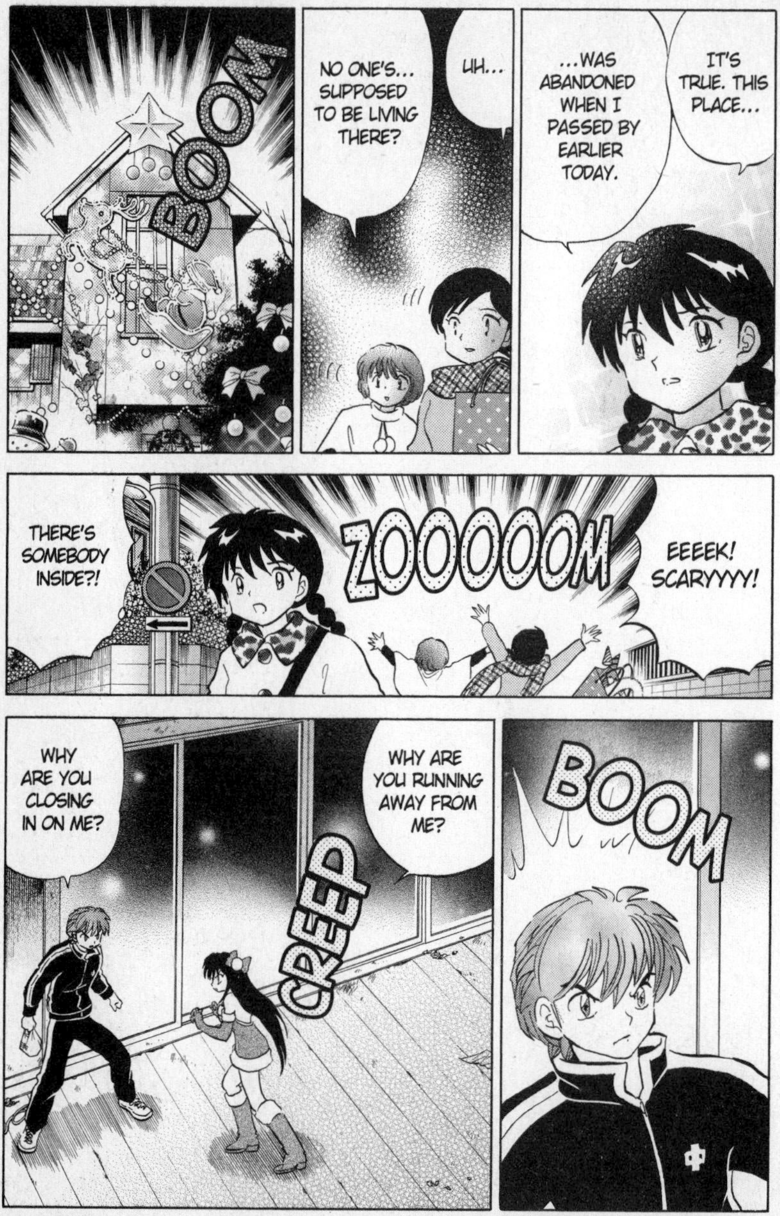
IT'S TRUE. THIS PLACE...
...WAS ABANDONED WHEN I PASSED BY EARLIER TODAY.
UH...
NO ONE'S... SUPPOSED TO BE LIVING THERE?
BOOM
EEEEK! SCARYYYY!
ZOOOOOM
THERE'S SOMEBODY INSIDE?!
BOOM
WHY ARE YOU RUNNING AWAY FROM ME?
CREEP
WHY ARE YOU CLOSING IN ON ME?

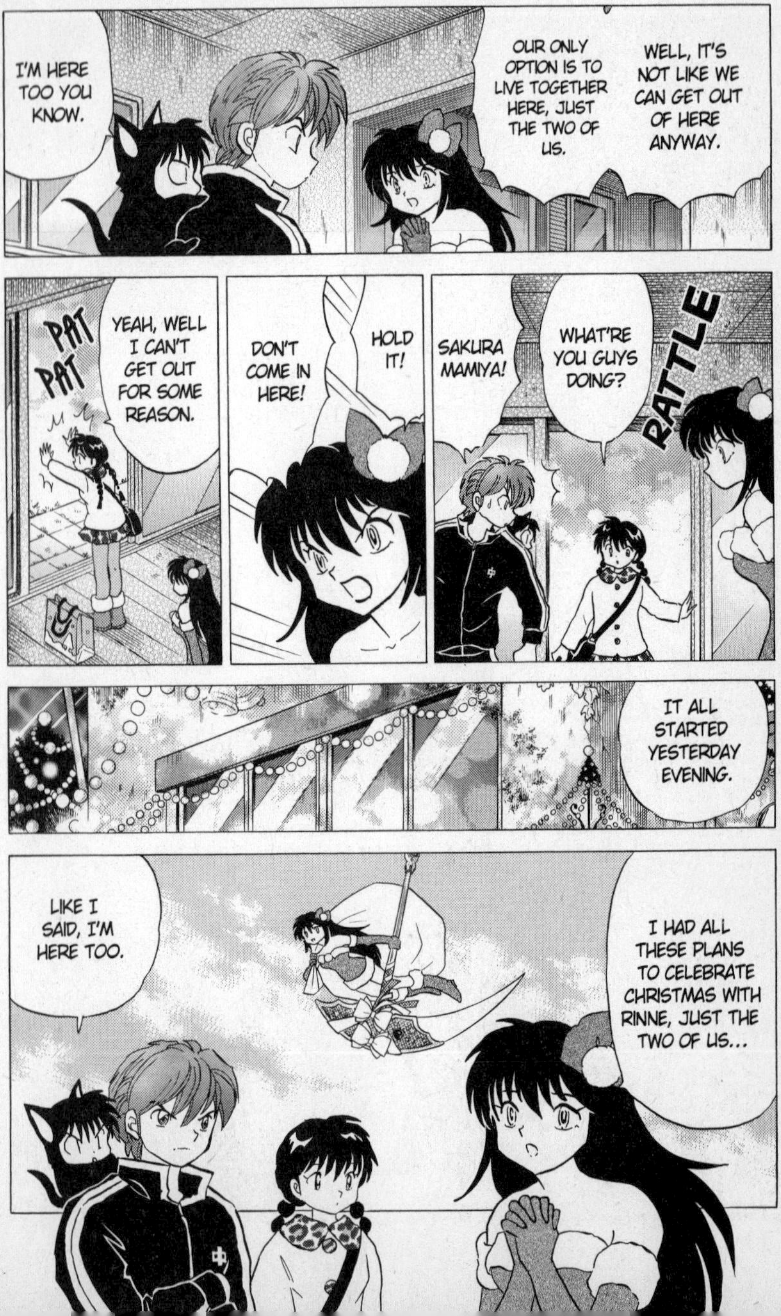
WELL, IT'S NOT LIKE WE CAN GET OUT OF HERE ANYWAY.
OUR ONLY OPTION IS TO LIVE TOGETHER HERE, JUST THE TWO OF US.
I'M HERE TOO YOU KNOW.
RATTLE
WHAT'RE YOU GUYS DOING?
SAKURA MAMIYA!
HOLD IT!
DON'T COME IN HERE!
YEAH, WELL I CAN'T GET OUT FOR SOME REASON.
PAT PAT
IT ALL STARTED YESTERDAY EVENING.
I HAD ALL THESE PLANS TO CELEBRATE CHRISTMAS WITH RINNE, JUST THE TWO OF US...
LIKE I SAID, I'M HERE TOO.

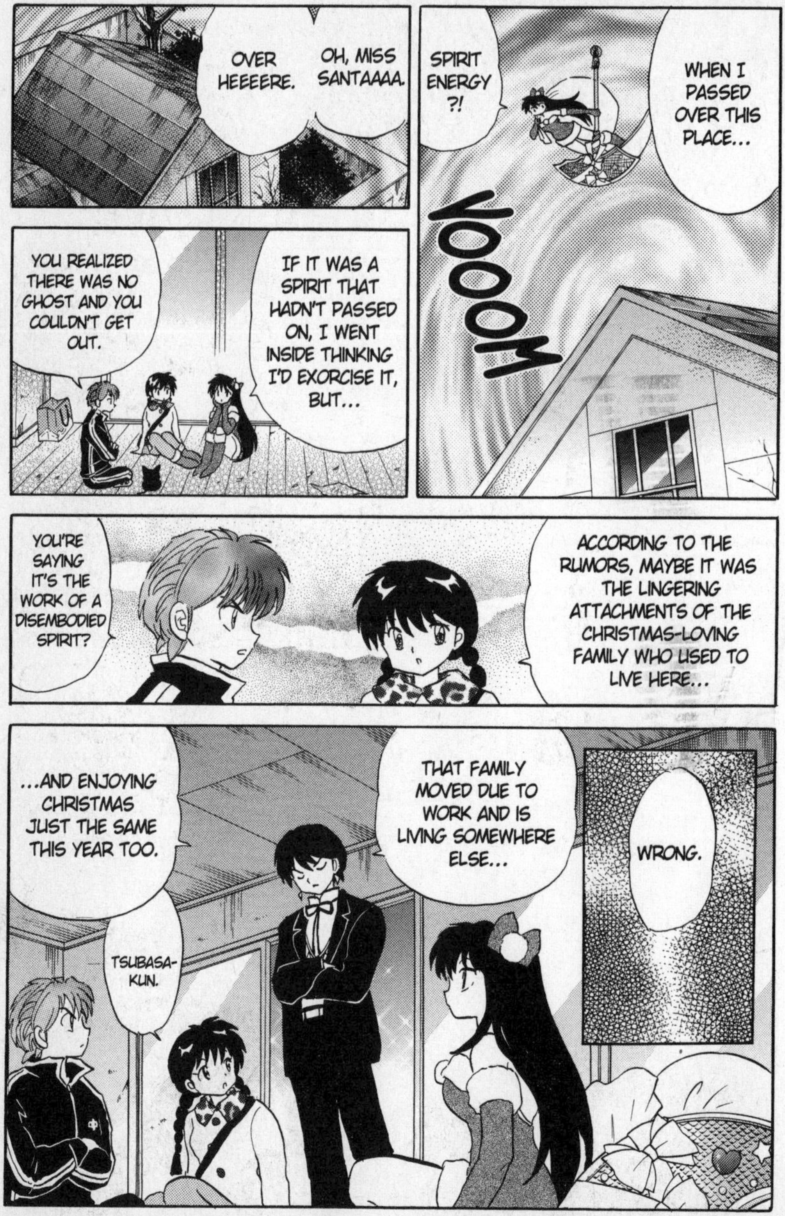
WHEN I PASSED OVER THIS PLACE...
SPIRIT ENERGY ?!
VOOOOM
OH, MISS SANTAAAA.
OVER HEEEERE.
IF IT WAS A SPIRIT THAT HADN'T PASSED ON, I WENT INSIDE THINKING I'D EXORCISE IT, BUT...
YOU REALIZED THERE WAS NO GHOST AND YOU COULDN'T GET OUT.
ACCORDING TO THE RUMORS, MAYBE IT WAS THE LINGERING ATTACHMENTS OF THE CHRISTMAS-LOVING FAMILY WHO USED TO LIVE HERE...
YOU'RE SAYING IT'S THE WORK OF A DISEMBODIED SPIRIT?
WRONG.
THAT FAMILY MOVED DUE TO WORK AND IS LIVING SOMEWHERE ELSE...
...AND ENJOYING CHRISTMAS JUST THE SAME THIS YEAR TOO.
TSUBASA-KUN.

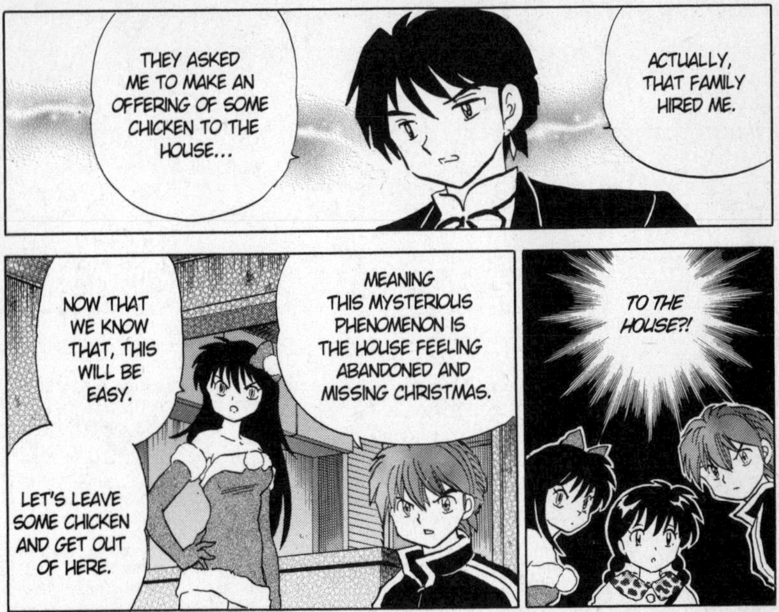
ACTUALLY, THAT FAMILY HIRED ME.
THEY ASKED ME TO MAKE AN OFFERING OF SOME CHICKEN TO THE HOUSE...
TO THE HOUSE?!
MEANING THIS MYSTERIOUS PHENOMENON IS THE HOUSE FEELING ABANDONED AND MISSING CHRISTMAS.
NOW THAT WE KNOW THAT, THIS WILL BE EASY.
LET'S LEAVE SOME CHICKEN AND GET OUT OF HERE.

*In Japan, Christmas Eve is celebrated with fried chicken and cake.

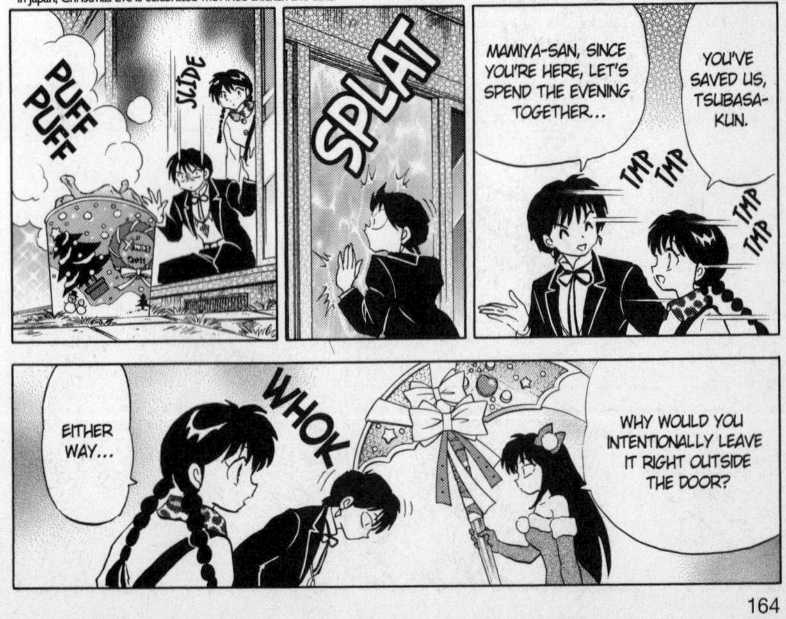
YOU'VE SAVED US, TSUBASA-KUN.
MAMIYA-SAN, SINCE YOU'RE HERE, LET'S SPEND THE EVENING TOGETHER...
TMP TMP
TMP TMP
SPLAT
SLIDE
PUFF PUFF
WHY WOULD YOU INTENTIONALLY LEAVE IT RIGHT OUTSIDE THE DOOR?
WHOK
EITHER WAY...

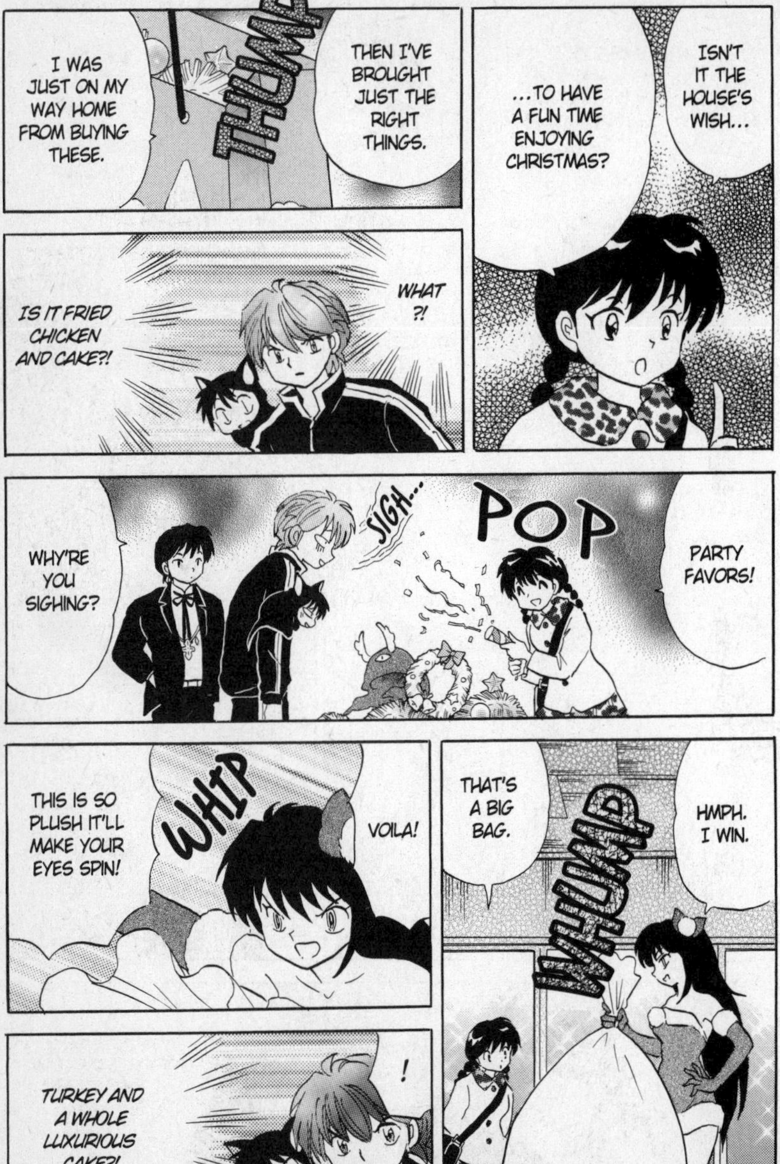
ISN'T IT THE HOUSE'S WISH...
...TO HAVE A FUN TIME ENJOYING CHRISTMAS?
THEN I'VE BROUGHT JUST THE RIGHT THINGS.
THUMP
I WAS JUST ON MY WAY HOME FROM BUYING THESE.
WHAT?!
IS IT FRIED CHICKEN AND CAKE?!
PARTY FAVORS!
POP
SIGH...
WHY'RE YOU SIGHING?
HMPH. I WIN.
WHUMP
THAT'S A BIG BAG.
VOILA!
WHIP
THIS IS SO PLUSH IT'LL MAKE YOUR EYES SPIN!
!
TURKEY AND A WHOLE LUXURIOUS CAKE?!

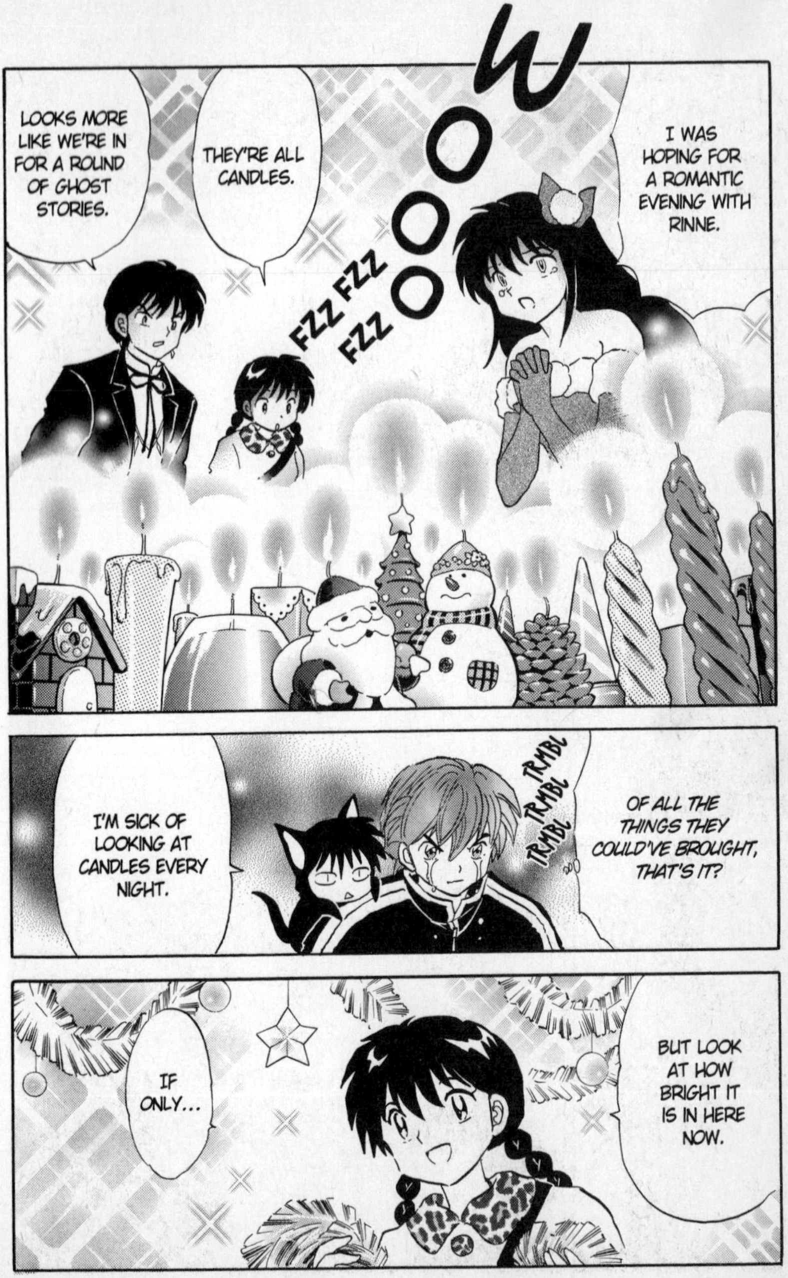
WOOOO
I WAS HOPING FOR A ROMANTIC EVENING WITH RINNE.
FZZ FZZ FZZ
THEY'RE ALL CANDLES.
LOOKS MORE LIKE WE'RE IN FOR A ROUND OF GHOST STORIES.
OF ALL THE THINGS THEY COULD'VE BROUGHT, THAT'S IT?
TRMBL TRMBL TRMBL
I'M SICK OF LOOKING AT CANDLES EVERY NIGHT.
BUT LOOK AT HOW BRIGHT IT IS IN HERE NOW.
IF ONLY...

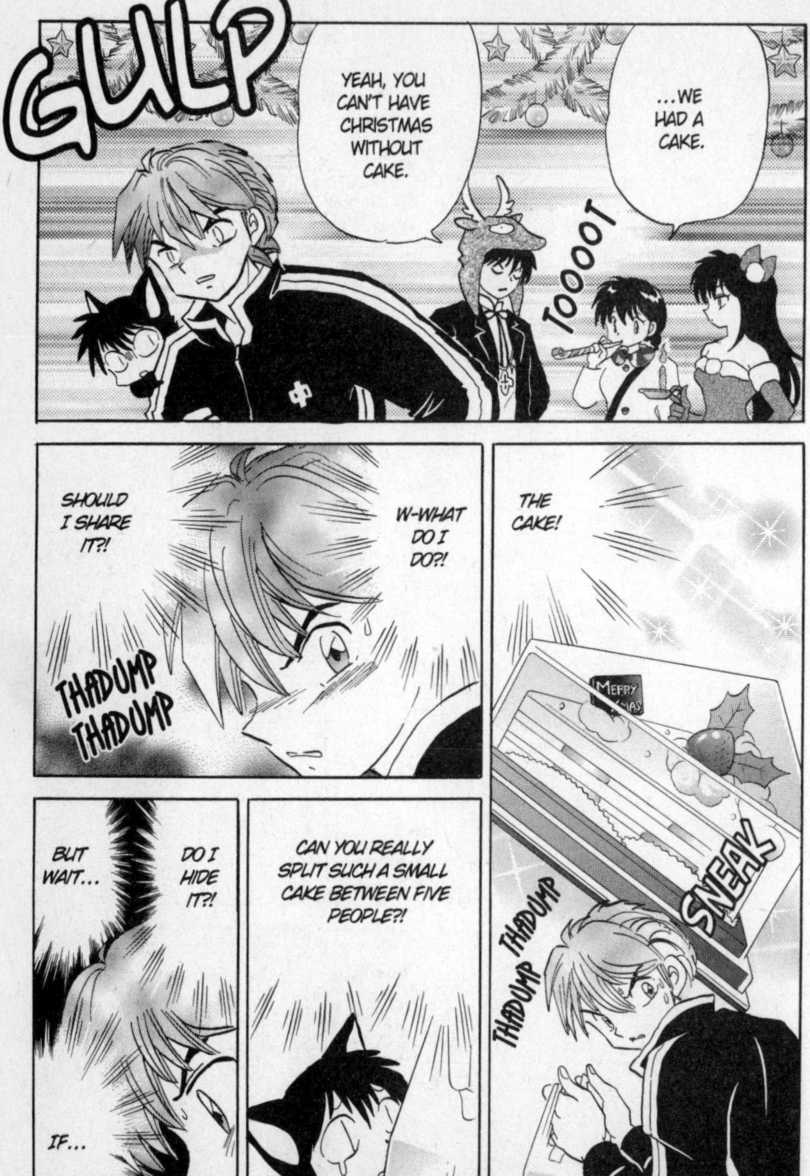
...WE HAD A CAKE.
YEAH, YOU CAN'T HAVE CHRISTMAS WITHOUT CAKE.
TOOOOT
GULP
THE CAKE!
W-WHAT DO I DO?!
SHOULD I SHARE IT?!
THADUMP THADUMP
MERRY
SNEAK
THADUMP THADUMP
CAN YOU REALLY SPLIT SUCH A SMALL CAKE BETWEEN FIVE PEOPLE?!
DO I HIDE IT?!
BUT WAIT...
IF...

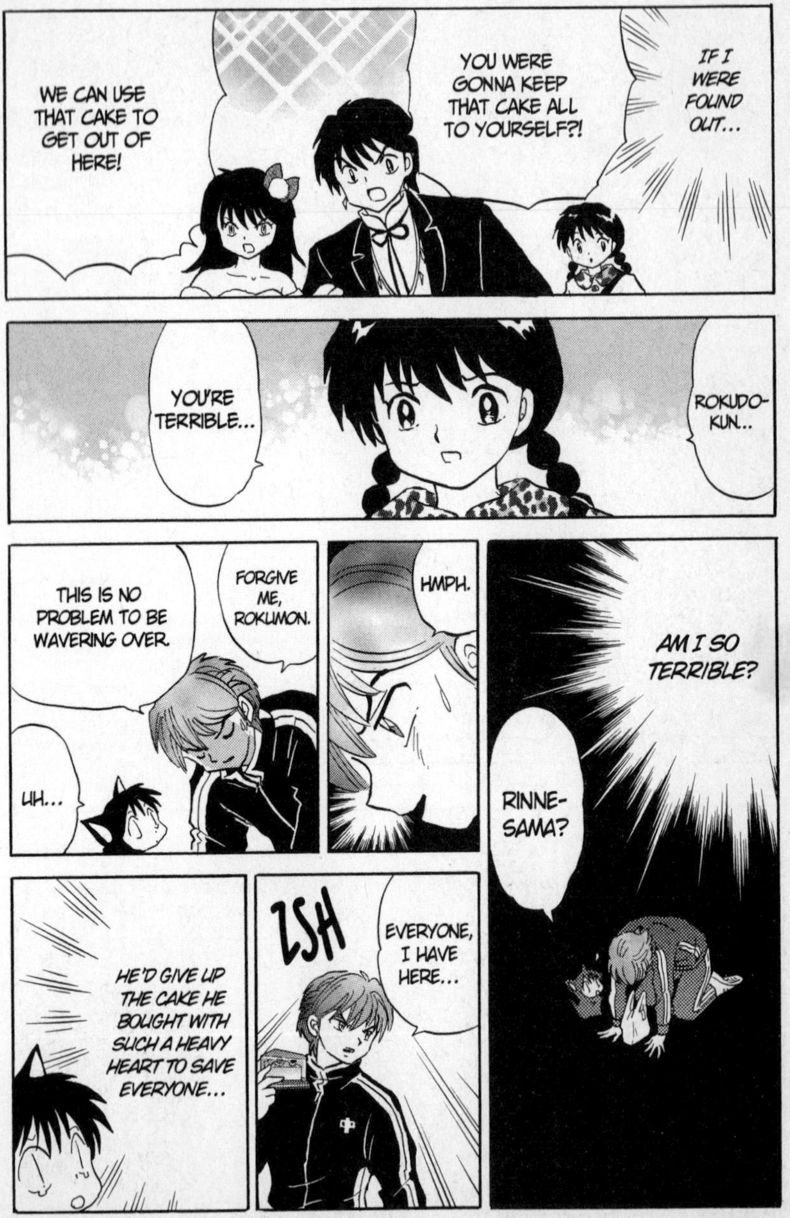
IF I WERE FOUND OUT...
YOU WERE GONNA KEEP THAT CAKE ALL TO YOURSELF?!
WE CAN USE THAT CAKE TO GET OUT OF HERE!
ROKUDO-KUN..
YOU'RE TERRIBLE...
AM I SO TERRIBLE?
RINNE-SAMA?
HMPH.
FORGIVE ME, ROKUMON.
THIS IS NO PROBLEM TO BE WAVERING OVER.
UH...
ZSH
EVERYONE, I HAVE HERE...
HE'D GIVE UP THE CAKE HE BOUGHT WITH SUCH A HEAVY HEART TO SAVE EVERYONE...

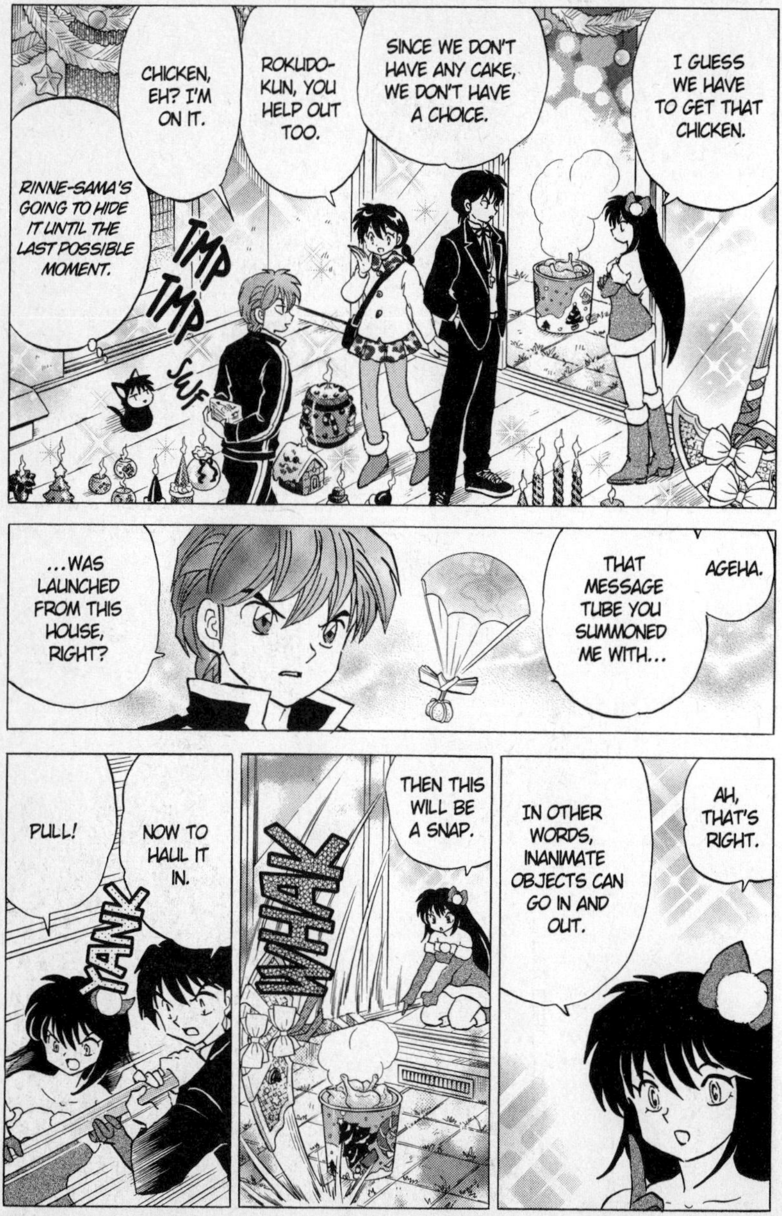
I GUESS WE HAVE TO GET THAT CHICKEN.
SINCE WE DON'T HAVE ANY CAKE, WE DON'T HAVE A CHOICE.
ROKUDO-KUN, YOU HELP OUT TOO.
CHICKEN, EH? I'M ON IT.
RINNE-SAMA'S GOING TO HIDE IT UNTIL THE LAST POSSIBLE MOMENT.
TMP TMP
SUF
AGEHA.
THAT MESSAGE TUBE YOU SUMMONED ME WITH...
...WAS LAUNCHED FROM THIS HOUSE, RIGHT?
AH, THAT'S RIGHT.
IN OTHER WORDS, INANIMATE OBJECTS CAN GO IN AND OUT.
THEN THIS WILL BE A SNAP.
WHAK
NOW TO HAUL IT IN.
PULL!
YANK

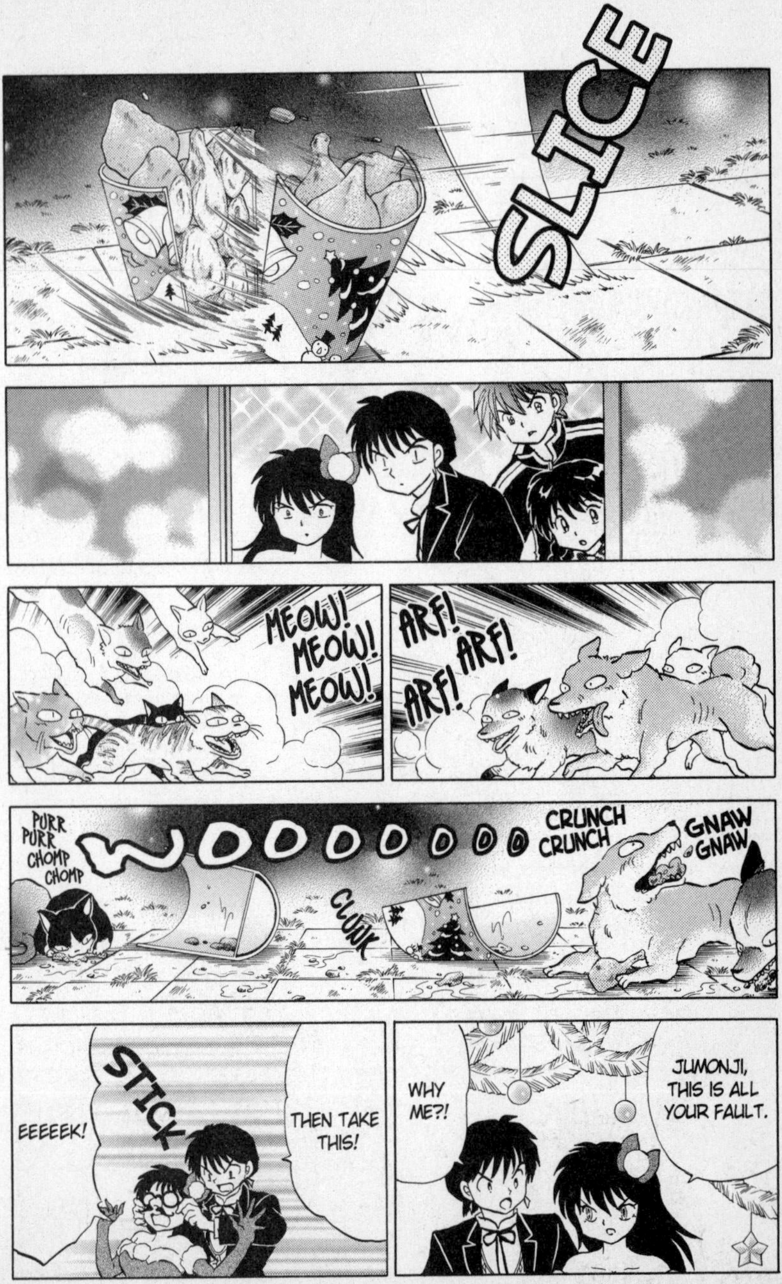
SLICE
ARF! ARF! ARF!
MEOW! MEOW! MEOW!
GNAW GNAW
CRUNCH CRUNCH
WOOOOOOO
CLUNK
PURR PURR CHOMP CHOMP
JUMONJI, THIS IS ALL YOUR FAULT.
WHY ME?!
THEN TAKE THIS!
STICK
EEEEEK!

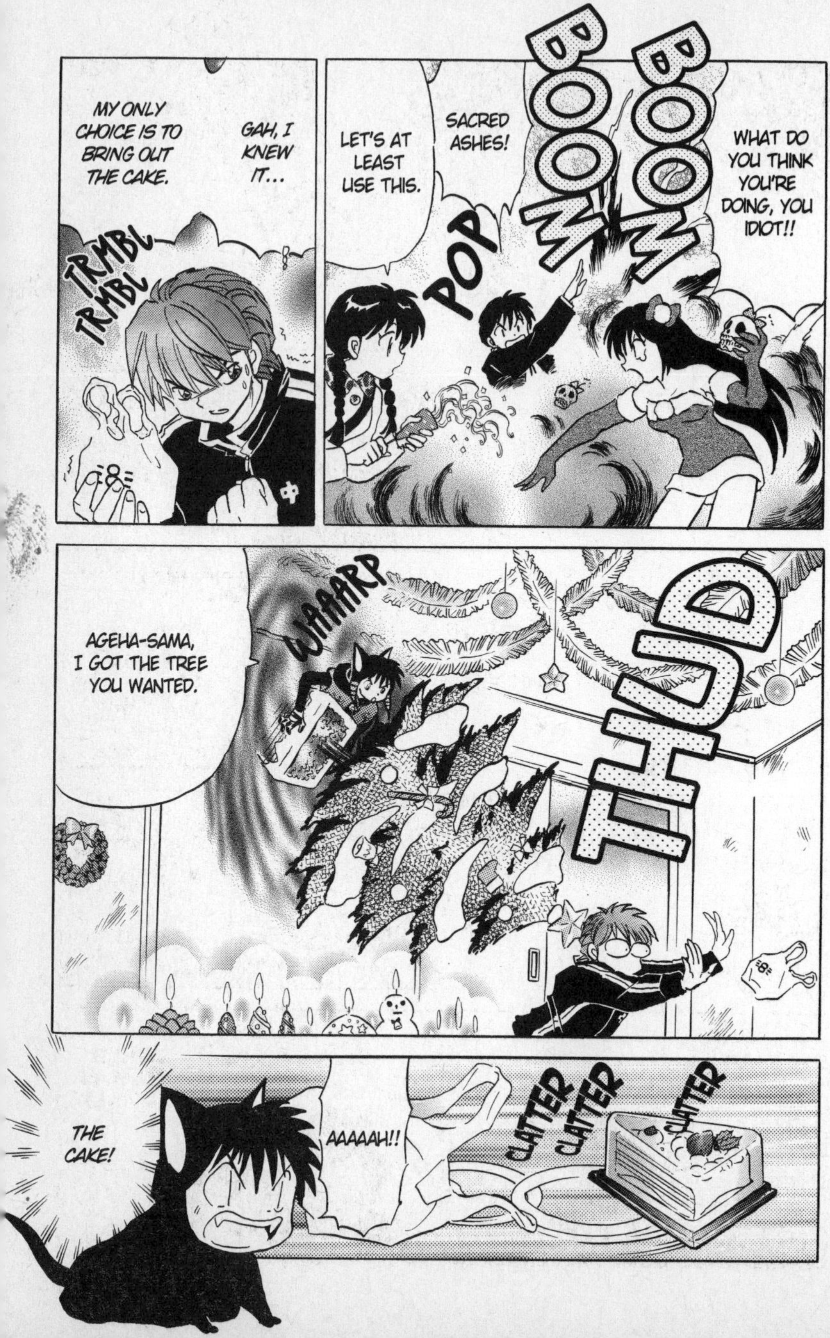

WHAT DO YOU THINK YOU'RE DOING, YOU IDIOT!!
BOOM
BOOM
SACRED ASHES!
LET'S AT LEAST USE THIS.
POP
GAH, I KNEW IT...
MY ONLY CHOICE IS TO BRING OUT THE CAKE.
TRMBL TRMBL
THUD
WAAARP
AGEHA-SAMA, I GOT THE TREE YOU WANTED.
CLATTER
CLATTER CLATTER
AAAAAH!!
THE CAKE!

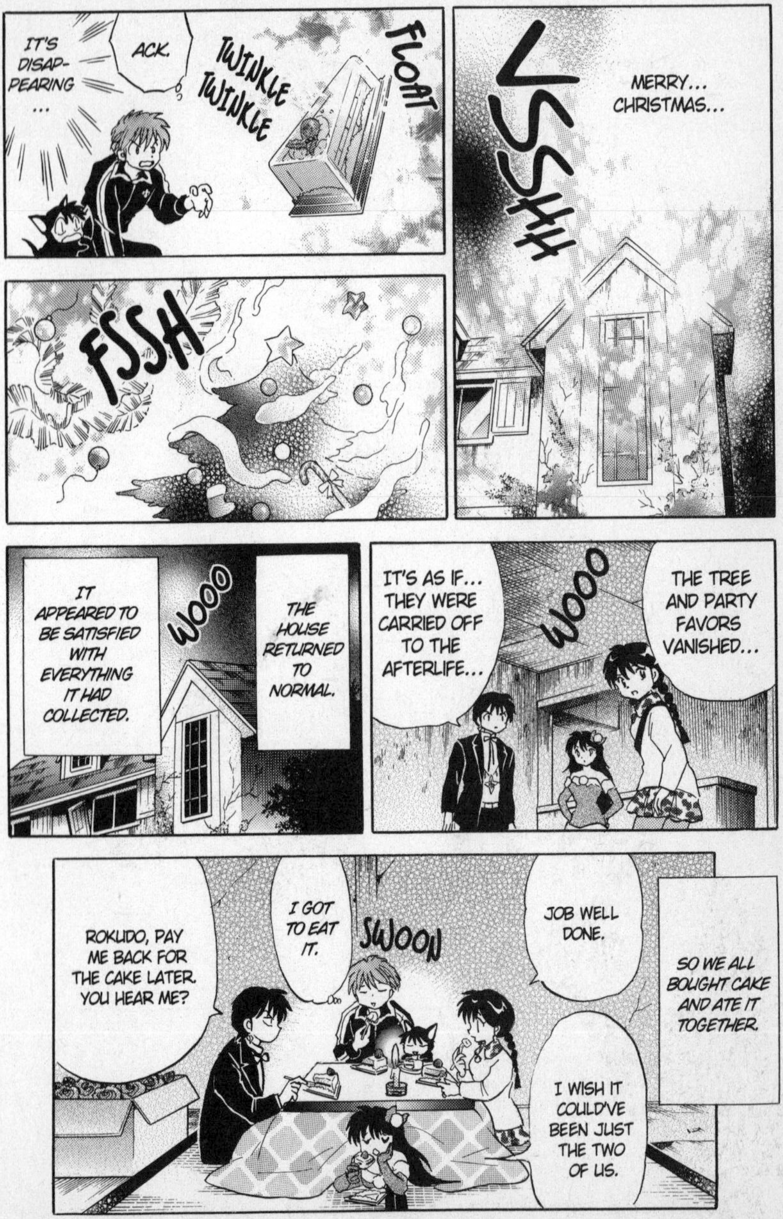
MERRY... CHRISTMAS...
VSSHH
FLOAT
TWINKLE TWINKLE
ACK.
IT'S DISAP-PEARING ...
FSSH
THE TREE AND PARTY FAVORS VANISHED...
WOOO
IT'S AS IF... THEY WERE CARRIED OFF TO THE AFTERLIFE...
THE HOUSE RETURNED TO NORMAL.
WOOO
IT APPEARED TO BE SATISFIED WITH EVERYTHING IT HAD COLLECTED.
SO WE ALL BOUGHT CAKE AND ATE IT TOGETHER.
JOB WELL DONE.
I WISH IT COULD'VE BEEN JUST THE TWO OF US.
SWOON
I GOT TO EAT IT.
ROKUDO, PAY ME BACK FOR THE CAKE LATER. YOU HEAR ME?

CHAPTER 128: THE BLANK PRAYER PLAQUE

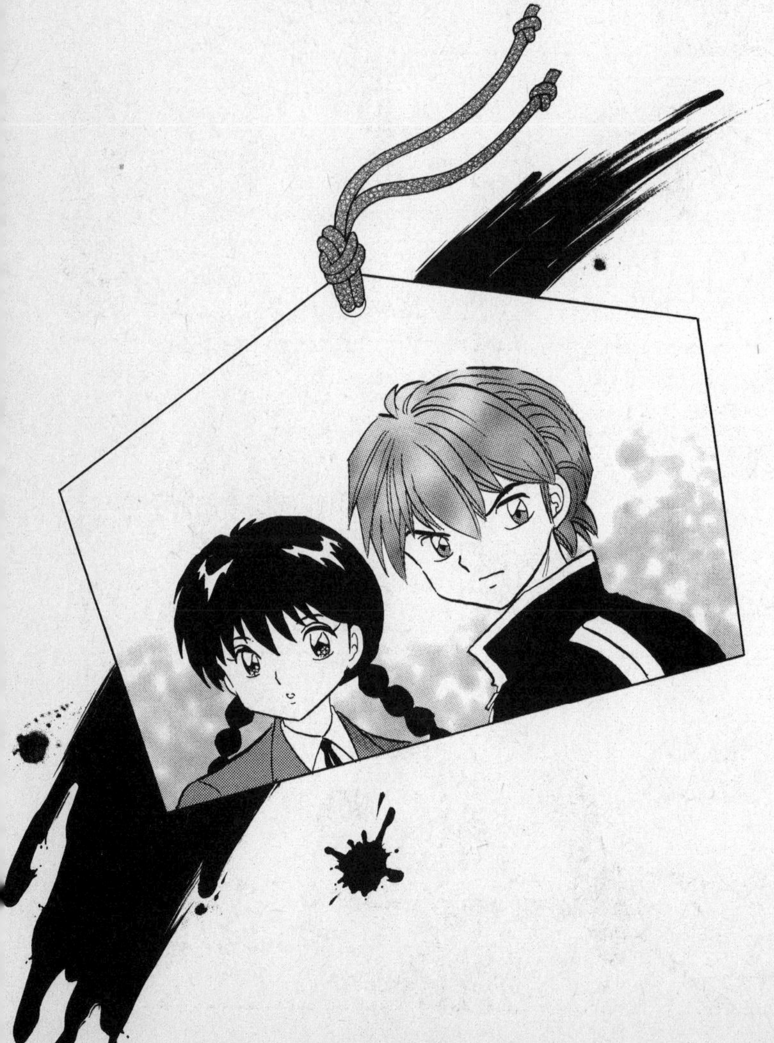

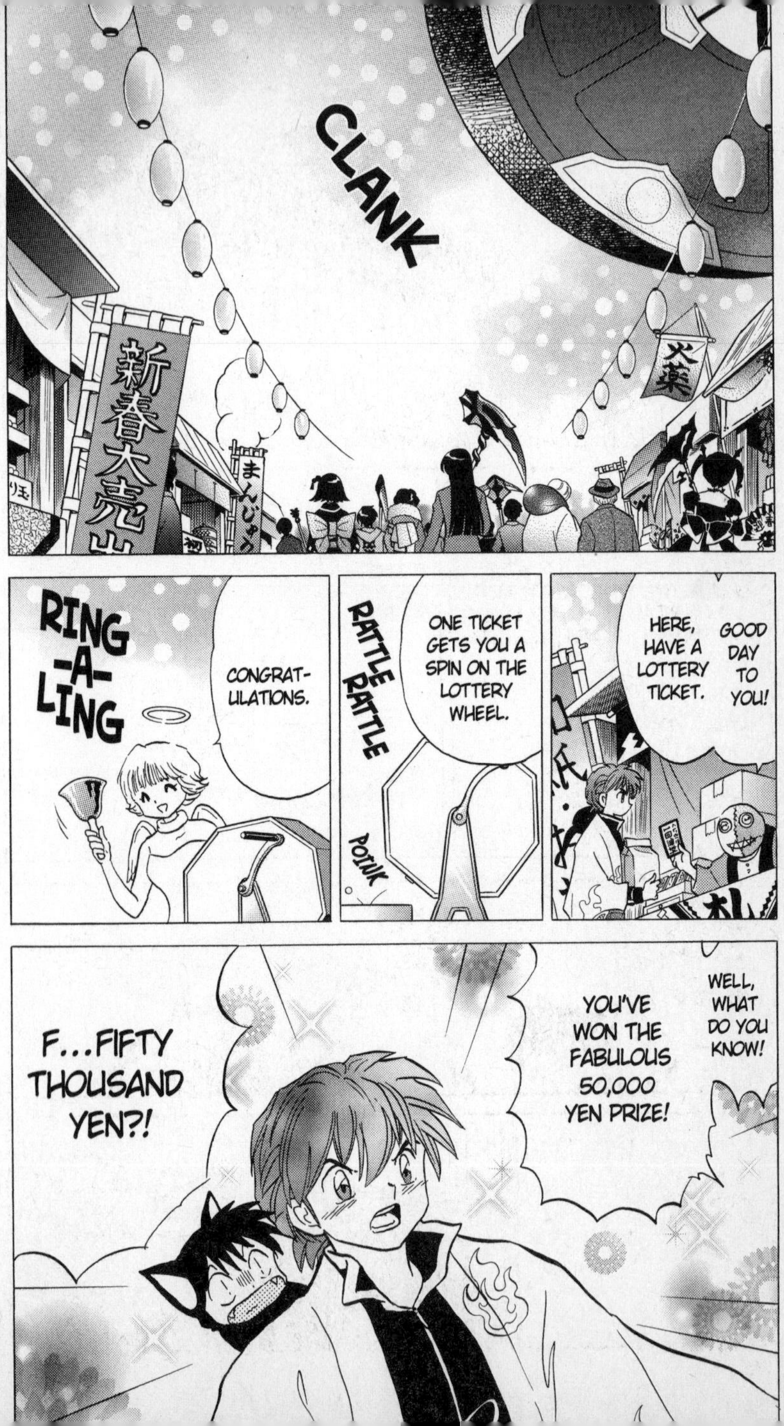
CLANK
新春大売
まんじゅう
火薬
GOOD DAY TO YOU!
HERE, HAVE A LOTTERY TICKET.
ONE TICKET GETS YOU A SPIN ON THE LOTTERY WHEEL.
RATTLE RATTLE
POINK
CONGRAT-ULATIONS.
RING-A-LING
WELL, WHAT DO YOU KNOW!
YOU'VE WON THE FABULOUS 50,000 YEN PRIZE!
F...FIFTY THOUSAND YEN?!

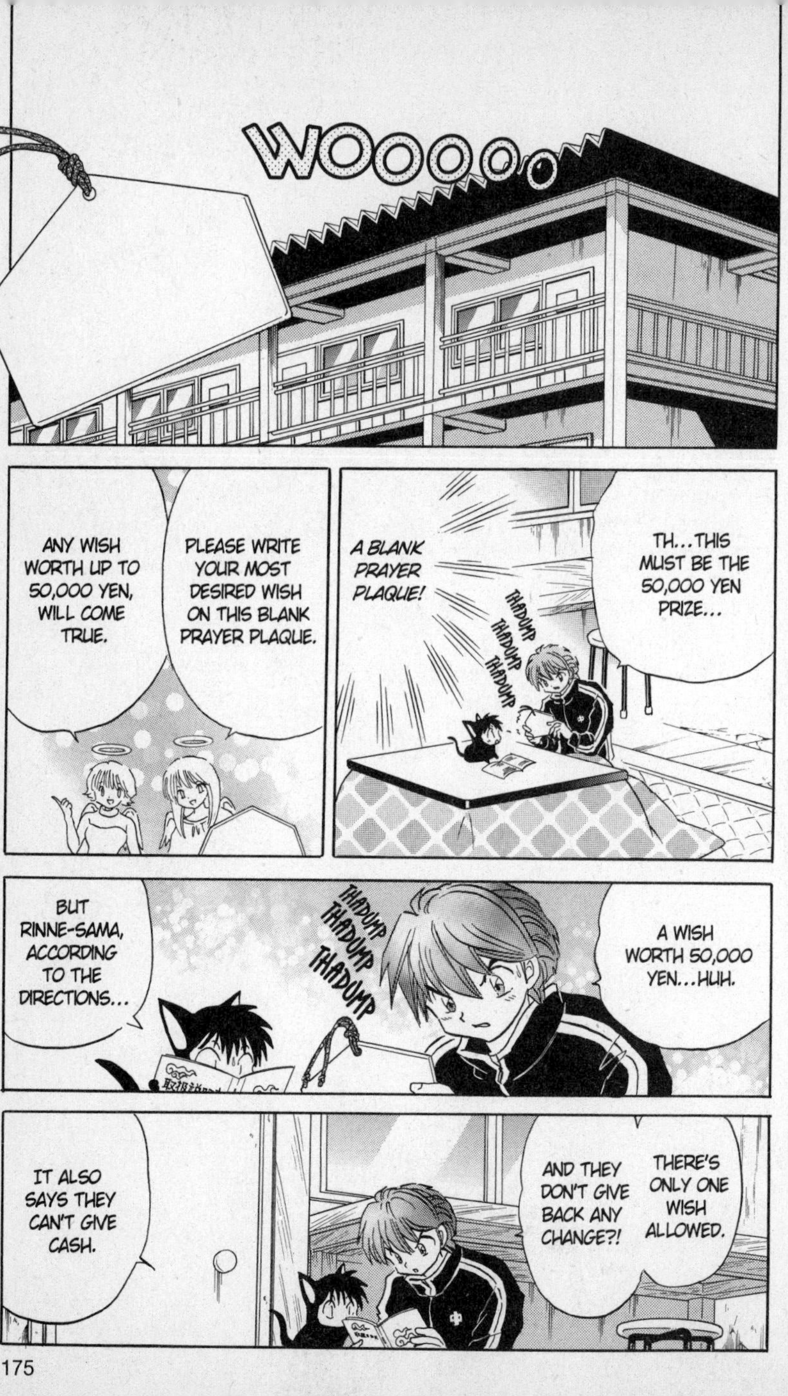
WOOOOO
TH…THIS MUST BE THE 50,000 YEN PRIZE…
A BLANK PRAYER PLAQUE!
THADUMP THADUMP THADUMP
PLEASE WRITE YOUR MOST DESIRED WISH ON THIS BLANK PRAYER PLAQUE.
ANY WISH WORTH UP TO 50,000 YEN, WILL COME TRUE.
A WISH WORTH 50,000 YEN…HUH.
THADUMP THADUMP THADUMP
BUT RINNE-SAMA, ACCORDING TO THE DIRECTIONS…
THERE'S ONLY ONE WISH ALLOWED.
AND THEY DON'T GIVE BACK ANY CHANGE?!
IT ALSO SAYS THEY CAN'T GIVE CASH.

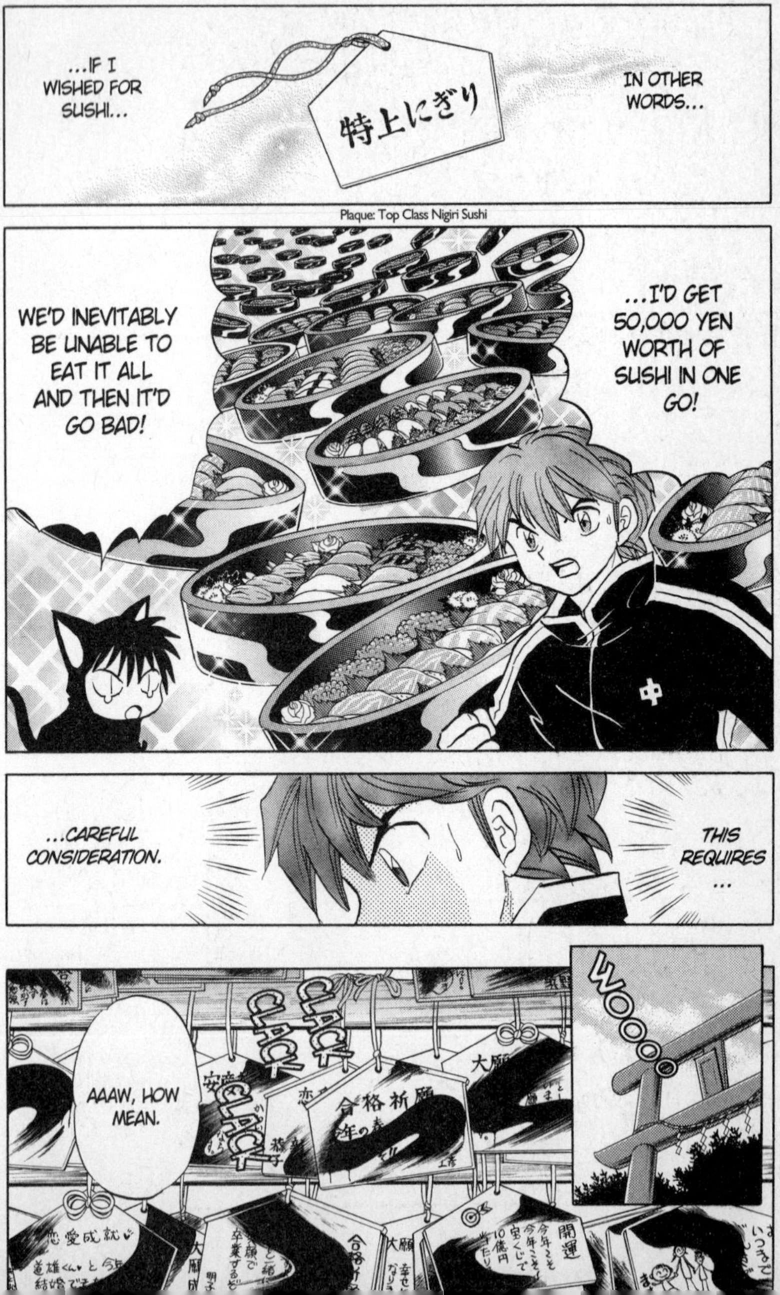
IN OTHER WORDS...
特上にぎり
...IF I WISHED FOR SUSHI...
...I'D GET 50,000 YEN WORTH OF SUSHI IN ONE GO!
WE'D INEVITABLY BE UNABLE TO EAT IT ALL AND THEN IT'D GO BAD!
THIS REQUIRES...
...CAREFUL CONSIDERATION.
WOOOO
CLACK
CLACK
CLACK
AAAW, HOW MEAN.
合格祈願
大願
恋愛成就
開運
Plaque: Top Class Nigiri Sushi

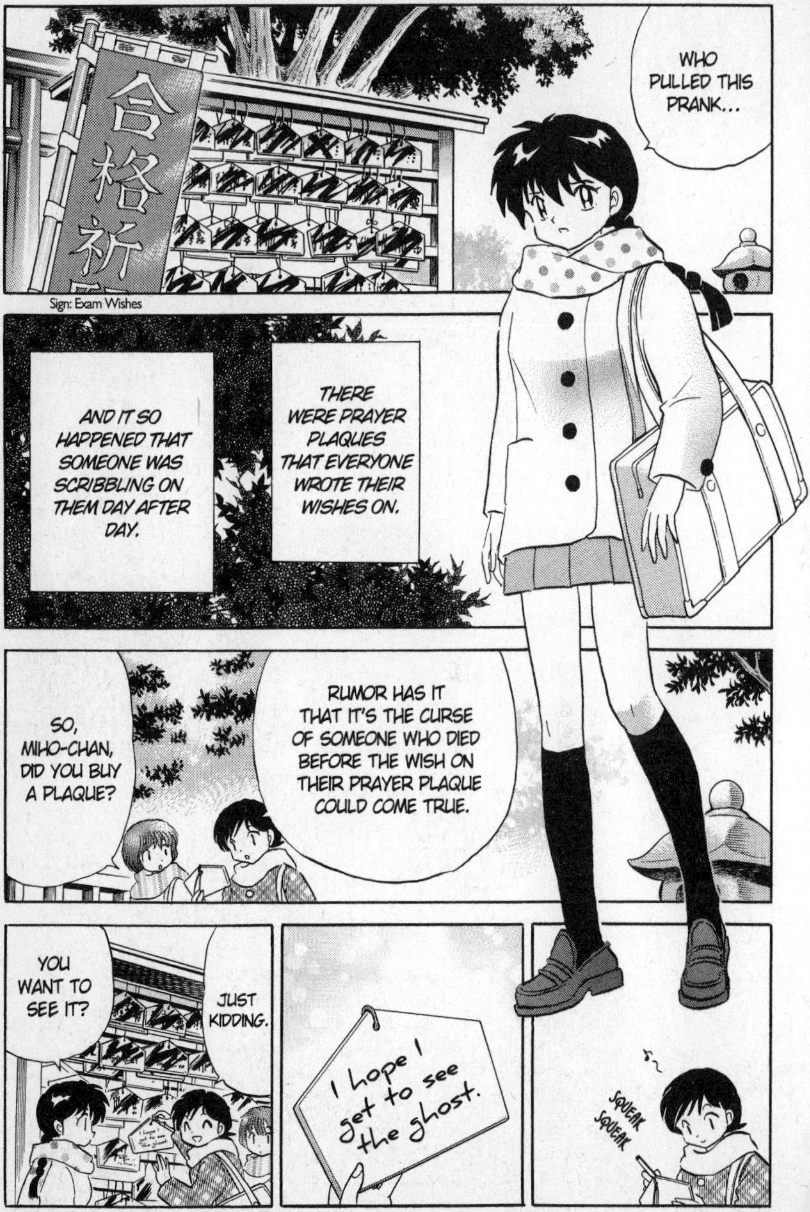
WHO PULLED THIS PRANK...
合格祈
Sign: Exam Wishes
THERE WERE PRAYER PLAQUES THAT EVERYONE WROTE THEIR WISHES ON.
AND IT SO HAPPENED THAT SOMEONE WAS SCRIBBLING ON THEM DAY AFTER DAY.
RUMOR HAS IT THAT IT'S THE CURSE OF SOMEONE WHO DIED BEFORE THE WISH ON THEIR PRAYER PLAQUE COULD COME TRUE.
SO, MIHO-CHAN, DID YOU BUY A PLAQUE?
SQUEAK SQUEAK
I hope I get to see the ghost.
YOU WANT TO SEE IT?
JUST KIDDING.

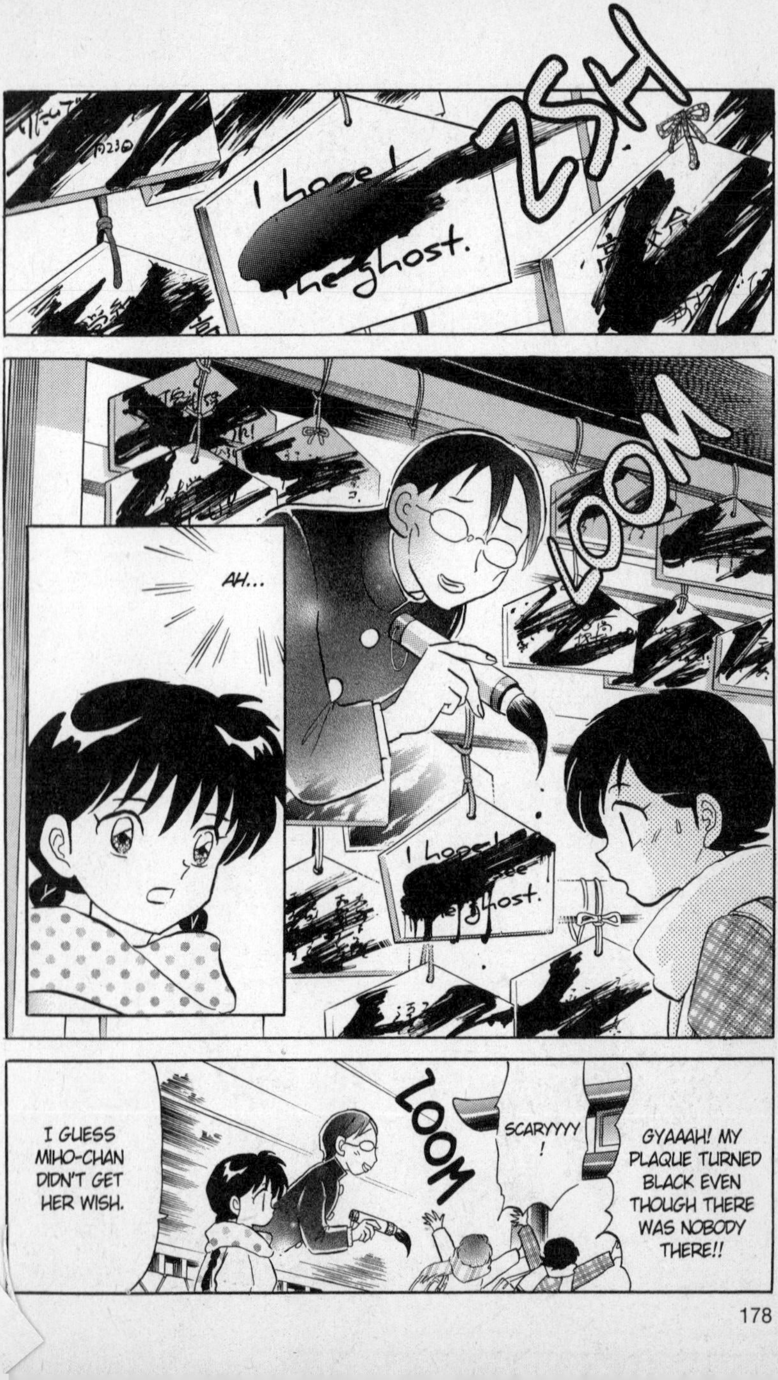
ZSH
I hope I
the ghost.
LOOM
AH...
I hope I
ghost.
GYAAAH! MY PLAQUE TURNED BLACK EVEN THOUGH THERE WAS NOBODY THERE!!
SCARYYYY!
LOOM
I GUESS MIHO-CHAN DIDN'T GET HER WISH.

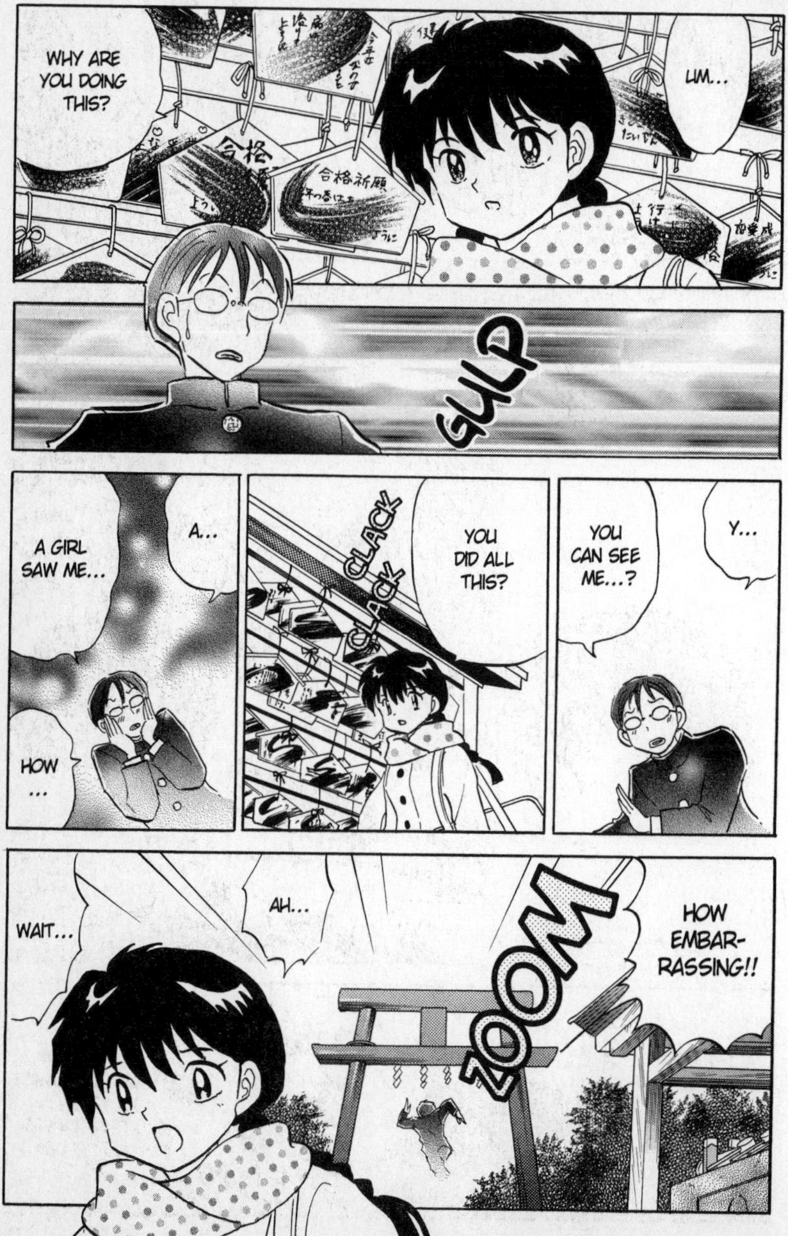
UM...
WHY ARE YOU DOING THIS?
GULP
Y...
YOU CAN SEE ME...?
YOU DID ALL THIS?
CLACK CLACK
A...
A GIRL SAW ME...
HOW ...
HOW EMBAR-RASSING!!
ZOOM
AH...
WAIT...

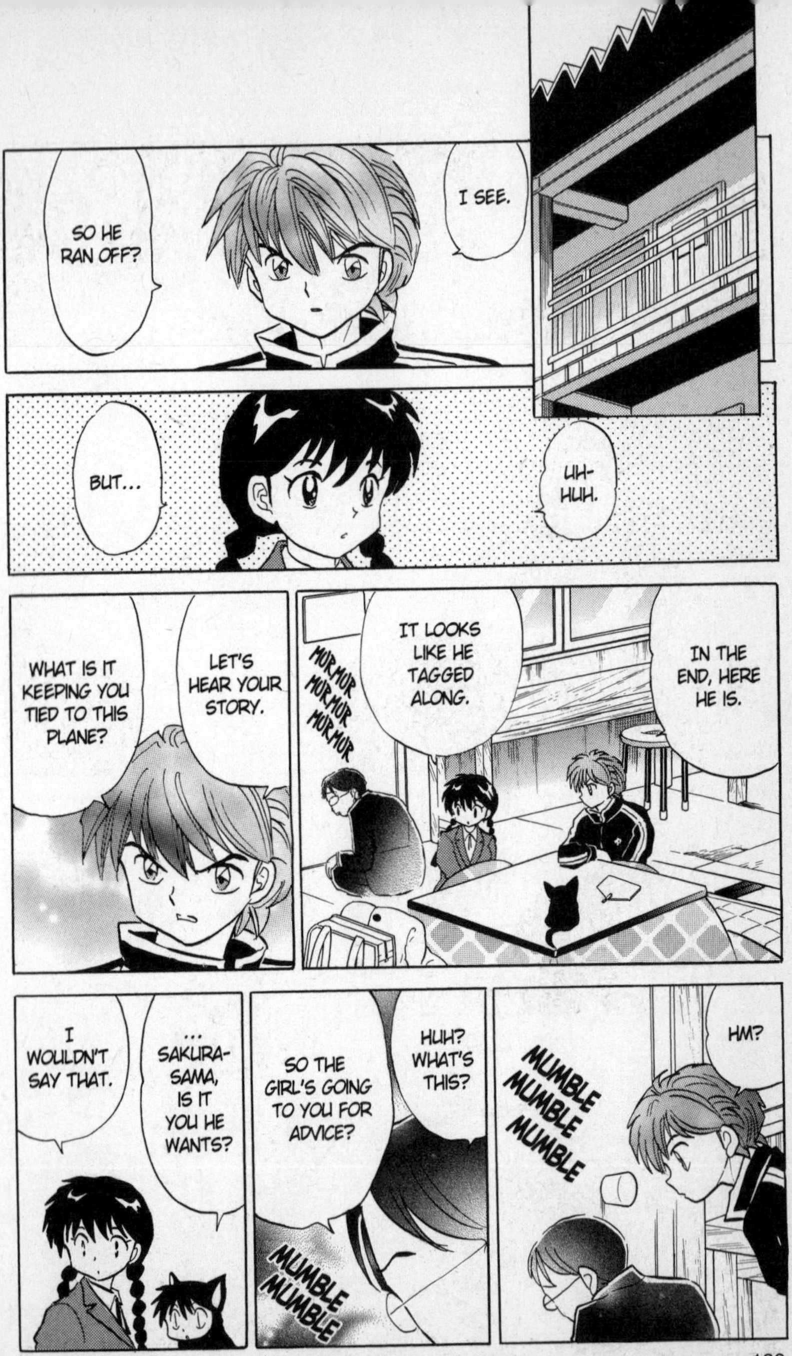
I SEE.
SO HE RAN OFF?
UH-HUH.
BUT...
IN THE END, HERE HE IS.
IT LOOKS LIKE HE TAGGED ALONG.
MURMUR MURMUR MURMUR
LET'S HEAR YOUR STORY.
WHAT IS IT KEEPING YOU TIED TO THIS PLANE?
HM?
MUMBLE MUMBLE MUMBLE
HUH? WHAT'S THIS?
SO THE GIRL'S GOING TO YOU FOR ADVICE?
MUMBLE MUMBLE
... SAKURA-SAMA, IS IT YOU HE WANTS?
I WOULDN'T SAY THAT.

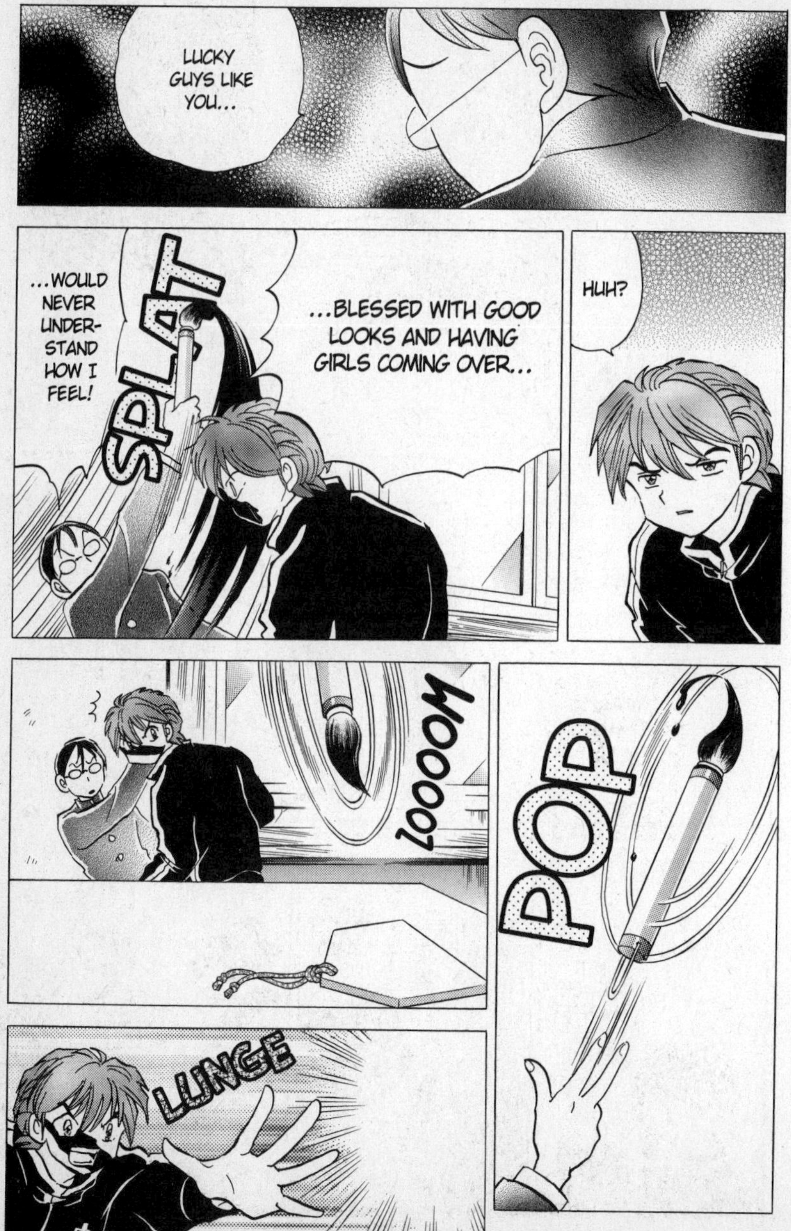
LUCKY GUYS LIKE YOU...
HUH?
...BLESSED WITH GOOD LOOKS AND HAVING GIRLS COMING OVER...
SPLAT
...WOULD NEVER UNDER-STAND HOW I FEEL!
POP
ZOOOOM
LUNGE

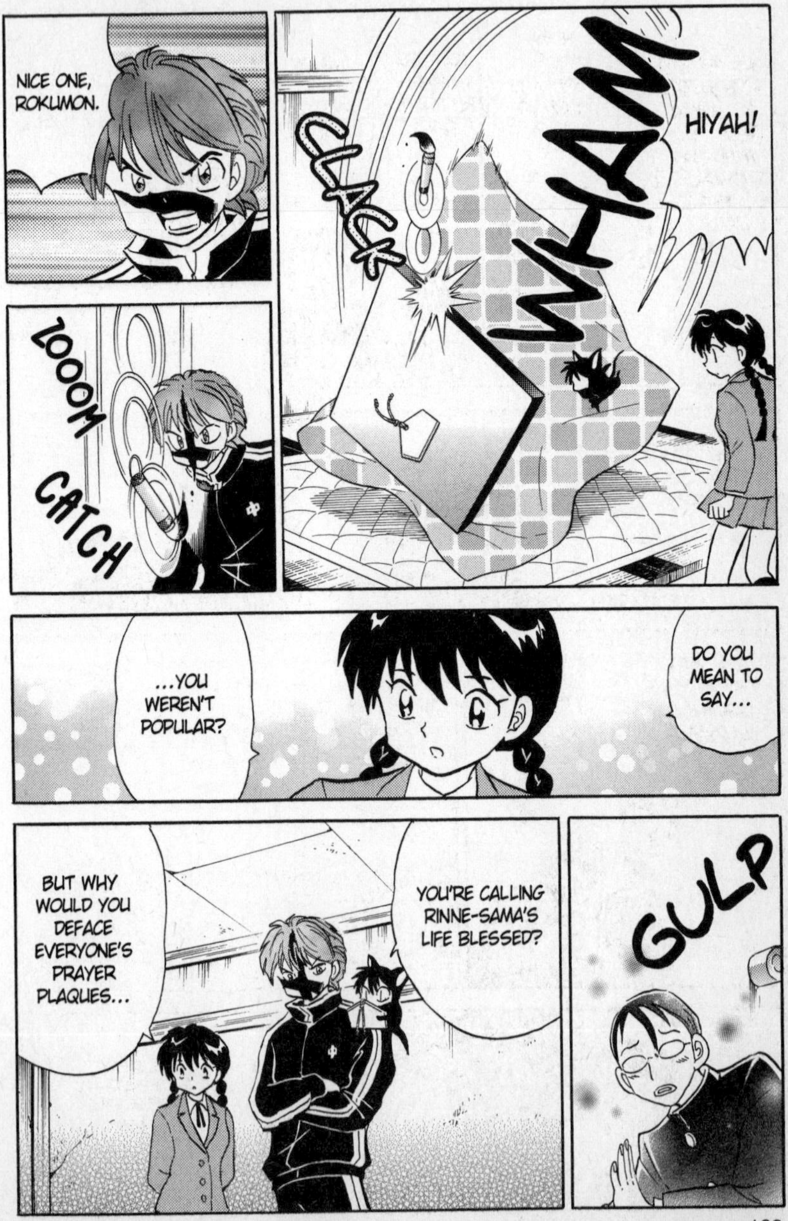

WHAM
HIYAH!
CLACK
NICE ONE, ROKUMON.
ZOOOM
CATCH
DO YOU MEAN TO SAY...
...YOU WEREN'T POPULAR?
GULP
YOU'RE CALLING RINNE-SAMA'S LIFE BLESSED?
BUT WHY WOULD YOU DEFACE EVERYONE'S PRAYER PLAQUES...

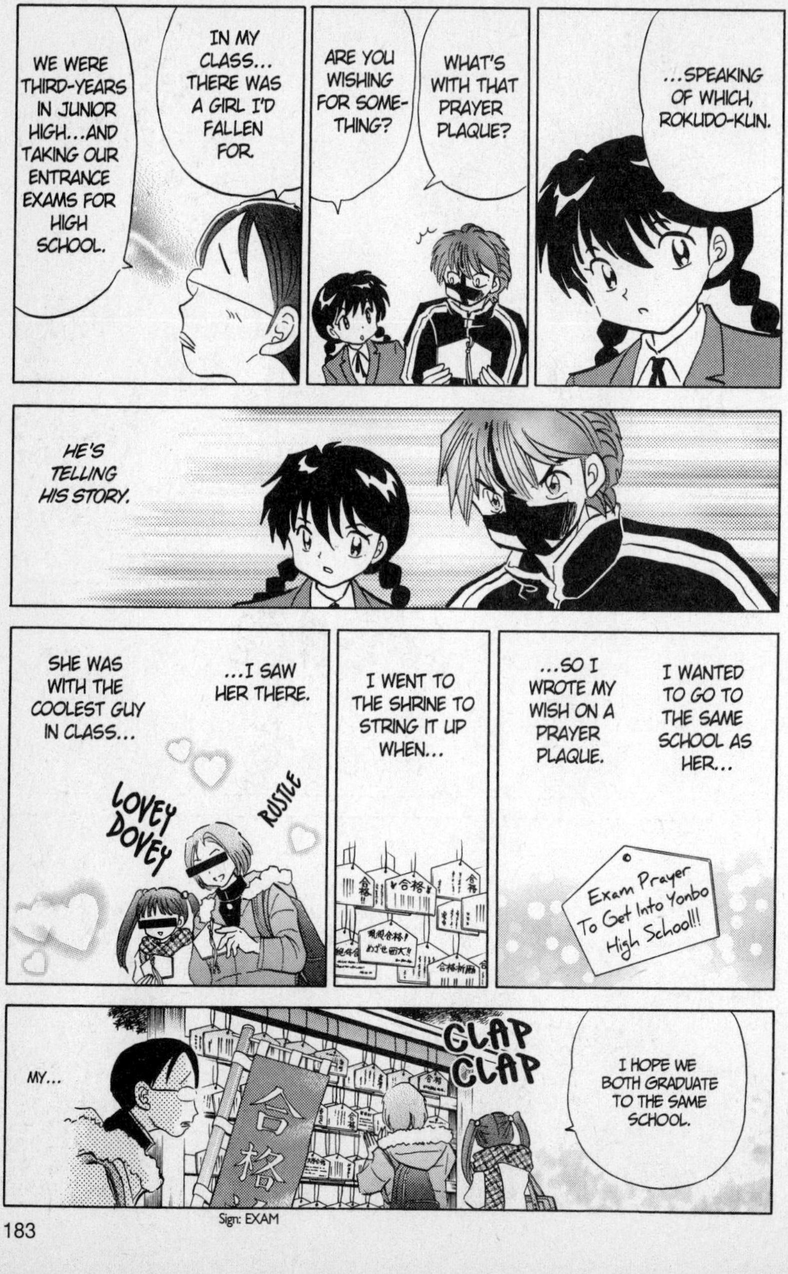
...SPEAKING OF WHICH, ROKUDO-KUN.
WHAT'S WITH THAT PRAYER PLAQUE?
ARE YOU WISHING FOR SOME-THING?
IN MY CLASS... THERE WAS A GIRL I'D FALLEN FOR.
WE WERE THIRD-YEARS IN JUNIOR HIGH...AND TAKING OUR ENTRANCE EXAMS FOR HIGH SCHOOL.
HE'S TELLING HIS STORY.
I WANTED TO GO TO THE SAME SCHOOL AS HER...
...SO I WROTE MY WISH ON A PRAYER PLAQUE.
Exam Prayer To Get Into Yonbo High School!!!
I WENT TO THE SHRINE TO STRING IT UP WHEN...
...I SAW HER THERE.
SHE WAS WITH THE COOLEST GUY IN CLASS...
RUSTLE
LOVEY DOVEY
I HOPE WE BOTH GRADUATE TO THE SAME SCHOOL.
CLAP CLAP
MY...
Sign: EXAM

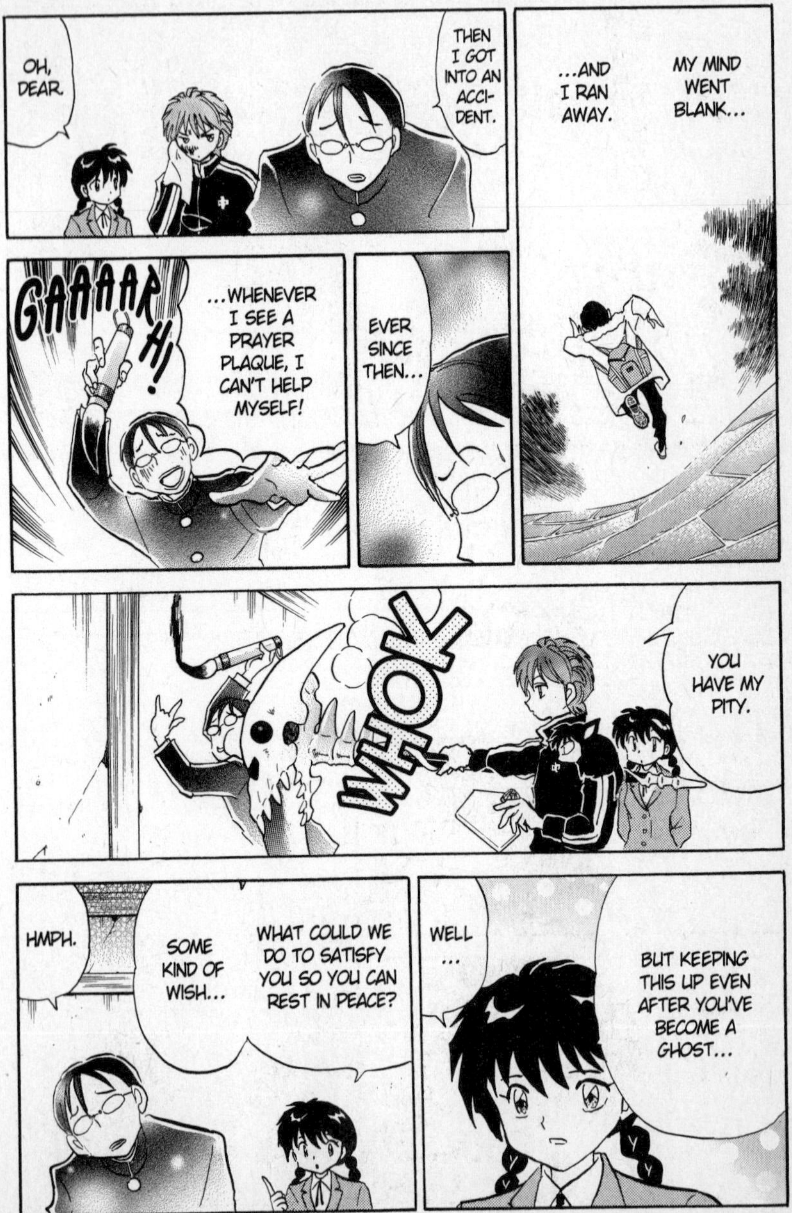
MY MIND WENT BLANK...
...AND I RAN AWAY.
THEN I GOT INTO AN ACCI-DENT.
OH, DEAR.
EVER SINCE THEN...
...WHENEVER I SEE A PRAYER PLAQUE, I CAN'T HELP MYSELF!
GAAAARH!
YOU HAVE MY PITY.
WHOK
BUT KEEPING THIS UP EVEN AFTER YOU'VE BECOME A GHOST...
WELL ...
WHAT COULD WE DO TO SATISFY YOU SO YOU CAN REST IN PEACE?
SOME KIND OF WISH...
HMPH.

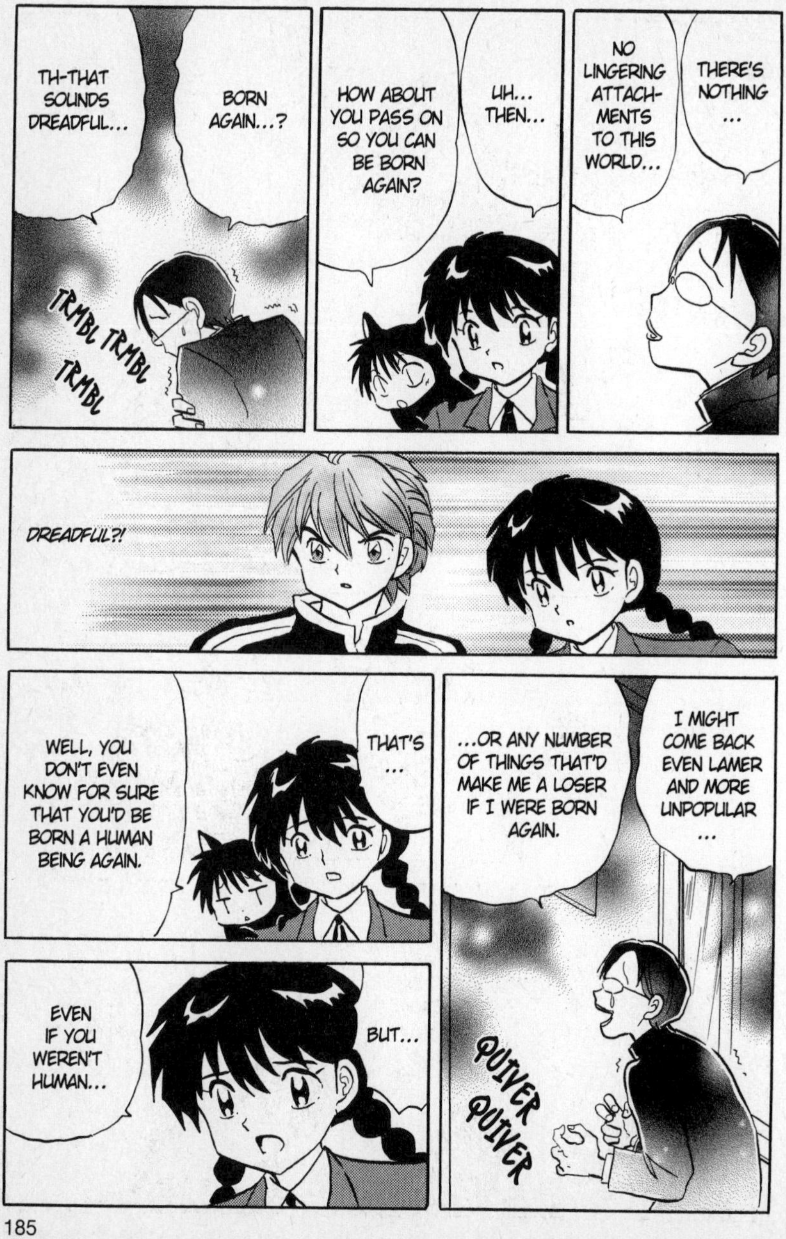
THERE'S NOTHING ...
NO LINGERING ATTACHMENTS TO THIS WORLD...
UH... THEN...
HOW ABOUT YOU PASS ON SO YOU CAN BE BORN AGAIN?
BORN AGAIN...?
TH-THAT SOUNDS DREADFUL...
TRMBL TRMBL TRMBL
DREADFUL?!
I MIGHT COME BACK EVEN LAMER AND MORE UNPOPULAR ...
...OR ANY NUMBER OF THINGS THAT'D MAKE ME A LOSER IF I WERE BORN AGAIN.
QUIVER QUIVER
THAT'S ...
WELL, YOU DON'T EVEN KNOW FOR SURE THAT YOU'D BE BORN A HUMAN BEING AGAIN.
BUT...
EVEN IF YOU WEREN'T HUMAN...

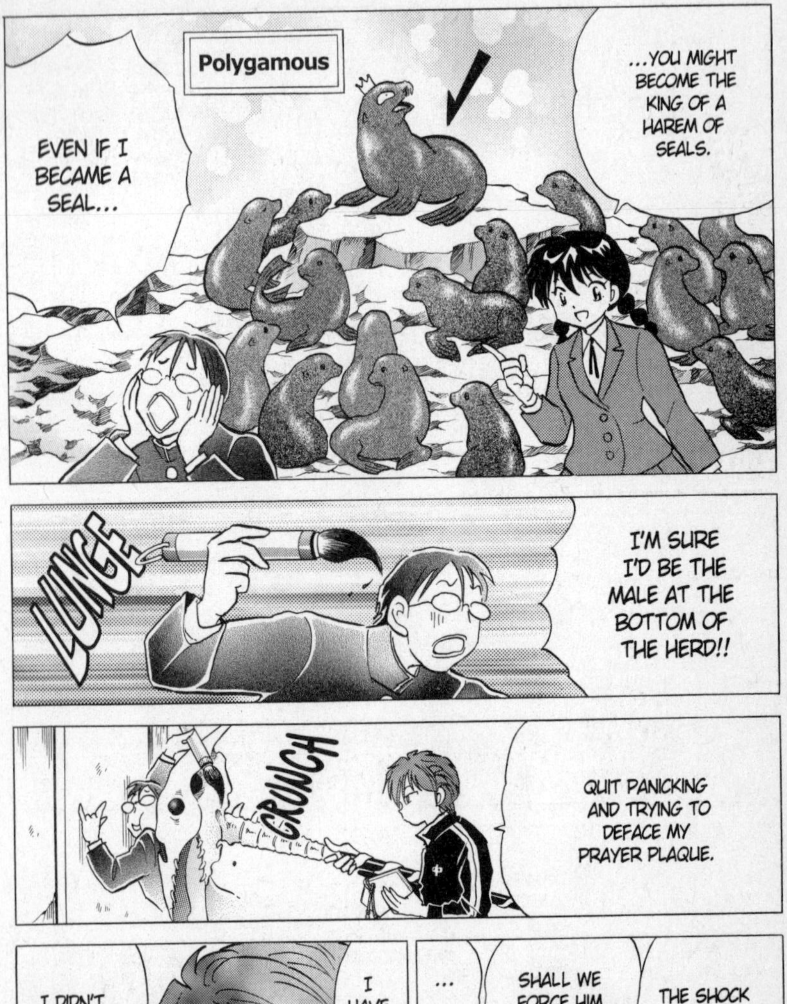
...YOU MIGHT BECOME THE KING OF A HAREM OF SEALS.
Polygamous
EVEN IF I BECAME A SEAL...
I'M SURE I'D BE THE MALE AT THE BOTTOM OF THE HERD!!
LUNGE
QUIT PANICKING AND TRYING TO DEFACE MY PRAYER PLAQUE.
CRUNCH
THE SHOCK OF LOSING HIS LOVE SHATTERED HIS CONFIDENCE.
SHALL WE FORCE HIM TO PASS ON?
...
I HAVE NO CHOICE...
I DIDN'T WANT TO HAVE TO USE THIS, BUT...

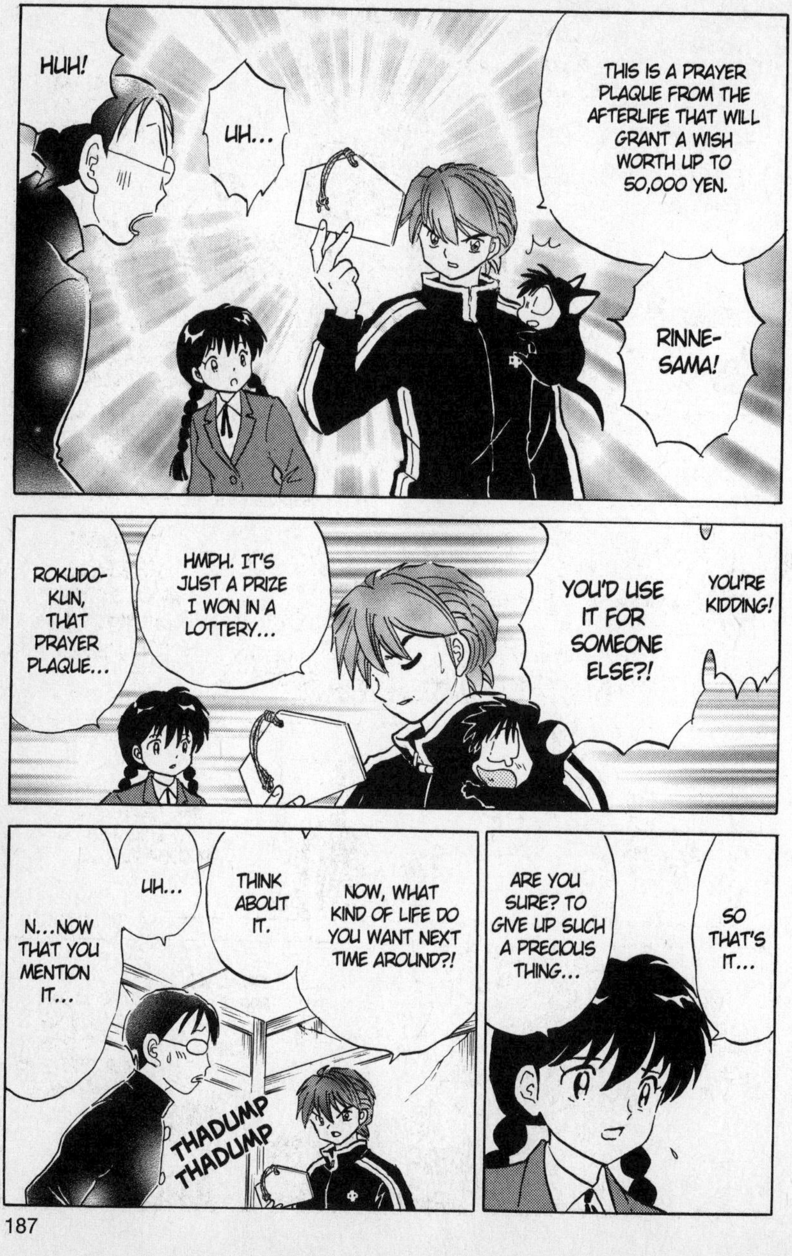
THIS IS A PRAYER PLAQUE FROM THE AFTERLIFE THAT WILL GRANT A WISH WORTH UP TO 50,000 YEN.
RINNE-SAMA!
UH...
HUH!
YOU'RE KIDDING!
YOU'D USE IT FOR SOMEONE ELSE?!
HMPH. IT'S JUST A PRIZE I WON IN A LOTTERY...
ROKUDO-KUN, THAT PRAYER PLAQUE...
SO THAT'S IT...
ARE YOU SURE? TO GIVE UP SUCH A PRECIOUS THING...
NOW, WHAT KIND OF LIFE DO YOU WANT NEXT TIME AROUND?!
THINK ABOUT IT.
UH...
N...NOW THAT YOU MENTION IT...
THADUMP THADUMP

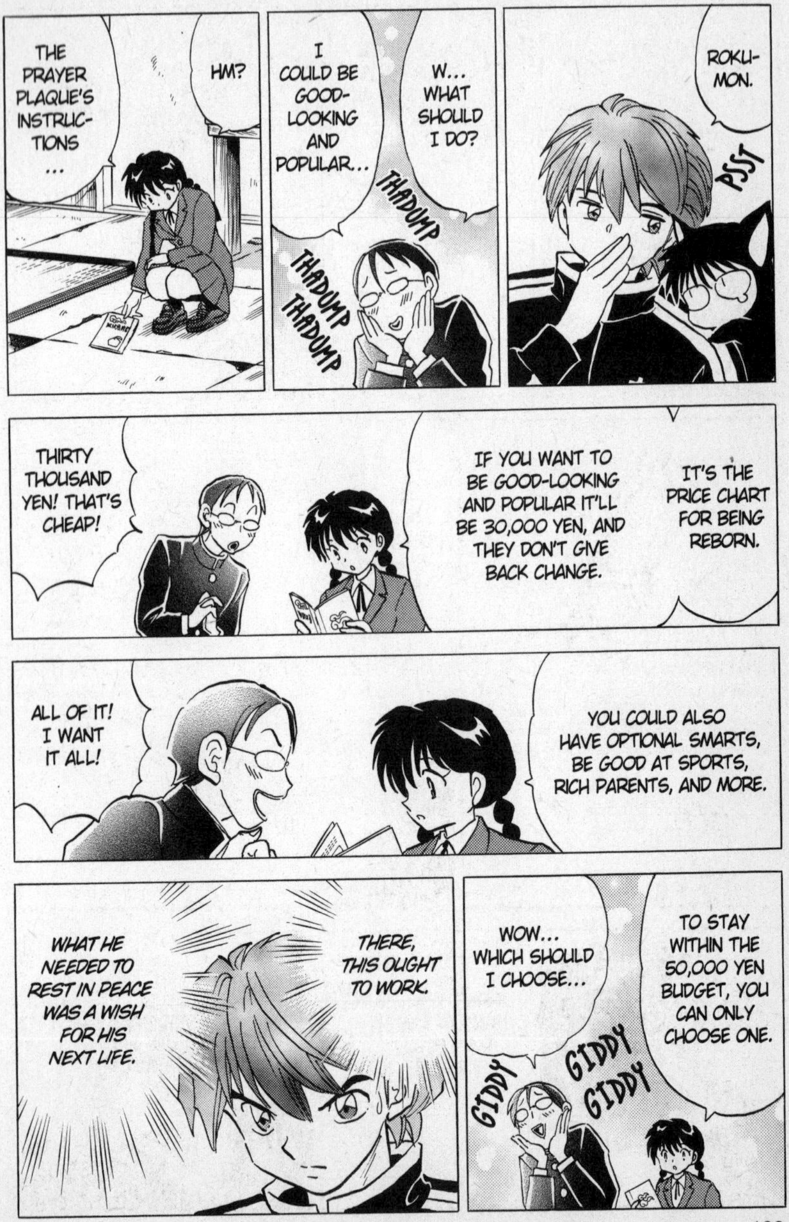
ROKUMON.
PSST
W... WHAT SHOULD I DO?
I COULD BE GOOD-LOOKING AND POPULAR...
THADUMP
THADUMP THADUMP
THADUMP
HM?
THE PRAYER PLAQUE'S INSTRUCTIONS ...
IT'S THE PRICE CHART FOR BEING REBORN.
IF YOU WANT TO BE GOOD-LOOKING AND POPULAR IT'LL BE 30,000 YEN, AND THEY DON'T GIVE BACK CHANGE.
THIRTY THOUSAND YEN! THAT'S CHEAP!
YOU COULD ALSO HAVE OPTIONAL SMARTS, BE GOOD AT SPORTS, RICH PARENTS, AND MORE.
ALL OF IT! I WANT IT ALL!
TO STAY WITHIN THE 50,000 YEN BUDGET, YOU CAN ONLY CHOOSE ONE.
WOW... WHICH SHOULD I CHOOSE...
GIDDY GIDDY
GIDDY
THERE, THIS OUGHT TO WORK.
WHAT HE NEEDED TO REST IN PEACE WAS A WISH FOR HIS NEXT LIFE.

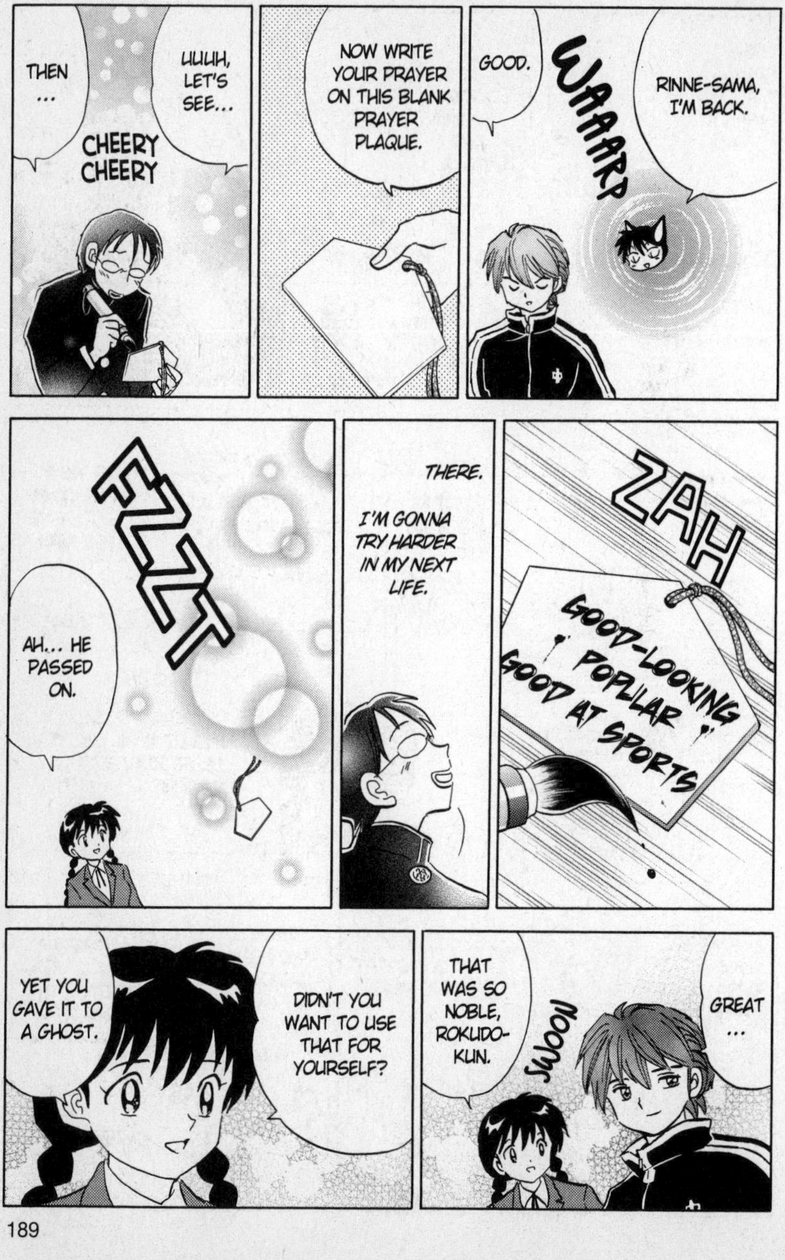
RINNE-SAMA, I'M BACK.
WAAARP
GOOD.
NOW WRITE YOUR PRAYER ON THIS BLANK PRAYER PLAQUE.
UUUH, LET'S SEE...
CHEERY CHEERY
THEN ...
ZAH
"GOOD-LOOKING POPULAR GOOD AT SPORTS"
THERE.
I'M GONNA TRY HARDER IN MY NEXT LIFE.
FZZT
AH... HE PASSED ON.
GREAT ...
THAT WAS SO NOBLE, ROKUDO-KUN.
SWOON
DIDN'T YOU WANT TO USE THAT FOR YOURSELF?
YET YOU GAVE IT TO A GHOST.

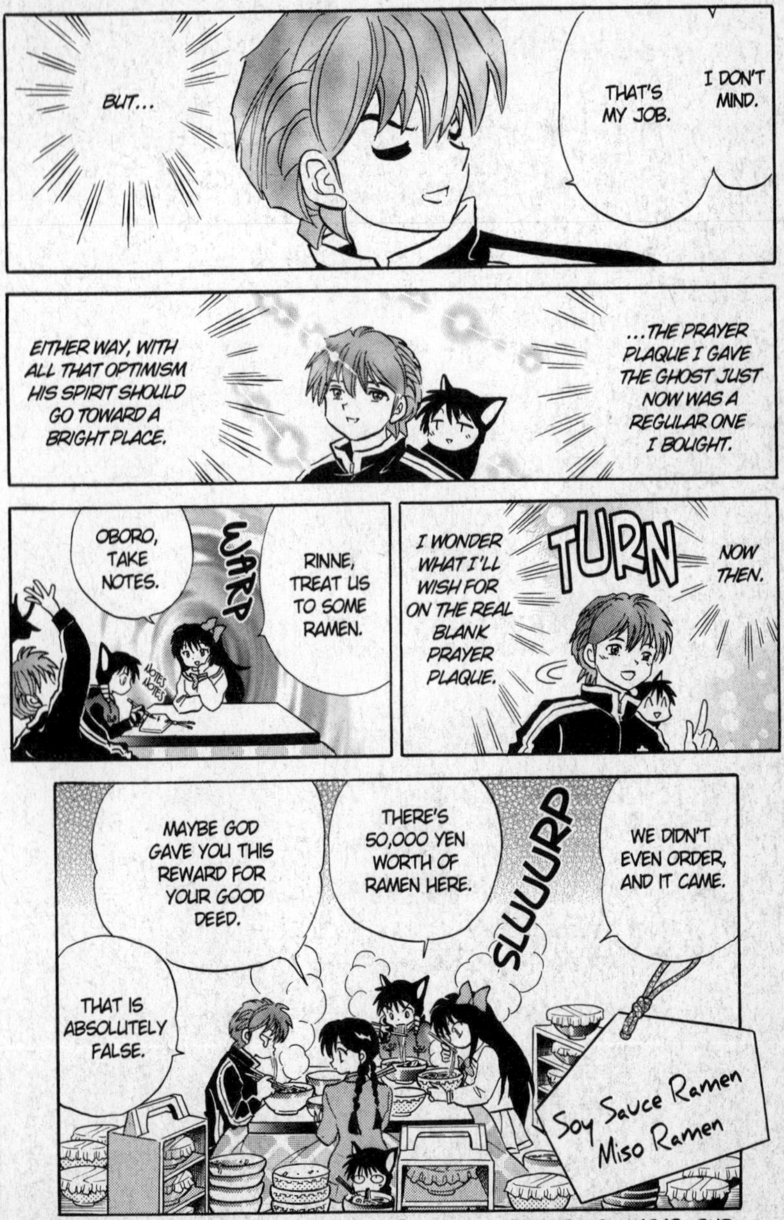
I DON'T MIND.
THAT'S MY JOB.
BUT...
...THE PRAYER PLAQUE I GAVE THE GHOST JUST NOW WAS A REGULAR ONE I BOUGHT.
EITHER WAY, WITH ALL THAT OPTIMISM HIS SPIRIT SHOULD GO TOWARD A BRIGHT PLACE.
NOW THEN.
TURN
I WONDER WHAT I'LL WISH FOR ON THE REAL BLANK PRAYER PLAQUE.
RINNE, TREAT US TO SOME RAMEN.
WARP
OBORO, TAKE NOTES.
NOTES NOTES
WE DIDN'T EVEN ORDER, AND IT CAME.
SLUUURP
THERE'S 50,000 YEN WORTH OF RAMEN HERE.
MAYBE GOD GAVE YOU THIS REWARD FOR YOUR GOOD DEED.
THAT IS ABSOLUTELY FALSE.
Soy Sauce Ramen
Miso Ramen

RIN-NE VOLUME 13 -END-

Hey! You're Reading in the Wrong Direction!

This is the end of this graphic novel!

To properly enjoy this VIZ graphic novel, please turn it around and begin reading from right to left. Unlike English, Japanese is read right to left, so Japanese comics are read in reverse order from the way English comics are typically read.

This book has been printed in the original Japanese format in order to preserve the orientation of the original artwork. Have fun with it!

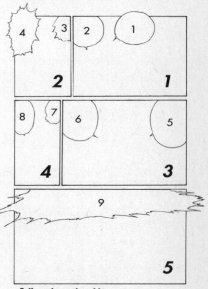

Follow the action this way